New Histories of Village Life at Crystal River

Florida Museum of Natural History: Ripley P. Bullen Series

New Histories of Village Life at Crystal River

THOMAS J. PLUCKHAHN
AND VICTOR D. THOMPSON

University of Florida Press
Gainesville

Copyright 2018 by Thomas J. Pluckhahn and Victor D. Thompson
All rights reserved
Published in the United States of America

First cloth printing, 2018
First paperback printing, 2025

30 29 28 27 26 25   6 5 4 3 2 1

Library of Congress Cataloging-in-Publication Data
Names: Pluckhahn, Thomas J. (Thomas John), 1966– author. | Thompson, Victor
    D., author.
Title: New histories of village life at Crystal River / Thomas J. Pluckhahn
    and Victor D. Thompson.
Other titles: Ripley P. Bullen series.
Description: Gainesville : University of Florida Press, 2018. | Series:
    Florida Museum of Natural History: Ripley P. Bullen series | Includes
    bibliographical references and index.
Identifiers: LCCN 2017031785 | ISBN 9781683400356 (cloth) | ISBN 9781683405412 (pbk.)
Subjects: LCSH: Crystal River (Fla.)—History. | Crystal River
    (Fla.)—Antiquities. | Cities and towns—Growth—Case studies. |
    Excavations (Archaeology)—Florida—Crystal River. | Citrus County
    (Fla.)—History.
Classification: LCC F319.C79 P58 2017 | DDC 975.9/72—dc23
LC record available at https://lccn.loc.gov/2017031785

University of Florida Press
2046 NE Waldo Road
Gainesville, FL 32609
http://upress.ufl.edu

GPSR EU Authorized Representative: Mare Nostrum Group B.V., Mauritskade 21D, 1091 GC Amsterdam, The Netherlands, gpsr@mare-nostrum.co.uk

To Becky and Ella, with love and thanks—T.J.P.

To Amanda, Fish, and Fin, with love and thanks—V.D.T.

Contents

List of Figures ix

List of Tables xiii

Acknowledgments xv

1. Crystal River and the Archaeology of Early Village Societies in the American Southeast (and Beyond) 1
2. Context 25
3. A Center Emerges 71
4. From Vacant Center to Early Village (Phase 1) 101
5. From Early Village to Regional Center (Phase 2) 117
6. From Regional Center to Mound-Residential Compound (Phase 3) 155
7. New Centers Emerge (Phase 4) 168
8. The Early Village at Crystal River in Broader Perspective 194

Afterword: Why Early Villages Still Matter 209

References Cited 215

Index 263

Figures

1.1. Location of the Crystal River site, the Roberts Island Shell Mound Complex, and other sites mentioned in the text   7
1.2. View north of Mound A at Crystal River from the river   10
1.3. View northeast across Mound G to Mound H at Crystal River   10
1.4. View north of the reconstructed Main Burial Complex at Crystal River   11
1.5. Copper ornament recovered by Moore from the Main Burial Complex at Crystal River, possibly representing a bear and completed in a style typical of Hopewell   12
1.6. View west of Mound K and a portion of the midden at Crystal River   14
2.1. Location of Crystal River and Roberts Island   26
2.2. Location of Crystal River and Roberts Island with respect to major geomorphic divisions   27
2.3. Location of Crystal River and Roberts Island with respect to major hydrologic communities   29
2.4. Map of Crystal River   31
2.5. Map of Roberts Island   32
2.6. View of Mound A on site 8CI41 at Roberts Island   33
2.7. View of Mound B on site 8CI40 at Roberts Island   33
2.8. View of site 8CI36 and Mound C at Roberts Island   34
2.9. Comparison of 1952 and 1969 aerial photographs of Crystal River showing development of the area   36
2.10. 1964 photograph showing extensive damage to the east side of Mound A at Crystal River   37

2.11. Aerial view of the former trailer park at Crystal River 38
2.12. Moore's map of Crystal River 41
2.13. Moore's maps of the Main Burial Complex at Crystal River 41
2.14. Two maps of Crystal River by Ripley Bullen 44
2.15. Conducting resistance survey in the plaza at Crystal River, with Mound H in the background 49
2.16. Resistance survey data from Crystal River 50
2.17. Conducting GPR survey on a portion of the midden at Crystal River, with Mound A in background 51
2.18. Using a GeoProbe coring device at Crystal River 52
2.19. Cores excavated at Crystal River 53
2.20. Locations of trenches at Crystal River 55
2.21. Excavation of Trench 1 at Crystal River, with Mound K in the background 56
2.22. Profile of Trench 1 at Crystal River 57
2.23. Excavation of Trench 2 at Crystal River 58
2.24. Profile of Trench 2 at Crystal River 58
2.25. Excavation of Trench 3 at Crystal River 59
2.26. Profile of Trench 3 at Crystal River 60
2.27. Excavation of Trench 4 at Crystal River 60
2.28. Profile of Trench 4 at Crystal River 61
2.29. Excavation of a shovel test at Roberts Island 62
2.30. Locations of shovel tests and trenches at Roberts Island 62
2.31. Excavation of Trench 2 at Roberts Island 63
2.32. Profile of Shovel Test 4 on Roberts Island 63
2.33. Profile of Trench 2 on Roberts Island 64
2.34. Excavation of Trench 1 on Mound A at Roberts Island 65
2.35. Excavation of Trench 3 on Mound B at Roberts Island 65
3.1. Manatees pack Three Sisters Spring on a cold morning in February 2016 72
3.2. The site plan at Crystal River in the last few centuries B.C., before village formation 81
3.3. Selected plummets of local limestone from Moore's work in the Main Burial Complex 85

3.4. Selected plummets of nonlocal stone from Moore's work in the Main Burial Complex 86
3.5. Selected copper plummets from Moore's work in the Main Burial Complex 87
3.6. Selected crystalline quartz artifacts from Moore's work in the Main Burial Complex 88
3.7. Selected reddish stone beads and pendants from Moore's work in the Main Burial Complex 89
3.8. Selected ceramic vessels from Moore's work in the Main Burial Complex 90
3.9. Copper plummet with traces of leather cap, cordage, and adhesive from Crystal River 91
3.10. Portions of the same ceramic vessel recovered by Moore in 1903 and 1906 95
4.1. Close-up of the shell-dense matrix in Trench 3 at Crystal River 102
4.2. The settlement plan at Crystal River during Phase 1 104
4.3. Arc of post features in the Phase 1 level at the bottom of Trench 2 106
4.4. Horizontal "slices" of the radar data from an area north of Mound A at increasing depths 107
4.5. Cross sections of sherds from Crystal River under magnification 110
5.1. The settlement plan at Crystal River during Phase 2 120
5.2. Generalized description of the soil core from Mound H at Crystal River 129
5.3. Generalized description of the soil core from Mound K at Crystal River 130
5.4. GPR profile from Grid 4, on the summit of Mound K 131
5.5. Generalized description of the soil core from Mound H at Crystal River 132
5.6. GPR profile from Grid 2, on the western half of the summit of Mound H 133
5.7. Generalized description of the soil core from Mound A at Crystal River 134

5.8. GPR profile from Mound A at Crystal River 135
5.9. Photograph of Bullen's cut into the ramp on Mound A at Crystal River 136
5.10. Ripley Bullen with Stela 1 at Crystal River in 1964, with inset of Stela 1 close-up 142
5.11. Bullen's notes on Stela 1, recorded in 1964 at the time of its discovery 143
5.12. View to the southwest of Stela 2 at Crystal River, with Mounds J and K in background 144
5.13. Selected shell plummets from Moore's work in the Main Burial Complex 146
5.14. Selected shell gorgets from Moore's work in the Main Burial Complex 147
5.15. Tabbed Circular Artifacts (TCAs) from Moore's work in the Main Burial Complex 150
6.1. The settlement plans at Crystal River and Roberts Island during Phase 3 157
6.2. View from the summit of Mound A 163
6.3. View of the ramp on Mound A 164
7.1. The settlement plans at Crystal River and Roberts Island during Phase 4 173
7.2. View of Trench 2 and the "water court" area on Roberts Island 178
7.3. Reflection of a GPR transect on the western side of Mound A at Roberts Island 179
7.4. Profile of Trench 1 in Mound A at Roberts Island 180
7.5. Trench 1, partially backfilled with oyster shell to show apparent stepped construction 182
7.6. Photograph of a shell mound in the Crystal River area, possibly Mound B at Roberts Island 184
7.7. Profile of the trench on Mound B at Roberts Island 185
7.8. Spatial relationships among the mounds at Roberts Island and possible relations to astronomical events 187

Tables

1.1. Outline of Major Periods in the Prehistory and History of the American South 2
1.2. Temporal Divisions of the Woodland and Mississippian Periods for Regions of the Eastern Gulf Coast 5
2.1. Modeled Phases of Midden Deposition at Crystal River and Roberts Island 68
2.2. Modeled Phases of Midden Deposition at Crystal River and Roberts Island 69

Acknowledgments

The successful completion of the research summarized and synthesized in this book owes much to the help of a number of individuals and organizations. First and foremost, we thank Nick Robins and John Lakich, former and current park managers, respectively, for their support of the research. For permission to work at the park, we also thank Triel Lindstrom and William Stanton (former and current archaeologists for the Bureau of Natural and Cultural Resources, respectively), Ryan J. Wheeler and Mary Glowacki (former and current state archaeologists, respectively), and Louis Tesar and Julia Byrd Duggins (former and current archaeologists with the Florida Bureau of Archaeological Research, respectively).

Our stay at Crystal River was greatly facilitated by the staff of Crystal River State Archaeological Park. We are particularly indebted to Mike Petellat and Leroy Smith for their considerable logistical support and good-natured humor.

Rich Estabrook and Jason Moser, past employees of the Florida Public Archaeology Network (FPAN), provided assistance for the first few field seasons. Jeff Moates, Rebecca O'Sullivan, and Nigel Rudolph, currently with FPAN, have been great friends and colleagues for more recent fieldwork.

Grateful appreciation is also extended to the sponsors of our work. This material is based upon work supported by the National Science Foundation under Grant No. 1026248. Any opinions, findings, and conclusions or recommendations expressed in this material are those of the authors and do not necessarily reflect the views of the National Science Foundation. Additional support was provided by a small grant from the University of South Florida, Office of Research, New Researcher Grant Program. We are also grateful for support provided by the Departments of Anthropology of the University of South Florida, the University of West Florida, the Ohio State University, and the University of Georgia.

Advice, encouragement, and information were extended by a number of colleagues. We are particularly grateful to colleagues Neill Wallis and John Krigbaum for sharing radiocarbon dating results from Crystal River. For additional advice and encouragement we thank friends and colleagues David Anderson, Bob Austin, Dave Carballo, Gary Ellis, Steve Kowalewski, George Luer, Bill Marquardt, Asa Randall, Chris Rodning, Mike Russo, Ken Sassaman, Jeffrey Shanks, Jan Simek, Sarah Taylor, Karen Walker, Neill Wallis, and Greg Waselkov. Brent Weisman was integral to the success of the early stages of the project. Jeff Mitchem, Bill Marquardt, and Keith Stephenson provided helpful comments on a draft of the manuscript. Amy Gatenbee assisted with the indexing of the book, and Jelane Wallace helped check the page proofs.

Graduate students at the University of South Florida have been sorting shell from our excavations for many years now. We are thankful for the laboratory assistance provided by Beth Blankenship, Alexander Delgado, Trevor Duke, Josh Foster, Jana Futch, Ashley Humphries, Kassie Kemp, Shannon McVey, Lori O'Neal, Katherine Padula, Liz Southard, Jelane Wallace, Shaun West, and Colette Witcher.

Donna Ruhl, Bill Marquardt, Irv Quitmyer, and Neill Wallis were instrumental in providing access to artifacts and archives at the Florida Museum of Natural History; Ann Cordell, at the same institution, cheerfully provided advice on pottery analysis. Dave Dickel, Marie Prentiss, and Dan Seinfeld facilitated our use of collections at the Florida Bureau of Archaeological Research. Victoria Cranner assisted with access to the collections at the National Museum of the American Indian. Kathy Turner Thompson provided much-appreciated help with the archives of the Citrus County Historical Society.

Finally, we are indebted to the many students and volunteers who have participated in the field for their hard work and for making our research at Crystal River a fun and rewarding experience. Graduate students who have spent time on the project include Beth Blankenship, Ellen Burlingame Turck, Trevor Duke, Randee Hunter, Kassie Kemp, Nick Laracuente, Sarah Mitchell, Sean Norman, Lori O'Neal, Katherine Padula, Christina Perry Sampson, Adrianne Sams, Maggie Spivey, Amanda Roberts-Thompson, and Colette Witcher. The long list of undergraduates who contributed to our understanding of Crystal River includes India Anderton, Timothy

Avalos, Kira Benton, Tatiana Bourey, Brett Briggs, Shawnna Callaghan, Stephanie Charles, Jessica Chevrolet, Janna Clevinger, Kyle Dalton, Alexander Delgado, Alexa Doyle, Sean Filnan, Amanda Gostelle, Leslie Haas, Kevin Hageman, Kristopher Head, Daren Hoffman, Danielle Hopping, Teddy Horowitz, Catherine Keckler, Benjamin Keller, Stephanie Lonergan, Daniel Lowery, Michael Marotti, Joseph McCormack, Shannon McGuffey, Travis McMullen, Marty Menz, Michelle Moretz, Stephanie Nelson, Melissa Norris, Kathryn Parker, Renae Presto, Emily Rempe, Brianna Ridge, Matthew Rooney, Erin Rosenthal, Jacob Rouden, Savannah Rudolph, Debra Sparr, Jessica Stanton, Kimi Swisher, Robert Taylor, Matt Touchton, Sarai Weaver, Shawn Westerman, Rachel Westfall, Eric Wyrock, Brittany Yabczanka, and Karrie Zezlina. To our volunteers, who are too numerous to mention by name, we also say thanks.

1

Crystal River and the Archaeology of Early Village Societies in the American Southeast (and Beyond)

In the archaeology and history of the American Southeast, the Woodland period—beginning at roughly 1000 B.C. and lasting to around A.D. 1050 (Table 1.1)—is not conventionally understood as an interval marked by significant "firsts." The first human settlement of the region came much earlier, during the Paleoindian period (before 10,000 B.C.). The first pottery was invented during the immediately preceding Archaic period (ca. 10,000 to 1000 B.C.), to which we can also credit the first experiments with horticulture, the first monument building, and the first patterned and persistent networks of long-distance exchange. The first intensive agriculture and social ranking on the scale ascribed to neoevolutionary social formations known as chiefdoms and states arguably dates to the subsequent Mississippian period (ca. A.D. 1050 to 1540).

But we believe that one important first marked the Woodland period: it is during this time that we see the widespread appearance of sedentary villages, often associated with large-scale public works (Pluckhahn 2010b; Wright 2016). These public works took many forms, from earthen enclosures, to large shell mounds, and even to the first platform mounds. The co-occurrence of these two traditions marks a dramatic change in the way people related to one another in the American Southeast.

Isolated examples of sedentary villages with public architecture appeared during the Archaic period, most famously at the Poverty Point site in Louisiana (Gibson 2001; Kidder 2011; Sassaman 2005), but these were few and far between. In contrast, the population aggregations of the Woodland period in the American Southeast, like village formations in many other areas (Kowalewski 2013:203), occurred as a regional process. Thus, this first was not simply the addition of new traditions onto existing

Table 1.1. Outline of Major Periods in the Prehistory and History of the American South

Dates	Periods
1800	Historic
1500	Mississippian
1000	Late Woodland
500	
0	Middle Woodland
500	Early Woodland
1000	
1500	
2000	
2500	Late Archaic
3000	
3500	
4000	

Years BP	Period
4000	
4500	
5000	
5500	Middle Archaic
6000	
6500	
7000	
7500	
8000	
8500	Early Archaic
9000	
9500	
10,000	
10,500	Paleoindian
11,000	
11,500	

social structure that emerged during the Archaic, but rather, as Anderson and Sassaman (2012:107) state, "a region-wide restructuring of the cultural landscape." This historical change, we argue, is crucial for understanding Woodland societies. Likewise, the understanding of how this restructuring of the cultural landscape played out in the American Southeast contributes to our knowledge of early village formation as a broader historical process.

We focus primarily on one of the most important archaeological sites of the Woodland period in the American Southeast, the Crystal River site on Florida's central Gulf Coast (Figure 1.1). Crystal River earned notoriety among archaeologists thanks to the early work of antiquarian Clarence B. Moore (1903, 1907, 1918). The site was a standard reference in archaeological syntheses of the middle twentieth century (e.g., Griffin 1946; Phillips et al. 1951:173–74; Sears 1962; Willey 1966:288; Willey and Phillips 1958:160). Two principal features made it stand out among its peers: elaborate mounds of earth and shell, and exotic artifacts of stone, bone, shell, mineral, and metal. The latter established Crystal River as the southernmost major expression of what would become known as the Hopewell Interaction Sphere, a network of trade and ceremony that linked distant portions of North America during the Middle Woodland period, from around 100 B.C. to A.D. 600 (Caldwell 1964). However, the site's fame has been eclipsed by the under-reporting of previous work and, until recently, the paucity of archaeological investigations using modern techniques.

A very short distance downstream from Crystal River is another mound complex that is important to the research we present here. In contrast with Crystal River, Roberts Island became known to archaeologists only in the 1960s, when it was first noted in passing by Adelaide and Ripley Bullen (1961:69). It went practically unnoticed for another three decades before Brent Weisman (1995b) visited the site and prepared a brief report. Weisman described the series of islands that had previously been reported as separate sites as the Roberts Island Shell Mound Complex (for simplicity, we will generally use "Roberts Island"). At the center of the complex is a large shell midden with a small but well-formed and exceedingly well-preserved platform mound. Nearby are two other small platform mounds and several smaller midden piles.

The societies that flourished at Crystal River and Roberts Island during the Woodland period are typical of those often referred to as "complex hunter-gatherers." We avoid drawing too heavily on this characterization

Table 1.2. Temporal Divisions of the Woodland and Mississippian Periods for Regions of the Eastern Gulf Coast (with primary diagnostic ceramics)

Dates	Regions		
	Central-Peninsular Gulf Coast	Southwest Florida	Northern Gulf Coast
1500	Pinellas (Safety Harbor) (Safety Harbor Incised; Pinellas Incised)		Ft. Walton (Lake Jackson Plain, Fort Walton, and other incised types)
1450		Caloosahatchee IV (Glades Tooled)	
1400			
1350			
1300		Caloosahatchee III (Belle Glade Plain; St Johns Check Stamped; Pinellas Plain)	
1250			
1200			Weeden Island 5 (Wakulla Check Stamped; cob-marked)
1150			
1100			
1050			
1000	Englewood (Safety Harbor) (Englewood Incised; Sarasota Incised)	Caloosahatchee IIB (Belle Glade Plain and Red)	Weeden Island 4 (Wakulla Check Stamped; various Weeden Island incised and punctated types)
950			
900			
850	Very Late Manasota (Wakulla Check Stamped; St Johns Check Stamped)		Weeden Island 3 (decline in stamped pottery; various Weeden Island incised and punctated types; Wakulla Check Stamped)
800			
750			
700		Caloosahatchee IIA (Belle Glade Plain; sand tempered plain)	
650			
600	Late Manasaota (Pasco Plain; sand-tempered plain)		Weeden Island 2 (Swift Creek Complicated Stamped; various Weeden Island incised and punctated)
550			
500			
450			
400			Weeden Island 1 (Swift Creek Complicated Stamped; Weeden Island Incised; Carrabelle Incised and Punctated)
350			
300			
250			

(continued)

Table 1.2—*Continued*

Dates	Regions		
	Central-Peninsular Gulf Coast	Southwest Florida	Northern Gulf Coast
600	Late Manasaota (Pasco Plain; sand-tempered plain)	Caloosahatchee IIA (Belle Glade Plain; sand tempered plain)	Weeden Island 2 (Swift Creek Complicated Stamped; various Weeden Island incised and punctated)
550			
500			
450			
400			Weeden Island 1 (Swift Creek Complicated Stamped; Weeden Island Incised; Carrabelle Incised and Punctated)
350			
300			
250	Early Manasota (Deptford Check Stamped; Swift Creek Complicated Stamped)		
200			Late Deptford (Deptford Check Stamped; Swift Creek Complicated Stamped)
150			
100			
50	Deptford (Deptford Check Stamped)		
0		Caloosahatchee I (sand-tempered plain)	
50			
100			Middle Deptford (Deptford Check Stamped)
150			
200			
250			
300			
350			Early Deptford (Deptford Check Stamped; fiber-tempered pottery)
400			
450			
500			

Sources: Based on Luer and Almy 1982; Marquardt 2013; Milanich 1994; Mitchem 1989; Percy and Brose 1974; Willey 1949a.

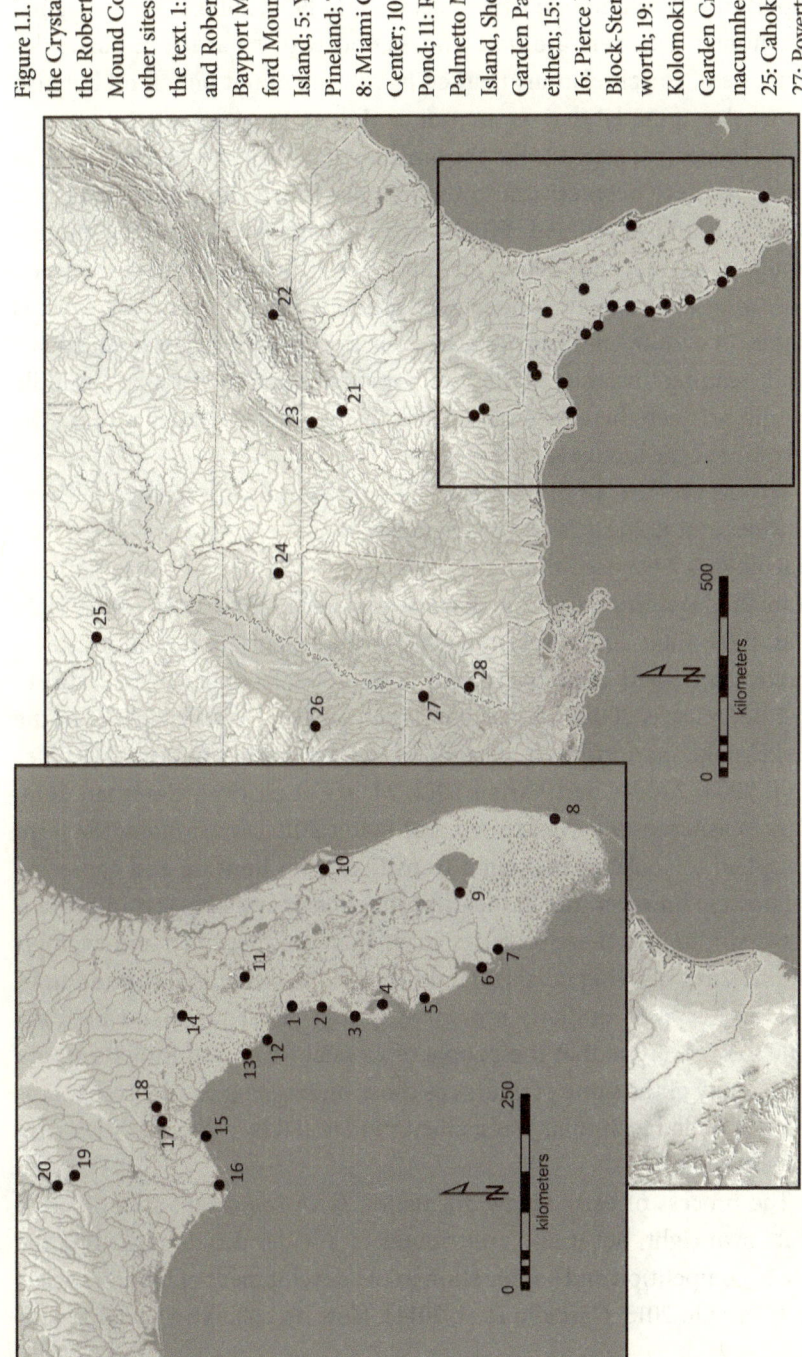

Figure 1.1. Location of the Crystal River site, the Roberts Island Shell Mound Complex, and other sites mentioned in the text. 1: Crystal River and Roberts Island; 2: Bayport Mound; 3: Safford Mound; 4: Weeden Island; 5: Yellow Bluffs; 6: Pineland; 7: Mound Key; 8: Miami Circle; 9: Fort Center; 10: Windover Pond; 11: River Styx; 12: Palmetto Mound, Deer Island, Shell Mound; 13: Garden Patch; 14: McKeithen; 15: Yent Mound; 16: Pierce Mound; 17: Block-Sterns; 18: Letchworth; 19: Mandeville; 20: Kolomoki; 21: Leake; 22: Garden Creek; 23: Tunacunnhee; 24: Pinson; 25: Cahokia; 26: Toltec; 27: Poverty Point; 28: Feltus.

for several reasons. First, the term is not an accurate descriptor of the mode of production at Crystal River and Roberts Island. Next, and more importantly, contemporary theorists (Ingold 1999, 2000:47) have argued that hunter-gatherers are best understood with regard to a particular structure of social relations marked by sharing of not only food but also knowledge, a model that we are not confident is appropriate to our case study. Indeed, we suggest that the breakdown in these sorts of social relations may have been critical to the manner in which Crystal River and Roberts Island developed. Finally, the archaeological study of hunter-gatherers has become deeply divided along theoretical lines, between those who adopt an evolutionary framework and others whose work is framed of contingent histories and theories of practice (Sassaman 2004). While leaning toward the latter, we hope to forge something of a middle ground between these extremes, a task that is arguably easier without the polemics of the hunter-gatherer debate.

We choose instead to conceptualize the Woodland societies at Crystal River and Roberts Island as examples of an "early village society." Archaeologists have used this term to describe societies in diverse settings, from the Neolithic period in Europe and Asia (Byrd 1994, 2005; Hole et al. 1969; Kuijt 2000; Nelson 2004), to the Formative period in Mesoamerica and South America (Bandy 2004, 2006; Flannery 1976; Lesure et al. 2013; Marcus 2008; Marcus and Flannery 1996; Whalen 1983), to the Basketmaker and Pithouse periods in the American Southwest (Kohler et al. 2004; Kohler and Varien 2012; Mabry et al. 1997; Rautman 2014, 2016; Wilshusen 1991; Wilshusen and Potter 2010). Most often, the term is applied to societies making a transition from hunting and gathering to farming; however, the mode of production is arguably less important to the similarities these societies share than are the social and ecological pressures of living in larger and more stable residential communities in a landscape of similarly organized groups (Rosenberg and Redding 2000:41). We argue that the people of Crystal River and Roberts Island faced many of the same pressures as those undergoing similar transitions and responded in similar ways, albeit moderated by particular historical circumstances.

The process of early village formation is an important area of study in its own right, but it also contributes to a wider debate regarding the role of competition and cooperation in the development of human societies (Carballo 2013; Carballo et al. 2014). How do collective social groups form in light of the obstacles posed by the pursuit of self-interests? The dynamic between competition and cooperation has emerged as a major topic of intellectual concern, as evidenced by its inclusion on the journal *Science*'s list of the "big questions" in contemporary science (Pennisi 2005). It is one of only a few topics on the list pertaining to the social sciences (Steckel 2007).

Theories of cooperation and conflict have developed largely in political science and evolutionary ecology. As other archaeologists have recently noted (Blanton and Fargher 2016:9–12; Carballo 2013; Carballo et al. 2014), much of this work is based on abstract game-theoretical modeling, short-term ethnographies, and anecdotal historical case studies. Archaeology, with its material and diachronic orientation, provides potential strength and depth to these studies. Thus far, however, archaeologists have made relatively few contributions to this issue. As Pauketat (2009:xvi–xiii) recently noted, archaeologists have paid surprisingly little attention to conflict, particularly among the native prehistoric societies of North America. On the opposite side of the coin, as Blanton and Fargher (2008:1) observe, anthropologists have largely abdicated the study of cooperation and collective action to scholars in other disciplines.

One obvious correlate of increasing cooperation is the choice people make to begin living together in larger and more permanent communities, although the process of village formation may also involve competition for cultural or material capital. Later in this chapter, we further develop the rationale for looking to early villages to understand the role of cooperation and competition in human societies. First, however, we provide a brief introduction to the Crystal River site.

Crystal River as Famous, and Then Largely Forgotten, "Enigma"

It has been more than a century since noted antiquarian Clarence B. Moore steered his steamship the *Gopher* up the clear waters of the Crystal River from the Gulf of Mexico. Crystal River was one of Moore's earliest stops on a 1902 excursion that would lead him down the west coast of Florida from Cedar Key to Tampa (Moore 1903:363). Moore's attention was undoubtedly drawn first to the huge, roughly rectangular mound of shell (which he referred to as Mound A) (Figure 1.2) along the northern bank of the river a short distance downstream from the town of Crystal River and the bubbling springs that serve as the river's source. However,

Figure 1.2. View north of Mound A at Crystal River from the river.

his previous work at other archaeological sites in the region had taught him that flat-topped mounds such as this, no matter how impressive, did not yield the burials and accompanying grave goods he desired. Moore likewise ignored the smaller platform mound (Mound H) at the northern end of the site, with its unusually long, narrow summit and ramped entrance (Figure 1.3).

Figure 1.3. View northeast across Mound G to Mound H at Crystal River.

Figure 1.4. View north of the reconstructed Main Burial Complex at Crystal River.

Instead, Moore turned his attention to a smaller suite of mounds—what he referred to as the Main Burial Complex—near the center of the site (Figure 1.4). Unlike most of the other mounds at the site, these appeared to be composed primarily of sand, rather than shell—a sign that they were more likely to contain the burials Moore sought. Moore (1903:382) would later note that "though the shell-heap on Crystal River is a famous one, the sand mound was unknown to the inhabitants of the town of Crystal River, even the owner being unaware of the existence of this mound."

Moore and his men set to work on the dome-shaped sand mound (Mound F) at the center of the complex, where they encountered burials rich with artifacts of copper and stone obviously imported from vast distances (Figure 1.5), as well as equally impressive but presumably local artifacts of bone and shell (Moore 1903). It seems safe to say that the results of Moore's work here exceeded his expectations; he would return to Crystal River twice, beginning in 1906 (Moore 1907). As before, he focused on the Main Burial Complex but this time directed his efforts to the "elevation" or platform (Mound E) surrounding the central burial mound and to a lesser extent the circular embankment (Mound C) that defines the

Figure 1.5. Copper ornament recovered by Moore from the Main Burial Complex at Crystal River, possibly representing a bear and completed in a style typical of Hopewell. Reproduced from Moore 1903:Figure 54.

limits of the complex. He found a number of burials in both locations, but most here lacked the exotic artifacts of copper and quartz crystal found in Mound F. Moore made his final visit to the site about a dozen years later, in 1917 (Moore 1918). He continued working in the circular embankment, where he identified a number of burials with shell and limestone artifacts.

Jerald Milanich (1999:7) has estimated that Moore spent a combined total of around three weeks of work at Crystal River, during which he excavated more than 400 burials. Gordon Willey (1949a:317) suggested that these burials may have represented more than 500 or 600 individuals. Modern archaeologists—and, of course, the Native American descendants of those buried in the mound—cringe at the thought of the coarseness of the excavations. Yet Moore's work has an upside; it established the importance of Crystal River among archaeologists and the public. The notoriety that the site achieved mainly from Moore's work led to its preservation as a Florida State Park and a National Historic Landmark.

Moore recognized the unusual nature of the artifacts at Crystal River, specifically their similarity to those from sites in the American Midwest that would soon come to be known as Hopewell, after a mound site in Ohio. He consulted Charles Willoughby, who had recently completed work at the Hopewell site, and Frederick Ward Putnam, excavator of the Turner Mound site, another Hopewellian mound complex (Moore

1903:409-410). Both men confirmed the similarities between artifacts from Crystal River and Ohio sites, the latter finding these proof of the "close connections of the prehistoric peoples of Florida . . . with those of the Ohio Valley region" (Moore 1903:422). One of Moore's other contemporaries, E. F. Greenman (1938), would later make this case more persuasively, arguing that Florida Hopewell diverged no more from that of Ohio than the latter region diverged from neighboring Illinois.

Why and how did artifacts from distant regions of the interior of North America find their way to peninsular Florida? Neither Moore nor Greenman were particularly concerned with these very basic, intriguing questions. Like most of their contemporaries of the cultural historical era of American archaeology, they considered these sorts of connections a natural result of the diffusion of ideas and the migration of people from one area to the next.

Nor would these questions trouble the next generation of archaeologists to work at Crystal River. Ripley Bullen (1951, 1953, 1965, 1966b), Hale Smith (1951), and Gordon Willey (1948a, 1948c, 1949b) were more intrigued with some of the site's other unusual features. Of the three, Bullen was by far the most heavily invested in Crystal River; he excavated in the Main Burial Complex, in another burial mound (G), and in the village, while Smith dug only a few small pits, and Willey conducted only surface collections and pottery analysis. Initially, the most vexing issue for these archaeologists concerned the site's platform mounds—a third example of which (Mound K) (Figure 1.6) was identified by Bullen (1966b) in an area of the site that was overgrown at the time of Moore's visit. The emerging cultural historical sequences (e.g., Ford and Willey 1941) suggested that these "temple" mounds dated later (to what we now recognize as the Mississippian period), when agricultural societies led by powerful chiefs constructed similar monuments throughout the Southeast. Constrained by the power of this idea, all three set out to prove that Crystal River dated at least partially to the Mississippian period (Bullen 1953; Smith 1951; Willey and Phillips 1944), despite the strong presence of Hopewellian artifacts and the preponderance of contemporaneous Middle and Late Woodland period ceramics in the village middens (Willey 1949a). They were ultimately stymied in their efforts to find any conclusive evidence of Mississippian connections (Willey 1948c). The apparent contradiction—a Woodland period "temple" mound—led Bullen (1951:142) to describe

Figure 1.6. View west of Mound K and a portion of the midden at Crystal River.

Crystal River as "enigmatic" and one of the "unsolved problems of Floridian archaeology" (see Russo [1994] and Pluckhahn [2007] for other examples of Bullen's reluctance to break with existing cultural historical sequences).

Where Bullen and Smith turned to later prehistory to explain the unusual features at Crystal River, other archaeologists looked to neighboring regions. McMichael (1960, 1964) argued that flat-topped mounds and other unusual features must have been introduced to Crystal River by immigrants from the Maya lowlands, then spread north to the Midwest to stimulate the "Hopewell Climax." James Ford (1969) offered a similar, if less specific, model for the flow of people and ideas from Mesoamerica.

Equally problematic or more so than the presence of platform mounds was the discovery of two limestone slabs at Crystal River (Bullen 1966b) (a possible third slab was discovered later [Hardman 1971]). One of these bears an inscribed figure, at least part of which appears to have some antiquity (Bullen 1966b). Bullen referred to the slabs as "stelae," a term used mainly in Mesoamerica to refer to stone with written inscriptions. Although the similarities are tenuous, the use of this term has stuck. The "stelae" have fueled additional speculation about possible connections between Crystal River and the Maya or others in Mesoamerica (Hardman 1971), despite a lack of any more definitive evidence.

There has been little archaeological study at Crystal River since Bullen's last excavations in the 1960s. Modern field investigations have been limited to park management and improvement (Ellis 1999, 2004, 2008b; Ellis et al. 2003; Glowacki 2002; Weisman 1992, 1993; Wheeler 2001). A few studies have been conducted on the human remains excavated by Bullen (Green 1993; Judd 1997; Katzmarzyk 1998; Mabulla ca. 1990), but the artifacts recovered from earlier excavations have attracted little attention (for exceptions, see Estabrook [2011] and Weisman [1995a]). Moore's artifacts, after several moves, are now mostly curated at the National Museum of the American Indian [NMAI] in Washington, D.C. Apart from Moore's basic published descriptions, they have—until now—never been studied or reported. The artifacts from Bullen's excavations are curated at the Florida Museum of Natural History (FLMNH); these were briefly tabulated by Weisman (1995a) but only recently studied in greater detail (Blankenship 2013; Kemp 2015).

As a result of the limitations of previous work and the lack of concerted research using modern methods, Crystal River has gone from famous to largely forgotten enigma. Once a standard reference in discussions of Hopewell and Middle Woodland period archaeology (e.g., Griffin 1946; Phillips et al. 1951:173–174; Sears 1962; Willey and Phillips 1958:160; Willey 1966:288), Crystal River is now often neglected (e.g., Price 2006:313) or mentioned only in passing (e.g., Neusius and Gross 2007:478).

Crystal River as a "Complex Hunter-Gatherer" Society

The monumental architecture and long-distance exchange that made Crystal River famous are two of the primary material manifestations of the type of social formations that anthropologists refer to as complex societies. Given the absence of any indications of horticulture, Crystal River would be classified by many as an example of "complex hunter-gatherers" (or "hunter-gatherer-fishers") similar to societies of the Late Pacific period on the Northwest Coast or Southern California or the late Mesolithic Natufian period of the Levant (Arnold 1996a). The recognition that some hunter-gatherers have more complex social relations than envisioned by earlier generations of anthropologists is a significant achievement (see Sassaman and Holly 2011). But there are problems with the term "complex hunter-gatherers" and its application.

The first problem is how to measure and define complexity with regard to hunter-gatherers. William Prentiss and Ian Kuijt (2004) have summarized the various ways archaeologists have approached this problem; briefly, these range from trait-based approaches that look for markers such as monuments and long-distance exchange (e.g., Brown 1985; Price 1985), to organization approaches that focus on status distinctions and control over labor or resources (e.g., Arnold 1993, 1996b; Hayden 1995), to what they refer to as "subsistence security" approaches that focus on the degree of population packing and the pressure to intensify production (Binford 2001).

The problems extend beyond "complex" to include the term "hunter-gatherer" itself. As Madonna Moss (2011:27) has noted for the native peoples Northwest Coast, the term is a misleading characterization of coastal dwellers whose subsistence focused largely on estuaries and the sea, and who actively owned and managed these marine resources (her concern would seem only weakly mitigated by the appendicized term "hunter-gatherer-fisher"). In a point that has relevance for our discussion of Crystal River and Roberts Island, Moss argues that the native people of the Northwest Coast were actually food producers, and in this respect more akin to horticulturalists than hunter-gatherers as traditionally conceived.

Timothy Ingold (2000:77–87) takes exception to the conventional dichotomy between collection and production invoked by Moss, among many others, to differentiate hunter-gatherers from horticulturalists and pastoralists. Significantly, however, Ingold (1999) argues that hunter-gatherers are differentiated in another respect: by a distinctive form of sociality marked by immediacy, autonomy (trust), and sharing (see also Lee 1988, 1990, 1992). Ingold's argument is too dense to fully relate here; at the risk of oversimplifying, his position is that social relations among hunter-gatherers "are constituted more by the sharing of food, residence, company, and memory, than by specific commitments and obligations incumbent on the occupants of positions within a formally instituted structure of social rules and obligations" (Ingold 1999:65).

Ingold's (1999) insights into hunter-gather sociality are profound. But are they universally applicable to hunter-gatherers? His discussion centers mainly on the small-scale social formations anthropologists have traditionally referred to as bands, but he uses this term interchangeably with "hunter-gatherer," and it is in relation to the latter that his ideas are often invoked by archaeologists (e.g., Sassaman and Holly 2011:5). Sassaman and Holly (2011:5) argue that it is incumbent on archaeologists to explain not only how the sort of sociality Ingold ascribes to hunter-gatherers is derived and maintained, but also "the conditions under which this sort of sociality is transformed into institutions of mistrust and exclusion." While we would not too heavily stress words like "mistrust" and "exclusion" in relation to the societies at Crystal River, it seems only logical that larger and more sedentary communities such as this required a different sort of sociality—with more formal structures of social rules and obligations. It thus may be more appropriate to consider these under a different rubric than "complex hunter-gatherer."

Crystal River and the Historical Process of Becoming Villagers

Recalling some of the same problems we cited above with regard to the literature on complex hunter-gatherers, Sassaman (2004:230) has observed,

> Clearly, the term "hunter-gatherer" does not carry the unified conceptual weight it once did, and we have to ask ourselves why and how the concept of complex hunter-gatherers truly differs from pastoral tribes or agricultural chiefdoms. Through some theoretical lenses, the differences blur indeed.

We agree. For us, the most salient features of the Woodland societies at Crystal River and Roberts Island are the ecological, social, and political milieu of life in larger and more permanent villages composed increasingly of people who were unrelated, in a landscape that was becoming full of villages of similar size. Through this theoretical lens, the societies of Crystal River and Roberts Island are more similar to the first village societies that developed elsewhere in the world, many of which were beginning to cultivate crops and herd animals.

Bandy and Fox (2010:2) define early villages as "a set of societies that are in the process of undergoing broadly comparable transformations in the face of broadly comparable and novel social and ecological conditions." They (Bandy and Fox 2010:3–4) describe the early village social process ("the process of becoming villagers") as shaped by four factors:

(1) the availability of an intensifiable system of food production (normally agriculture), (2) relatively permanent residence in nucleated

settlement clusters, (3) political autonomy of the village or settlement cluster, and (4) nearness in time to the origins of sedentary village life.

Certainly, these factors are not without ambiguity. As Bandy and Fox (2010:4–5) note, while the process of becoming villagers is usually associated with farming, this is not necessarily so; the critical factor here is population density, which is equally achievable in regions with intensifiable estuarine and marine resources, as at Crystal River. Taking this a bit further, Rosenberg and Redding (2000:41) argue that the organizational features associated with the Neolithic farming life developed before agriculture: "The reason for this is apparently that such organizational features are necessary for sedentary life, whatever subsistence base it is predicated on."

The term "sedentary village" is also open to interpretation, but is clearly applicable to Crystal River when defined in its simplest terms as "relatively permanent, multifamily residential clusters" (Bandy and Fox 2010:6). The concept of "autonomous villages" is likewise problematic, as villages are always linked to other communities (see Kowalewski 2012), but we take the term to mean that regional political hierarchies are only weakly developed, as we think was the case at Crystal River. Finally, as we noted above, we do not deny the appearance of earlier sedentary villages but suggest that these were largely isolated cases and still relatively near in time to the Woodland period.

We believe the process of becoming villagers suitably describes the Woodland period societies at Crystal River and Roberts Island. First, Bandy and Fox (2010) are careful to define this as a historical process, instead of an evolutionary type—as "hunter-gatherer" is too often perceived. By "historical process," as noted above, they mean one that played out in "broadly comparable" ways in different areas and times. Following Bandy (2006:13), we see early village societies as an example of what Julian Steward (1955:8) described as a "phenomenon of limited occurrence," which we take to describe commonalities falling between the generality of evolutionary approaches and the particularism of many historical approaches.

Competition and Cooperation in Early Villages

Walking a line between process and particularism is not easy in the polarized intellectual milieu regarding the historical development of social groups. On the one hand, some scholars see this as a process guided by universal human tendencies toward competition that must be overcome in order for people to live together. Others see the process as determined mainly by historically contingent changes in production or other factors.

"How We Conquered the Planet" declares the title on the cover of the August 2015 issue of the *Scientific American*, with the subtitle "Our Species Wielded the Ultimate Weapon: Cooperation." The author of the cover article, paleoanthropologist Curtis W. Marean, argues that the colonization of the Earth by *Homo sapiens* was the result of a genetically encoded trait that he refers to as "hypersociality"—an extreme brand of cooperation that "made us, on one hand, peerless collaborators and, on the other, ruthless competitors" (Marean 2015:34). Marean thinks this tendency toward hypersociality would have emerged in conditions of conflict, as groups with higher numbers of "prosocial" people worked together more effectively and passed the genes for this behavior on to the next generation (Marean 2015:36; see also Marean 2014).

Marean's explanation for the development of larger social collectives is typical of evolution-minded scholars in anthropology, biology, ecology, and other fields, for whom the impetus for cooperation resides somewhat paradoxically in the competitive nature of individuals, a tendency that they believe was overcome sometime deep in our evolutionary history. Drawing insights from evolutionary ecology (e.g., Richerson et al. 2003; Smith 2003; Smith and Bird 2005) and game theory (e.g., Axelrod 1984, 1997), these theorists assume—based on natural selection—that individuals act according to their self-interests. This presents an impediment to the development of larger and more complex social formations, in that "free-riders" can reap the benefits of collective action without participating. Still, in a landscape where there is conflict for scarce resources, larger social groups offer a competitive advantage, and evolution favors populations that can overcome the tendency to self-interest. For Marean, the key to overcoming this tendency is genetics, but many evolution-oriented archaeologists posit instead the institution of social mechanisms to enforce participation, especially "costly" rituals that signal one's commitment to play by the rules (e.g., Bonhage-Freund and Kurland 1994; Kantner 1996;

Kohler 2004; Kohler and Van West 1996; Kohler et al. 2000; Kohler et al. 2004; Peacock and Rafferty 2013; Stanish 2004; Stanish and Haley 2005). Carballo et al. (2014:101) note that evolutionary approaches to cooperation like these generally typically focus on the individual or small groups; tend to the theoretical and are hence prone to general explanations; and are usually based on limited empirical evidence that is "only peripherally linked to the ethnographic and archaeological records." Criticizing the assumption that human societies have been basically cooperative since sometime deep in our evolutionary past, Blanton and Fargher (2016:10–11) note that this "seems quaint when we recall the numerous examples in which the social fabric of a society is constructed principally out of the coercive and exploitative power of a particular person, faction, or social class."

Evolutionary approaches to cooperation can be compared with recent work under the rubric of collective action theory (Carballo et al. 2014:110; DeMarrais 2016). Modeling human behavior from the perspective of rational choice theory, collective action theorists focus on how societies develop institutions to overcome the tensions between individual and group interests (Blanton and Fargher 2016:3). Much of the work in collective action shares with evolutionary approaches a concern with the management of free-riders (DeMarrais 2016:4). However, collective action theorists recognize that a number of variables influence the decision to cooperate. Research in this vein (e.g., Blanton and Fargher 2008; Levi 1988; Ostrom 1990, 2000) tends to focus on larger social groups, gives greater weight to cultural and historical differences, and typically draws on empirical data drawn from the ethnographic and archaeological records (Carballo et al. 2014:110). Blanton and Fargher (2008), for example, examine a number of case studies of larger social groups to understand variation in the extent to which, and manner in which, they are integrated. They argue that collective or corporate leadership is common among social groups where leaders are more dependent on local populations for their economic support. Autocratic leadership, on the other hand, is more typical of societies where leaders demand less from the local population.

DeMarrais (2016:3) has described a third body of work, perhaps less cohesive than the previous two, as "social cohesion approaches." In general, archaeologists working from this perspective consider decisions regarding competition and cooperation as complex and historically contingent, rather than as determined by natural selection or uniform variables such as group size. Many draw from theories of agency and practice (Bourdieu 1977, 1980; Giddens 1979, 1984). As DeMarrais (2016:3) summarizes the common premise,

> kinship and shared cosmology, propinquity and collective experience, and the sense of familiarity that builds up over time act as "social glue," providing a foundation for consensus and coalition-building at the local level.

Emphasis is placed on the manners in which bodily and sensory experiences, shared habitus, and rituals build solidarity. However, much of this work is rooted in Marxist theories that see such seemingly communal understandings as components of ideologies that mask social divisions (e.g., Bender 1990; Gilman 1981; McGuire 1992; Nassaney 1992, 2000, 2001; Pauketat 2000; Pauketat and Alt 2005; Sassaman 1993; Varien and Potter 2008). Others, especially those working with materials from the historical era, describe how cooperation develops in groups that coalesce around issues of class or race (Leone and Potter 1999; McGuire and Paynter 1991; Saitta 2007).

A number of authors have suggested the need for rapprochement between these approaches (Blanton and Fargher 2016; Carballo et al. 2014; Roscoe 2013; Saitta 2013). Carballo and colleagues (2014; see also Roscoe 2013) suggest building common ground on the recognition of a few basic principles. First is the acceptance that people are not simply self-interested but instead have multiple interests. As Blanton and Fargher (2008:16) note, "any social actor may be cooperative or not at the same time, or both at the same time with respect to different situations." Or, further, as Carballo et al. (2014:99) observe, "complex societies comprise fluid networks of individuals who cooperate and compete in differing social domains."

Next is the recognition that there are different forms of cooperation and collective action, and these may operate at different temporal and spatial scales. For example, where collective interests are ephemeral, we may expect temporary coalitions such as task groups, while more enduring cooperation might be expected with respect to longer-term challenges (Carballo et al. 2014:111; Roscoe 2013:60). Cooperative efforts may be community-wide or might involve only a subset of the population

(Carballo et al. 2014:116). And, as a final example, cooperative relations may be informal or formalized through rituals or economic relationships, among other means.

As Carballo and colleagues (2014:116) note, more explicit consideration of the logic of cooperation over space and time "provides an avenue capable of productively investigating the recursive relations between individuals and institutions, commoners and elites, agency and structure, top-down and bottom-up processes, and biology and culture." Crystal River, Roberts Island, and related early villages of the Gulf Coast make an ideal field laboratory for the study of competition and cooperation in the formation and growth of social groups, because—as Dye (2009:98) has noted—the societies here challenge some of our traditional expectations (see also Carr 2008a:644–647 for Hopewell societies generally). The scale of public architecture and scope of prestige goods exchange are suggestive of the sort of complex societies characterized by exclusionary political strategies, competition, and conflict (Anderson 1998; Coon 2009; Dye 2009). However, there is little evidence of warfare (Hutchinson 2004:155) and much of the ritual associated with mounds appears to have been corporate in nature (Knight 1990, 2001; Pluckhahn 2003; Thompson and Pluckhahn 2012). These facts suggest to us that competitive and cooperative social practices alternated or even overlapped at different temporal and spatial scales.

Approaching Early Villages at Crystal River and Beyond

We suggest that the forces that shaped early villages were complex and not reducible to mechanical relationships and motivations. Indeed, the recognition of the complexity of factors shaping the process of becoming villagers is one of the principal attractions for the application of this perspective to Crystal River and Roberts Island. Previous work suggests that early village societies grappled creatively with a number of issues, some biological, others ecological, and still others social. The historical process of becoming villagers therefore includes both broad-scale, long-term structural constraints and opportunities and the shorter-term motivations of individuals or smaller groups. For example, we know that increased fertility and, ultimately, higher population density accompanied the higher residential stability of early villages (Bandy 2010) and that this sometimes precipitated a need to intensify food production to feed larger populations (Bandy and Fox 2010). We also know that early village life presented health problems as more people and more waste are crowded into smaller spaces (Goring-Morris and Belfer-Cohen 2010). But it is also commonly recognized that social life in early villages presented novel challenges in terms of the organization of decision making and labor (Fletcher 1995; Johnson 1982; Kowalewski 2013). We focus particularly on the maintenance of egalitarianism (or the ideology thereof) as the sociality of sharing was transformed.

Our goal in this volume is to elucidate Crystal River and Roberts Island as examples of the historical process of early village societies. This is historical process without the benefit of written records, which requires the theory, method, and data of archaeology. In Chapter 2, we summarize archaeological work at Crystal River and Roberts Island, focusing especially on investigations conducted in association with the Crystal River Early Village Archaeological Project, or CREVAP.

One part of "historical process" is history. Following Rautman (2014:35), we are interested in understanding how this early village "worked" as a living organization within a landscape of similar small-scale, early village societies. By this we mean the particular details of how a vacant ceremonial center developed on the landscape at Crystal River (Chapter 3), how this set the stage for the development of a village (Chapter 4), and how this village grew to become a regional center for population and ceremony (Chapter 5). We also consider how the village ultimately declined (Chapter 6) and was eclipsed by the growth of new centers at Roberts Island and elsewhere in the region (Chapter 7).

The second part of "historical process" is process, by which we mean how the particular details of Crystal River's history may or may not be typical of other societies undergoing the same transition. In Chapter 8, we look for correspondence between Crystal River and neighboring and contemporaneous sites on the Gulf Coast. We also look for parallels with early village societies elsewhere in the world. In doing so, we hope to contribute to the broader literature on the development of early villages, as well as to the question of why this form of sociality emerged among groups across the ancient world.

We also hope to contribute in some small way to contemporary public discourse regarding the social and ecological dynamics of human societies. For us, the communities at Crystal River and Roberts Island attest to the creativity and resilience of early villages in regard to ecological challenges, as well as the inherent tensions of living in larger social collectives. In the Afterword, we consider the implications of our work for contemporary debates regarding, first, individual versus collective responsibility for social welfare and, second, the human role in and response to environmental change.

2

Context

The archaeological site of Crystal River has been the target of speculation since at least 1859, when D. G. Brinton (1859:178–179; 1867:356–357) published the earliest known written description of Mound A. For perspective, this was two years before the onset of the Civil War and Abraham Lincoln's election as president, at a point when archaeology was just emerging as a field of scientific inquiry. At the time, many people still believed that mounds like this were built by a mythical race—perhaps a lost race of giants or people from Europe—rather than Native Americans (Silverberg 1986). Unfortunately, a long history of attention to Crystal River has not automatically led to clarity of understanding; the site has remained, at least until recently, poorly understood. Roberts Island, which was first recorded as an archaeological complex comparatively recently (around fifty years ago), has remained even more of an enigma.

This book describes the fruits of recent research at Crystal River and Roberts Island. In this chapter we present an overview of the methods that we employed in our investigations at the sites. Our research builds on the work of earlier generations of archaeologists, from C. B. Moore in the early 1900s; to Gordon Willey, Hale Smith, and others in the middle twentieth century; and on to Ripley Bullen and others in the later twentieth century. We present a brief overview of this earlier work, which has been summarized elsewhere: first and in considerable detail by Brent Weisman (1995a), and more recently and succinctly by Pluckhahn et al. 2009 and Pluckhahn et al. 2010. However, we begin with a brief overview of the sites and their setting on the central peninsular Gulf Coast of Florida.

The Crystal River Site and Roberts Island Complex and Their Setting

Crystal River and Roberts Island are located in Citrus County, Florida, approximately 3 km (2 miles) west and 1.6 km (1 mile) north of the city of

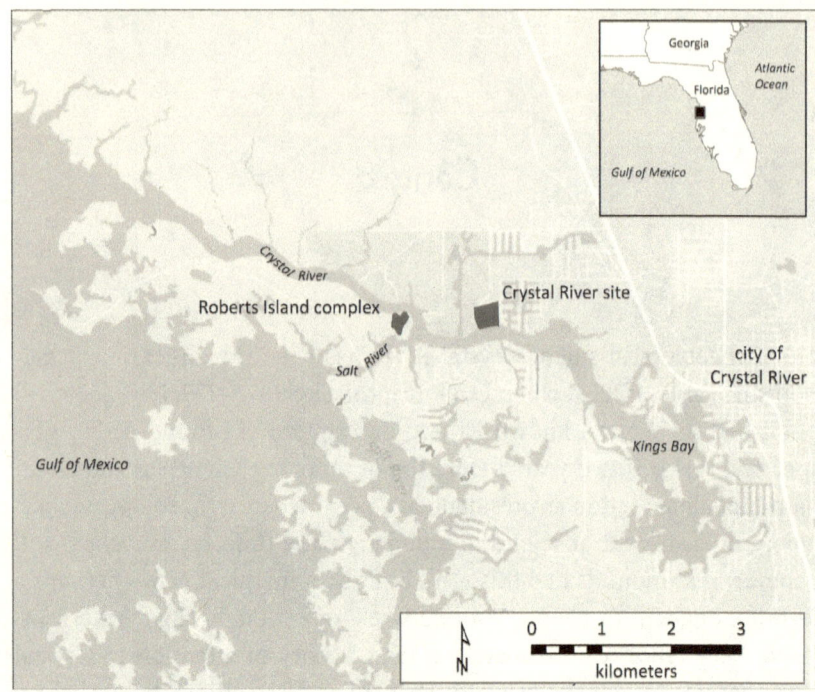

Figure 2.1. Location of Crystal River and Roberts Island.

Crystal River (Figure 2.1). The Crystal River, which directly borders the Crystal River site to the south, originates a short distance to the southeast at a series of springs in Kings Bay (Florida Department of Environmental Protection [hereinafter FDEP] 2000:14). The river flows west and slightly north for about 10 km (6 mi) before emptying into the Gulf of Mexico. The Crystal River site is located almost halfway between the river's source (at a series of springs at Kings Bay) and its mouth (at Crystal Bay and the Gulf of Mexico). Roberts Island is located only a short distance downstream, at the junction of the Crystal and Salt rivers.

Crystal River and Roberts Island lie in the Gulf Coastal Lowlands geomorphic division of the mid-Florida Peninsula, specifically at the interface between the coastal swamps and terraces (Cooke 1945; White 1970) (Figure 2.2). These lowlands, which border the entire Florida coast at elevations of less than 30 m (100 ft), are widest in southern Florida but narrow somewhat in the vicinity of the sites (Cooke 1945:10). To the east of the Coastal Lowlands in the vicinity of Crystal River site is the Brooksville Ridge section, part of the Central Highlands.

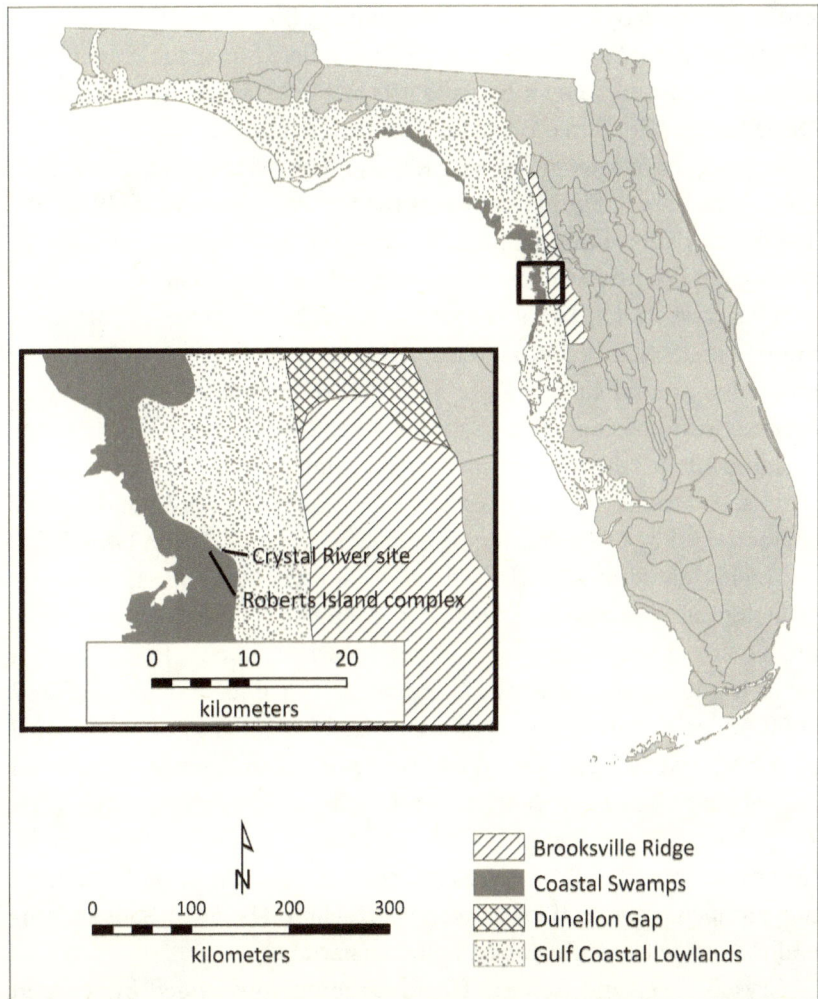

Figure 2.2. Location of Crystal River and Roberts Island with respect to major geomorphic divisions. Divisions based on White (1970), with GIS data provided by the Florida Department of Environmental Protection.

Composed of a series of marine terraces formed as Pleistocene shorelines, the Coastal Lowlands can be described as gently sloping plains with escarpments that face seaward (Cooke 1945:11; FDEP 2000:10). The Crystal River site lies on the Pamlico terrace, found at elevations less than 7.6 m (25 ft) above sea level. This is the most extensive plain in Florida, covering most of southern Florida, as well as broad strips along both coasts to the north. The Pamlico terrace is composed of sand and clayey sand,

and is underlain by limestone and dolomite of Eocene and Oligocene age (FDEP 2000:10). Specifically, the sites are situated on a substrate of undulating limestone known to geologists as the Williston member of the Ocala Group (Goodbred 1995:14).

In terms of hydrology, Crystal River and Roberts Island sites are located in an area of Florida known as the Springs Coast (Wolfe 1990:211). The spring rivers of this region flow across the shallow carbonate layer to produce an extensive marsh system. Indeed, the central Gulf Coast is one of the largest stretches of marsh shoreline in North America, extending more than 250 km (155 mi) (Goodbred 1995:2). Within this unique area, the region around Crystal River is further differentiated by its position between two physiographic divisions: to the south is the marsh archipelago, a salt marsh and mangrove swamp composed of hundreds of small islands, and to the north is the shelf embayment, a marsh-bound estuary characterized by extensive shore-parallel oyster bars (Hutton 1986:1).

The low elevations on which the Crystal River and Roberts Island archaeological sites reside are hydric hammocks (FDEP 2000:18). Hammocks are characterized by well-developed hardwood forests with a variable understory generally dominated by palms and ferns (FDEP 2000:Addendum 4). The understory typically includes sabal palm (*Sabal palmetto*) and saw palmetto (*Serenoa repens*). Tree species include red cedar (*Juniperus silicola*), and slash pine (*Pinus eliottii*), swamp bay (*Persea palustris*), sweet bay (*Magnolia virginiana*), and southern magnolia (*Magnolia grandiflora*), as well as live oak (*Quercus virginiana*) and other nut-producing species (Goodbred 1995:42; Hutton 1986:76). Soils are generally sandy with considerable organic material.

Crystal River and Roberts Island are both surrounded by wetland marshes (Cowardin et al. 1979; FDEP 2000:18) (Figure 2.3). Those nearest the sites are classified as freshwater emergent wetlands and freshwater forested shrub wetlands, both of which are tidal (Cowardin et al. 1979). These natural areas are composed of expanses of grasses, rushes, and sedges along coastlines of low-wave-energy rivers (FDEP 2000:Addendum 4). Typical plants include saltgrass (*Distichlis spicata*), cordgrass (*Spartina*), rushes (*Juncus*), marsh elder (*Iva annua*), cattail (*Typha*), and bulrushes (*Scirpus*). Animals characteristic of these environments include: various species of small terrestrial and marine snails; marsh clams (*Polymesoda caroliniana*), eastern oysters (*Crassostrea virginica*), and other bivalves; fiddler (*Uca pugilator*) and blue (*Callinectes sapidus*) crabs; American

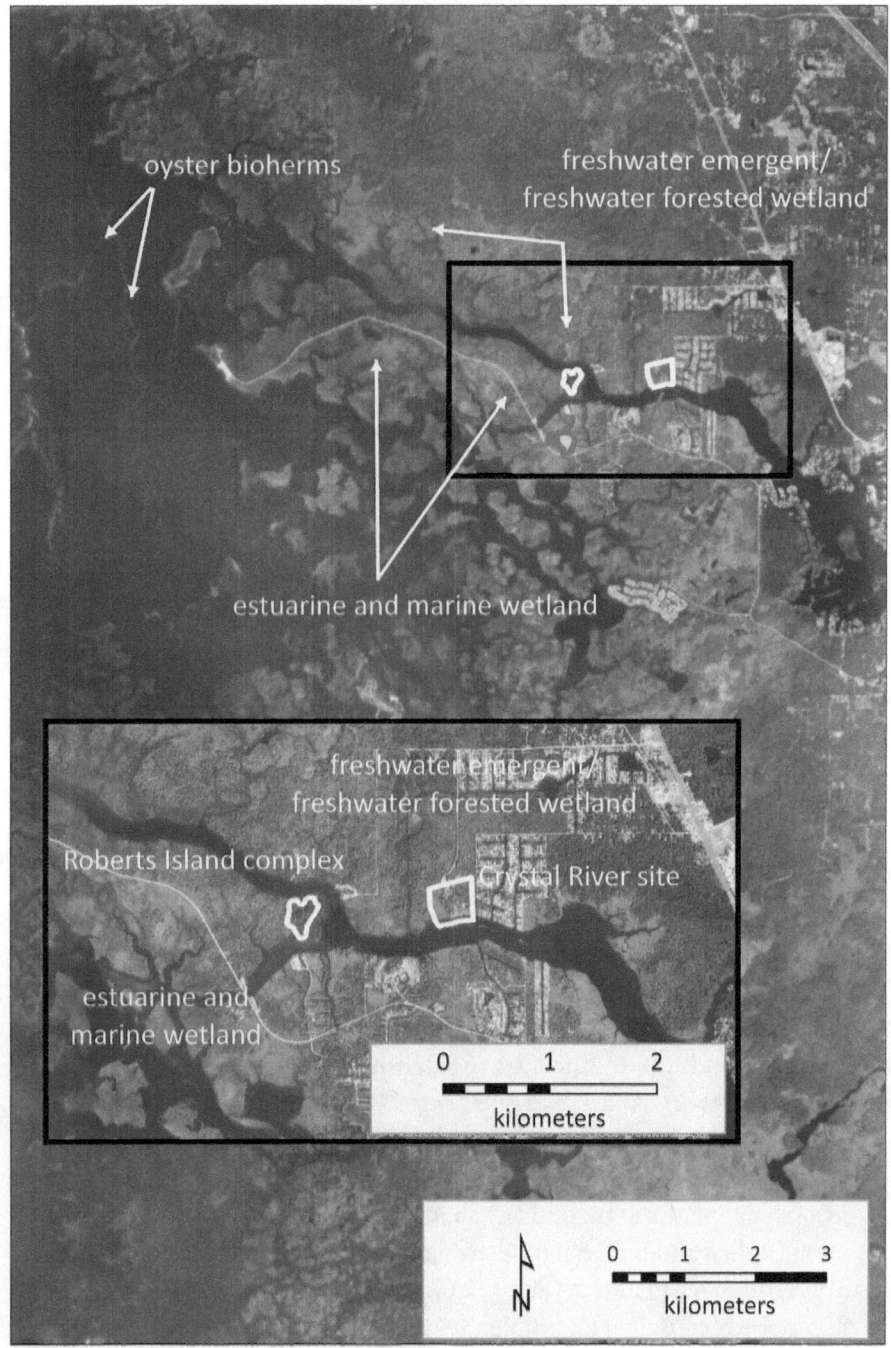

Figure 2.3. Location of Crystal River and Roberts Island with respect to major hydrologic communities. Community definitions based on Cowardin et al. (1979), with GIS data provided by the U.S. Fish and Wildlife Service and the National Wetlands Inventory.

alligators (*A. mississippiensis*) and various smaller reptiles; various species of turtles; osprey (*Pandion haliaetus*), marsh wrens (*Cistothorus palustris*), and other species of small birds; as well as deer (*Odocoileus virginianus*), raccoon (*Procyon lotor*), and other mammals. Various types of fishes are also common in tidal marshes. To the west and south of the sites, estuarine and marine wetlands are more common (Cowardin et al. 1979). These are subtidal and dominated by aquatic vascular plants.

As we describe in the chapters that follow, the landscapes at Crystal River and Roberts Island are not pristine but have been modified by people for thousands of years. Until relatively recently, most of this landscape modification was the result of the actions of Native Americans in the first millennium A.D. The Crystal River site includes an 8-m-high platform mound (A) (see Figure 1.2), as well as several smaller platform mounds (Figure 2.4). One of these smaller platform mounds (Mound H) (see Figures 1.1–1.3) anchors an open area—an apparent plaza—that is bordered by two burial complexes, one discrete (Mound G) and the other comprising several interrelated parts (Mounds C–F) (see Figure 1.1–1.4). Another small platform mound (K) (see Figure 1.6) and an irregularly shaped mound (J) stand north of Mound A on a portion of the shell ridge or midden. Finally, the site includes three upright limestone boulders (two bearing inscribed images) that have been described as "stelae" (Bullen 1965, 1966b).

As defined by Weisman (1995b), the Roberts Island Shell Mound Complex includes five separate sites originally recorded by Adelaide and Ripley Bullen (1961; see also site forms at the Florida Master Site File [hereinafter FMSF], Tallahassee) (Figure 2.5). Site 8CI41 is the largest site in the complex, and occupies the main area of elevated ground known as Roberts Island. The site includes an extensive midden, described by Weisman (1995b:1–2) as "a broad shell ridge" with "several lower mounded areas" together totaling 6–8 ha (15–20 ac). Site 8CI41 also includes the largest and best preserved monumental construction in the complex, a rectangular platform mound (A) about 4 m (13 ft) high, with an apparent ramp (Bullen and Bullen 1961; Weisman 1995b) connecting the summit to a plaza-like area to its east (Figure 2.6). A second mound (B), also possibly flat-topped (cf. Bullen and Bullen 1961:69), is located to the northeast on site 8CI40; it now serves as a foundation for a home that was constructed in the 1950s (Figure 2.7). Recent survey suggests the presence of a third

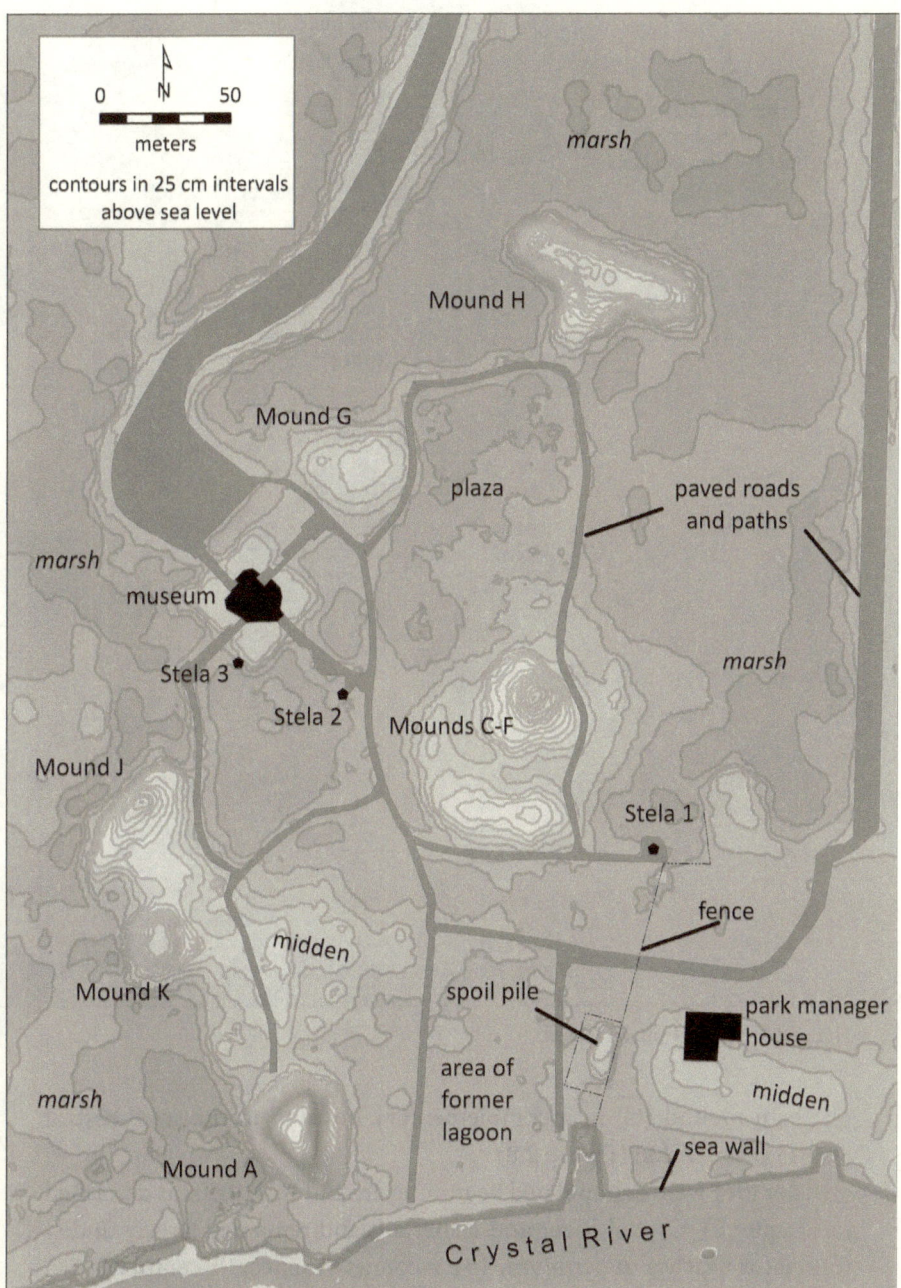

Figure 2.4. Map of Crystal River.

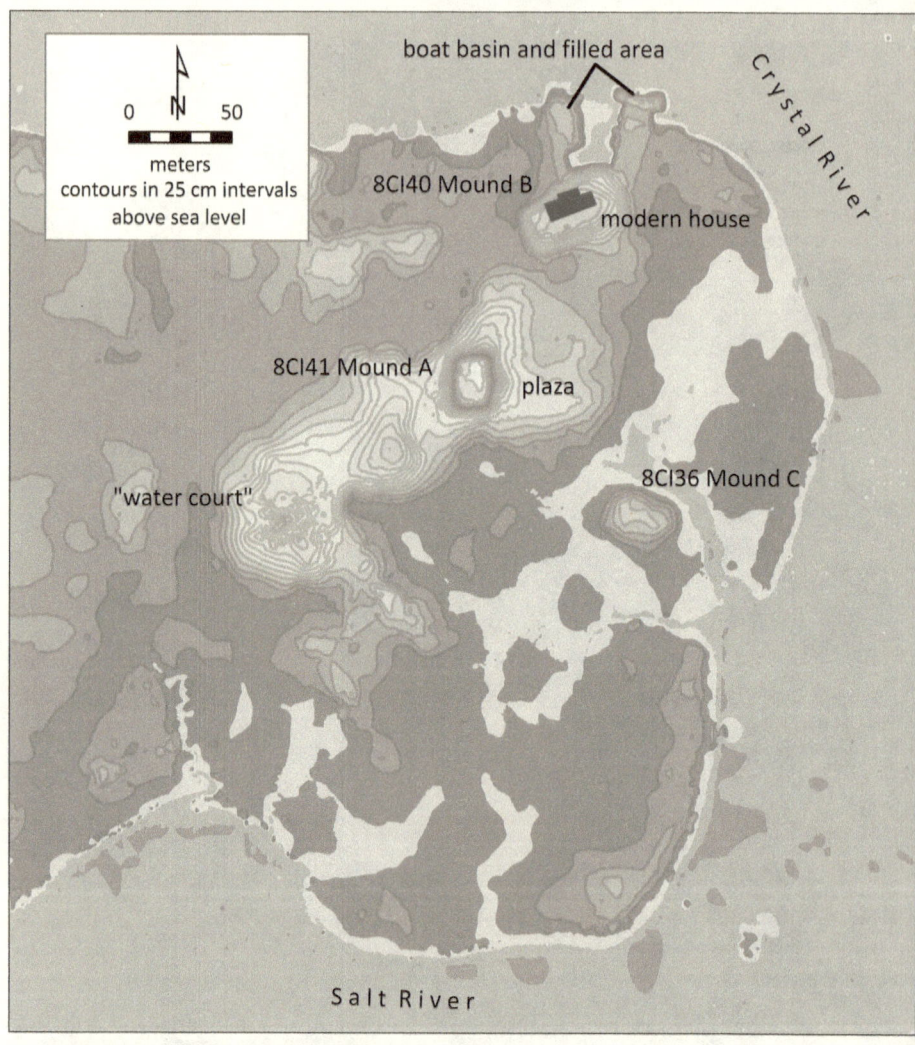

Figure 2.5. Map of Roberts Island.

platform mound (C) in a complementary position to the southeast of 8CI41 on site 8CI36 (Figure 2.8).

After they were depopulated beginning around A.D. 1050 (as described in Chapter 7), Crystal River and Roberts Island remained largely undisturbed for nearly a millennium. The accounts of sixteenth-century Spanish explorers suggest native settlement of the area was slight at the time of contact (Hudson 1998). It remained so even as settlers of European and African descent began moving to Florida in greater numbers under

Figure 2.6. View of Mound A on site 8CI41 at Roberts Island.

Figure 2.7. View of Mound B on site 8CI40 at Roberts Island.

Figure 2.8. View of site 8CI36 and Mound C at Roberts Island.

Spanish, British, and—eventually—American rule. An 1847 survey plat map shows only a few houses and fields in the vicinity of Crystal River (map on file on Land Boundary Information System [LABINS], Florida Department of Environmental Protection [FDEP]), Division of State Lands, Bureau of Survey and Mapping). These include one house that probably stood somewhere in the vicinity of the modern park ranger's home (FDEP 2003).

Settlement increased gradually after the Civil War. By 1885 the population of Citrus County had reached around 4,000 (Dunn 1977:74). An 1882 guide to Florida noted Crystal River as one of the principal "little farming or lumbering settlements" of the Gulf Coast (Barbour 1964 [1882]:147). The principal industry was the manufacture of pencils from the cedar trees that were abundant in the area (Dunn 1977:92).

R. J. Knight, who owned the Crystal River property when C. B. Moore visited for the first time in 1903 (Moore 1903:379), is listed in the poll taxes for 1898–1901 as a naval store manufacturer (records on file at the Citrus County Historical Society [CCHS], Inverness, Florida). The same year as Moore's visit, Knight gave the Crystal River Lumber Co., of which he was part owner, covenant to the timber on numerous parcels that probably include the current park property (Deed Book 23:257, CCHS).

The population of the area began to boom in the 1960s. The effects of this growth are evident in aerial photographs of the Crystal River site and adjoining properties (Figure 2.9). A 1952 aerial photograph shows minimal development. By the time of the 1969 aerial photograph, new canals had been excavated, and a housing subdivision was completed to the east of the site. Perhaps as a result of this development, the wetland buffer between the river and Mound A seems to have disappeared.

The accelerated development brought increasingly direct impacts to the archaeological site. In a visit to the site in 1951, John Goggin noted that lower area of Mound A had been partially bulldozed (Florida Site File card on file at the FLMNH, Gainesville). In 1960 Ripley Bullen noted that the ramp or "graded way" had been "very recently removed" by the landowner at the time (letter from Ripley Bullen to George C. Dyer, November 11, 1960, on file at the FLMNH, Gainesville).

In response to these and other incidents, Ripley Bullen began discussion with the landowners regarding the possibility that the property might be acquired by the State of Florida (Weisman 1995a:17). The first and principal acquisition in 1962 was a 7.3-ha (18-ac) tract that included all of the major mounds, except for a large portion of Mound A that remained in private ownership. The Florida Board of Parks and Historic Memorials (the predecessor of the FDEP's Division of Recreation and Parks) obtained this tract via a donation by S. M. and E. A. Whitcraft and G. C. and I. Dyer.

Former landowner George Dyer maintained a strong interest in the development of the park and lobbied for public interpretation, including a museum (Weisman 1995a:17–18). The Florida State Museum began planning museum displays in 1964, with considerable input from Bullen (Weisman 1995a:18). The museum formally opened in 1965. Onsite interpretation included an in situ display of human burials excavated by Bullen in Mound C of the Main Burial Complex, since decommissioned out of respect to Native Americans.

Unfortunately, the state was slow to acquire the remaining parcel that included a portion of Mound A. By the time of a photo taken in 1964 (Figure 2.10), as much as two-thirds of the eastern portion of the mound had been removed for use as fill (Weisman 1995a:45).

Figure 2.9. Comparison of 1952 (*top*) and 1969 (*bottom*) aerial photographs of Crystal River showing development of the area. Photo credits: aerial photograph DCP-7H-69, flown 1-8-52, and aerial photograph DCP-ILL-252, flown 12-4-1969, Aerial Photography: Florida project, http://web.uflib.ufl.edu/digital/collections/FLAP/.

Figure 2.10. 1964 photograph showing extensive damage to the east side of Mound A at Crystal River. Reproduced courtesy of the FLMNH (Negative PN94.228.1250).

Ouida and Theron A. White purchased the tract of land that included the eastern portion of the mound and the lagoon to the east around 1965, with the intention of creating a 42-space trailer park, according to an article in the Ocala *Star-Banner* (1965). The article noted plans for the construction of a marina (capable of accommodating 52 boats) and the dredging of a deeper swimming area in the adjacent river. The article notes that "the top of Shell Mound will become a shaded patio-like resting place for residents and museum visitors."

The Whites followed through with the plan for the trailer park (Figure 2.11), but apparently not for the marina. A later newspaper article (Meier 1972) noted the presence of 42 trailer sites for "transients," another 32 for "regulars," and two docks that could accommodate 10 to 12 boats. Demand was evidently high; in a comparison jarring to contemporary readers, the article observed that "getting a set-up in the Crystal River Mobile Home Park is about as easy as ending the war in Vietnam." The article also noted that at that time the Whites still owned "the huge pile of oyster shells that forms a major feature of the museum." Regarding the earlier damage to the mound, Ouida White reported, "Some of the shells... were used by the government for road building but that was stopped when the site became a museum." But the article also related that Theron White had recently borrowed more shells "for fill that he needed." Some of the earth and shell that were removed from Mound A may have been used to fill a

Figure 2.11. Aerial view of the former trailer park at Crystal River.

lagoon to the east of the mound in anticipation of development. Museum officials reportedly protested the action, "but White insists he had every right in the world to act as he did."

The state acquired the privately owned portion of Mound A—or at least what remained of it—from the Whites around this time, as indicated by a 1973 appraisal conducted by the Florida Department of Natural Resources (Tolius 1973). The 1,520 square meters (16,355 square feet) of land was valued at around $4,000, while the 6,880 cubic meters (9,000 cubic yards) of oyster shell was valued at nearly $22,000. If this is an accurate indication of the value that was placed on shell mounds for construction fill in Florida, it is a wonder not that Mound A was damaged but that any of the mounds at Crystal River or elsewhere in the state were saved.

Today, Crystal River Archaeological State Park encompasses around 25 ha (61 ac). The Crystal River site was officially designated as a National Historic Landmark in 1990 (Weisman 1995a:ix).

As we discuss in Chapter 4, the 1993 "Storm of the Century" destroyed much of the mobile home park and set the stage for the final acquisition of the remaining portion of the White property by the state. The Florida Board of Trustees officially obtained the parcel from Ouida White in 1996 (Deed Book 1152:731, CCHS). Most of the remaining vestiges of the trailer park were removed in 2000 (Behrendt 2000).

The property that includes the Roberts Island site complex was purchased by the State of Florida in 1996 from Annie C. Roberts (formerly known as Annie Caroline Christian), A. H. Roberts, and Carol R. Brennan (Deed Book 1137:1192, CCHS). The property appears to have been in the possession of the Christian family for many years, but precisely how long is difficult to determine. In a site form dating sometime after 1951 (on file at the FMSF, Tallahassee), Ripley Bullen described the site complex as "Christian's Shell Mounds," an apparent reference to the owner at the time. However, Bullen also referred to a house that formerly stood on the site as "Edge's home." The 1942 tax roll provides no evidence that the Christians or Edge lived on the property; the roll lists the status of the property as "unknown."

Part or all of the tract that contains the Roberts Island complex may have been purchased by Annie C. Christian and John Lanier Christian from Mrs. Thelma Smith in 1931, but unfortunately, while a transaction between these parties is indexed, the corresponding deed (CCHS 78:600) is missing; thus, the precise property and nature of the transaction cannot be confirmed. Annie C. Christian was presumably the same person as, or a relative of, Annie C. Roberts, who sold the land to the state in 1996 (as noted above), but this is not clear from the historical records.

Potentially conflicting information regarding the timing of the Christians' purchase of the property is provided by the tax records (on file at the CCHS), which allow that Mrs. J. F. Smith was in possession of 120 acres in the same township and range that includes Roberts Island in 1929 and 1935—the latter perhaps suggesting it was still owned by Mrs. Smith and had yet to have been purchased by the Christians. In 1912 J. F. Smith and the Dixon Crucible Co. owned most of the land in this area (tax records on file at the CCHS). The company, based in New Jersey, was a major manufacturer of pencils and was named for Joseph Dixon, the inventor of the graphite pencil (Karnoutsos 2007). Unfortunately, neither J. F. Smith nor Mrs. J. F. Smith are listed in any of the extant poll tax registers for early-twentieth-century Citrus County.

The Roberts Island site is today preserved and protected as a part of the Crystal River Preserve State Park. The site has yet to be listed on the National Register of Historic Places, although it has been recommended as potentially eligible "without question" (Weisman 1995b:3). The work presented here should form the basis for a nomination.

We would be remiss if we did not pause to consider the substantial damage inflicted by uncontrolled development on Crystal River and Roberts Island in the modern era. Unfortunately, this story is far from unique in Florida or the American Southeast more generally. Hundreds of shell mounds across the state were mined for road fill and construction materials; we are fortunate that Crystal River and Roberts Island were acquired by the state. While we may hope that we now live in a more enlightened era with regard to the conservation of sites like these, climate change threatens the cultural heritage of our coasts, as we discuss more in the Afterword of this book.

Previous Archaeological Research

C. B. Moore (1903, 1907, 1918) conducted the earliest archaeological excavations at Crystal River. Moore spent a week at the site in 1903, mapping many of the site's major features and assigning to these the letter designations that are still used today (Moore 1903; Weisman 1995a:12–13) (Figure 2.12). Comparison of Moore's map with those produced by modern survey methods reveals that it is quite accurate (Pluckhahn et al. 2009; Pluckhahn et al. 2010). Notably, however, Moore's map does not mention several features described by later researchers (Mounds J and K and the presumed stelae), presumably because the site was very overgrown at the time of his visit (Weisman 1995a:60).

Moore focused his 1903 excavations on the Main Burial Complex, which he labeled Mounds C–F (Moore 1903). While work was conducted in all parts of the complex, he concentrated on the central sand mound (Mound F) (Figure 2.13). The excavations here produced many of the exotic artifacts for which the site would soon become famous.

Returning to Crystal River in 1906 (Moore 1907; Weisman 1995a:13), Moore again focused his excavations on the Main Burial Complex but this time directed his efforts to the "elevation" or platform (Mound E), and to a lesser extent the circular embankment (Mound C). As before, he found a number of burials. On his final visit to the site in 1918, Moore

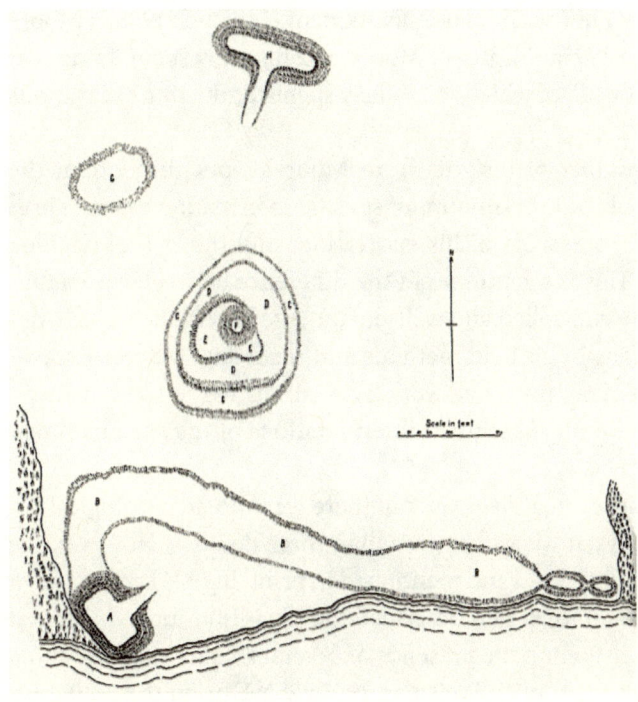

Figure 2.12. Moore's (1903) map of Crystal River.

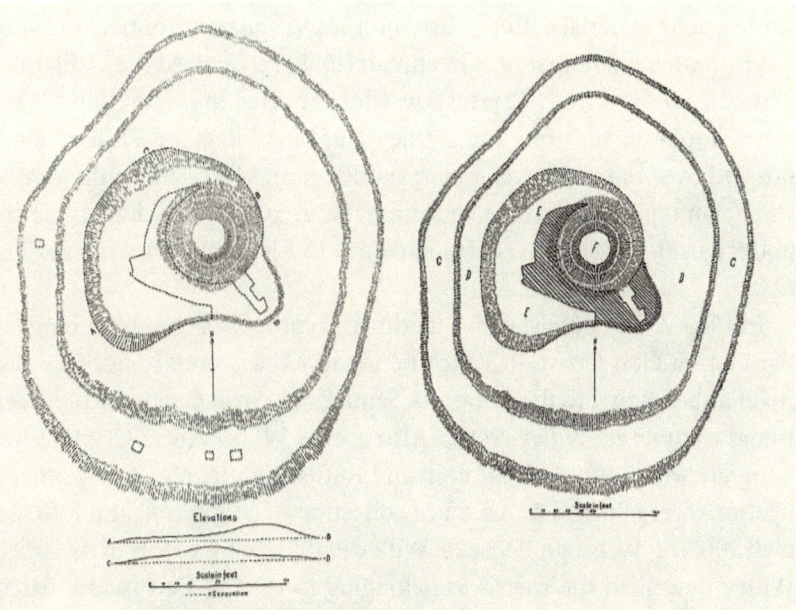

Figure 2.13. Moore's (1903:Fig. 17; 1907:406) maps of the Main Burial Complex at Crystal River.

continued working in the circular embankment (Milanich 1999:7; Moore 1918; cf. Weisman 1995a:13). In all, Moore and his crew spent 34 days at Crystal River, about 25 of which were likely spent conducting excavations (Milanich 1999:7).

We draw a number of insights from Moore's work throughout the course of this book, but the amount of specific information we can glean is limited by the coarseness of his excavations and the lack of detailed documentation. This is a reminder of the difference between casual digging and carefully controlled and well-documented excavations. Still, despite the limitations in his field methods and reporting, Moore's excavations remain the most intensive work ever conducted at Crystal River, and the baseline for all subsequent interpretations of the site (Weisman 1995a:12–14).

Following Moore's final field season, there were no archaeological investigations at Crystal River for more than three decades. However, the site was occasionally visited and mentioned in print. In 1924 botanist John Small toured Crystal River and described the "Spanish Mound" (Mound A), while also mentioning the presence of several smaller mounds and a village site (Small 1924, 1929; Weisman 1995a:25). During the 1930s and 1940s, archaeologists began assessing the significance of the site through studies of its material culture, chronology, and apparent connections with the Hopewell phenomenon. Greenman (1938) recognized the similarities between artifacts from Crystal River (as reported by Moore) and those from Hopewell sites in Ohio. Willey (1948a; Willey and Phillips 1944) puzzled over the pottery from Crystal River and its relationship to Mississippian types. After some confusion, he eventually concluded that the pottery from Crystal River was ancestral to Mississippian types (Willey 1948c).

In 1949 Willey published his landmark synthesis of the archaeology of the Florida Gulf Coast, in which he identified the pottery from Crystal River as belonging to the Deptford, Santa Rosa–Swift Creek, and Weeden Island complexes (Willey 1949a). Also in 1949 Willey visited Crystal River for a day with Antonio Waring Jr. and Rufus Nightingale. Willey's investigations were limited to a surface collection of Mounds C and F (Milanich 2007:22; Weisman 1995a:28; Willey 1949b). In his report of this work, Willey described the sherds as belonging to the Weeden Island, Pasco, and St. Johns series. Willey pointed out that the dating of Mound A was still unresolved but suggested the possibility that the mound could date to the Santa Rosa–Swift Creek or Weeden Island I periods. Bullen (1951) took exception to Willey's chronology and argued that Crystal River dated mainly to later Weeden Island.

To resolve questions about the relative ordering of the pottery series and mound construction at Crystal River, Hale Smith conducted limited work at the site in February 1951 (Smith 1951; Weisman 1995a:14, 28–29). His investigations included one 2-×-2-ft (.6-×-.6-m) test in the midden area (Mound B), another test of equal size in Mound H, several tests in Mounds C and E, and a surface collection of Mound A. Smith's analysis suggested that at least a portion of the Mound C embankment was constructed late in the Weeden Island period, refining Willey's earlier temporal assignment.

A short time later, in June 1951, Ripley Bullen initiated the first of several seasons of fieldwork at Crystal River (Bullen 1953; Weisman 1995a:28–29). Bullen's work at Crystal River, like Moore's before him, is fundamental to the interpretation of the site. Unfortunately, while Bullen's excavations were more carefully controlled than Moore's (in keeping with improvements in archaeological technique), they are perhaps even less thoroughly documented. Bullen apparently preferred to write from memory, without taking notes in the field, but few of his excavations at Crystal River were written up before he passed away in 1976 (Wilkerson 1978). As with Moore's work, this is another cautionary tale regarding the importance of documentation to the process of archaeology.

Bullen's 1951 investigations included two stratigraphic excavations in the midden (Mound B) to test his idea that the site (and particularly the burial mound complex) was in use for more than one period (Bullen 1951). On the basis of this work, Bullen postulated three periods of occupation and mound construction: Santa Rosa–Swift Creek (lower levels of Mound F), Weeden Island (the Mound E platform and Mound C embankment), and late Weeden Island or Safety Harbor (the upper levels of Mound F).

Bullen completed extensive excavations at Crystal River in 1960 (Weisman 1995:37–38). Perhaps most significantly, these investigations included topographic mapping that led to the identification of two additional mounds and an extension of the midden area (Mound B) to the north of Mound A (Figure 2.14). Bullen described Mound J as an "irregularly shaped imminence of shell" (Weisman 1995:37), while Mound K was described as a flat-topped deposit resembling a small temple mound. Tests were excavated into these two mounds. Another test was excavated

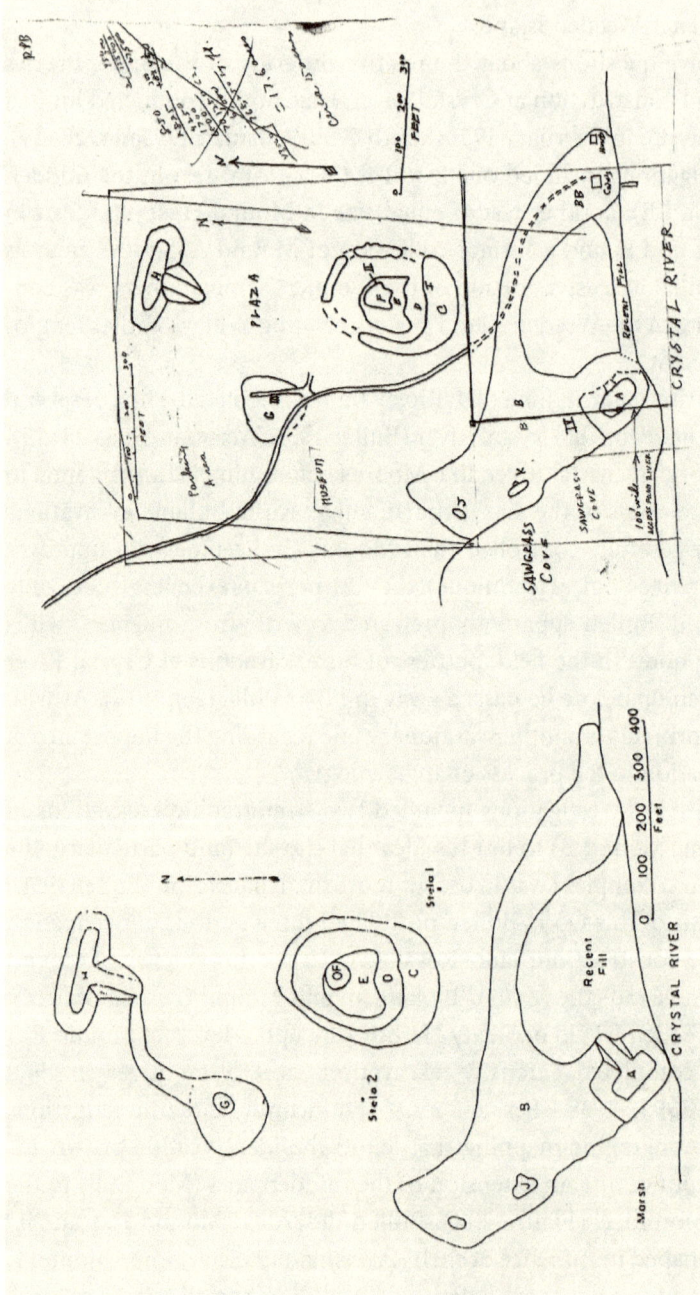

Figure 2.14. Two maps of Crystal River by Ripley Bullen. *Left*: reproduced by permission of the Society for American Archaeology from *American Antiquity* 31(6), 1966. *Right*: from 1960 correspondence between Bullen and George Dyer, reproduced courtesy of the FLMNH.

into Mound G, where 35 burials were identified in a 10-×-20-ft (3-×-6-m) trench. Finally, Bullen identified undisturbed burials in the Mound F platform and Mound C embankment. Unfortunately, the only record of most of this work is a brief letter Bullen wrote to landowner George Dyer (on file at the FLMNH), an accompanying summary (Bullen 1960b), and two other very brief overviews (Bullen 1960b, 1965). The Florida Museum of Natural History has photographs of the excavations in Mounds C and G that permit at least limited insight into their construction history.

In 1964, as the site was being cleared for the creation of the state park, two upright limestone slabs were discovered (Bullen 1965, 1966b; Weisman 1995:31–32). Bullen referred to these as "stelae," a term used primarily in Mesoamerica to refer to vertically placed slabs (often with writing). Stela 1 was pecked and incised with a representation of a human face and torso, the former apparently done in antiquity. Bullen (1966b) excavated the area around Stela 1, identifying a small concentration of animal bones and other artifacts. A third limestone boulder, also possible carved, was reported by Hardman (1971) after it was apparently displaced by the construction of the museum. The presence of these possibly carved stones has fueled speculation about connections between Crystal River and Mesoamerica (Bullen 1966b; Ford 1966, 1969; Hardman 1971), although the links remain conjectural at best.

Contemporary fieldwork at Crystal River has been limited. In 1985 Brent Weisman and Jeffrey Mitchem excavated core samples and two 2-×-2-m test units in the midden north of Mound A, with the goal of obtaining samples from the Safety Harbor component on the site (Weisman 1985, 1995a:35–36). These excavations penetrated only to a relatively shallow depth and have not been thoroughly reported. Weisman, Barbara Purdy, Ray McGee, and Erica Hill excavated five auger samples in the area around Mound A to determine if a wet site component was present. A brief report of this investigation (Anonymous 1995) indicates that most of the auger samples encountered limestone at relatively shallow depth; however, a sample immediately west of the mound penetrated to a depth of 220 cm.

A number of small projects have been conducted at Crystal River over the past three decades in response to natural disasters and general park maintenance (Ellis 2004, 2008b; Glowacki 2002; Weisman 1992; Wheeler 2001). Among the most substantial of these was the documentation of damage caused to several of the mounds by trees felled by a tornado spawned by the 1993 "Storm of the Century" (Weisman 1993). Also noteworthy was the mitigation of a seawall restoration project by Gary Ellis (1999), which resulted in the identification of intact midden deposits buried below fill in the area east of Mound A. Ellis and colleagues (2003) also documented artifacts recovered from midden displaced during the dredging of a boat slip.

In 2005, with support from the Florida Department of Environmental Protection, Weisman, Lori Collins, and Travis Doering began laser scanning of site features, resulting in new visual presentations of the overall site plan and documenting the scarplike exposed eastern and southern profiles of Mound A (Collins and Doering 2009; Weisman et al. 2007).

The Crystal River Early Village Archaeological Project (CREVAP)

Previous research—especially Moore's work in the Main Burial Complex—established Crystal River as one of the most important sites in North America. As we noted above, by the 1950s, the site was a standard reference in textbooks summarizing the archaeology of the continent. However, as archaeology boomed in the 1970s and beyond, the Crystal River site remained poorly understood, owing to both the limited scope and underreporting of previous investigations and the lack of any modern excavations. The stature of the site appears to have suffered as result; although Crystal River still figures prominently in many scholarly treatments of Hopewell and Woodland period archaeology (e.g., Ruhl 1981; Seeman 1979), it earns only fleeting reference—if it is mentioned at all—in most syntheses of the prehistory of North America and the Southeast (e.g., Neusius and Gross 2007; Smith 1986; Steponaitis 1986).

It was in this context that we initiated archaeological research to better understand the history of Crystal River. In 2008 we began a pilot study at Crystal River (Pluckhahn 2009, 2010; Thompson and Pluckhahn 2010). We conducted detailed topographic mapping and compared the resulting maps to those that had completed by Moore (1903) and Bullen (1966b), finding that both had done admirable jobs documenting the major features and their spatial arrangements. We also completed geophysical survey—ground-penetrating radar (GPR) and electrical resistance—of select areas of the site. This provided insight into both mound construction and the location and extent of buried midden deposits (Thompson and Pluckhahn 2010).

Leveraging the results of the 2008 fieldwork, we formulated several proposals to the National Science Foundation to fund additional work. In 2010 we (Pluckhahn, Thompson, and Brent Weisman) were awarded funding for a three-year study to examine the dynamic between cooperation and competition in the formation of early village societies, using Crystal River as a case study.

We focused on three categories of material remains reasonably easy to identify archaeologically: prestige goods, public architecture, and feasting debris. Depending on the context, these may be associated with relations that are inclusive and cooperative or exclusive and competitive. Evaluating these possibilities, we reasoned, would require a methodology finely attuned to variations in their distribution in space and time. With regard to the former, we planned investigations to determine the manner in which these material remains are distributed spatially at Crystal River and related settlements, to ascertain if access was open or restricted. We also planned fine-grained studies of the timing of these phenomena, building on the recognition that cooperative relationships rely on timely reciprocity and regular reinforcement of social commitments (Bonhage-Freund and Kurland 1994; Stanish 2004). The project employed two general methods for accomplishing a fine-grained study of these remains, while respecting the need for site conservation: 1) reanalysis of the collections from previous investigations; and 2) systematic, minimally invasive new fieldwork to correct both the biases and limited scope of previous studies.

Regarding the first general method, the artifacts from Moore's excavations are mainly curated by the National Museum of the American Indian (NMAI). The authors visited the collection facilities of the NMAI in Suitland, Maryland, to conduct photography and basic description of the artifacts. The results of these analyses, necessarily limited because of restrictions intended to maintain their safekeeping, are forthcoming. However, we draw on these analyses in the chapters that follow.

The collections from the work at Crystal River by Ripley Bullen are housed primarily at the Florida Museum of Natural History in Gainesville. Fortunately, the flaked stone in these collections has already been thoroughly documented by Estabrook (2011). In addition, Katzmarzyk (1998) has already inventoried and analyzed the human remains. Kassie Kemp (2015) analyzed the ceramics in these collections for CREVAP, identifying, counting, and weighing more than 16,000 fragments of pottery. Beth Blankenship (2013) identified the shell tools and ornaments.

The faunal remains from Bullen's excavations have yet to be analyzed but are probably of relatively little value for understanding subsistence, given that the recovery methods were biased to larger bone fragments.

Three seasons of new fieldwork were conducted at Crystal River and Roberts Island from 2011 to 2013. To create more detailed maps of the modern landscapes of Crystal River, we combined the total station survey data generated in 2008 with publically accessible airborne LiDAR data that became available in the years that followed. Briefly, LiDAR is based on the principle that distance can be measured on the basis of the time it takes light to travel from an instrument to a target and return; a laser emitter-receiver mounted on a plane sends hundreds of thousands of pulses of light per second to the ground and measures how long it takes each pulse to reflect back to the unit (Andersen et al. 2006). The result is a point cloud that can be used to create very detailed maps of the ground surface. However, with the publicly available LiDAR data, there are often voids introduced by the misclassification of elevation anomalies, including archaeological surface features such as mounds and shell middens (for Crystal River, see Collins et al. 2012:77; for a discussion of a case study elsewhere in Florida, see Pluckhahn and Thompson 2012). Total station survey helped us fill these voids. We combined the approximately 18,000 surface elevations at Crystal River and 3,000 at Roberts Island with around 200,000 and 340,000 LiDAR data points from these sites (respectively) to model the contemporary surface of the sites and the surrounding landscape (see Figures 2.4 and 2.5).

We employed several types of geophysical survey to form initial impressions regarding the nature and distribution of subsurface mound and midden deposits (Pluckhahn et al. 2010; Thompson and Pluckhahn 2010). The first, resistance survey (Figure 2.15), works by inducing a known electrical current to measure ease of flow (Somers 2006:113); archaeological features can be of either higher or lower resistance than the surrounding soil matrix (Dalan et al. 1992:51; Thompson et al. 2004:195). Resistance survey proved particularly effective in regard to identifying buried shell midden, largely confirming previous accounts of a dense and well-preserved linear concentration of shell extending south from Mound A to Mound J at Crystal River (Figure 2.16). The signature became less continuous in the area where the midden turned east, consistent with the disturbance introduced by the trailer park. However, the resistance data included anomalies supporting the notion that midden

Figure 2.15. Conducting resistance survey in the plaza at Crystal River, with Mound H in the background.

might be preserved in some areas, an observation later confirmed by our excavations.

The second type of geophysical survey, ground-penetrating radar (GPR), is better known to both the general public and most archaeologists (Johnson 2006). GPR uses an antenna to transmit high-frequency radar pulses into the ground (Conyers 2013:2) (Figure 2.17). The device measures the time between transmission and return after the signal is reflected back from buried materials or sediments. GPR survey was conducted in selected blocks in the midden area at both Crystal River and Roberts Island, and we draw on these data in the chapters that follow. At the former site, although limited by the nearly 2-m depth of the midden in some areas, the GPR data seemed to indicate a transition in the composition of the midden around 50 cm below surface (cmbs) (Pluckhahn et al. 2009; Pluckhahn et al. 2010; Thompson and Pluckhahn 2010). We draw on these data in the chapters that follow.

GPR survey was also conducted on the three platform mounds at Crystal River, and on two of the three mounds at Roberts Island. For Mound H at Crystal River, the GPR data seemed to show alternating layers of

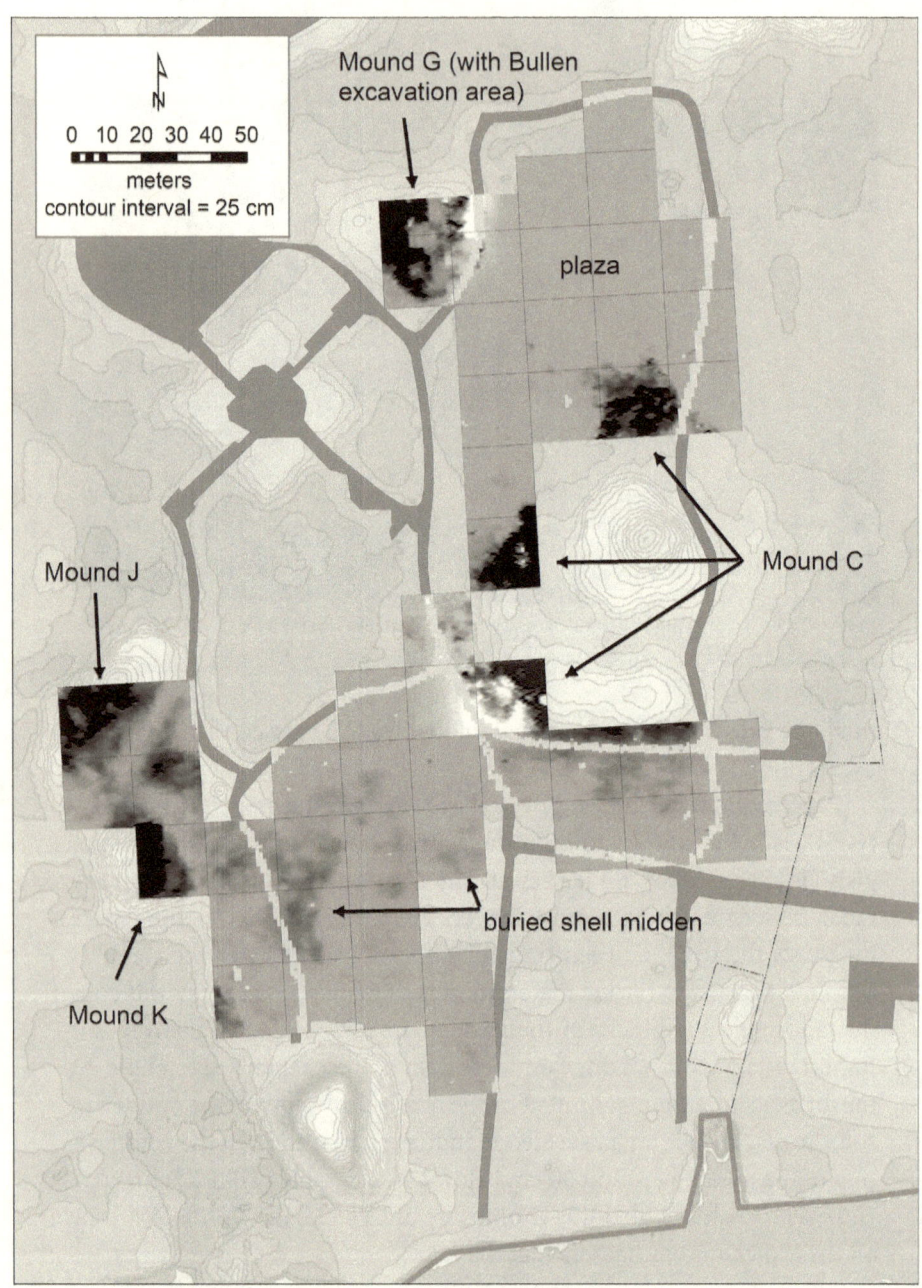

Figure 2.16. Resistance survey data from Crystal River.

Figure 2.17. Conducting GPR survey on a portion of the midden at Crystal River, with Mound A in background.

highly reflective shell and less reflective sand but also suggested that the mound kept the same basic form from beginning to end (Pluckhahn et al. 2009; Pluckhahn et al. 2010; Thompson and Pluckhahn 2010). Mound K at Crystal River, as well as Mounds A and B at Roberts Island, appeared to be composed almost entirely of shell and perhaps in single episodes. The GPR data from Mound A at Crystal River supported the existence of at least one earlier mound stage. Subsequent investigations both confirmed and refined these observations, as we discuss in the chapters that follow.

Geophysical survey can provide much information, but some form of excavation is usually necessary to corroborate the data, and to recover samples of artifacts and other materials for dating and other specialized studies. At Crystal River we began minimally invasive excavation in the form of small-diameter coring. Coring was conducted at 20-m (66-ft) intervals across the site, with the assistance of Glen Doran and Grayal Farr, using a GeoProbe Model 6620DT (Figure 2.18). This is a hydraulic coring device that hammers a metal tube containing a plastic sleeve about 4.5 cm (1.8 in) in diameter and around 116 cm (4 ft) long. The sections are retrieved one at a time, progressing deeper with each section. The off-mound cores at Crystal River varied from one to three sections deep. The cores in mounds were at least three sections deep; in the case of Mound A,

Figure 2.18. Using a GeoProbe coring device at Crystal River.

it took nine sections to penetrate through the mound and the underlying, earlier midden.

In total, we retrieved 51 GeoProbe cores at Crystal River (Figure 2.19). Seven of these were collected from four mounds (none from the burial mounds), and the remainder from the off-mound areas. For the majority of these cores, we split the tubes from each section in half. One half of each section was used to document the soils, with soil samples taken for pollen and other specialized studies. The other half of each section was screened for artifacts using .32 cm (.125 inch) mesh.

Five of the GeoProbe cores, including four from the mounds and one from the area between Mounds J and K, were collected specifically for

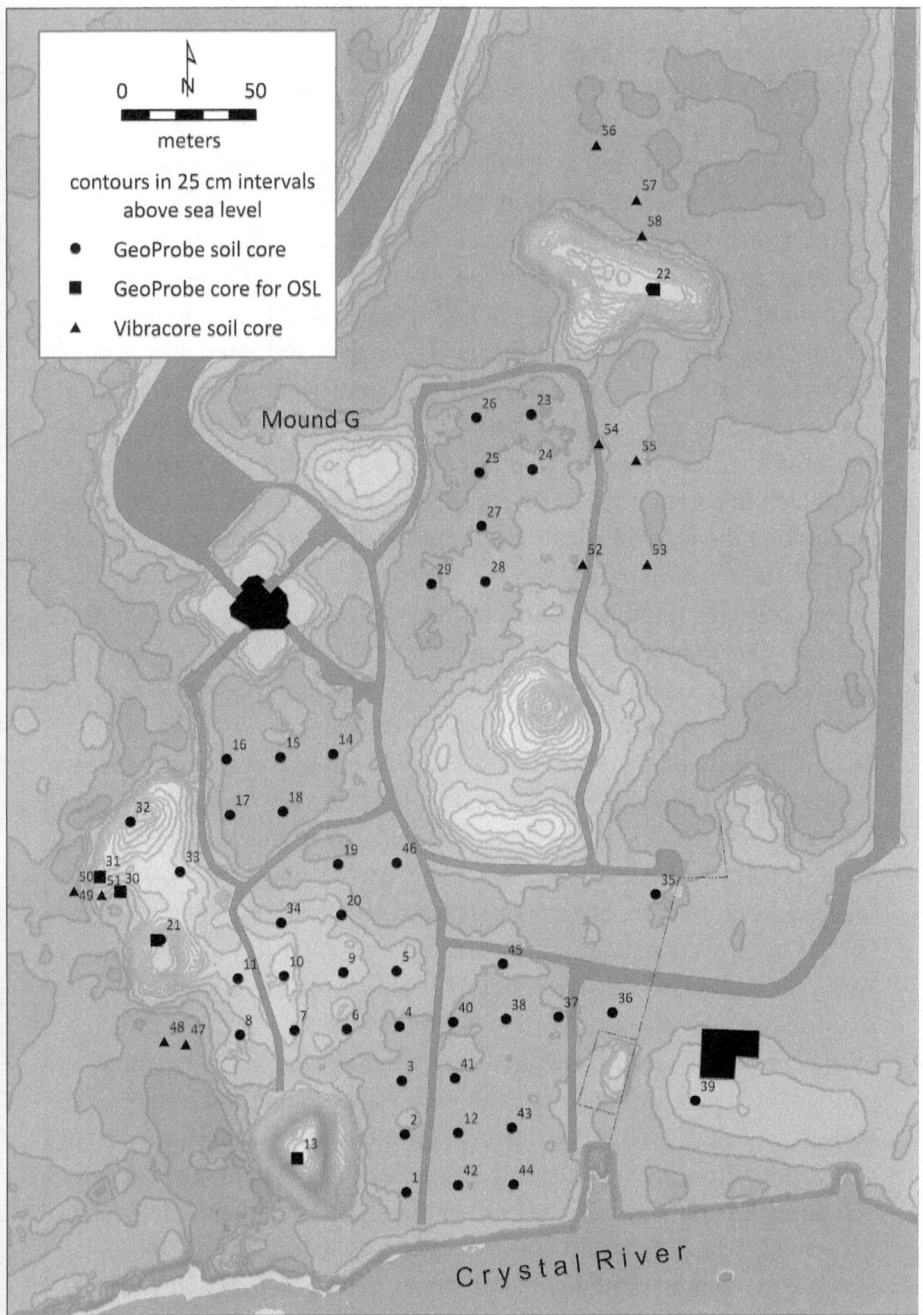

Figure 2.19. Cores excavated at Crystal River.

optically stimulated luminescence (OSL), which measures the last time mineral grains were exposed to light (thereby resetting their electron traps). This requires that the sediments not be exposed to light, so these sections were collected with black plastic tubes. Geologist Jack Rink and his students Alex Hodson and Robert Hendricks processed these samples at McMaster University (Hodson 2012; Pluckhahn, Hodson, et al. 2015).

Sean Norman (2014) documented the soils in the cores from Crystal River, and we draw insights from his work in reconstructing the history of mound and midden formation. Beth Blankenship (2013) documented the artifact assemblages from the cores. Briefly, the occurrences of shell and ceramics in these cores track historical descriptions of the midden, with the addition of shell in the former lagoon area that likely represents material displaced from the grading of Mound A. Pottery was surprisingly abundant in cores on the northern edge of the former trailer park, again suggesting the possibility that some areas within the former trailer park escaped destruction.

We collected additional cores from the edges of the site and the surrounding wetlands using a vibracore device provided by Gary Ellis. As the name implies, a vibracore uses vibration to penetrate the ground surface. The vibracore we employed was capable of taking only one section from each core. In total, we collected 12 vibracores, but this includes several where the tube encountered obstructions that the device could not penetrate. In severe cases the cores were not retained. Otherwise, these cores were processed in the same manner as those taken with the GeoProbe. Kendal Jackson (2016) analyzed pollen samples from some of these cores to aid in our understanding of past environmental conditions, and we draw on his research at several points in the chapters that follow.

In addition to the cores, at Crystal River we placed four trenches across the extent of the midden (Figure 2.20). These provided larger samples of artifacts and presented a better window on stratigraphy and features. The trenches were all 1 m (3.3 ft) wide and varied from 2 to 4 m (6.6 to 13.1 ft) in length but were excavated in 1-×-1-m sections. We employed a combination of natural and arbitrary 10-cm levels and sifted the soil through .32-cm (.125-inch) mesh. In two of the trenches, we excavated 25-×-25-cm (.8-x-.8-ft) column samples in levels not exceeding 4 cm (1.6 inches). The soil from these column samples was used for dating and other specialized analyses. These larger excavations merit more detailed description, which

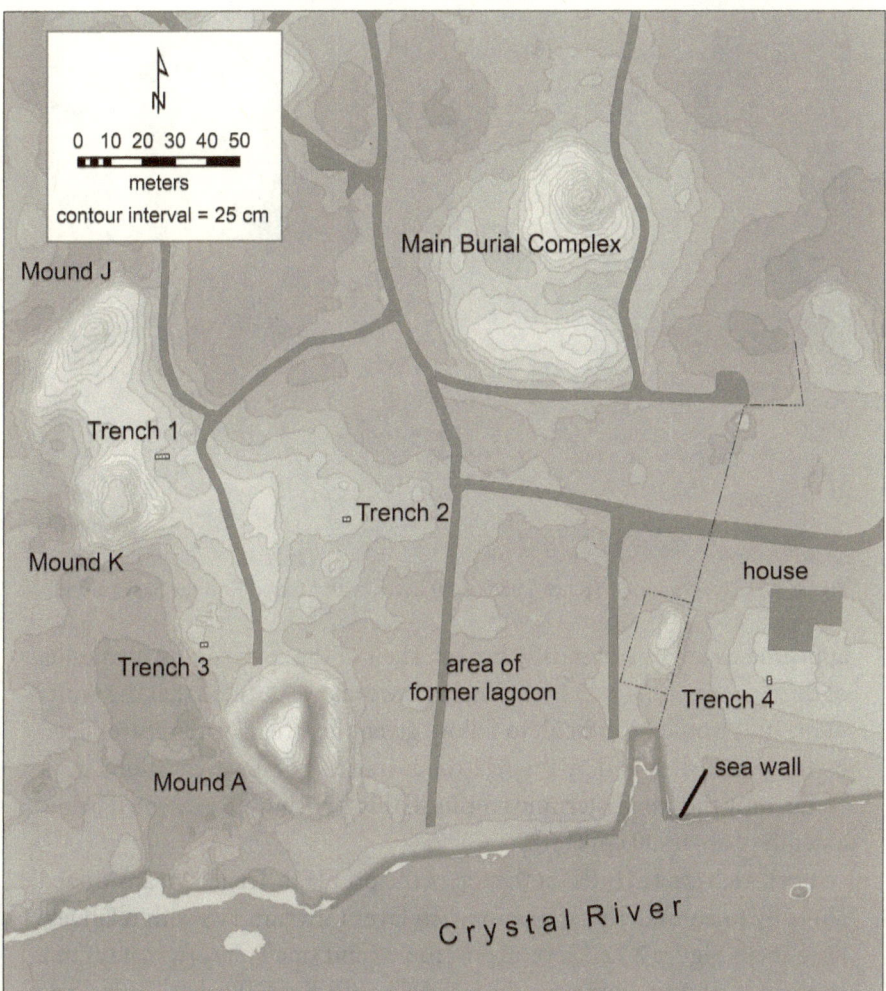

Figure 2.20. Locations of trenches at Crystal River.

we have presented elsewhere (Pluckhahn, Thompson, and Cherkinsky 2015) and repeat only in brief here.

Trench 1 was located on the highest and best-preserved part of the shell ridge, a short distance east of Mound K (Figure 2.21). Our intention here was to sample this portion of the midden, but we also hoped to intercept and reexcavate a test excavation completed by Bullen and better document the stratigraphy he observed and thus provide better context for his artifact collections. We were successful in intercepting his unit, which

Figure 2.21. Excavation of Trench 1 at Crystal River, with Mound K in the background.

appeared as an area of mostly broken shell in the easternmost two units of this 1-×-4-m (3.3-×-13.1-ft) trench. However, we decided that the limits of his unit would be difficult to follow, given the irregularities introduced by the dense shell and by the relative coarseness of his excavations. As a result, only the two easternmost units in this trench were excavated below a depth of about 30 cm (1 ft).

Shell-rich strata (I–III) at the top of the profile in Trench 1 transitioned abruptly to an underlying organic-rich layer (Stratum IV) with relatively little shell (Figure 2.22). Several post molds and small pits originate at this stratum, a pattern corresponding closely with the GPR data. This horizon appears to represent a period of intensive occupation, but with little in situ shell disposal. The features originating at this level intruded into a shell deposit (Stratum V), with shell density suggestive of a period of rapid deposition. We noted no obvious stratigraphic changes or features within this shell-dense layer, but variation in the quantity of oyster by level suggests possible breaks in the deposition.

The other trenches at Crystal River, all measuring 1 × 2 m (3.3 × 6.6 ft), represent variations of the theme established by Trench 1. Trench 2 was located to the east of the first trench in the area of the former trailer park (Figure 2.23). The uppermost portion of the midden was truncated by grading, and a layer of yellow sand (Stratum II) had been added for

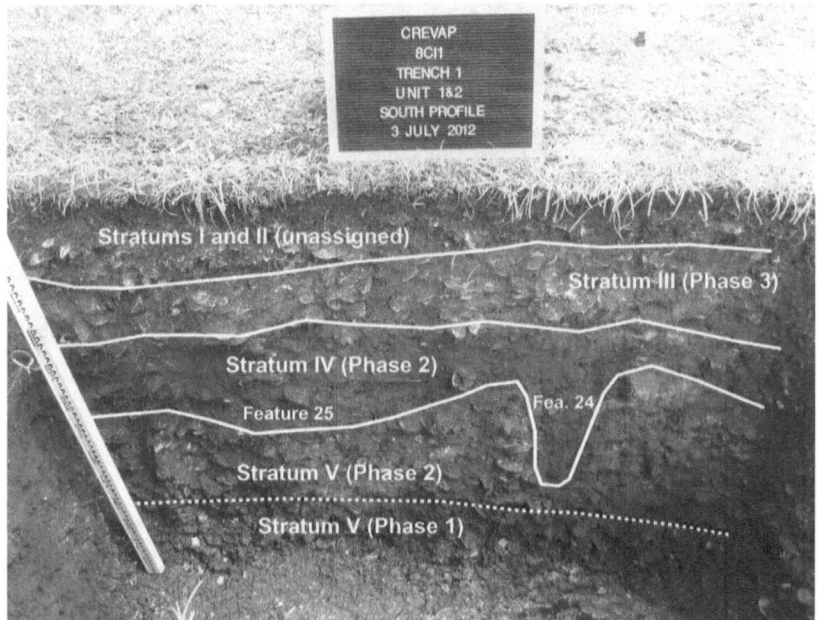

Figure 2.22. Profile of Trench 1 at Crystal River.

a mobile home pad (Figure 2.24). A great many armadillo bones were found at the base of the yellow sand; since the armadillo is a recent (early-twentieth-century) migrant to Florida, we suppose this individual might have been an unfortunate victim of the trailer park development. Regardless, below this modern disturbance, the midden was well preserved. As in Trench 1, a layer of dark sediment with moderately dense shell gave way to a zone darker in color with much reduced shell content (Stratum III). And as with Trench 1, there were a number of features originating from this surface. Here, however, we were able to observe features originating at slightly different depths, indicating their formation across a prolonged period. Radiocarbon dates on three distinct features confirm this and demonstrate temporal contemporaneity with the feature-rich strata in Trench 1. The features intruded into an underlying layer of dense shell similar to those in Trench 1, although here the shell appeared to have been deposited in overlapping shell-filled pits rather than a "sheet" of midden. In the lowermost level of Trench 2, we encountered a dark layer of sediment (Stratum IV), which was almost completely free of both shell and artifacts but which included a series of post features. A date on soil-charcoal

Figure 2.23. Excavation of Trench 2 at Crystal River.

Figure 2.24. Profile of Trench 2 at Crystal River.

Figure 2.25. Excavation of Trench 3 at Crystal River.

here is only 10 years removed from a stratigraphically equivalent sample from Trench 1.

Trench 3 was located on the western ridge to the south of Trench 1 and just north of Mound A (Figure 2.25). Here again dense shell layers (Strata I and II) near the surface gave way to a dark sediment with reduced shell content (Stratum III) similar to those observed in Trenches 1 and 2 (Figure 2.26). As in those trenches, this dark layer likewise represented a surface from which several features originated. However, radiocarbon dates indicate the reduced-shell layer here dates slightly later. The layer of dark sediment was underlain by a horizon composed of dense shell (Stratum IV). However, unlike in Trenches 1 and 2, this layer included very little sediment other than shell, and no stratigraphic breaks or features. This would appear to represent a relatively rapid depositional episode, perhaps a deliberate attempt to expand the shell ridge south in association with the construction of Mound A.

Trench 4 was positioned at the eastern edge of the shell ridge (Figure 2.27). Shell-rich layers (Strata I and II) near the surface gradually gave way to darker sediments with significantly less shell (Strata III and IV) (Figure 2.28). This layer continued deep into the unit, and the relatively narrow temporal spread of three radiocarbon dates on soil-charcoal sample of variable depths (from 40 to 102 cm [16 to 40 in] below the ground surface)

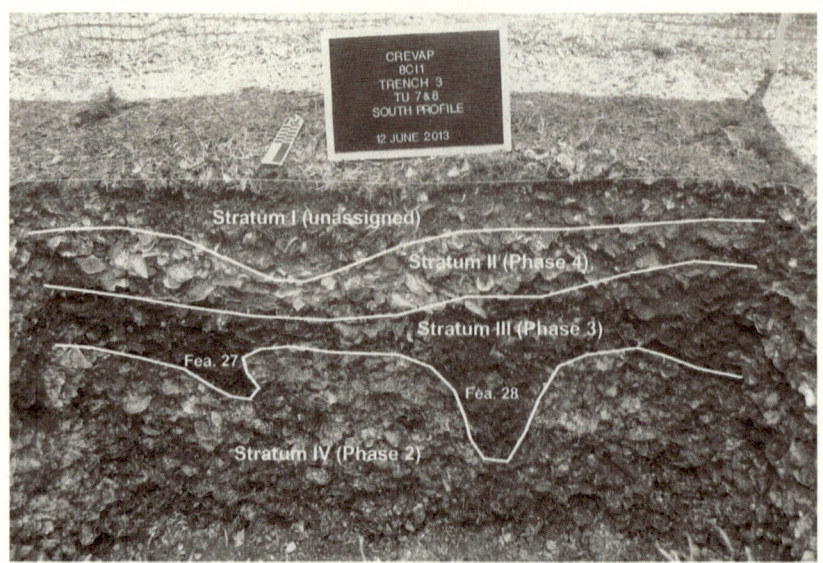

Figure 2.26. Profile of Trench 3 at Crystal River.

Figure 2.27. Excavation of Trench 4 at Crystal River.

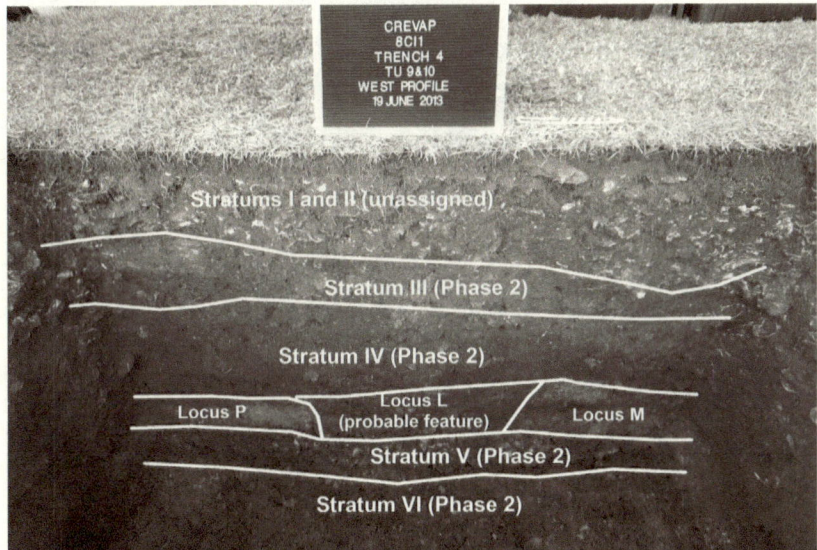

Figure 2.28. Profile of Trench 4 at Crystal River.

suggests a period of continuous midden formation akin to and coeval with that in Trenches 1 and 2. Near the base of this trench, we encountered a layer of even darker sediment (Stratum V) with dense shell and several features. A soil-charcoal sample from this layer returned a date only slightly later than the dates on the lowermost midden layers in Trenches 1 and 2. The lowermost stratum (VI) consisted of a lighter-colored riverine sand mainly devoid of oyster and other artifacts.

The bulky and heavy GeoProbe coring device could not be easily transported to Roberts Island, so instead we employed shovel tests and a single test trench to sample the midden (Figure 2.29). The shovel tests measured 50 × 50 cm (20 × 20 inches) and were generally placed at 20-m (66-ft) intervals (Figure 2.30). Trench 2, which measured 1 × 2 m, was located in a low area (as described in Chapter 7, a presumed "water court") (Figure 2.31). We excavated both shovel tests and the trench using the same methods cited above for units at Crystal River.

These excavations indicated that the island is almost completely anthropogenic in origin, with midden deposits extending below the modern water table in some areas. Even more so than many areas at Crystal River, the midden here is composed principally of oyster shell. However, we noted A horizons with comparatively little shell in shovel tests across the island (Figure 2.32). Trench 2, because it was positioned at a lower

Figure 2.29. Excavation of a shovel test at Roberts Island.

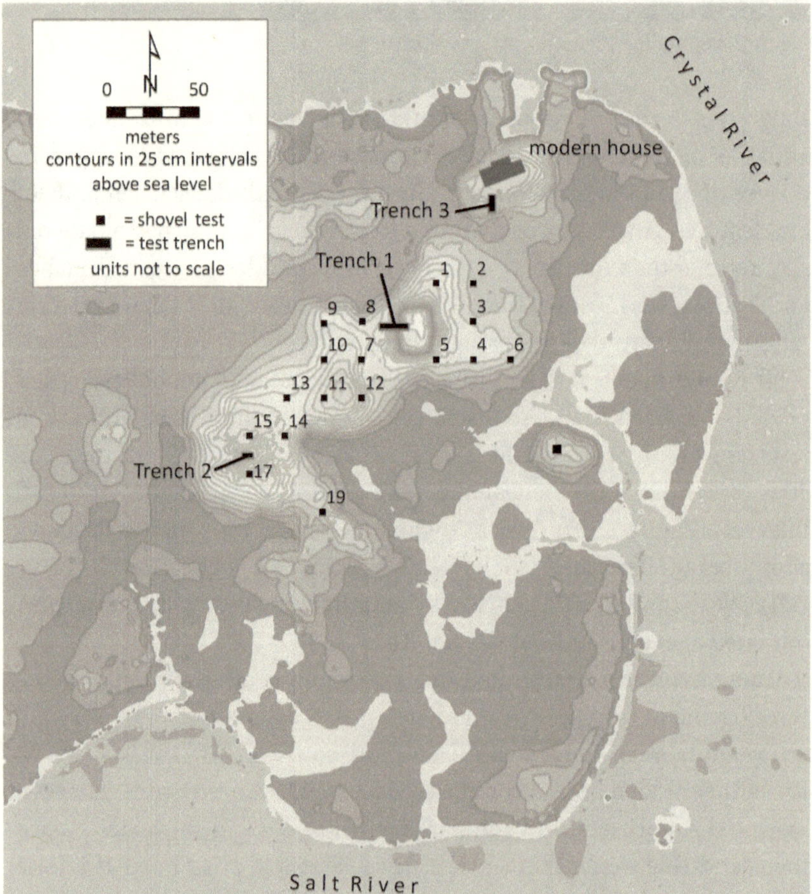

Figure 2.30. Locations of shovel tests and trenches at Roberts Island.

Figure 2.31. Excavation of Trench 2 at Roberts Island.

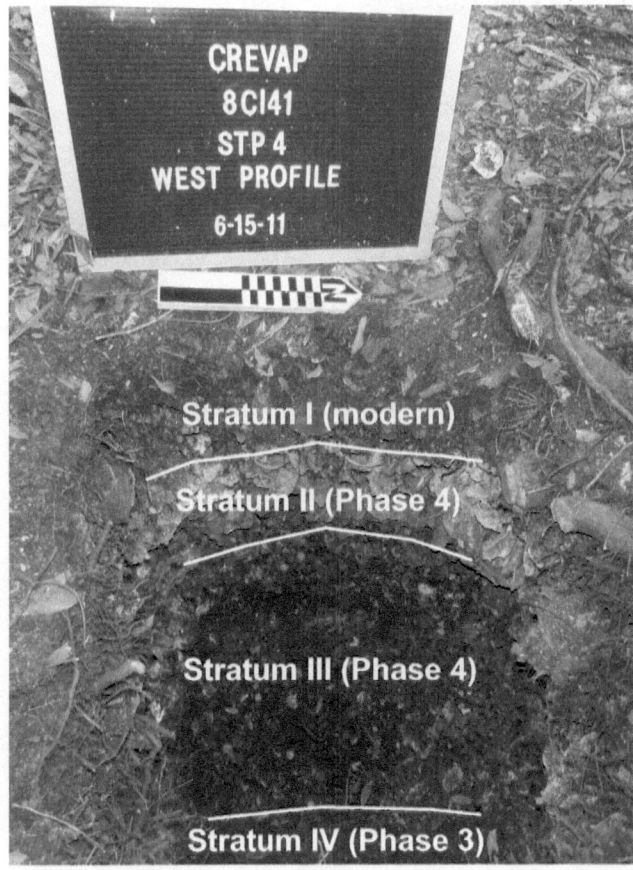

Figure 2.32. Profile of Shovel Test 4 on Roberts Island.

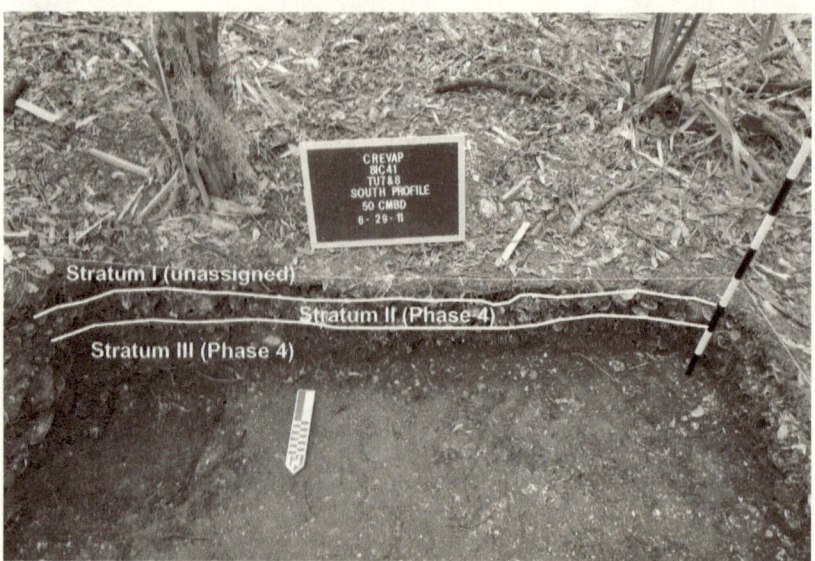

Figure 2.33. Profile of Trench 2 on Roberts Island.

elevation, exhibited a shallower soil profile (Figure 2.33). There was little break in the dark soils, but we did note variation in the quantity and wholeness of shell.

We also excavated test trenches on Mounds A and B at Roberts Island, to better understand the construction history of these monuments. The trench on Mound A was placed on the western slope, in an area of recent surficial disturbance (Figure 2.34). This trench measured 1 × 6 m (3.3 × 19.7 ft). Owing to the slope and the instability of the shell matrix, we generally terminated the excavation of a 1-×-1-m section when we reached the ground surface in the adjacent downslope unit, thus forming a stepped trench that facilitated excavation. For Mound B at Roberts Island, we excavated a 1-×-4-m (3.3-×-13.1-ft) trench on the southern slope of the mound's better-preserved western half (Figure 2.35). These trenches were excavated using the same basic procedures as the others. We discuss the profile of these trenches and their implications in Chapter 7.

The shovel test and test unit excavations have been reported in several student theses. In her honors thesis, Sarah Gilleland (2013) summarized the invertebrate faunal remains from shovel tests at Roberts Island. Rachel Thompson (2016) reported the ceramic assemblages from shovel tests and test units at both Crystal River and Roberts Island. Lori O'Neal (2016) has done the same for bone, stone, and shell tools. Additional analyses of shell

Above: Figure 2.34. Excavation of Trench 1 on Mound A at Roberts Island.

Left: Figure 2.35. Excavation of Trench 3 on Mound B at Roberts Island.

tools were conducted by Martin Menz (2013). Samples of faunal remains from test units and shovel tests at Roberts Island have been analyzed by Matthew Compton (2014), while those from Crystal River have been analyzed by Elizabeth Reitz, Maran Little, and Kelly Brown (Little and Reitz 2015; Reitz and Brown 2015). Trevor Duke (2015) summarized temporal trends in the exploitation of vertebrate fishes and estuarine invertebrates in his thesis.

We have thus far focused our summary of recent work primarily on our investigations of the form and spatial extent of mounds and middens, but as we noted at the start of this section, we were also very much concerned with timing. Toward this end, we have retrieved a total of 70 radiocarbon dates from Crystal River and Roberts Island. This represents a tenfold increase over the dates that have been previously obtained from Crystal River. It makes Crystal River perhaps the most thoroughly dated Woodland period archaeological site in eastern North America, surpassing the previous claim to this title for the Pinson Mounds site in Tennessee (based on 39 dates) (Mainfort and McNutt 2013:191).

We have elsewhere described our efforts to develop a chronology of midden deposition based on 47 radiocarbon dates from such contexts at Crystal River and Roberts Island (Pluckhahn, Thompson, and Cherkinsky 2015). Intending to develop a local correction for oyster shell, given that it is plentiful in both mounds and midden, we first dated stratigraphically equivalent samples of oyster shell, terrestrial mammal bone, and charcoal from Trench 1. Unfortunately, our dates on shell proved inconsistent with both other shell in terms of stratigraphy and with dates on other materials in the same levels, perhaps due to a hard-water effect introduced from the limestone substrate (Cherkinsky et al. 2014). However, bone and soil-charcoal samples displayed good correspondence both with each other and by depth. We attribute the positive results here to the fact that small fragments of charcoal are abundant in the midden at Crystal River, allowing us to date very small samples of sediment. In addition, the midden is generally very compact and high in shell density, which together may impede the vertical displacement of materials through the profile by ants and other organisms (see Pluckhahn, Hodson, et al. 2015; Tschinkel et al. 2012).

To model the distribution of radiocarbon dates from the midden into phases, we utilized the Bayesian modeling capabilities of OxCal 4.2

(©Christopher Bronk Ramsey 2013; Bronk Ramsey 2009). Bayesian modeling is based in Bayes' Theorem, plainly summarized here by Bayliss et al. (2011:19):

> This approach is fundamentally probabilistic and contextual. It simply means that we analyse the new data we have collected about a problem ("the standardised likelihoods") in the context of our existing experience and knowledge about and our new data (our "prior beliefs"). This enables us to arrive at a new understanding of the problem which incorporates both our existing knowledge and our new data (our "posterior beliefs"). . . . We do this by the use of formal probability theory, where all three elements of our model are expressed as probability density functions.

For example, to model phases of midden formation at Crystal River and Roberts Island, we use the proposed phases as prior certainties and the calibrated radiocarbon dates as observed likelihoods (Bayliss et al. 2011; Bronk Ramsey 2009; Schilling 2013). Of course, since a considerable amount of "lumping" is inherent to any archaeological phase, we do not expect the dates to be in perfect agreement.

Because models of this sort can have many possible outcomes, OxCal uses a Markov Chain Monte-Carlo (MCMC) model to build up a representative sample of possible solutions (Bronk Ramsey 2014). The extent to which it is able to do so is measured by convergence (C), with good convergence indicated by a value above 95. The solution is also evaluated using an agreement index to determine if the data are consistent with the model (Bronk Ramsey 1995). OxCal calculates agreement indices for individual dates (A), the model (A_{model}), and the overall agreement between the agreement indices ($A_{overall}$). The critical value for these results, or $A'c$, is 60.0; anything above this is considered significant agreement.

As described in more detail by Pluckhahn, Thompson, and Cherkinsky (2015) we omitted a number of outlying radiocarbon dates (principally those on shell), and modeled a total of 26 from the trenches and shovel tests in the middens at Crystal River and Roberts Island. Our best model is a four-phase, sequential ordering, which produced agreement indices well above critical values (A_{model} = 101.7; $A_{overall}$ = 102.0). Table 2.1 summarizes the 68 percent and 95 percent posterior density estimates for the modeled start and end dates for the four phases of midden deposition. In

Table 2.1. Modeled Phases of Midden Deposition at Crystal River and Roberts Island

Phase	Modeled Start		Modeled End	
	68%	95%	68%	95%
4	cal A.D. 779 to 867	cal A.D. 723 to 881	cal A.D. 902 to 982	cal A.D. 891 to 1060
3	cal A.D. 521 to 605	cal A.D. 478 to 634	cal A.D. 671 to 747	cal A.D. 663 to 810
2	cal A.D. 238 to 292	cal A.D. 221 to 321	cal A.D. 441 to 499	cal A.D. 434 to 544
1	cal A.D. 125 to 199	cal A.D. 69 to 225	cal A.D. 180 to 242	cal A.D. 144 to 265

keeping with convention, when we discuss these modeled date ranges in the chapters that follow, we use italics to distinguish them from the simple calibrated dates (Bayliss et al. 2011:21).

As summarized elsewhere (Pluckhahn, Hodson, et al. 2015; Pluckhahn et al. 2016; Pluckhahn and Thompson 2017), we have obtained 23 radiocarbon and eight OSL dates from mounds at Crystal River and Roberts Island, greatly expanding the few obtained previously by Bullen (1966b) and Katzmarzyk (1998). To model the construction histories of these monuments, the radiocarbon and OSL dates were positioned with respect to the boundaries for the start and end dates for mound construction episodes, based on stratigraphic relationships. Thus, for example, dates from the pre-mound layers represent a priori information for the start of the first mound construction episode in Mound H at Crystal River, while dates from the second mound layer provide a priori information for the cessation of this first layer and the initiation of the second. In cases where we had multiple dates from the same mound construction episode, these were modeled stratigraphically if their ages corresponded with their relative superpositioning. However, it is not unexpected that the dates from a single construction episode might exhibit variation and even stratigraphic inversion, given the probabilistic nature of radiocarbon dating, the mixing of sediments that is often evident in mound construction, and the temporal "lumping" inherent to archaeological phases and construction episodes. Thus, in cases where the ordering of dates for a single construction episode did not correspond with their stratigraphic position, we modeled these together as a phase of mound construction, rather than as a sequence. Only Mound J proved problematic for modeling, in that we have only one date from what appears to have been an early stage of mound construction and this predates one date for a lower,

Table 2.2. Modeled Phases of Mound Construction at Crystal River and Roberts Island

Site	Mound	A_{model}	$A_{overall}$	Mound Stage	Modeled Start 68%	Modeled Start 95%	Modeled End 68%	Modeled End 95%
Crystal River	Mound A	78.3	75.6	stage 3	cal A.D. 617 to 940	cal A.D. 578 to 1756	cal A.D. 629 to 1166	to cal A.D. 2548
				stage 2	cal A.D. 434 to 579	cal A.D. 481 to 548	cal A.D. 612 to 739	cal A.D. 573 to 920
				stage 1	cal A.D. 398 to 480	cal A.D. 357 to 532	cal A.D. 437 to 521	cal A.D. 394 to 557
	Mound C	99.6	99.6	single stage	2043 to 913 cal B.C.	2049 to 899 cal B.C.	766 cal B.C. to cal A.D. 471	772 cal B.C. to cal A.D. 478
	Mounds E/F	93	93.4	single stage	256 to 42 cal B.C.	723 cal B.C. to cal A.D. 4	41 cal B.C. to cal A.D. 145	94 cal B.C. to cal A.D. 632
	Mound G	94.1	93.7	single stage	80 cal B.C. to cal A.D. 125	483 cal B.C. to cal A.D. 222	cal A.D. 372 to 618	cal A.D. 263 to 1026
	Mound H	111.5	110.4	stage 2	cal A.D. 425 to 534	cal A.D. 403 to 552	cal A.D. 451 to 555	cal A.D. 426 to 622
				stage 1	cal A.D. 340 to 475	cal A.D. 284 to 526	cal A.D. 389 to 495	cal A.D. 338 to 542
	Mound J	100.2	100.2	stage 2	cal A.D. 561 to 640	cal A.D. 426 to 653	cal A.D. 593 to 688	cal A.D. 558 to 1013
				stage 1	cal A.D. 324 to 628	cal A.D. 133 to 634	cal A.D. 452 to 634	cal A.D. 255 to 646
	Mound K	99.2	99.1	stage 2	cal A.D. 427 to 541	cal A.D. 394 to 569	cal A.D. 446 to 566	cal A.D. 423 to 721
				stage 1	cal A.D. 335 to 476	cal A.D. 280 to 535	cal A.D. 390 to 510	cal A.D. 331 to 552
Roberts Island	Mound A	88.7	88.7	single stage	cal A.D. 865 to 1045	cal A.D. 791 to 1115	cal A.D. 1046 to 1168	cal A.D. 925 to 1168
	Mound B	96.9	96.9	single stage	cal A.D. 1055 to 1165	cal A.D. 1034 to 1200	cal A.D. 1169 to 1233	cal A.D. 1102 to 1233

pre-mound stratum. Modeling of the mound construction sequence with this date omitted provided acceptable agreement indices.

Table 2.2 provides the results of our Bayesian modeling of mound construction episodes, along with the agreement indices. We provide additional detail on the stratigraphy of the mounds and our modeling in the chapters that follow but refer readers to the previous published summaries (Pluckhahn and Thompson 2017; Pluckhahn et al. 2016) for more detailed descriptions. As with the modeled phases of midden formation, we use italics to differentiate the modeled probability ranges for the posterior density estimates for mound construction. We focus on the modeled start dates for mound construction, because the end dates are often unconstrained by a priori assumptions and thus the probable date ranges for the posterior densities are very broad. For similar reasons, we focus mainly on the 68 percent probability ranges.

As we have noted at several points above, more detailed descriptions of various facets of our investigations have been published in journal articles and theses, and longer technical reports are forthcoming. Our aim in this book is to synthesize these studies into a detailed history of Crystal River and Roberts Island. In the chapter that follows, we begin telling this history.

3

A Center Emerges

The city of Crystal River, Florida, is famous today among the general public not for the ca. 2,000-year-old mounds that lie just up the highway at Crystal River Archaeological State Park, but instead for a series of springs that bubble up near the old downtown. In colder weather the near-constant 70-degree temperature of the springs makes them a haven for the cold-intolerant manatees that frequent southern Florida waters. On particularly cold (for Florida) winter mornings, manatees pack the crystal-clear waters of these springs—most famously the Seven Sisters Spring (Figure 3.1). The spectacle attracts tourists from around the state and much farther afield who come to watch the manatees and perhaps even swim with them (at least for the time being—as White (2013) reported for *National Geographic*, many conservationists would prefer to end the practice). These "sea cows" have earned iconic status in Crystal River—likenesses of manatees adorn the city hall and many of the town's homes and businesses.

One naturally wonders if it might have been this same manatee spectacle that attracted native peoples to the area of Crystal River some 2,000–3,000 years ago. But we must bear in mind that the environment we know today is much changed from that encountered by the first settlers of the Crystal River area. Sean Norman (2014) studied the sediments from the core samples that were taken from Crystal River, and Kendal Jackson conducted analysis of pollen from selected cores. Their work, when situated in the context of geological studies in the region, provides insights into the natural environment that existed when people first began coming to the site.

At the end of the last ice age (the Pleistocene) around 12,000 years ago, sea levels were about 6 m (20 ft) lower than present (Goodbred 1995:19; Scholl et al. 1969). The coast would thus have been much farther west than it is presently, especially given that the limestone shelf in this area of the

Figure 3.1. Manatees pack Three Sisters Spring on a cold morning in February 2016.

Gulf Coast is broad and gently sloping. As we noted in the last chapter, this limestone is gently undulating; at higher elevations in the vicinity of Crystal River, it lies exposed at or near the surface, but elsewhere it is buried by accumulated sediments. Norman's (2014:Fig. 5.29) research suggests that at Crystal River there are three areas where the limestone is found at higher elevation, all now buried by more recent sediment (Norman 2014:91–93): one on the northeastern end of the site as we now know it (in the area where Mound H would later be built), another on the western margin of the site (where people would eventually construct Mounds J and K), and the third on the eastern end of the site near the river. These high spots likely trapped sand blown about by the cold, dry winds of the ice age. Hodson (2012; see also Pluckhahn, Hodson, et al. 2015) used OSL to date sand grains below Mound H to the end of the ice age around 14,000 years ago.

People were settling in Florida about this time, in the Paleoindian period—if not even slightly earlier (Clausen et al. 1979; Purdy 2008). But the sand ridge at Crystal River would have been high and dry; it was far from the coast, and the river may not have been flowing, since the springs that feed the river would have been less active due to reduced rainfall and a lower water table. Crystal River thus may not have been a particularly attractive place to settle for Paleoindian hunter-gatherers. Only two Paleoindian sites have been recorded in the general vicinity of Crystal River; the closest is three miles away (records of the Florida Master Site Files, Tallahassee). Reports of a Paleoindian find at Crystal River (Bullen 1967) appear to have been unfounded (Neill and McKay 1968).

With the end of the last ice age and the beginning of the Holocene, the global climate became warmer, and with the melting of polar ice and increased precipitation, sea level began to rise. Recent research suggests that instead of a gradual warming, there were six intervals of rapid climatic change between the end of the ice age and our current era (Mayewski et al. 2004). Likewise, instead of a continuous rise in sea level, we now know that there were several pulses over the course of the Holocene (Walker 2013). The timing and magnitude of these climatic changes and sea level pulses varied locally, so global models must be taken with caution (Kidder et al. 2008).

Mayewski et al. (2004) suggest that one episode of rapid climatic change occurred between 6,000 and 5,000 years ago. This roughly corresponds with a highstand in global mean sea level modeled by Tanner (1993), and with a pulse in sea level that has been suggested for the Gulf Coast in general (Balsillie and Donoghue 2004; Stapor et al. 1991) and the Crystal River area specifically (Goodbred 1995; Robbin 1984; Scholl et al. 1969).

Geomorphological studies of the Suwanee Delta to the north of Crystal River by Wright and colleagues (2005) suggest a slightly different pattern, with sea level rising at a relatively rapid rate of about .16 cm/year between 7500 and 5500 BP (roughly 5500 to 3500 B.C.). Beginning around 5500 years ago and continuing to 2500 B.P. (3500 to 500 B.C.), the rate of sea level rise may have decreased to around .07 cm/year. However, the cumulative rise over the course of the two millennia was enough to top the low-gradient limestone shelf, at which point the shoreline would have transgressed (i.e., moved landward) rapidly across. This is indicated by the development of estuaries and oyster beds in the Suwanee Delta.

These same changes appear to have also been taking place at Crystal River. Jackson (2016:68–77) studied pollen from Core 11, from the western midden ridge. Stratum 11 from this core, consisting of a thin humic layer lying directly above the limestone substrate at a depth of 159–160 cmbs (62.6 to 63.0 inches), produced a radiocarbon date calibrated to 2620 to

2475 cal B.C. (95 percent). Based on the associated pollen assemblage, Jackson suggests that this early deposit formed along the shoreward side of a freshwater marsh along the river. Seaward of these marshes, a series of long, linear oyster reefs—now inactive—at the mouth of the Crystal River at Crystal Bay probably also formed around this time, when the coast was only slightly west of its current location (Goodbred 1995:84).

The interval of initial coastal estuary and oyster bioherm formation corresponds with the end of the Late Archaic period in the prehistory of the Southeast. In some areas of Florida and nearby states, the people of the Archaic period began building massive circular rings of shell (Russo 1991, 1994; Russo and Heide 2001; Thompson 2007, 2010; Thompson and Andrus 2011; Trinkley 1980, 1985). Archaeological sites of the Late Archaic period are more common in the vicinity of Crystal River than those of the preceding Paleoindian period, but the settlement here remained light, and no large monuments appear to have been constructed (records of the FMSF, Tallahassee).

As discussed below (see also Pluckhahn and Thompson 2017), there is radiocarbon evidence for burials at Crystal River perhaps as early as 1000 B.C., but certainly by a century or two of the start of the first millennium A.D. The latter date corresponds generally with the onset of the Roman Warm Period, or the Wulfert High as it is known on the Gulf Coast (Balsillie and Donoghue 2004; Stapor et al. 1991). Karen Walker and William Marquardt (Marquardt and Walker 2013:876; Walker 2013:38–39), who have devoted considerable study to sea level change in the Calusa area of southwestern Florida, date this interval of episodic warmer temperatures and correspondingly higher sea levels from around A.D. 1 to 550 on the Gulf Coast. The higher sea levels, higher precipitation, and warmer temperatures of the Wulfert High would have created an environment more similar to the one we know today, providing a home for most of the flora and fauna we now consider native to the Gulf Coast.

We are not certain, however, that manatees were among those native fauna. One or two manatee bones have been reported from archaeological sites in the vicinity of Crystal River (Cumbaa 1980:9; Milanich 1994:135; Thulman 2004). Another was identified from the site itself in midden dredged from a boat slip (Ellis et al. 2003:10). Bullen (1953) suggested that a bone tool recovered by Hale Smith might have been fashioned from a manatee rib. However, the contexts for all of these finds are less than ideal.

Although much remains to be analyzed, no manatee specimens have been identified in the tens of thousands of bone fragments that have thus far been identified in association with the work conducted by CREVAP.

While surprising given the abundance of manatee in the area today, the paucity of manatee remains at Crystal River is consistent with archaeological work elsewhere in the state; David Thulman (2004) reviewed the archaeological evidence for manatees on prehistoric sites in Florida and found that they were extremely uncommon. In the 1950s a biologist (Moore 1951a, 1951b) (see also Laist and Reynolds 2005) concluded that before the construction of power plants (which produce a warm-water discharge that provides a haven for manatees during cold weather), manatees were not present north on the Gulf Coast of Charlotte Harbor, around 100 miles (160 km) to the south of Crystal River. It seems safe to assume that if manatees were present at all two millennia ago when the prehistoric site of Crystal River was initially settled, they were not present in the numbers that now frequent the waters of the region.

Still, the clear springs that form the Crystal River were probably active by the time the site was founded, and these might have been a spectacle equally worthy of attracting prehistoric settlement. Early settlers certainly found the springs worthy of description. A travel guide for Florida and other southern states published in the late 1800s described the beauty of the springs at the source of the nearby Homosassa River:

> The transparency of the river waters is something wonderful. On the springs the floating boat seems poised in mid-air, and small objects are as distinct at a depth of 60 feet as if seen through a sheet of window glass. Even here innumerable fish from river and gulf of all variety and size, impeded in their upward course, linger and play as if loath to leave so bright a pool. As one passes up or down the river, shoals of fish beneath dart away in such crowds it seems as if the very bottom were moving from underneath. The banks are fringed with a growth of the greatest luxuriance, the marvellous richness of the soil declaring itself in gigantic and picturesque oaks, bays, magnolias, palms and cedars, with a dense undergrowth of strange and tropical beauty. (Hillyard 1887:216)

Springs of such amazing clarity were not unusual in Florida before the explosive development of the late twentieth century. But it was unusual even for prehistoric Florida to have springs in such close proximity to the coast—as we noted in the previous chapter, it is a short distance from the source of the Crystal River to its mouth at the Gulf of Mexico.

Jerald Milanich (1999:20) has suggested that Crystal River is fortuitously placed in one of the few areas along the Gulf coast where hardwood hammocks reached the coast (pine and scrub forests were more typical). This location would have offered several other advantages, one being the proximity of mast-bearing trees. The combined resources of fresh, salt, and brackish water make the Springs Coast the most diverse and productive wildlife habitat in the region (Simons 1990:155). In addition, the wide, shallow continental shelf on this stretch of the Gulf Coast reduces wave energy (Goodbred 1995:27). This reduces tidal variation—the mean annual wave height is just 30 cm (1 ft) and the average spring tide only around 90 cm (25 in) (Hine and Belknap 1986). The unique physiography would have facilitated communication and transportation along the rivers and coast, and offered protection from the storms that regularly blow in from the Gulf of Mexico.

Milanich (1999:20) cites this favorable setting as an explanation for the eventual growth of the settlement of Crystal River, arguing that "the people of Crystal River placed their village in a place that gave them an economic advantage over their neighbors." There is no doubt truth to this statement, but it also risks oversimplifying the circumstances of Crystal River's founding in two important ways. First, the emphasis on competition and economics in the choice of settlement location belies the possibility that the location of Crystal River—especially its proximity to the springs—might have been equally important for religious or spiritual reasons. Romain (2009) has noted that Hopewell sites in the American Midcontinent are frequently positioned with respect to natural features, including bodies of waters. We have extended this observation to Crystal River and several of the other large ceremonial centers of the Middle Woodland period in the American South (Pluckhahn and Thompson 2013). From such evidence, Pauketat (2012:76) suggests that the Middle Woodland period was characterized by "... relational ontologies wherein juxtapositions of powers and people were central and where agency was vested in places, things, and ... bodies other than people." Explanations like this that are rooted in belief are notoriously difficult to prove empirically but also consistent with the very clear evidence that Middle Woodland societies were heavily vested in ritual.

Our second qualification to Milanich's observation is more basic: the evidence suggests that Crystal River began not as a village but as a vacant ceremonial center, by which we mean a center for rituals with little or no permanent habitation. As discussed in the chapter that follows, based on extensive radiocarbon dating we can now say with confidence that the village formed in the first or second century A.D. (see also Pluckhahn, Thompson, and Cherkinsky 2015). As is always the case in archaeology, additional testing and radiocarbon dating of other areas could produce earlier dates that challenge this assumption. However, we doubt this, since we have now dated the lowermost midden layers in four widely spaced portions of the site.

We are less confident in our dating of the onset of mound construction, because our efforts here have been hindered by the poor resolution of the excavations by Moore and Bullen and the lack of datable materials other than human bone and marine shell, which have thus far produced erratic dates (Cherkinsky et al. 2014; Katzmarzyk 1998; Milanich 1999; Pluckhahn and Thompson 2017; Pluckhahn et al. 2009; Pluckhahn, Thompson, and Cherkinsky 2015). These inconsistent dates may be due to the introduction of older carbon from the ocean (the marine reservoir effect) or the limestone substrate (the hard-water effect), or both (Cherkinsky et al. 2014).

Bearing in mind this caveat, current radiocarbon evidence suggests that the first mound to be initiated at Crystal River was Mound C, the circular embankment that forms a part of the Main Burial Complex. A recently obtained date on Bullen's Burial 19 has a calibrated range that begins at the start of the last millennium B.C. and extends for another two and a half centuries (Pluckhahn and Thompson 2017) (notes on file at the FLMNH, Gainesville, indicate that this individual was interred with six plummets, while most of the other burials from the circular embankment apparently had few funerary offerings). A second date on another set of human remains from the same mound has a calibrated range only slightly more recent. Modeling the onset of Mound C is imprecise owing to the paucity of dates and their lack of stratigraphic associations, but we can say generally that construction began between *2049 and 899 cal B.C. (95 percent)*, probably between *2043 and 913 cal B.C. (68 percent)* (Pluckhahn and Thompson 2017) (see Table 2.2). Bullen's recovery of tetrapodal vessels in association with burials in the lower levels of the embankment (Bullen 1965; Weisman 1995a:56–58) lends some support for both the earlier radiocarbon dates and the relative dating of the initiation of Mound C before that of the village; these ceramic treatments are common in the first millennium B.C. and exceedingly rare in the midden at Crystal River (Kemp 2015:41).

The possibility that the circular embankment is the earliest monument at the site is intriguing. Recent work by Ken Sassaman, Micah Monés, and colleagues suggests that small, circular enclosures were also constructed (albeit of shell, rather than earth) up the coast from Crystal River at the Deer Island and Shell Mound sites; both monuments appear to have been initiated in the Deptford period, at least by the first century A.D. (Monés et al. 2010; Sassaman et al. 2013). As we noted above, circular monuments of shell were common to parts of the coasts of Florida and Georgia during the preceding Late Archaic period, so this would mark a continuity of form. Unlike earlier shell rings, however, the circular embankment at Crystal River was composed mainly of sandy midden materials, and it was heavily laden with human burials (Moore 1903:379). Still, this might also mark continuity with the past; Mound C was positioned on a low spot on the landscape, not unlike those that Archaic period peoples of the Florida peninsula had used for burying their dead, as evidenced most famously by the Windover Pond site near Cape Canaveral (Doran 2002). Wetlands might have been conceived as liminal zones appropriate for the recently deceased (Cooney 2004:326).

Small geometric enclosures are also common to Adena and Hopewell traditions in the Midwest (e.g., Burks 2014; Byers 2004; Clay 1987; Henry et al. 2014; Webb and Snow 1945) and occur more occasionally at related sites in the lower Southeast (e.g., Mainfort 2013; Toth 1974; Wright 2014a, 2014b, 2016). The closest analogues to Mound C at Crystal River in terms of size and material are the circular embankments completed at the River Styx site to the north (Wallis et al. 2014) and Fort Center site to the south (Sears 1982:146, 198).

As with Mound C, a few of the radiocarbon dates on the two conical burial mounds also predate the earliest evidence for village occupation. Unfortunately, in the case of Mound G, some of the dates are contradictory. Early dates obtained by Cheryl Katzmarzyk (1998:Tables 3.8, 3.9) for Bullen's Burials 1 and 20 are contradicted by newly obtained dates on the same individuals that have more recent ages (Pluckhahn and Thompson 2017). The later dates obtained on Burials 1 and 20 are in greater agreement with two others from Mound G, including one we retrieved from Bullen's

Burial 30 and another obtained by Katzmarzyk (1998: Tables 3.8, 3.9) on Burial 35. Omitting the presumably errant dates on Burials 1 and 20 obtained by Katzmarzyk, our modeling suggests that Mound G was initiated between *483 cal B.C. and cal A.D. 222 (95 percent)*, probably between *80 cal B.C. and cal A.D. 125 (68 percent)* (Pluckhahn and Thompson 2017) (see Table 2.2). Surprisingly, given this range, Mound G produced none of the Hopewellian artifacts common to the Main Burial Complex, and few burial goods in general (Katmarzyk 1998:30–31; Weisman 1995a:59).

Turning from Mound G across the plaza to Mound F in the Main Burial Complex, there is better evidence for interments beginning in the last two centuries B.C. As we noted above, Moore's excavations revealed that extended burials and Hopewellian artifacts of copper and exotic stone were most common in the lowermost burials of this mound; the lack of such artifacts and variations in burial treatments suggested to him that the upper portions of the mound and the surrounding platform (Mound E) were later additions (see also Bullen 1953; Weisman 1995:52–58; Willey 1949a:316–317). Bullen's excavation of a small portion of Mound F that had not been previously disturbed by Moore indicated that there were two layers of burials in the mound, as summarized in a letter he wrote to then-landowner George Dyer (Ripley Bullen to George C. Dyer, November 11, 1960, letter on file at the FLMNH). He suspected that the upper layer of Mound F might have been added last, that is, after the surrounding platform. In a later chapter we suggest this was not the case, but for now we simply focus on the dating of Mound F, for which we have three dates from what we assume to have been the upper levels of the mounds: one we recently obtained on human bone (Pluckhahn and Thompson 2017), and two others on bulk carbon from the core of ceramic sherds (Pluckhahn et al. 2010:Table 1). Considering these three dates as a single phase of construction in Mound F, our model suggests it was initiated between *723 cal B.C. and cal A.D. 4 (95 percent)*, probably between *256 and 42 cal B.C. (68 percent)* (Pluckhahn and Thompson 2017) (see Table 2.2). Successful dating of the lowermost burials would presumably extend this range back a century or two earlier.

This modeled range for the start of Mound F is consistent with the prevalence of Hopewell artifacts in the mound's lowermost burials. The modeled range is also consistent with the ceramic assemblage from Mound F, which includes a number of vessels with podal supports (i.e., small "feet" on the bottom of the pot) (Moore 1903:387–393). As we noted above in regard to Mound C, these are a feature common to pots of the last millennium B.C. but are rare later in the Woodland period, and almost completely absent from the village middens (Kemp 2015:41–42; Thompson 2016; see also Pluckhahn et al. 2017).

Thus, the evidence suggests that people were interred on the site prior to the formation of the village—perhaps as much as a millennium earlier in the circular embankment, and a few centuries prior in the case of at least one of the burial mounds (Figure 3.2). This leads to two obvious questions: Who participated in the ceremonies that led to the creation of these first burial mounds at Crystal River? Where did the builders of these mounds live, if not at Crystal River?

Most of the area around Crystal River has unfortunately never been systematically surveyed for archaeological sites. However, Adelaide and Ripley Bullen recorded a number of the more obvious and accessible sites in the area during the 1950s and 1960s (Bullen and Bullen 1961; records on file at the FMSF). Brent Weisman and Christine Newman also recorded several sites in the area (Weisman 1990; Weisman and Newman 1991). Many more have been recorded in reconnaissance surveys by Gary Ellis, Jonathan Dean, and colleagues (Dean and Ellis 2004; Dean et al. 2004; Ellis and Dean 2004; Ellis et al. 1993; Ellis et al. 1995). A bit farther afield, Brent Weisman and Jeff Mitchem surveyed the Cove of the Withlacoochee to the south of Crystal River (Mitchem and Weisman 1987; Weisman 1986). The combined data suggest that Woodland period sites can be found on just about every marsh island, hammock, or other piece of high ground in the area surrounding Crystal River.

Many of these Woodland sites have been identified as bearing pottery of the Deptford series, which would date them to around the time of Crystal River's founding as a ceremonial center. One of the largest Deptford sites in the area may have been at the Wash Island site, just downstream from Crystal River. Adelaide and Ripley Bullen (1961:69) described Wash Island as "a narrow shell midden, 5 to 30 feet wide and 250 feet long, which at its highest point is only about 3 feet above present sea level." Ripley Bullen (1966a) excavated additional low-lying Deptford middens on Burtine Island, about 1 km (.5 mi) from the mainland and 10 km (6 mi) from Crystal River. However, like many sites on the Gulf Coast with Deptford components (Willey 1949a:353), the Burtine Island and Wash Island sites appear to have been reoccupied in later periods (Bullen and Bullen 1961; Bullen 1966a; Ellis 2008a), making it difficult to judge the intensity

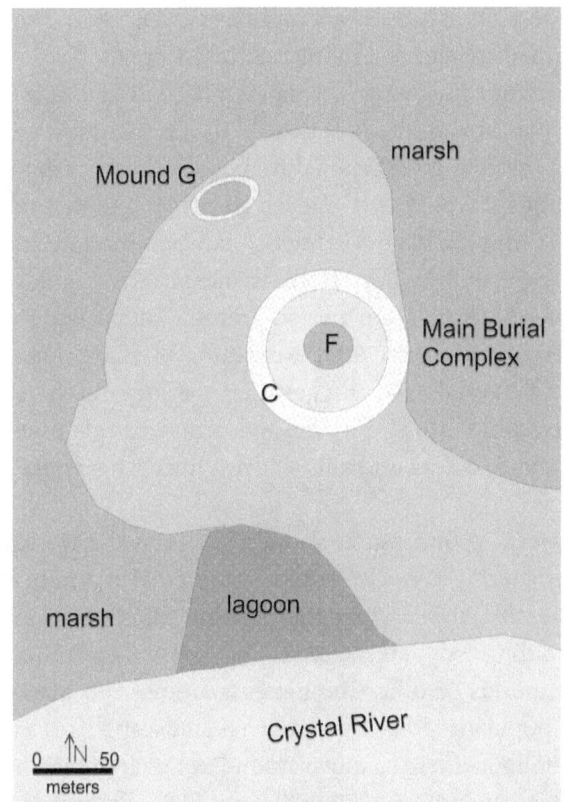

Figure 3.2. The site plan at Crystal River in the last few centuries B.C., before village formation.

of Deptford occupation. In light of the relative scarcity of "pure" and deep middens, Willey (1949a:353) suggested that Deptford society consisted of "probably small, autonomous bands based upon kinship affiliations."

Crystal River likely began as a ceremonial center for such small and dispersed family groups. In the chapter that follows, we provide some evidence that these kin groups shared a common identity, based on the analysis of ceramics associated with the earliest phase of the village at Crystal River. On the other hand, however, there are intriguing suggestions in the built environment that different communities may have been interacting at the site from very early in the settlement's history. The spatial arrangement of partially contemporaneous burial mounds—with Mound G and the Main Burial Complex opposing each other across an apparent plaza—suggests that they may have served distinct groups of people, perhaps communities to the north and south along the coast, or maybe different lineages or clans. The latter would be groups of people who share a common ancestor, either distant and perhaps fictive in the case of clans or more immediate and real in the case of lineages.

Crystal River may be unique in having two apparently contemporaneous burial facilities, but there are hundreds of sites on the Gulf Coast with small burial mounds like these, and perhaps a dozen or so others of comparable size (e.g., the Safford, Bayport, and Weeden Island Mound sites to the south of Crystal River, and the Pierce, Palmetto, and Yent mounds to the north) (Moore 1903, 1907, 1918; Willey 1949a). Isolated burial mounds were common in the later Safety Harbor period around Tampa Bay to the south (Mitchem 1988). But Moore's (1903) excavations of many of the mounds in the vicinity of Crystal River suggest that the majority here date to the Middle Woodland period. Why did the people of this time period—relative to those both before and after—invest their labor in the creation of burial mounds?

Archaeologists who work in this region and elsewhere in the world where similar formal cemeteries were constructed have posited a number of motivations, generally emphasizing the possible functions that mounds and mound building may have served. One possibility is that cemeteries marked by mounds or other monuments are used to mark territories, especially as population density in a given landscape rises to levels where people are no longer free to move around as much in search of necessary resources (Goldstein 1976, 1980, 1981; Saxe 1970). Several archaeologists have made this case for Middle Woodland societies in the Midcontinent (Buikstra and Charles 1999; Ruby et al. 2005:171; Seeman and Branch 2006), proposing that some Hopewell era mounds served to announce corporate ownership of portions of particular drainages (a practice that may have had its roots in the preceding Archaic period). Weisman (1995:83) has conjectured the same for the burial mounds at Crystal River.

As we noted above, the landscape surrounding Crystal River may have become more densely settled in the last few centuries B.C., around the same time that the first burials were interred at the site. However, as we also noted above, most of the area has not been surveyed. In addition, much of the pottery in this region is plain or check stamped, and these decorations were employed for thousands of years. Moreover, sea level was probably lower than at present in the first few centuries B.C. (Balsillie and Donoghue 2004; Stapor et al. 1991; Tanner 1993; Walker et al. 1995), and thus some associated sites from this early period in Crystal River's history are likely underwater. The problem has been exacerbated by recent sea level rise; indeed, several of the sites in the vicinity of Crystal River that were recorded by Bullen just 50 years ago are now almost completely underwater, even at the lowest of neap tides.

As a result of these limitations, we can't know for sure what the density of population was in the area at the time people began coming to Crystal River to bury their dead. We would be reluctant to say that there was any population pressure, but it might be true that the landscape had filled to the point that groups began staking out territories, especially with regard to relatively fixed resources like oyster beds. On the other hand, however, the placement of the burial mounds at Crystal River in inconspicuous locations on low ground away from the river would seem to cast doubt on the interpretation that these were meant as territorial markers.

An alternative perspective also views burial monuments as markers of difference but situates this difference among individuals or smaller social groups within—rather than between—larger collectives. To this way of thinking, mound building emerges as individual positions of leadership or power become more developed, either to highlight or mask these differences in status (for varied examples from the American Southeast, see Pauketat [1994], Peebles and Kus [1977], Muller [1997]; for a summary, see Cobb [2003]). Aspiring leaders are better able to marshal the labor required for monument construction through appeals to authority or religion, and these sorts of higher-status individuals are often assumed to be represented by special burials in mounds accompanied by more lavish burial goods. There is, however, a truism in mortuary archaeology that we do well to bear in mind: "the dead did not bury themselves" (Parker Pearson 2008:3). Accordingly, we must consider the possibility that these special burials say as much about the succession of authority as about the status of the departed individuals themselves.

Relatedly, some suggest that the act of monument construction and the commingling of remains serve to reinforce the cohesiveness of the social group or groups (Birch and Williamson 2015). Monument construction at Crystal River was probably tied to communal feasts that involved copious quantities of oyster; along the base of Mound F, Moore (1903:382) noted a "ledge of shell about 2 feet high and 20 feet broad" from the eastern margin to the center. This type of solidarity building through communal feasting, ceremony, and labor projects may have become particularly necessary when important people passed away, given that positions of leadership and other rights and responsibilities would need to be renegotiated (see Clay 1992 for an ethnographic example).

Perhaps consistent with the notion that early mound building at Crystal River revolved around the negotiation of social differences within the community or continuity of leadership, the earliest internments in Mound F seem to have been particularly rich in terms of grave goods. Moore (1903:408) noted that "practically all articles of especial interest" were found in the southern portion of this burial mound, and that "all came from considerable depths in the mound, from 4 to 8 feet." By "especial interest," Moore appears to mean ornaments of copper and exotic stone, which were concentrated in these early burials in Mound F (Moore 1903:408; Weisman 1995:53–54).

These and other artifacts that Moore excavated from Crystal River are now carefully curated by the staff of the Museum of the American Indian at its facility in Suitland, Maryland, a short bus ride from the museum on the National Mall in Washington, D.C. As archaeologists who look at material remains day in and day out, it is easy to become inured to the beauty of the artifacts we study. The artifacts from the mounds at Crystal River challenge this complacency.

Not surprisingly, there are numerous plummets and other objects made from the sort of limestones that could be acquired locally (Figure 3.3). However, many of the objects are finely crafted of materials exotic to the Florida peninsula, and even the American Southeast more broadly. Several stone plummets are made of granites and other igneous rocks that must have originated at least 400 miles from Crystal River, in the Piedmont region (Figure 3.4). The copper used to make plummets and other artifacts found at Crystal River (Figure 3.5) has never been sourced but must have come from sources no closer than the southern Appalachians more than 500 miles distant, and perhaps even copper quarries much farther afield in the Great Lakes area (Goad 1978, 1979). Quartz crystals (Figure 3.6) may have likewise come from the southern Appalachians or, perhaps, more distant sources in the Ozark Mountains. Some of the stone pipes and pendants have a reddish color that appears characteristic of catlinite, a type of stone restricted mainly to southern Minnesota, or perhaps Citronelle gravels, found in Louisiana, Alabama, and Mississippi (Figure 3.7). Many of the ceramic vessels bear unusual forms, pastes, and decorations that suggest they were also imported from other areas (Figure 3.8).

Figure 3.3. Selected plummets of local limestone from Moore's work in the Main Burial Complex. National Museum of the American Indian, Smithsonian Institution (Catalog Number 171617.001). Photographs by the authors.

Handling the objects like Moore once did—albeit now with much greater care—one can't help but wonder: How did they travel so far? What were they were used for? How did they ultimately end up being deposited in these burial mounds?

Beyond their beauty and exotic nature (relative to lithic- and mineral-poor Florida), one of the more striking characteristics of these early burial items at Crystal River—as with those found on Hopewell sites generally—is that they lean heavily toward nonutilitarian items, perhaps especially

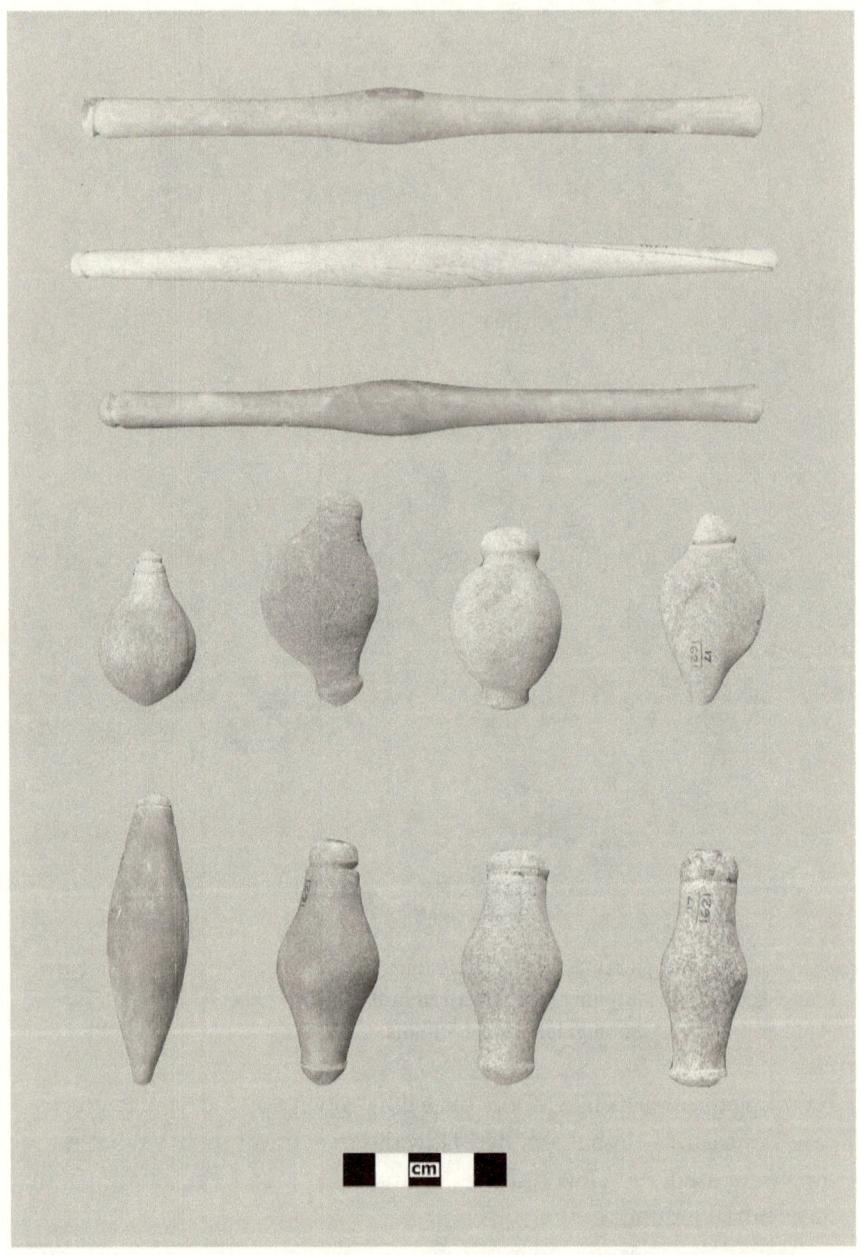

Figure 3.4. Selected plummets of nonlocal stone from Moore's work in the Main Burial Complex. National Museum of the American Indian, Smithsonian Institution (Catalog Numbers 171621.000, 171621.002, 171621.002, 171625.001, 171627.000). Photographs by the authors.

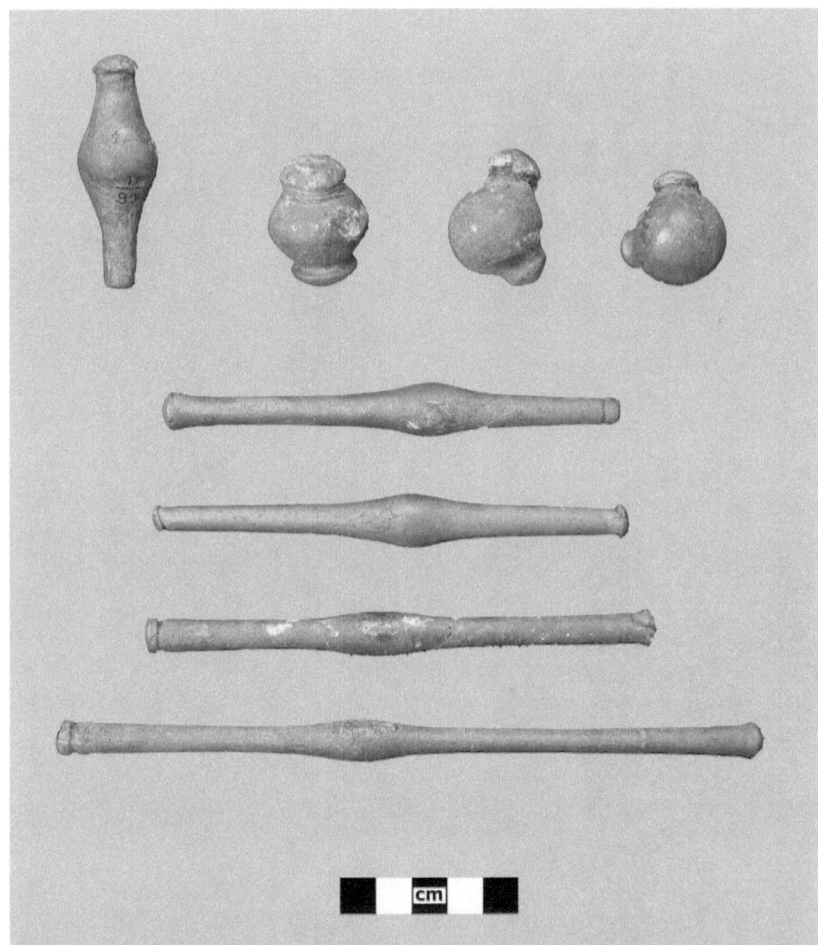

Figure 3.5. Selected copper plummets from Moore's work in the Main Burial Complex. National Museum of the American Indian, Smithsonian Institution (Catalog Numbers 170090.000, 170091.000, 170092.000, and 170093.000). Photographs by the authors.

objects of personal adornment. Projectile points (spear points and arrowheads) and other weaponry are rare. Ceramics are more common, but as noted above, these tend toward specialized vessel forms with unusual decorations, suggesting these were not used for cooking (an observation reinforced by the fact that many were ritually "killed" by puncturing a hole in the base). By far the most abundant class of artifact in these early burials at Crystal River consists of adornments of stone, shell, mica, and copper.

Figure 3.6. Selected crystalline quartz artifacts from Moore's work in the Main Burial Complex. National Museum of the American Indian, Smithsonian Institution (Catalog Numbers 171077.000, 171078.000, 171093.000, 171094.000, 171095.000, and 171622.000). Photographs by the authors.

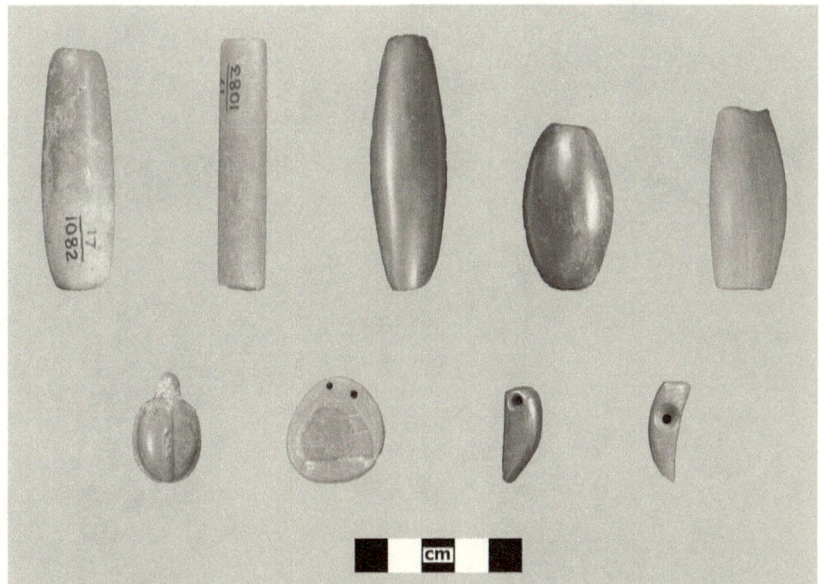

Figure 3.7. Selected reddish stone (possible catlinite, hematite, or Citronelle gravel) beads (*top*) and pendants (*bottom*) from Moore's work in the Main Burial Complex. National Museum of the American Indian, Smithsonian Institution (Catalog Numbers 171081.000, 171082.000, 171083.000, 171085.000, 171087.000, 171088.000). Photographs by the authors.

Plummet-pendants of stone, shell, and copper are particularly prevalent at Crystal River (Thompson et al. 2017). In his description of his Crystal River excavations, Moore took pains to make the case that these plummets were worn on belts or sashes, describing their orientation with respect to bodies and thus the manner in which they would have hung, and citing the sixteenth-century drawings of Jacques LeMoyne that show similar items of dress (Moore 1903:399, 424). His case is substantiated by his recovery of several stone plummets still bearing the leather "caps" and cordage from which they were suspended (Moore 1903:408). We have seen these firsthand at the NMAI, and the preservation of the 2,000-year old organic remains is remarkable; one can even see the "bitumen" (we suspect that in reality this was probably a plant-based adhesive) that Moore describes for some of the specimens (Figure 3.9).

Items of personal adornment have been popular burial accoutrements for the native peoples of eastern North America for at least the last few

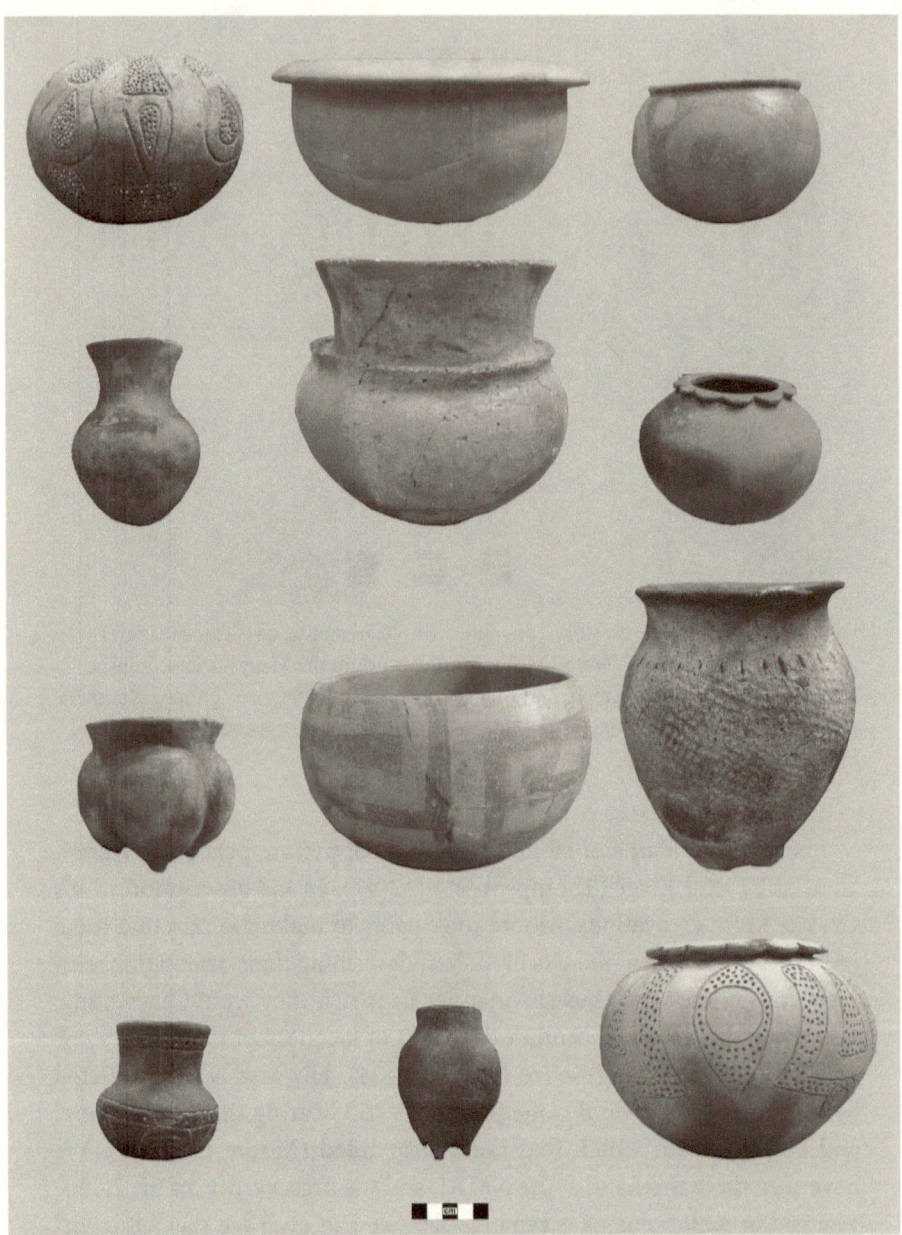

Figure 3.8. Selected ceramic vessels from Moore's work in the Main Burial Complex. National Museum of the American Indian, Smithsonian Institution (Catalog Numbers 173520.000, 173522.000, 173523.000, 173525.000, 173526.000, 173871.000, 173872.000, 174497.000, 180324.000, 180326.000, and 180327.000). Photographs by the authors.

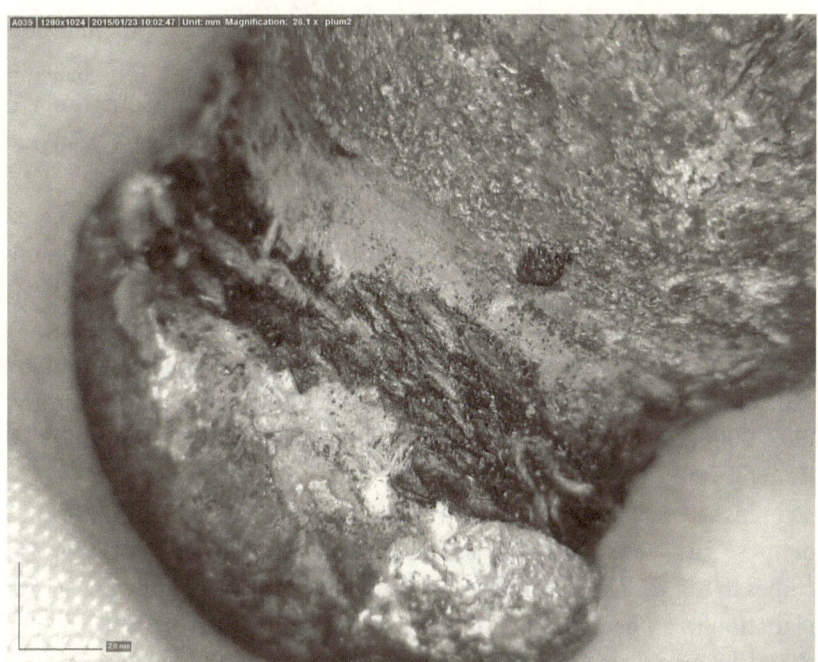

Figure 3.9. Copper plummet with traces of leather cap, cordage, and adhesive from Crystal River. Magnified approximately 26X. National Museum of the American Indian, Smithsonian Institution (Catalog Number 170093.000). Photographs by the authors.

thousand years. But in the later Mississippian period, these often bore themes relating to warfare or supernatural beings (Knight 1989). The burial goods from Crystal River and other Hopewellian sites, in contrast, lack any clear iconographic content of this sort. With the exception of one depiction of human hands on a ceramic vessel (described below) and another potsherd bearing a human face (Moore 1903:384), the only clear representations are of plants and animals. The former include a shell gorget carved in a form representing a flower (Moore 1903:397). Animal representations are more common and include two copper plates with abstract designs interpreted as bears (Moore 1903:409), several carved stone replicas of carnivore teeth (e.g., Moore 1903:406), a stone pendant in the form of a turtle (Moore 1903:419), a pot with a clearly incised depiction of a bird in flight (Moore 1903:411), and two possible bird-effigy vessels (Moore 1903:412–413). Most of the plummets are teardrop in form, some are more elongated, a few may represent stylized birds (Moore 1903:399), and one—as we noted above—may represent a manatee. Also common are animal "power parts," including the teeth of dogs, bears, pumas, deer, and dolphins recovered by Moore from the Main Burial Complex. We have likewise recovered a few teeth of pumas, sharks, and bears from our excavations in off-mound areas at Crystal River.

Some of these items of personal adornment may have marked membership in clans or sodalities; Carr et al. (2006) make this case for many of the animal power parts found in the Midwest. Others may have been markers of personal prestige or skill. But archaeologists have long associated many of these sorts of Hopewellian and Adena artifacts and their exchange with ritual and ritual specialists (priests or shamans) (Brown 1997, 2006; Carr 2008b; Carr and Case 2006; Griffin 1952:359; Otto 1975; Romain 2009; Webb and Baby 1957).

In his satirical book *Bluff Your Way in Archaeology*, Paul Bahn (1989:62) defines "ritual" as "all-purpose explanation used where nothing else comes to mind." The joke may genuinely reflect an overuse of ritual as explanation in archaeology, but in the case of Hopewellian artifacts such as these, the case seems convincing. First, the representation of animals, and especially birds, is typical of shamans, who often symbolically transform themselves during rituals and take flight to other realms (Devlet 2001:44; Eliade 1964; Harner 1981; Pearson 2002:134; VanPool 2003; VanPool and VanPool 2007; see Carr and Case [2006:192] for an extension of this to the Hopewell Midwest, and Pluckhahn [2010a] for the Woodland Southeast). Next, the qualities of many of these artifacts are consistent with an association with medicine or other forms of esoteric knowledge; for example, copper, silver, and meteoric iron are all transformative, in that their shiny and light surfaces age to dark but can be restored again with polishing (Carr 2008b; Carr and Case 2006:200–201). Finally, the artifacts are often restricted to contexts—especially burial mounds—that are clearly ritual in nature.

The argument for ritual specialists has been extended to the lowermost layers of Mound F, where, as we have noted, many of the more exotic Hopewellian artifacts were concentrated (Weisman 1995:3; see also Milanich 1994:140). Of particular note was the burial of an adult, found lying extended with three copper pendants, 39 stone pendants, two parts of the lower jaw of a puma (drilled for attachment), and four ground black bear teeth (Moore 1903:399–401). Brown (1997:473) notes that for native peoples of the Eastern Woodlands during the historic era, pumas were regarded "as animals imbued with special powers as top predators of the . . . forests" and that "bears have an even larger history as special animals." Also noteworthy was a "bunched" burial (Moore's term for a bundle of bones) interred with three quartz crystal pendants, one double quartz crystal, and 16 stone ornaments (Moore 1903:400). The latter include carved representations of carnivore teeth, beads, a small gorget with incised lines, and an amethyst quartz plummet described by Moore (1903:400) as "a perfect gem, a triumph of aboriginal endeavor." One can easily imagine that the individuals who were adorned with suites of ornaments such as these were considered somehow better connected to spirit worlds and thus held privileged roles in ritual performances—if not also in everyday life.

Some of these exotic artifacts may have served not—or not only—as items of personal adornment, but also as ritual paraphernalia. But a more obvious case for ritual accoutrements may be highlighted by the large soapstone and limestone pipes and smaller ceramic pipes and tubes that Moore (1903:393–395) recovered from Mound F. Pipes enter the archaeological record of the American Southeast as early as 1000 B.C. but are found in much greater quantities in the Middle Woodland period, and the coincidence with other Hopewellian artifacts and mounds suggests use in ritual contexts (Brown 1997:474–475; Carr 2008b; Wright 2016). More broadly, the smoking of tobacco (the seeds of which have also been found in Middle Woodland contexts in the Midwest [Asch and Asch 1985]) seems to have been associated with shamanistic visions and transformations across much of the Americas (VanPool 2003, 2009; VanPool and VanPool 2007).

The shell cups recovered by Moore (1903:393–394) from the Main Burial Complex likely also represent ritual paraphernalia. In the Mississippian and historic eras, large lightning whelk (*Sinistrofulgur sinistrum*) (formerly *Busycon sinistrum*) cups were used for the ritual consumption of cassina, or black drink, a tea made from the leaves of the yaupon holly (*Ilex vomitoria*) (Kozuch and Marquardt 2016; Milanich 1979) (although the Seminoles and some other groups substituted other plants [Hudson 1976:373]). The shells of the lightning whelk may have been favored because of their unusual sinistra (left-handed) opening; when viewed from the apex, this shell spirals clockwise and may thus have been associated with the sun and its movement (Kozuch 2013:38–42; Kozuch and Marquardt 2016).

If we can count smoking and drinking as part of a suite of ritual activities reflected by artifacts from Mound F at Crystal River, perhaps we should also consider music; VanPool (2009:178) notes that noisemakers and instruments are frequently associated with ritual specialists. Panpipes, consisting of conjoined tubes of copper that probably covered reeds, have been described as "uniquely Hopewellian" (Seeman 1979:142), since they do not appear in either earlier or later contexts. Most of the known examples are from Ohio; Crystal River is one of only a handful of sites in the American Southeast that has produced artifacts of this type (Moore 1903:411). Reis (2013) replicated a number of panpipes found on Hopewell sites and found that they were mostly tunable to a limited scale of musical notes.

One other artifact from Crystal River hints at the possibility of religious specialists. On his first trip to Crystal River, Moore (1903:384) recovered a portion of a pot incised with a depiction of a human hand, on the back of which are several abstract designs (Figure 3.10). To his astonishment, Moore (1907:411) recovered another fragment of the same vessel from his own backdirt on a trip to Crystal River a few years later; this fragment also bore a depiction of a human hand, as well as the image of a bird in flight (perhaps toward the sun). The fingernails on the hands are clearly depicted, a stylistic convention common on much later (Mississippian period) engraved shell cups and possibly linked to the shamanistic practice of defleshing the bones of the dead (Phillips and Brown 1978) (although Willey [1948c] felt that the fingers were more "delicately tapered" than the "broader and stubbier" Mississippian examples). The design on the back of the hand could represent an early prototype of the Mississippian "Nonconforming Eye" or "bilobed arrow" design elements (Willey 1948c).

One must be cautious about the use of later ethnographies and historical accounts to interpret ancient societies thousands of years removed, but it is clear both that religious specialists were common to the native societies of the Southeast in the seventeenth and eighteenth centuries and that these individuals often invoked identification with birds. In his observations of the native peoples of the region in the 1770s, William Bartram observed,

> The junior priests or students, constantly wear the mantle or robe, which is white, and they have a great owl skin cased and stuffed very ingeniously, so well executed, as almost to represent the living bird,

having large sparkling glass beads or buttons fixed in the head for eyes; this insignia of wisdom and divination, they wear sometimes as a crest on top of the head, at other times the image sits on the arm, or is borne on the hand. These bachelors are also distinguishable from the other people, by their taciturnity, grave and solemn countenance, dignified step, and singing to themselves songs or hymns, in a low sweet voice, as they stroll about the towns. (Waselkov and Braund 1995:123)

We find the case for shamans at Crystal River and other Hopewell sites compelling, if admittedly not entirely conclusive; the suite of artifacts we have described above, in combination with their occurrence in mortuary contexts, constitutes what VanPool (2009:188) has termed a "shamanic sacra." Beck and Brown (2011:73) note, "Novel religious or charismatic movements often achieve traction during moments of social crisis, when existing ideals and ideologies fail to make sense of the world as it

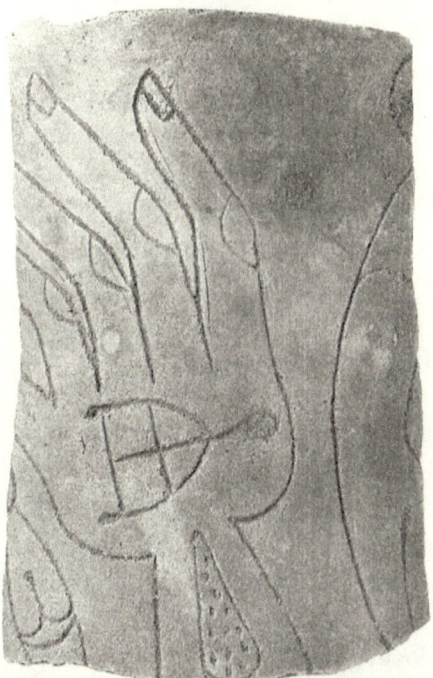

Figure 3.10. Portions of the same ceramic vessel recovered by Moore in 1903 (Moore 1903:384) and 1906 (Moore 1907:411).

is experienced." The transition to settled village life may be an example of this sort of "structural disjunction" (Sewell 2005), and the apparent religious specialists represented in some of the burials in Mound F may signal the appearance of the sort of charismatic leaders that sometimes step up in these moments of crisis to point the way to a new or revitalized ideology better suited to the emerging structures of life.

The recognition of ritual specialists does not, however, entirely clarify the mechanisms by which these exotic artifacts were produced and exchanged. Most of the hundreds of Middle Woodland burial mounds of the Gulf Coast that were excavated by C.B. Moore contain small numbers of nonlocal craft items, principally the same sort of ornaments of copper, shell, mica, and stone that we have described for Crystal River and which are considered typical of Hopewellian exchange (Seeman 1979:116). Seeman's (1979:131) seminal analysis of the distribution of these and other Hopewell artifacts suggested close connections between the Gulf Coast and the Scioto region of Ohio. He suggested that some objects, such as bicymbal copper ear spools and panpipes, were likely made in Ohio and exchanged with groups to the south (Seeman 1979:131, 144). The Ohio drainage is also a likely source for a small fragment of cannel coal (Seeman 1995:102) recovered from one of our test units in the village. On the other hand, plummets and shell gorgets may have been made primarily on the Gulf Coast and moved north to Ohio (Seeman 1979:163–164). Certain artifacts from Crystal River may reflect more complicated itineraries and influences; for example: a copper breastplate from Crystal River was probably made locally from imported copper (Seeman 1979:132); a marine shell crescent gorget mimics the form of copper examples found primarily in Ohio (Seeman 1979:140); mica mirrors may have been made in Ohio from raw materials imported from the southern Appalachians (Seeman 1979:151); and the oversized stone pipes were probably made in the Copena area of Tennessee (Seeman 1979:160–162).

Brose (1979; see also Brose and Percy 1974) argued that the ceremonial exchange of exotics among the Middle Woodland societies of Gulf Coast functioned to facilitate access to resources from different environmental zones, an adaptation to higher population densities. Anderson (1998:288) has suggested that participation in Hopewellian exchange may have been motivated by "greed, rather than need"; specifically, he suggests that the concentration of Hopewellian exotics at major Middle Woodland centers along the Gulf Coast derived in part from the ability of elites to control the procurement and movement of marine shell to the interior (Anderson 1998:278–280). Seeman (1988) and Buikstra and Charles (1999) have advanced similar arguments for the competitive display of valuables by aspiring Hopewell leaders. Goad (1979) made a parallel argument for Crystal River in particular, based on the disproportionate representation of copper.

Carr (2006:577) suggests that attempts such as these to explain the "entire expanse of interregional exchange" by some single economic phenomenon or motivation are misguided (see also Seeman 1995 and Wright 2014a, 2014b, 2016). In their stead, Carr (2006) offers a variety of mechanisms by which artifacts may have moved from one location to another. For example, in some cases individuals may have made pilgrimages to places in nature, especially sources of exotic materials, and returned to their communities with some of these materials. Medicine people or their patients may have traveled for healing ceremonies that involved ritual paraphernalia. Individuals from one community may have been ceremonially adopted as the spirit of a deceased member of another; this practice of "spirit adoption" was common to historic Indian groups, for whom it was facilitated by smoking from special pipes (see Hall 1979, 1997). Travel to distant lands to acquire specialized knowledge was likely a common practice among shamans, religious specialists, and emergent leaders in the ancient world (see Helms 2014). The exotic objects that were exchanged—many already probably symbolically charged owing to their shininess, translucence, or other unusual properties—probably became imbued with further special qualities owing to their itineraries (Van de Noort 2011:39).

Following this logic, individuals or small groups from Crystal River may have traveled to distant mound sites to trade, or to participate in ceremonies, or to be tutored or treated by religious specialists. They may have brought—or returned with—items for trade, or tokens of remembrance, or symbols of newfound knowledge and skills that gave them special status. Likewise, people from other communities probably came to Crystal River.

Based on the relatively widespread occurrence of small numbers of Hopewellian artifacts at mound sites along the Gulf Coast (Moore 1900; 1903, 1907, 1918), we can imagine that the community that came together for ceremonies at Crystal River was enmeshed in various forms of exchange and ceremony with villages throughout the region. However, the quantity and variety of Hopewellian artifacts that Moore recovered from Mound F provide ample evidence that Crystal River had already emerged as a better-connected node in regional and extraregional networks of exchange. Shell artifacts are relatively rare in these early burials, suggesting either that control of the import and consumption of marine shell was not a significant factor in the early development of complexity at Crystal River or that these shells were, as yet, such precious commodities that they remained in circulation. Assuming the former, which seems more likely given the interment of copper, to what can we credit the appearance of these exotics in some of the earliest burials at Crystal River?

As noted above, we disagree with several of the premises of Milanich's assertion that the environs of Crystal River afforded residents a natural economic advantage over neighboring communities. Still, we would agree more generally that this stretch of coast was propitious in terms of resources. Oyster beds were undoubtedly developing in the tidal rivers and estuaries by the last few centuries B.C. We are not certain that marine resources here would have been any more abundant than up the coast at Cedar Key, where other—potentially competing—ceremonial centers were developing around this same time (Wallis and McFadden 2016; Wallis et al. 2015). But perhaps Milanich is correct that the location of Crystal River at a point where hardwood hammocks reach the coast offered an advantage relative to the locations of neighboring coastal communities, where pine and scrub forest are more typical. Proximity to a prominent upland (the Brooksville Ridge) might have afforded advantageous access to overland trails that connected to communities in the interior. Particular communities and factions within them may have differentially exploited potential advantages like these, fueling imbalances in population (Widmer 1988:270–271), as well as in the scale and elaboration of ceremony.

These scalar differences are evident not only in the number and diversity of Hopewellian artifacts at Crystal River, but also in public architecture. By the first century A.D., if not earlier, the still vacant ceremonial center at Crystal River had developed a complexity unparalleled among its peers, with one burial mound surrounded by an encircling embankment, and another singular burial mound across an apparent plaza. Like Milanich, we see the elaboration of mortuary construction at Crystal River as an indication that ceremonies here were attracting more, and more varied, people.

To summarize, Crystal River emerged as a center for ceremony in the last millennium B.C., perhaps as early as 1000 B.C. but certainly by the last few centuries B.C. Since there is no apparent village occupation at Crystal River in this interval, and since no contemporaneous domestic sites in the surrounding area have been excavated using modern methods, we can't say much about subsistence or population density in this period. But the fact that the site began as a vacant ceremonial center would seem to belie the notion that the early village at Crystal River formed as result of population circumscription, resource stress, or conflict. Still, we assume that the local population burgeoned as sea levels rose and the landscape in the area took on something resembling what we know today, with tidal rivers and estuaries teeming with fish and shellfish and forests full of mammals. Given the dispersed nature of settlement, we doubt that collective labor had yet extended to hunting and fishing, as seems to have been the case in later phases.

People from the surrounding area apparently came together at certain times of the year to bury their dead in the circular embankment and Mound F. These events were probably a way for the dispersed community to negotiate or assert access to resources and to maintain some degree of collective identity and cooperation through communal labor projects and feasting.

Communal ceremonies no doubt also provided an opportunity for individuals and households to establish and maintain ties based on kinship and trade, with others in the area and perhaps some from farther away. The probability that some individuals or households were better able to exploit such relations to gain access to prestige and its trappings is indicated by the unequal treatment of burials at Crystal River. As Berle Clay (2014:147) has noted for the Adena and Hopewell societies in the Midwest that were developing around this very same time, most individuals never made it to burial mounds. We don't know where or how these individuals were disposed of in death, but we can assume that their bodies were scattered "in dispersed and isolating circumstances that may be difficult to identify archaeologically today." As Clay notes, "it took deliberate actions of agents or teams to deploy some of their dead or their transformed remains in contrived archaeological contexts." There is a great deal of "interpretive ambiguity" (Clay 2014) in the diversity of burial treatments seen in the early layers of the burial mounds of earth and shell at Crystal River, but it seems clear that the individuals who were buried with the plummets, copper plates, and other finery—or perhaps the people who buried them—enjoyed a higher status than those who were buried without such objects, or in isolated locations away from mounds. It is possible that the filling in of the landscape favored corporate groups that controlled the best hunting or fishing grounds, leading to imbalances in wealth and status (Widmer 1988:271). Still, the apparent emphasis on ritual paraphernalia and animal imagery suggests that high status may have been tied primarily to religious leadership and that such positions were not yet fully institutionalized, as Carr and Case (2006) suggest for Hopewell sites of the same time period.

At a broader scale of analysis, it is clear that all communities were not equal (cf. Willey 1949a:369). Crystal River, with its circular embankment and burial mound, was emerging as the paramount center for ceremony in the local area. In scale and elaboration, it already exceeded other ceremonial centers on the peninsular Gulf Coast. Its closest peers were at the Yent and Pierce sites in the Florida Panhandle, and the Mandeville site in the interior of the Chattahoochee River Valley of southwestern Georgia, where we see similarly elaborate mounds and comparable quantities of exotic Hopewell artifacts (Milanich 1994:135–136; Sears 1962; Smith 1975, 1979; Willey 1949a:369). There was no doubt competition between these centers and their respective leaders for access to exotic goods, and in attracting people.

4

From Vacant Center to Early Village (Phase 1)

Shell middens are notoriously difficult to excavate archaeologically for a variety of reasons. In cases where shell is the dominant constituent of the sediment, as exemplified by our Trench 3 at Crystal River (Figure 4.1), the profiles of excavations become prone to collapse. The process of excavation becomes something like the game Jenga—in fact, we recall one graduate student on CREVAP coming to tears when the removal of one too many oyster shells from the wall of the unit caused an avalanche of shell. In addition to the problem of instability, features like posts and pits are often difficult to see, in that they may be marked only by small variations in the type, orientation, or frequency of shell. Screening is difficult, because the copious quantities of shell obscure smaller items like pottery and bone.

Shell middens are also challenging to interpret with confidence. The remains of marine organisms like shells and fish bones are tricky to radiocarbon-date effectively, due to marine reservoir effects, as we noted in the previous chapter. Variations in the density or composition of shellfish in middens may represent breaks in occupation, but these may also simply indicate short-term (perhaps even one-time) targeting of specific resources (Claassen 1998:194–195; Marquardt 2010; Waselkov 1987). Shells may have been deposited in proximity to houses, or they instead may have been dumped away from habitations, to intentionally fill low spots or to keep living areas clean, among many other potential reasons.

These complications need to be kept in mind as we attempt to understand the process of village formation at Crystal River. They are especially relevant when it comes to the earliest period of village formation, since these are the deepest layers at Crystal River—buried to a depth of 1.5 m (6 ft) or more below the contemporary ground surface. In fact, these layers are today underwater at high tide, a good indication that sea levels were

Figure 4.1. Close-up of the shell-dense matrix in Trench 3 at Crystal River.

probably at least a few feet lower than present when the village was first occupied.

Radiocarbon dates from the lowermost levels in our trenches suggest that the midden at Crystal River began to form in the first century A.D. From our modeling, the first phase of midden deposition began between *cal A.D. 69 and 125 (95 percent probability)*, probably between *cal A.D. 125 and 199 (68 percent)*, and ended between *cal A.D. 144 and 265 (95 percent)*, probably between *cal A.D. 180 and 242 (68 percent)* (Pluckhahn, Thompson, and Cherkinsky 2015) (see Table 2.1). Relative to other periods, Phase 1 was relatively short; our modeling suggests that it lasted between *0 and 161 years (95 percent)*, probably between *0 and 73 years (68 percent)*.

There is radiocarbon evidence for Phase 1 midden deposition on the western portion of what would come to be the Midden B shell ridge, as evidenced by two samples from our Trench 1. A sample from Trench 2 produced a remarkably similar date and indicates midden was also being deposited in the central portion of the site on the fringes of the former lagoon. Current radiocarbon evidence suggests midden formation began slightly later (in Phase 2, as discussed in the chapter that follows) in the area of Trench 4, to the east. We also have no evidence for Phase 1 occupation in Trench 3, just north of where Mound A would eventually be built. Together, the evidence suggests that the early village at Crystal River was an abbreviated version of its later crescent shape, extending from the Mound J area at the north to the northern fringes of the lagoon (Figure 4.2).

This crescent (or in many cases circular) village plan is common to sites of the Middle Woodland period in the region (Pluckhahn 2010b; Russo et al. 2006; Stephenson et al. 2002), as it was also to ceremonial centers of the preceding Late Archaic period (Claasen 2015:167–168). It is perhaps notable that the crescent-shaped midden at Crystal River opened toward the northeast and the Main Burial Complex; Claasen (2015:168) relates the C-shape with portals to other worlds.

Recent excavation data provide suggestions that life in the Phase 1 village was oriented toward the ceremonial sphere. Pluckhahn, Thompson, and Cherkinsky (2015) compared the quantity of midden observed in excavations with the length of time it took for these layers to form. The first phase in the growth of the early village at Crystal River included relatively fast accumulation of food remains. However, the Phase 1 midden layers, while rich in shell and bone, contain relatively few other artifacts. This pattern of lots of food remains with few other artifacts may indicate that people were living at the site seasonally, or perhaps only coming to the site for special occasions like feasts.

Recent isotopic studies of shellfish remains by Thompson, Isabelle Holland Lulewicz, and colleagues (Lulewicz et al. 2017; Thompson et al. 2015) provide some support for the interpretation of seasonal settlement during

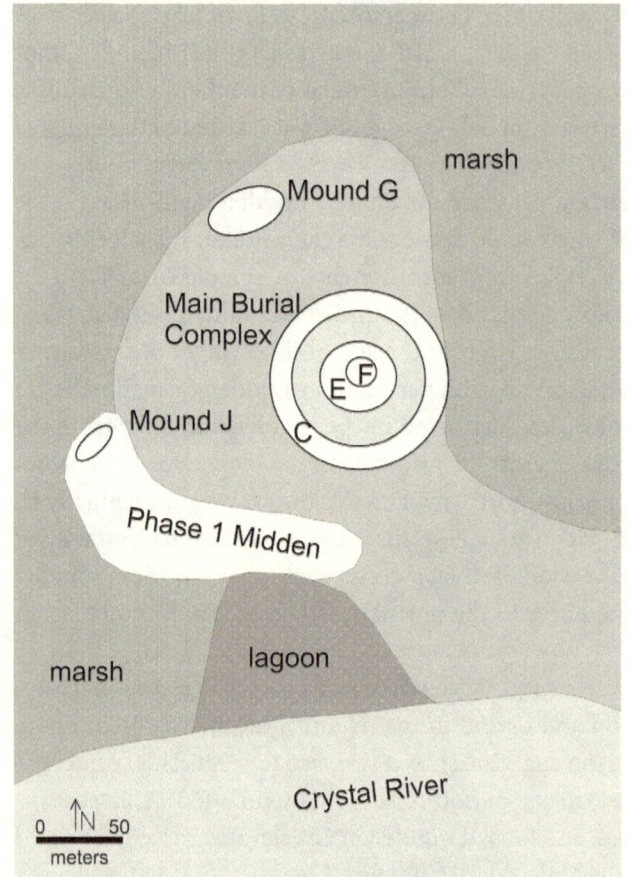

Figure 4.2. The settlement plan at Crystal River during Phase 1.

Phase 1. Oysters put on annual growth rings, and we can cut the shell in half to see these in cross section. The thickness of these rings varies with seasons, but also with age and other variables, so we can't determine when the oyster was procured by just looking at the rings. However, the rings include oxygen isotopes that are indicative of water temperature when they formed, and thus also the season they were captured. Fred Andrus and Orinda Dras at the University of Alabama used a mass spectrometer to measure the oxygen isotopes on samples from Crystal River. The samples from Phase 1 midden contexts, in contrast with those from later phases, were gathered exclusively during cooler months of the year. Further study of subsistence remains by graduate students Elizabeth Southard (at USF) and Lulewicz (at UGA) will clarify the picture, but the existing isotope data provide another indication that settlement at Crystal River in Phase may have been seasonal, perhaps associated with mortuary ceremonies and burial events.

Other aspects of the faunal assemblage provide hints that the occupation may have become more permanent over the course of Phase 1. Elizabeth Reitz, Maran Little, and Kelly Brown analyzed vertebrate faunal remains from the Phase 1 levels in Units 1 and 5 (Little and Reitz 2015; Reitz and Brown 2015). The assemblages from these two units are broadly similar overall, demonstrating a clear preference for aquatic resources. In the Phase 1 levels of Unit 1, 88 percent of the individuals (i.e., the Minimum Number of Individuals, or MNI, an estimate of the number of individuals of each species or taxon) are from aquatic habitats, and 7 percent of the individuals are terrestrial animals. In terms of biomass (an estimate of the meat that could be obtained from those individuals), 77 percent is from aquatic habitats, and 22 percent is from terrestrial ones. In the single Phase 1 level in Unit 5, 80 percent of the individuals are from aquatic habitats, and 8 percent of the individuals are terrestrial animals; 66 percent of the biomass is from aquatic habitats, and 31 percent is from terrestrial ones. This strong reliance on aquatic over terrestrial resources is characteristic of Woodland faunal assemblages from the coast, an area rich in aquatic resources from marine, estuarine, and freshwater biomes (Hadden 2015; Hoese and Moore 1998; Little 2015; Reitz et al. 2013).

When viewed level by level, however, the percentages of aquatic taxa in Unit 1 decline from earlier (Level 14) to later (Level 12) Phase 1, as the percentages of terrestrial taxa increase. Specifically, during the latter part of Phase 1, people may have chosen to more frequently target terrestrial fauna, specifically deer. This sort of change might be expected if people were beginning to live at the site more permanently, or at least for longer portions of the year. Of course, the sample sizes are relatively small, and we can't rule out other possibilities, such as change in the environment, to explain this apparent trend.

In keeping with this interpretation of seasonal and impermanent residence through at least much of Phase 1, we noted few features associated with this phase in our excavation units. This contrasts sharply with the midden layers dating to later occupations, where pits are so common they frequently overlap. One exception is our Trench 2, where we noted a semicircle of post molds of consistent size (about 20 cm [8 in] in diameter) and spacing (every 30 cm [1 ft]) (Figure 4.3). Unfortunately, these features were located below the modern water table, so they could not be

Figure 4.3. Arc of post features (marked by chaining pins) in the Phase 1 level at the bottom of Trench 2. Note water seepage at left due to high tide.

excavated. But the pattern is clear enough to suggest that a small circular or oval house (or similar structure) may have been present on the edge of the lagoon. Comparable houses are known from Deptford period sites elsewhere in Florida and Georgia (Milanich 1994:122–125).

Our few test units provide only a limited window on the early village at Crystal River. But the supposition that small structures were present is supported by the results of our work with ground-penetrating radar. Figure 4.4 shows a series of horizontal "slices" of the radar data from an area north of Mound A at increasing depths. The slices from the upper and middle layers of the midden show a great deal of reflection, consistent with a dense "sheet" of shell midden. However, the slices from the lower and earlier layers in the midden reveal more discrete areas of highly reflective sediment, possibly corresponding to the sort of widely spaced clusters of features we might expect with a spatial arrangement of scattered houses and accompanying midden. This pattern too is typical of Deptford period sites in the region (Milanich 1994:122).

Assuming that the posts we observed in Trench 2 were from a house, and that the GPR data reflect similar post patterns scattered in other parts

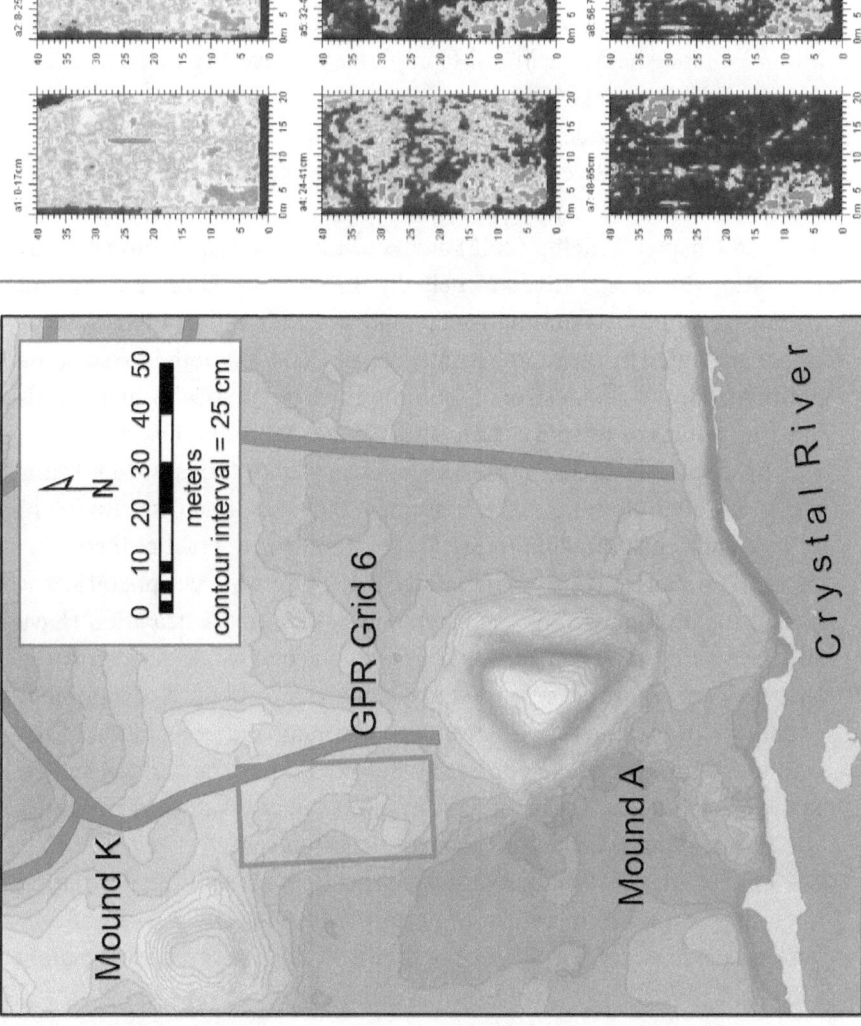

Figure 4.4. Horizontal "slices" of the radar data from an area north of Mound A at increasing depths. Note more-uniform, highly reflective upper layers indicative of a "sheet" midden of shell, and more spotty reflections in lower layers, perhaps indicative of features and feature clusters.

of the midden, we may be justified in imagining that the early village at Crystal River consisted of an arc of houses from Mound J to the lagoon. Milanich (1994:123–124), drawing on excavations at Deptford sites by himself and others (especially Bense [1985]), estimates that the typical village of this time period included five to ten houses, with a population of 25 to 60 people. We imagine, based on the size of the Phase 1 midden, that the population of Crystal River was at the higher end of this range.

Again bearing in mind the isotope data, however, the site seems to have been only seasonally occupied during Phase 1. People may have spent the warmer months of the year dispersed in smaller settlements, coming together at Crystal River in the late fall and staying through the winter. These seasonal aggregations would have been a good time for ceremonies, as reflected in mound construction. As we noted in the previous chapter, Mound G and the Main Burial Complex may have begun even before there was a village at Crystal River.

Pottery may provide one measure of the scale at which people were coming to Crystal River for ceremonies, and two recent thesis projects have approached this topic (see Pluckhahn et al. 2017 for a summary). As noted in Chapter 2, Kemp (2015) analyzed the collections from previous excavations at Crystal River, principally the work by Ripley Bullen; and Thompson (2016) has summarized temporal trends in the pottery assemblages generated by the more recent work of CREVAP. Both looked at the pottery from the perspective of "communities of practice," which developed in studies of learning (Lave and Wenger 1991) and has since been widely adopted by archaeologists (e.g., Eckert 2012; Garraty 2013; Lyons and Clark 2012; Roddick 2009; Sassaman 2005; Sassaman and Rudolphi 2001; Wendrich 2012a, 2012b). Briefly, communities of practice theory focuses on how an individual is integrated into a group by "peripheral learning," through imitation, observation, and graduated participation (Lave and Wenger 1991:29; Wenger 1998). Pottery making would seem particularly well suited to this type of study, since it is composed of a number of choices and learned skills—from procurement and preparation of the clay, to the forming of the vessel, to the decoration of the surface, and on to the firing process. These choices and skills can be assumed to be shared within communities of potters that regularly interact.

Kemp's (2015:137) analysis suggested that there was minimal variation in temper or surface treatment of pottery from the earliest levels of Bullen's excavations in the midden. The sherds from these levels were mainly tempered with limestone. Further, with the exception of a few sherds of the Deptford Check Stamped and Swift Creek Complicated Stamped types that are typical of this time period elsewhere, most of the pottery was plain; indeed, the dominance of plain pottery prompted Bullen (1953:34) to observe that "the inhabitants of the Crystal River site seem to have been 'conservative royalists' who did not adopt every passing fancy in pottery decoration." Although we would not go so far as Bullen, we agree with Kemp that at this time Crystal River was routinely visited by a single community of potters, resembling what Carr (2006b:75) has described as a "residential community," or one composed of "sets of households and people who live in close proximity and interact regularly on a face-to-face basis, whether they be clustered or dispersed over the landscape" (Carr 2006b:75).

On the other hand, however, there are intriguing suggestions that Crystal River may have begun as a ceremonial center that united not just one but two distinct communities. Looking at the better-controlled and well-dated pottery assemblages from the midden, Thompson (2016:67) (see also Pluckhahn et al. 2017) noted that the Phase 1 assemblage was almost equally split between sand- and limestone-tempered types, suggesting the possibility of two communities of potters. The assemblage from this phase was small and restricted mainly to one test unit, so our conclusions are limited. But looking at sherd cross sections under magnification, the extremes in tempering are striking: some sherds are densely packed with limestone, others lack limestone but are very sandy, and a minority appear to have no temper at all (Figure 4.5).

Crystal River is situated on one of many limestone outcrops in this area of the Gulf Coast. In core samples, we noted relatively pure clays (without limestone inclusions but with varying amounts of sand) lying just above the limestone substrate (see Norman 2014). These clays would have been suitable for pottery making. Ann Cordell (2016) conducted ceramic petrography of a sample from this clay layer and from three other clays in the surrounding area; she found that two samples had high sand content, and two had moderate amounts. One of these sherds also included sponge spicules, but none of the clays contained limestone.

It would thus seem that people living at Crystal River had a choice with regard to recipes for pottery clays; they had easy access to relatively pure clays and also to limestone that could be used as temper. Limestone outcrops are rare with increasing distance from the mainland, so we might

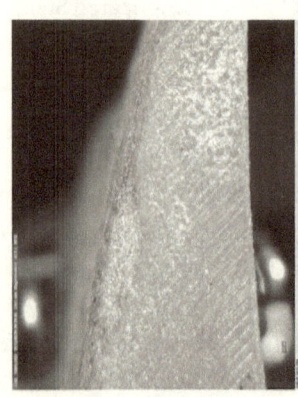

"temperless" (probably sponge-spiculate), typical of St Johns series pottery

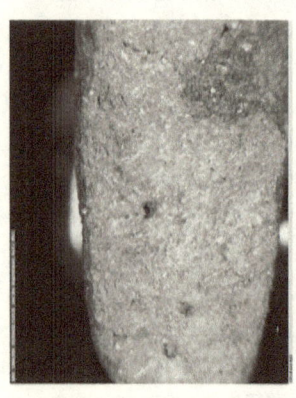

sand temper, typical of pottery of the Deptford, Swift Creek, and Weeden Island pottery series/types

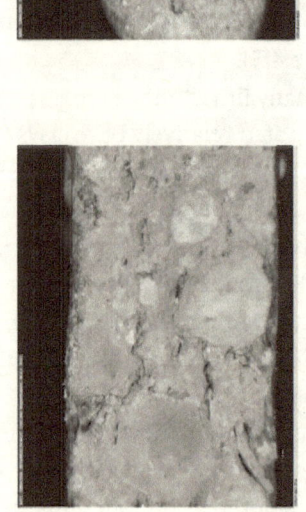

limestone temper, typical of Pasco series pottery

Figure 4.5. Cross sections of sherds from Crystal River under magnification (ca. 50X) to show variation in temper.

therefore expect this temper to have been less commonly utilized by people who resided on marsh islands downstream of Crystal River. Given the split between two temper categories, it seems possible that the dispersed community that congregated occasionally at Crystal River during Phase 1 was composed of distinct pottery making traditions: a local group of potters that preferred the addition of limestone to pottery clays and another from areas farther removed that favored sandier clays.

The ceramic assemblages from mounds suggest that such social divisions may have been mapped onto the landscape through the maintenance of distinct burial facilities, as we alluded to in the last chapter. Radiocarbon dates indicate that while Mound G may have been initiated earlier, its use continued through at least Phase 1. The assemblage from Bullen's work in Mound G is small, totaling only 155 sherds (Kemp 2015:49–50). Still, as with the Phase 1 midden assemblage, the majority (70 percent) of these are limestone tempered, with sand-tempered following at 18 percent, and spiculate pottery at 3 percent. Also consistent with the Phase 1 midden assemblage, most of the sherds from Mound G are plain, with the exception of isolated sherds of Deptford Check Stamped, Deptford Simple Stamped, Swift Creek Complicated Stamped, and several other types. This assemblage seems to indicate that Mound G was a burial facility for people who practiced local pottery-making traditions.

The pottery assemblages from Mounds E and F at the heart of the Main Burial Complex are clearly different from those from Mound G and the midden. The 2,012 total sherds from these mounds are dominated by sand-tempered and spiculate-tempered ceramics, at 38 percent and 37 percent respectively (Kemp 2015:52–53). Limestone-tempered sherds make up only about 20 percent of the total. Surface decorations also exhibit much more diversity here than in the assemblages from the midden and Mound G. Although the majority of the sherds are still plain, Weeden Island Red makes up 12 percent of the total. The other 27 percent of the collection is spread between at least six basic attributes and 17 types. The greater diversity in ceramics here probably reflects a longer period of use but may also reveal social differences; perhaps the Main Burial Complex was reserved either for people of nonlocal pottery-making traditions or, more likely, people who lived in the area but were better connected to these traditions.

Graves may further bear out these social differences, as well as shifts in the nature and extent of interaction. As we noted above, Moore's account suggests that the main burial mound (F) and surrounding platform (E) were built in at least three phases: two phases of construction in the mound and the addition of the platform (see Bullen [1953], Weisman [1995:52–58], and Willey [1949:316–317] for additional and largely similar attempts to interpret the mound stratigraphy from Moore's descriptions). It is difficult to precisely parse the burials and burial goods based on Moore's (1903, 1907, 1918) accounts of his excavations. We can say with some confidence, as we did in the previous chapter, that the burials in the lowermost portions of Mound F—dating to the period before the village formed—are the richest in terms of Hopewellian imports like copper and quartz crystal. These individuals also appear to have been more often interred in full, either resting on their backs or flexed on their sides (Moore 1903:382). The later Phase 1 burials above these appear to have more often taken the form of what Moore referred to as "bunch burials" (Moore 1907:408), or what we more commonly refer to today as bundles or secondary burials (wherein the deceased was defleshed, either by hand or by being temporarily buried elsewhere for a time, before being reburied). These bundle burials from the later and upper portion of the mound mostly lacked more exotic Hopewellian objects but were nevertheless rich in other grave goods, especially ceramics and marine shell ornaments and cups (Moore 1907:409–421). Moore (1907:416–418) noted in particular that shell pendants were "much in vogue" (in contrast, and to Moore's befuddlement, shell beads were rare throughout the mounds at Crystal River).

Thus, although the burials in the upper levels of Mound F may have lacked many of the classic Hopewell exotics found in the mound base, they were still far more elaborate than those in Mound G, which produced very few grave goods. In this sense, the social divisions that were evident in the earliest burials at Crystal River appear to carry through to the first phase of village life. Interment in the Main Burial Complex was probably reserved for people of higher status, as marked by the deposit of exotic ceramics and marine shell. Status may have been reinforced by the maintenance of separate burial facilities on opposing sides of the plaza.

The differences in burial goods in Mound F also demonstrate a shift in the nature of interaction and, by extension, perhaps in the way higher-status goods were procured or earned. The copper and quartz artifacts found in earlier burials suggest connections to Hopewellian centers to the north, not only to sites along the Gulf Coast but likely farther afield to sites like Tunnacunnhee (Jefferies 1976) and Leake (Keith 2013) in northern Georgia, and perhaps as far as the classic Hopewell communities in the Midwest. The unusual physical properties of these commodities and the distance they traveled to reach Crystal River suggest that these connections were important to the achievement of positions of status or skill, probably in many cases as religious specialists, as we noted in the previous chapter. In contrast, the apparently greater frequency of marine shell and ceramics in the later burials of Mound F suggests a contraction of interaction to the Gulf Coast and adjacent interior regions of the Southeast.

These pots and shell ornaments are less obviously associated with religious specialists than the quartz and copper objects prevalent in earlier burials. In the last chapter, we cited Beck and Brown's (2011) observation that charismatic leaders often appear during moments of structural disjunction. They further note that for these charismatic leaders to effect a durable transformation of structures, the authority must be institutionalized. Max Weber (1947:364) referred to this process as routinization and saw it necessary for the creation of both ideal and material stability (Beck and Brown 2011:73). Similarly, for the Hopewell Midwest, Carr and Case (2006:229) (see also Carr 2008b) suggest that the appearance of conch shells and shell spoons might be part of a trend toward greater segregation of leadership roles and may specifically mark positions that were not associated with shamanistic properties.

It also seems possible that these goods might simply reflect wealth accumulated by particular individuals or households. However, there are few indications that the possible distinctions in wealth and status that were marked in death carried over to life in the early village at Crystal River. The ceramic assemblages from the Phase 1 levels in Units 1 and 5 are small but generally comparable and lacking in any types that could be considered indicative of status—all of the sherds are either plain or check stamped (Thompson 2016:67). There is a single barrel-shaped bone bead from one of the levels from this phase in Unit 1 (O'Neal 2016:115–116), but it is hard to read too much into this single and relatively unremarkable artifact.

On the other hand, faunal remains provide an intriguing, if yet inconclusive, indication of possible status differences in the village. As we noted above, the Phase 1 assemblages from Units 1 and 5 are generally similar; the two components share 22 taxa (roughly 43 percent), and most of the taxa in both units are aquatic (Reitz and Brown 2015). The sources of meat, however, are considerably different: 25 percent of the biomass in the Phase 1 levels from Unit 1 is from deer and probable dolphin, compared to 71 percent for this phase in Unit 5. Probable dolphin specimens contributed only 4 percent of the biomass for this phase in Unit 1, but 45 percent in Unit 5.

Dolphins frequent the shallow waters of the Gulf region in high numbers (Widmer 1988:247) and are a relatively common sight in the Crystal and Salt rivers. They are high-return resources that might be interpreted as high-status animals in that they are difficult to hunt and could feed many people. Thus, the differential representation of this taxon could signal the presence of a higher-status household in the vicinity of Unit 5. In possible support of the association of dolphin hunting with higher status, it is worth noting that Moore recovered a number of perforated dolphin teeth from the Main Burial Complex (photographs on file at the NMAI), apparently a cache representing a necklace worn by one of the deceased. A single additional drilled porpoise tooth was recovered by Bullen (Weisman 1995a:98).

Of course it is also possible that the Unit 5 area was simply used for processing dolphin, as might be expected given its location near the lagoon. Additional dolphin specimens were recovered by Ellis and colleagues (2003) from the riverbank area. However, argument from utility does not clearly explain the higher representation of deer—another high-return prey—in Unit 5.

One could perhaps equally make a case for higher status for the residents of the area of Unit 1 based on a disparity in the amount of sea turtle present. The Phase 1 collection from Unit 1 has 126 specimens of Chelonioidea, the superfamily that includes leatherbacks and all other species of sea turtles, contributing 23 percent of the biomass (an estimate of the total contribution of meat). In contrast, the Phase 1 collection in Unit 5 has a single sea turtle specimen that contributes less than 1 percent of the biomass. Small sample size could be an issue here, especially since the assemblage from Unit 5 is limited to a single level. But the Phase 2 levels in Unit 5, which are also relatively small samples, do not lack for sea turtles. Further, Unit 1 shows a general increase in the use of sea turtle over the course of Phase 1; the Number of Individual Specimens Present (NISP), a simple measure of all bone and bone fragments, increases from Level 14 (N = 24) to 13 (N = 55) before declining slightly in Level 12 (NISP = 47). It seems possible that during Phase 1, the vicinity of Unit 1 was specifically used to process sea turtles or to dispose of refuse; particularly since 18 percent of the sea turtle specimens (N = 23) are burned. It is also possible that the residents of this portion of the village targeted sea turtles more often. Evolutionary anthropologists relate that sea turtle hunters in the Torres Strait in Australia enjoyed wide recognition for their accomplishments (Smith et al. 2003). It is not clear that sea turtle hunting on the Gulf Coast carried the same costs in terms of time or materials. One early historic account by Murphy (1890) notes that sea turtles were sometimes harpooned from boats, with divers bringing them to the surface (Seminole Indian divers were reportedly accomplished at this task, capable of bringing up an 800-pound turtle from a depth of 40 feet). However, in the summer when the turtles came to shore to lay eggs, they could probably be taken quite easily. Regardless, a large turtle would have generated a considerable amount of meat to be shared, and thus perhaps also some measure of prestige for the hunter.

Notwithstanding these tentative and somewhat conflicting lines of evidence for achieved status in the faunal remains, the seasonal village that developed at Crystal River during Phase 1 appears to have been relatively homogeneous, consistent with a high degree of cooperation. Roscoe (2009) has described how the modular organization of small-scale societies in New Guinea may have facilitated the transformation of cooperation from one form or context to another of larger scale. As summarized by Carballo et al. (2014:112),

> In this kind of nested or segmentary structure, groups focused on an end such as reproduction might combine with other such units to form subsistence optimization units, and these subsistence optimization units may in turn combine as security units against predation.

This model might help to explain how the dispersed households that cooperated in mortuary ceremonies at the vacant ceremonial center of Crystal River began to live together in a seasonal village during early Phase 1, and perhaps in a more permanent village by the end of this phase.

The households that chose to aggregate at Crystal River during Phase 1 would have enjoyed a number of benefits, such as proximity to kin and a greater sense of community membership (Spencer 2013:210). It seems likely that village life also promoted greater cooperation in subsistence endeavors (Kowalewski 2013), perhaps especially fishing with nets and weirs since these may require larger task groups to produce and use effectively

(Widmer 1988:266). Indeed, an emerging body of research known as "settlement scaling" (see Bettencourt 2013) suggests that ancient early villages such as this one exhibit many of the same economies of scale as modern metropolitan areas, in terms of increases in economic productivity and social interaction (Ortman and Coffey 2017; Ortman et al. 2016).

As Rautman (2014, 2016) has noted, however, periods of aggregation may also be times when existing ideas and organizational forms are contested. Life in the emergent village at Crystal River undoubtedly presented new challenges, especially the potential for conflict that comes with increased face-to-face contact. We assume that there was also a greater need to coordinate access to resource areas, especially the more dense and predictable inland fishing and shellfishing locations that had the potential to become the subject of contention as populations in the area grew larger (Widmer 1988:30–31).

These challenges appear to have remained manageable mainly through the continued tradition of mortuary ceremonialism and feasting. We can imagine the extended community coming together in the colder months to hold communal feasts that included lots of oyster, mullet and other fishes, and the occasional deer, dolphin, or sea turtle. These ceremonies would have provided an opportunity to work out differences and schedule access to resources. McNiven (2004) has described the "ritual orchestration of seascapes" by indigenous fishers of Australia, by which he refers to the manner in which public rituals, by invoking spirits of the sea and the dead, mediated marine tenure at various scales of inclusiveness, from household to clan and larger communities. But it seems possible too that the possible change in leadership noted above, from religious to more secular, signals the need for more institutionalized authority.

5

From Early Village to Regional Center (Phase 2)

Sharp-eyed visitors to Crystal River Archaeological State Park may be able to pick out remnants of the mobile home park that formerly occupied much of the riverfront. A portion of the midden was graded for the park, leaving a rectangular "ledge" carved into the shell midden, running north from Mound A before turning sharply east. In the former lagoon east of Mound A that was filled for the trailer park in the 1960s, one can spot occasional trailer tie-downs, old electrical cables, and drain pipes poking through the grass.

The mobile home park was destroyed in the superstorm of March 1993 that, although officially unnamed, has been unofficially referred to as the "Storm of the Century." The storm, which caused hundreds of deaths across the Atlantic seaboard, hit Florida's West Coast with hurricane-strength winds and a tidal surge as high as 3.5 m (12 ft) that moved as much as 3 km (1.5 mi) inland (Goodbred 1995:153; *St. Petersburg Times* 1998). The nuclear plant just north of Crystal River recorded sustained winds over 55 mph (50 knots) for a period of eight hours (Goodbred 1995:153). At the site of Crystal River, a tornado spawned by the storm crossed between Mounds A and K and continued across Mound G, uprooting a number of trees (Weisman 1993). The storm surge flooded not only the trailer park but also the museum, situated on an elevated berm a few hundred feet from the river's edge. Park rangers and docents gladly show inquisitive visitors the watermark on a chair that was free-floating in the flooded museum. Fortunately, the display cases remained elevated above the 48 cm (19 in) of water in the museum (Weisman 1993), but the trailer park was deemed a total loss; the state purchased the property, and the residents relocated.

Global warming was not yet a widely recognized phenomenon when the 1993 storm hit. We must always be cautious in relating short-term weather events like this to longer-term climate, but one wonders in retrospect if the storm wasn't a harbinger of what we recognize now as a broader trend toward higher sea levels, stronger storms, and more severe storm surges. If sea level rises even by the conservative estimate of three feet by the end of this century (IPCC 2014), the museum at Crystal River may be routinely flooded.

The archaeological record suggests that the residents of the Gulf Coast have been reacting to weather events and climatic changes for more than 2,000 years. We noted in the previous chapter that studies elsewhere suggest that sea level rose during the Roman Warm period, or the Wulfert High, as this interlude is known for the Gulf. Geologic evidence from Waccasassa Bay and the Suwannee Delta, just north of Crystal River, indicates that this increase was not slow and steady but instead came in pulses (Goodbred 1995; Goodbred et al. 1998; Wright et al. 2005). One of these pulses, perhaps around A.D. 200, was an order of magnitude higher than in the previous 2,000 years and resulted in a transgression of 2–4 km (1.2–2.5 mi) (Goodbred et al. 1998; McFadden 2015, 2016).

Several studies from southwestern Florida suggest that the relatively higher sea levels of the Wulfert High may have even exceeded those of the present day (Stapor et al. 1991; Walker et al. 1995; Widmer 1988). At Crystal River, we have seen no evidence of sediment deposition that would indicate higher-than-present sea levels in the first millennium A.D., consistent with geologic (Wright et al. 2005) and archaeological (Sassaman et al. 2011) investigations in the Suwannee Delta. Of course, it is possible that such a high stand occurred, but the resulting sediments were subsequently weathered or reworked; for example, the 2.5–5-cm (1–2-in) layer deposited in local marshes by the 1993 storm was soon obscured by normal soil weathering processes (Goodbred 1995). Regardless, we can say with some confidence that sea level approximated that of the present day.

The pulse in sea level rise that appears to have occurred around A.D. 200 probably would have led to the sort of occasional flooding that happens today at Crystal River during spring tides or when there is a strong onshore breeze. This would have been a minor inconvenience of life at Crystal River. However, it may have made life difficult for those living on lower-lying marsh islands closer to the Gulf. Sea level rise would have also changed the character of the vegetation on these islands, probably leading to a decline in species that are less salt tolerant, such as live oaks (Vince et al. 1989; Williams et al. 1999). The dispersed community that occupied these marsh islands may have decided to relocate.

Crystal River would have been an attractive location for resettlement, for several reasons. First, as described in previous chapters, by at least the last century B.C., it had emerged as a major ceremonial center, and during Phase 1 it became a seasonally occupied village. In addition, rising sea levels in the first centuries A.D., coupled with the accumulation of shell midden, would have turned Crystal River into the sort of elevated hammock that offered considerable advantages in terms of resources. We can assume that like the hammocks in the area today, the dominant vegetation included live oak and other nut-producing trees (Goodbred 1995:42; Hutton 1986:76). Hammocks develop on areas of near-surface limestone where lenses of fresh groundwater can be maintained (Hine and Belknap 1986). Limestone outcrops associated with hammocks often include small freshwater springs (Goodbred 1995:42). Even today there is an active spring on the southwestern margin of the state park, near the western edge of Mound A.

Given these developments, it is not surprising that recent testing suggests that the possible pulse in sea level around A.D. 200 corresponds with a sharp increase in the size of the early village at Crystal River. Our modeling of radiocarbon dates from the midden indicates that the second phase of village life started between *cal A.D. 221 and 321 (95 percent probability)*, probably between *cal A.D. 238 and 292 (68 percent)*, and ended between *cal A.D. 434 and 544 (95 percent)*, probably between *cal A.D. 441 and 499 (68 percent)* (Pluckhahn, Thompson, and Cherkinsky 2015:31). This phase lasted between *128 and 303 years (95 percent)*, probably between *166 and 256 years (68 percent)*. Phase 2 is well represented by radiocarbon-dated layers in Trenches 1, 2, and 4. We have no dates from this interval in Trench 3, but there is a massive deposit of oyster in this trench that we presume dates to the later part of Phase 2, based on slightly later dates on the layer above. Based on its strong representation in these four trenches, we can say that during Phase 2 the village grew to its full areal extent (Figure 5.1)—the shape of a "barbed fish hook," as it was rather colorfully described by Bullen (1951:142).

The midden also grew vertically. The dense shell layers in Trenches 1 and 2 were deposited during the early portion of Phase 2—perhaps in a deliberate effort to raise the height of the ridge. This reworking of the midden during Phase 2 may have been both practical and symbolic. With regard to the former, the construction of a higher living surface may have been a strategy for coping with seasonal high tides and storm surges,

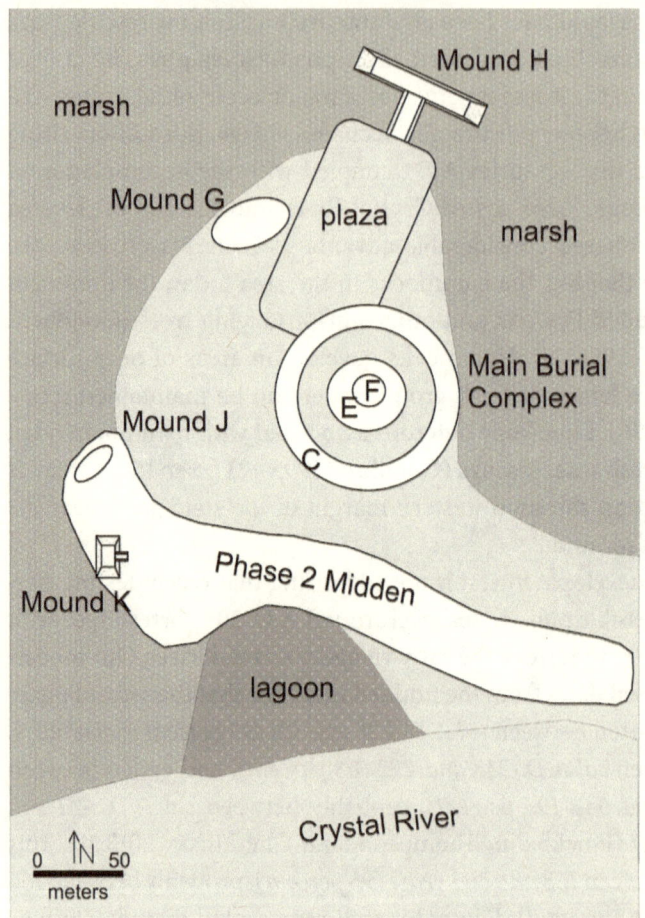

Figure 5.1. The settlement plan at Crystal River during Phase 2.

especially as these increased in frequency and severity along with the rise in sea level. But we also hypothesize that the dense deposits of oyster shell reflect a deliberate attempt to expand the ridge to the south and encircle the lagoon, creating a more formal and imposing entrance to the community for visitors coming by way of canoe. Traditionally, archaeologists have not tended to think of the accumulation of shell midden as a form of monumentality (Marquardt 2010; cf. Randall 2015; Randall and Sassaman 2010; Sassaman and Randall 2012), but the ridge of midden that developed at Crystal River during Phase 2 would have made a dramatic statement about the size of the community in relation to other, smaller villages and hamlets. The reworking of the midden may also speak to the manner in which these early villagers related to the sea. McNiven

(2004:344) suggests that Australian hunter-gather-fishers created stone monuments in the intertidal zone as a mechanism of spiritual control of extreme tidal regimes.

That the practical and symbolic aspects of midden growth may have been intertwined in the minds of the early villagers is illustrated by Sassaman's (2012:258) relation of shell mounding to the Earth Diver myth of historic Native Americans in the American Southeast. In the myth, land is created from a primordial watery world by a water beetle (or crawfish or other creature), which dives down to snatch a bit of mud from the sea floor. Mounding shell may have thus symbolically recreated the process of creation. Sassaman (2012:258) suggests that "by incorporating a familiar theme in mounding ritual, they rendered more predictable and routine a process that was unpredictable, and, at times, catastrophic."

The growth of the midden during Phase 2 appears to represent not only an increase in the size of occupation, but also its permanence. Isotopic studies of oyster shells from Phase 2 contexts suggest collection during all seasons, in contrast with the evidence for collection only during the cooler months for Phase 1 samples (Lulewicz et al. 2017; Thompson et al. 2015). We also see evidence for more-intensive occupation in the stratigraphy of our excavation units. Organic-rich sediment layers with higher densities of ceramics and most other artifacts covered the dense oyster deposits that were laid down early in Phase 2 in the areas of Trenches 1 and 2. We see a number of features originating from these layers in both trenches. The relative lack of oyster in the later Phase 2 strata may be another indication of more permanent settlement if we assume that sedentism encouraged disposal of such food remains elsewhere—on the flanks of the midden (as noted above) or in mounds (as noted below). We have less evidence for intensive occupation in the form of features in the Phase 2 layers of Trench 3, but there was nevertheless substantial midden accumulation, as indicated by the spread of radiocarbon dates across depths in our column sample.

Artifact assemblages from our test units also point to more-permanent occupation during Phase 2. O'Neal's (2016:121–122) comparison of the density of bone, stone, and shell tools and tool making debris through time revealed that the density of virtually all of the major classes of tools and their respective debris was higher in Phase 2 contexts than those dating to earlier or later phases. In most cases the differences were dramatic; the only exception consists of shell hammers, a tool type that seems to have been particularly associated with Phases 3 and 4 (as discussed in more detail in the chapters that follow). O'Neal's (2016:84–86) sourcing of stone tools and debris indicates a strong preference for raw materials that could have been procured in reasonable proximity to the site, consistent with earlier analyses of older collections by Estabrook (2011).

Pottery too provides evidence for greater permanence. First, as with most tools, the density of pottery is much higher in Phase 2 contexts. Next, there are differences in temper that suggest greater sedentism. In the pottery from Phase 2 midden contexts, limestone tempering comes to dominate over sand, forming over 70 percent of the assemblage relative to less than 20 percent for sand (Pluckhahn et al. 2017; Thompson 2016:67–68). This pattern is consistent across various sampling proveniences and suggests the establishment of a more uniform, local potting tradition and, by extension, community of practice. Surface treatments are also consistent with this; although a number of named types are present, more than 96 percent of the midden pottery from Phase 2 is plain. Further, a possible blending of pottery-making traditions or communities is indicated by the nearly 10 percent of sherds from Phase 2 midden contexts that appear to have a fabric composed of mixed sand and limestone.

The vertebrate faunal assemblages suggest slight changes in subsistence strategy that might also be consistent with more-permanent settlement during Phase 2. The Phase 2 collection contains 74,635 vertebrate specimens weighing 8,104.9 grams and representing the remains of an estimated 324 individuals from 64 taxa (Reitz and Brown 2015). This a larger sample than we have for Phase 1, and it is drawn from more varied contexts, so comparisons between the two phases should be considered tentative. Still, it is interesting that while the Phase 2 assemblage is richer (meaning more species are represented), it is also both less equitable and less diverse (meaning emphasis was placed on fewer species). This focus on two or three primary taxa, all of which could be obtained in close proximity to the village, might be expected as settlement became more permanent. Kowalewski (2013:209) suggests that this type of intensification way be typical of rapid population aggregation.

White-tailed deer, which were probably plentiful in nearby forests, contribute most of the terrestrial individuals and contribute the bulk of the overall biomass for Phase 2. This clearly contrasts with the faunal data from later phases, where deer are infrequent (Compton 2014).

Mullet (*Mugil* spp.) are the dominant fish taxon and make up the majority of the individuals for all taxa in Phase 2 contexts. The vertebrate fishes also include a relatively robust representation of hardhead catfishes (*Ariopsis felis*). On sites in southwestern Florida, sea catfishes, particularly the hardhead catfish, are among the most abundant fishes represented. Conversely, mullet remains are often conspicuously scarce (Fradkin 1976; Milanich et al. 1984; Walker 1992a:169, 1992b). In his recent review of Calusa archaeology, Marquardt (2014) addresses the apparent absence of mullet remains among faunal assemblages from the region and suggests it may be due to identification and sampling issues. The abundance of sea catfish and mullet here supports Marquardt's observation, although we also cannot rule out the possibility that these species are simply more abundant in our area. Hardhead catfish and mullet are generally abundant to highly abundant in shallow marine and estuarine environments along the Gulf Coast of Florida today (Lewis and Estevez 1988:88; Pattillo et al. 1997:8–9; Wolfe et al. 1990:188); they were likely taken in nets in the tidal creeks near the village.

The other taxa represented in the faunal assemblage are also consistent with the targeting of resources from nearby forests and fresh and brackish water creeks. In addition to mullet and sea catfish, the fish assemblages include lesser amounts of bowfins (*Amia calva*), golden shiners (*Notemigonus crysoleucas*), sunfishes (*Lepomis* sp.), and largemouth basses (*Micropterus salmoides*). In addition to deer, the collection also contains the remains of box turtles (*Terrapene carolina*), gopher tortoises (*Gopherus polyphemus*), alligators, diamondback terrapins (*Malaclemys terrapin*), sea turtles (*Cheloniidae*), softshell turtles (*Apalone* spp.), turkey (*Meleagris gallopavo*), an unspecified waterbird (Pelecaniformes), an unspecified marine mammal presumed to be dolphin (Cetacea), an otter (*Lontra canadensis*), and both nonvenomous (Colubridae) and venomous (Viperidae) snakes.

So the village at Crystal River grew dramatically in both size and permanence during Phase 2, and this may correspond with a sea level pulse that we speculate might have made life on the marsh islands more precarious. But while environmental stimuli seemingly provide a tidy (pun intended) explanation for cultural changes at the early village at Crystal River and elsewhere, in a larger sense such explanations are frequently wanting. First, the temporal resolutions of both past environmental and cultural changes are rarely fine enough to establish a clear correlation. This is a particular problem on the Gulf Coast, where sea level reconstructions frequently rely on the radiocarbon dating of shell (e.g., Goodbred 1995:57), which, as we noted above, can produce unreliable dates. Next, closer examination of the context of cultural change usually reveals that there is more to the story than environment alone. In the case of Crystal River, as we noted in the previous chapter, the village here was already growing, and the community had already established itself as one of preeminent ceremonial centers on the Gulf Coast. Finally, the growth of Crystal River during Phase 2 was part of a much broader shift in settlement and ceremony.

By the fourth century A.D., if not a century or more before, the Hopewellian Interaction Sphere had faded. In the Hopewell core in the Midwest, there was a decline in extralocal exchange, the construction of burial mounds ceased, and settlement shifted from floodplain to uplands (McElrath et al. 2000:14–16). This decline in extralocal exchange had implications for much of the American Southeast. Archaeologists today are often hesitant to use the word "collapse," largely due to the uncritical employment of this phrase by popular writers such as Jared Diamond (2005), but the suddenness of this transition suggests to many archaeologists that collapse is an appropriate characterization of this Middle to Late Woodland transition in the Midwest (Carr and Case 2008:28; McElrath et al. 2000:14–16; Yerkes 1988:1). Several of Crystal River's contemporaries in the American Southeast declined with the cessation of Hopewellian interaction—whether or not this was the cause. Mandeville, for example, seems not to have been occupied much past A.D. 300 (Smith 1975:178). But in a pattern common to past societies, a collapse in one area was accompanied by florescence in a neighboring region; at Crystal River and other sites along the Gulf Coast, mortuary ceremony and exchange continued and perhaps intensified, even as these declined elsewhere.

The material culture complex that marks this florescence is known as Weeden Island, after a site to the south of Crystal River on the outskirts of the modern city of St. Petersburg. Excavations at the Weeden Island site in the 1920s by J. W. Fewkes (1924) for the Smithsonian Institution revealed the distinctive punctate and incised pottery that archaeologists now recognize as typical of Weeden Island pottery. In an irony that is typical in archaeology, however, the site that gave Weeden Island its name is in many ways atypical of the complex to which its name is now attached.

C. B. Moore (1903:383), although without the name Weeden Island, had several decades earlier noted that pottery of this sort was most common on sites in the panhandle of Florida, and infrequent on the central Florida peninsula. In contrast with the more traditional vessel forms found at the Weeden Island site, on sites in the Panhandle, the punctate and incised designs were also frequently found on ceramic vessels formed in the likenesses of people and animals. Most of these vessels were ritually "killed" with a hole cut in the bottom that would have ended their use life; in some cases the pots were made with geometric shapes cut into the surface to make them seemingly useless for any practical purpose apart from ceremony. Finally, in contrast with the pattern at the Weeden Island site, the vessels at more northerly sites were often placed in burial mounds in caches, primarily on the eastern sides, before the mounds were sealed by a capping layer of earth or shell.

Moore excavated a number of the Weeden Island pottery caches from the northern Gulf Coast. Unfortunately, his work was done well before the invention of radiocarbon dating, and his rather poorly controlled digging mainly targeted burial goods that can't be directly dated. Thus, few Weeden Island burial mounds have been adequately dated. One exception is Mound C at the McKeithen site in central peninsular Florida, where Milanich and colleagues (1997) retrieved dates that with an updated calibration fall late in our Phase 2 or early in Phase 3 at Crystal River: two on the same pine post have ranges of cal A.D. 475 to 654 (UM-1436) and cal A.D. 434 to 636 (UM-1565), and a third date on an in situ pine post has a range of cal A.D. 543 to 655 (UM-1434) (all at 95 percent probability).

Crystal River was located on the southern periphery of Weeden Island and appears to have drawn selectively from the traditions that developed to the north and west. It lacks any type of pottery cache, as Moore (1903:383) noted:

> In this place of aboriginal abode it was evident that we were no longer among the mounds of the northwest Florida coast, with their great deposits of earthenware placed for the dead in common, in the eastern part of the mound.

Still, as Willey (1949a:318) notes, there is evidence from Moore's description for the presence of common burial deposits. Bullen identified surfaces of broken pottery in the circular embankment (Weisman 1995a:56–57), possibly representing a local variation on the caches found elsewhere.

And even though there was no cache of whole pots, Moore recovered several complete—or nearly so—Weeden Island vessels. One is a large fragment of a pedestaled effigy in the apparent form of a bird, a vessel form typical of assemblages from the Panhandle (Moore 1907:412–413). Several others have lobes, compound shapes, or decoration also typical of Weeden Island. Pots of this type seem to have been most common in Moore's excavations in what he referred to as Mound E or "the artificial elevation," the flat-topped apron surrounding Mound E (Moore 1907:411–415).

The higher concentration of Weeden Island pottery in the Mound E "artificial elevation" suggests to us that this was a Phase 2 addition to the existing burial mound. The temporal difference between the platform and the burial mound proper is also indicated by differences in burial treatment. Comparing his descriptions of the burials, it is apparent that a much higher percentage of those in the platform—perhaps as much as 95 percent—were placed in fully extended or flexed positions, compared with only around 68 percent of those in the upper levels of the burial mound. Moore (1903:383) also noted that "in the elevated ground surrounding the mound, masses of oyster-shells almost invariably lay above the burials and sometimes extended well to the sides"; this treatment seems to have been the exception in the burial mound proper.

Unfortunately, Moore provides little detail regarding the burials in the circular embankment, and Bullen's excavations here are mainly unreported. But Kemp's (2015:53–56) reanalysis of sherds recovered by Bullen from the circular embankment revealed a number of Weeden Island types, suggesting that the use of this feature continued into Phase 2 as well.

Weeden Island types are exceedingly scarce in Bullen's Mound G assemblage (Kemp 2015:49–50), but several radiocarbon assays indicate burials were added in Phase 2 (Katzmarzyk 1998:Table 3.8; Pluckhahn et al. 2010:Table 1). Taking these dates into account, our model suggests that Mound G continued in use until sometime between *cal A.D. 263 and 1026 (95 percent)*, probably between *cal A.D. 372 and 618 (68 percent)* (Pluckhahn and Thompson 2017) (see Table 2.2). We suspect that the later end of the 68 percent posterior density estimate is most accurate. However, we also note that in a draft manuscript, Bullen (1960b) rather cryptically suggested (without citing any substantiating evidence) that Mound G was once much larger than we know it to be, which would indicate that the mound may have continued in use even longer than we propose here (Katzmarzyk [1998:15] suggests the surface of the mound may have been graded for road construction). Regardless, it appears that the duality in mortuary facilities that began even before the village was established continued well after people settled permanently.

So mortuary ritual continued through Phase 2 at Crystal River, and in many of the same locations, even as a new tradition of ceramic decoration and burial mound ceremony emerged on the Gulf Coast. Yet mortuary rituals did not remain the same. As we noted above, there were differences in the way bodies were treated in death, with many more now interred as secondary burials. There were also differences in burial offerings, with fewer exotic artifacts interred with graves in Phase 2, and fewer grave offerings associated with particular individuals generally. As Moore (1907:425) noted:

> We know that when the mound proper [Mound F] was built a better class of objects was placed with the dead. Either the possessions of those living at that earlier period were of a higher grade than those of persons who later built the cemetery around the mound [Mounds C and E], or else the makers of the mound proper were endowed with a greater spirit of liberality than were those who came later.

Moore does not mention much in the way of specific associations of burial goods in Mound E. Only three of the dozen or so ceramic vessels that he individually describes for this mound were found in graves, one with a child and the other two with adults (Moore 1907:412–414).

On the other hand, however, shell tools and ornaments may have been more common in Mound E than in Mound F. Moore (1907:415) noted the recovery of 53 marine-shell drinking cups (most probably lightning whelks, and often ritually "killed" with a hole at the base), while also observing that "this number of cups, however, by no means represents the total of such cups in the tract dug through by us, inasmuch as many, probably as many again as have noted, were found badly decayed and broken into fragments." In addition to these cups, Moore recorded: 33 chisels and gouges made from columellae; 7 chisels and gouges made from outer whorls; 7 celts manufactured from outer whorls; "no fewer than forty gorgets of shell"; 72 shell pendants; and a number of other shell ornaments Moore deemed worthy of only passing mention. The prodigious quantity of shell here is a point we return to below.

Thus, mortuary ceremonialism in Phase 2 represents both continuity with long-standing traditions and the reinterpretation of these. There is also evidence for the invention of new traditions. The three definitively flat-topped mounds at the site—Mounds A, H, and K—were likely constructed at least partially during the second midden phase at Crystal River (Pluckhahn and Thompson 2017). Mound J, which we are less confident in describing as a platform mound, also may have been started in this interval.

Unfortunately, our core sample and geophysical survey present only a limited window on the construction and use of these mounds. In the case of Mound J, interpretation is particularly vexing, given its irregular shape and complicated stratigraphy (Pluckhahn and Thompson 2017). One date from what appears to be pre-mound midden is consistent with Phase 1 of the midden (Figure 5.2). This pre-mound midden layer appears to have been capped by alternating shell- and soil-dense layers that may represent an early mound stage, but a radiocarbon sample from one of the latter produced a date earlier than that from the pre-mound midden. Omitting this date, but including another from a subsequent mounding episode, our modeling broadly suggests that the first stage of construction in Mound J was initiated between *cal A.D. 133 and 634 (95 percent probability)*, probably between *cal A.D. 324 and 628 (68 percent)* (Pluckhahn and Thompson 2017) (see Table 2.2). The shell-dense layers at the top of the mound were added between *cal A.D. 426 and 653 (95 percent probability)*, probably between *cal A.D. 561 and 640 (68 percent)*. The first stage is mostly coeval with Phase 2 of the midden chronology, while the upper stage is more consistent with Phase 3.

We are more confident in the dating and interpretation of Mound K. Charcoal from a dark soil layer below the mound is consistent with Phase 2 of the midden chronology (Pluckhahn and Thompson 2017). The mound itself appears to have been constructed mainly of shell, as indicated by both our core and GPR data (Figures 5.3 and 5.4, respectively). It may have been constructed in a single episode, but we noted a layer of darker soil in the lower levels of the mound that may represent an initial low platform, similar to those observed on several other Woodland period platform mounds (Knight 1990; Wright 2014b). A date on soil-charcoal from this layer has a calibrated range consistent with Phase 2 of the midden chronology (Pluckhahn and Thompson 2017). Bayesian modeling of the two dates from Mound K suggests that construction of

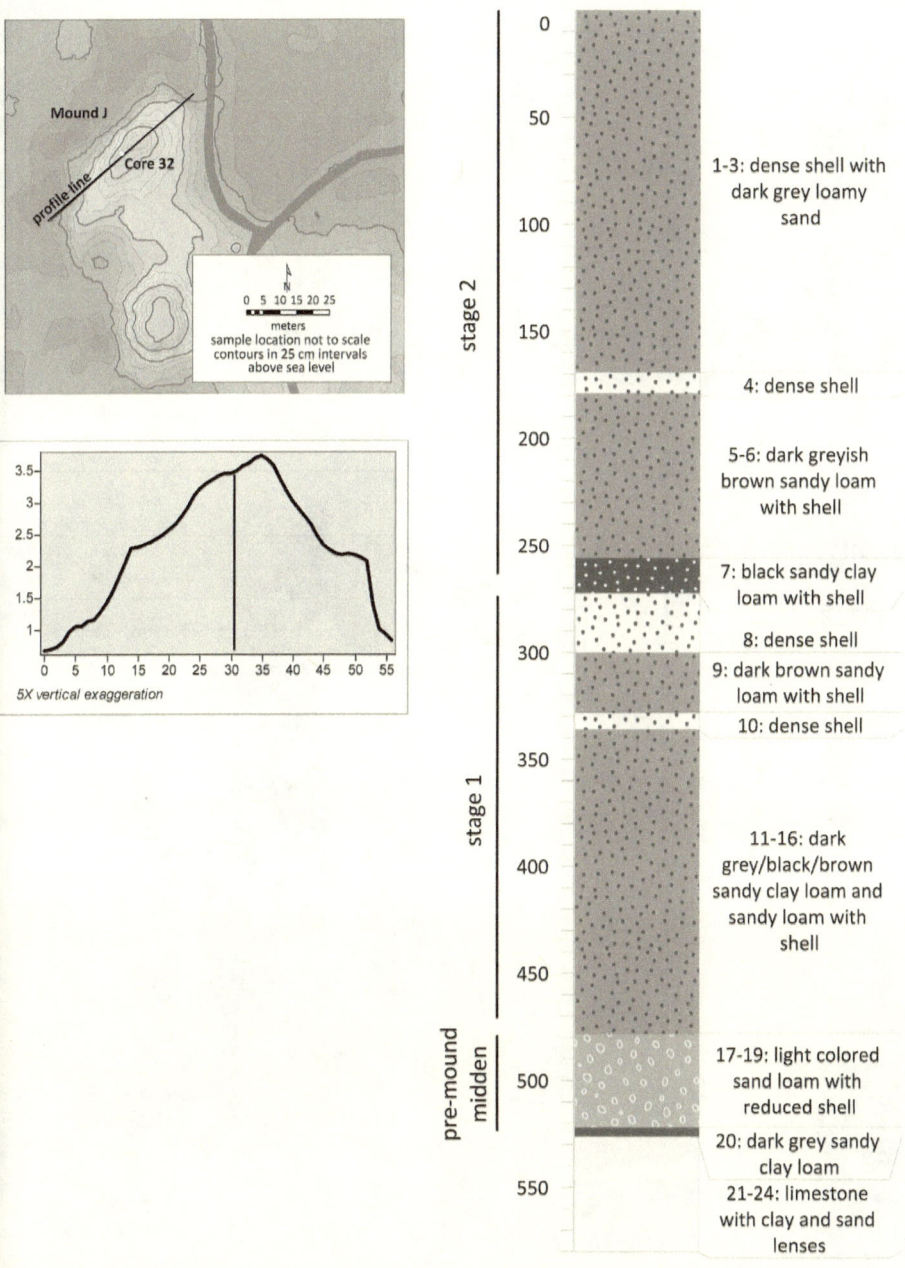

Figure 5.2. Generalized description of the soil core from Mound H at Crystal River.

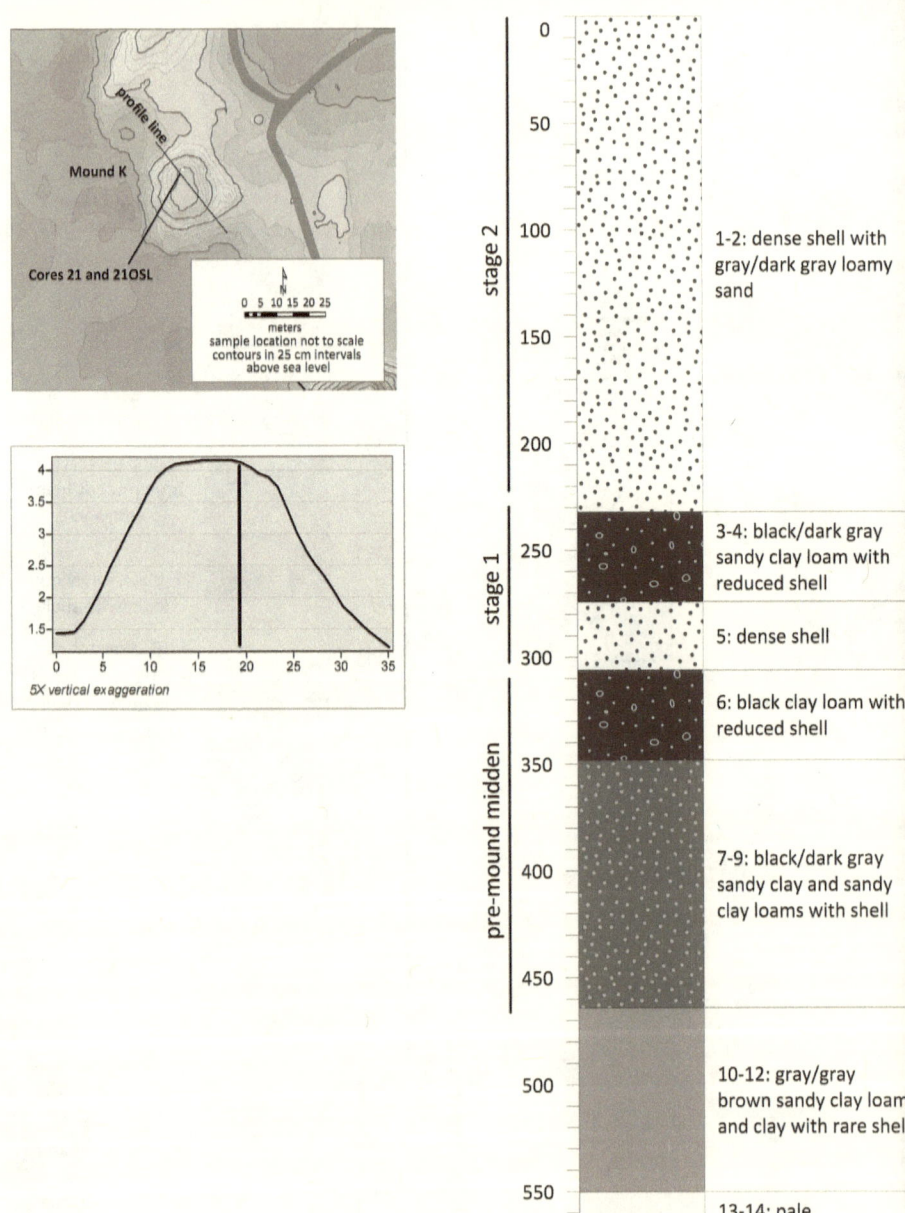

Figure 5.3. Generalized description of the soil core from Mound K at Crystal River.

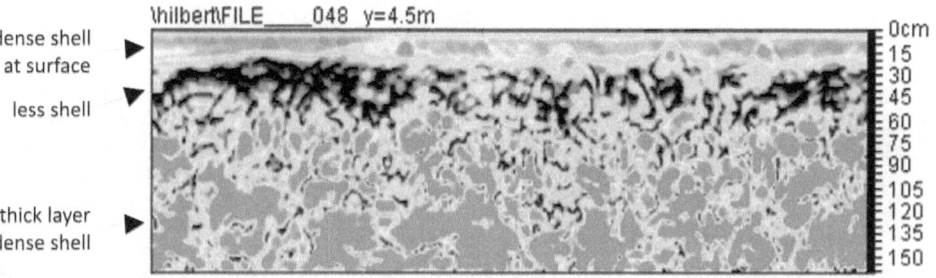

Figure 5.4. GPR profile from Grid 4, on the summit of Mound K. This is oriented north–south, with north to the right.

the lower mound stage began between *cal A.D. 280 and 535 (95 percent probability)*, probably between *cal A.D. 335 and 476 (68 percent)*. Our modeling suggests that construction of the upper stage began between *cal AD 394 and 569 (95 percent probability)*, probably between *cal AD 427 and 541 (68 percent)*. Thus, this mound was probably both initiated and completed during Phase 2 of the midden chronology.

Construction of Mound H began around the same time as that of Mound K. Below the mound, but above the Pleistocene sands that lie above the limestone substrate, we observed a dark soil layer that was present before the mound was built (Figure 5.5). Charcoal from this layer produced a date with a calibrated range that falls within Phase 2 of the midden chronology, and which corresponds almost exactly with our date on the pre-mound layer below Mound H (Pluckhahn and Thompson 2017). Above this was a layer of mottled soils perhaps indicative of a low platform similar to the one we hypothesize for Mound K and common to other mounds in the region. This was capped by alternating layers of yellow and white sands, which were eventually capped by a darker sand layer, and, finally, several feet of oyster. The GPR data are consistent with these alternating layers of highly reflective shell and less-reflective sand (Figure 5.6).

We doubt that the initial platform was in use for very long; instead it seems likely that Mound H was constructed in a short amount of time, possibly in a single episode and almost certainly in no more than two or three. This is indicated by the sand layers, which would have washed away if left uncovered in the rainy climate of central Florida. We also point to two radiocarbon dates, one on charcoal mixed with the sand at a depth

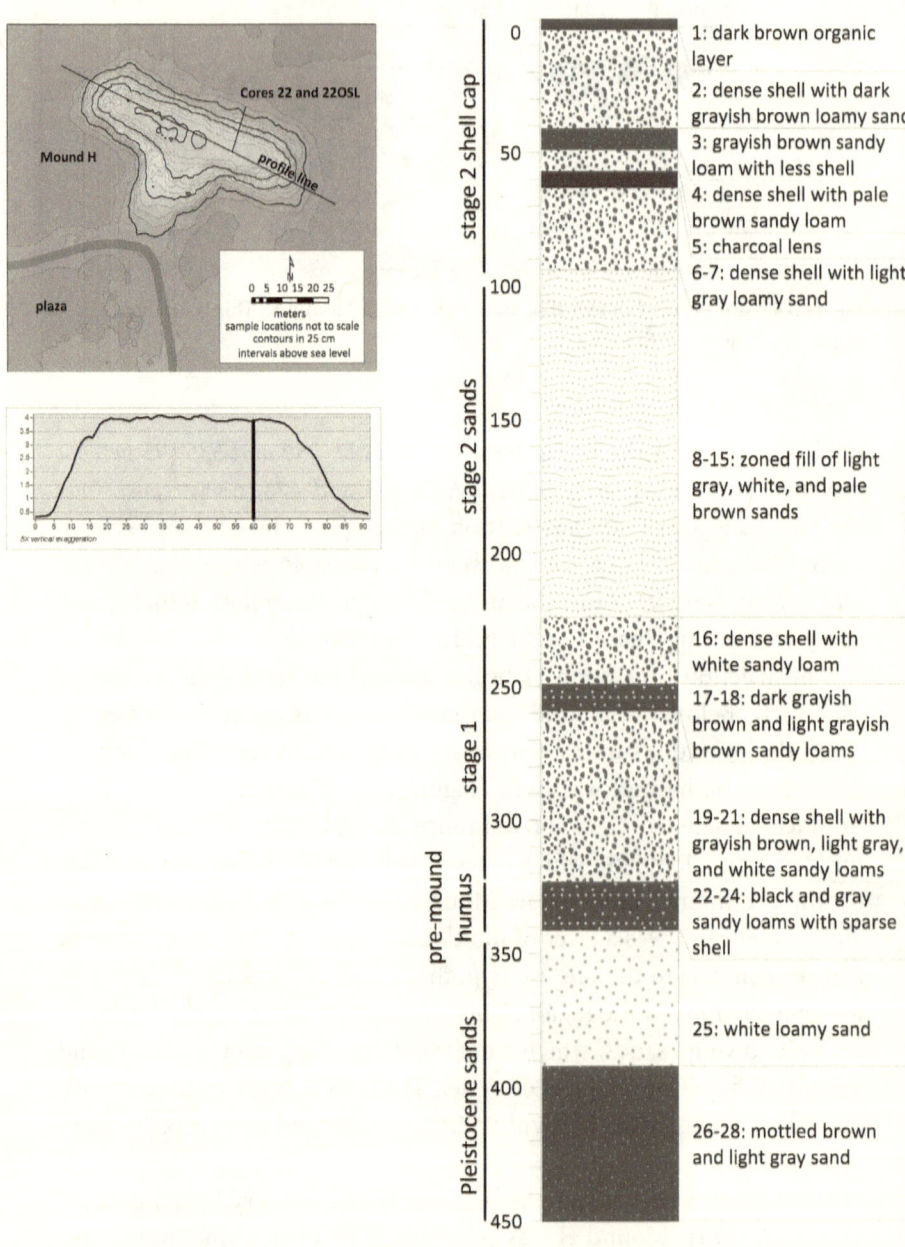

Figure 5.5. Generalized description of the soil core from Mound H at Crystal River.

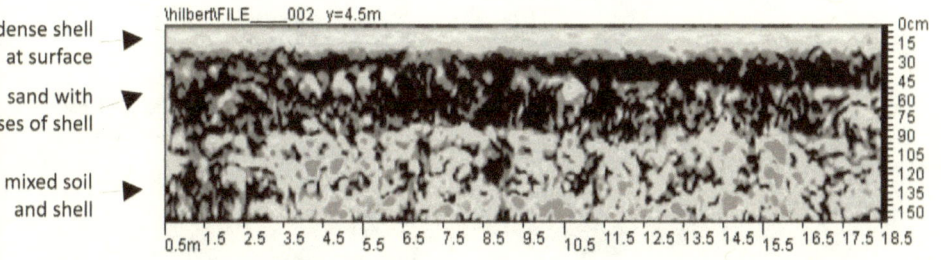

Figure 5.6. GPR profile from Grid 2, on the western half of the summit of Mound H. This is oriented northwest–southeast, with southeast to the right.

of 153–174 cm and another on a worked deer bone that Bullen recovered from the upper 31–61 cm (1–2 ft) in the shell cap. Despite the differences in depth, these dates are virtually indistinguishable and fall in the latter portion of Phase 2. Bayesian modeling of the three radiocarbon dates from within and below Mound H (Pluckhahn et al. 2010:Table 1), plus two acceptable OSL dates (Hodson 2012; Pluckhahn, Hodson, et al. 2015), suggests that construction of the lower stage began between *cal A.D. 284 and 526 (95 percent probability)*, probably between *cal A.D. 340 and 475 (68 percent)*. Our modeling suggests that the construction of the upper stage of this mound began between *cal A.D. 425 and 534 (95 percent)*, probably between *cal A.D. 403 and 552 (68 percent)*. Like Mound K, Mound H was therefore probably both started and completed during Midden Phase 2.

The stratigraphy of Mound A is more difficult to interpret than that of the others at Crystal River. Because of its height, the core required nine sections. Because the principal constituent of large portions of the mound is shell, the recovery was generally poor. The height and shell matrix also presented challenges for geophysical survey. Based on his observation of alternating shell-dense layers (presumed to represent construction episodes) and layers with more soil (possibly representing mound summits), Norman (2014:66–73) suggested that there may have been four construction episodes. While this may be true, it is difficult to say for certain based on the data at hand. For purposes of modeling the construction history of Mound A, we simplify the stratigraphy into three broad episodes (Figure 5.7). These were preceded by the premound midden, represented by the mix of dark soils and moderately dense shell in Layers 37–42. The generally dense shell deposits in Layers 31–35 represent the early phase of mound construction. Next, there is a middle stage represented alternating

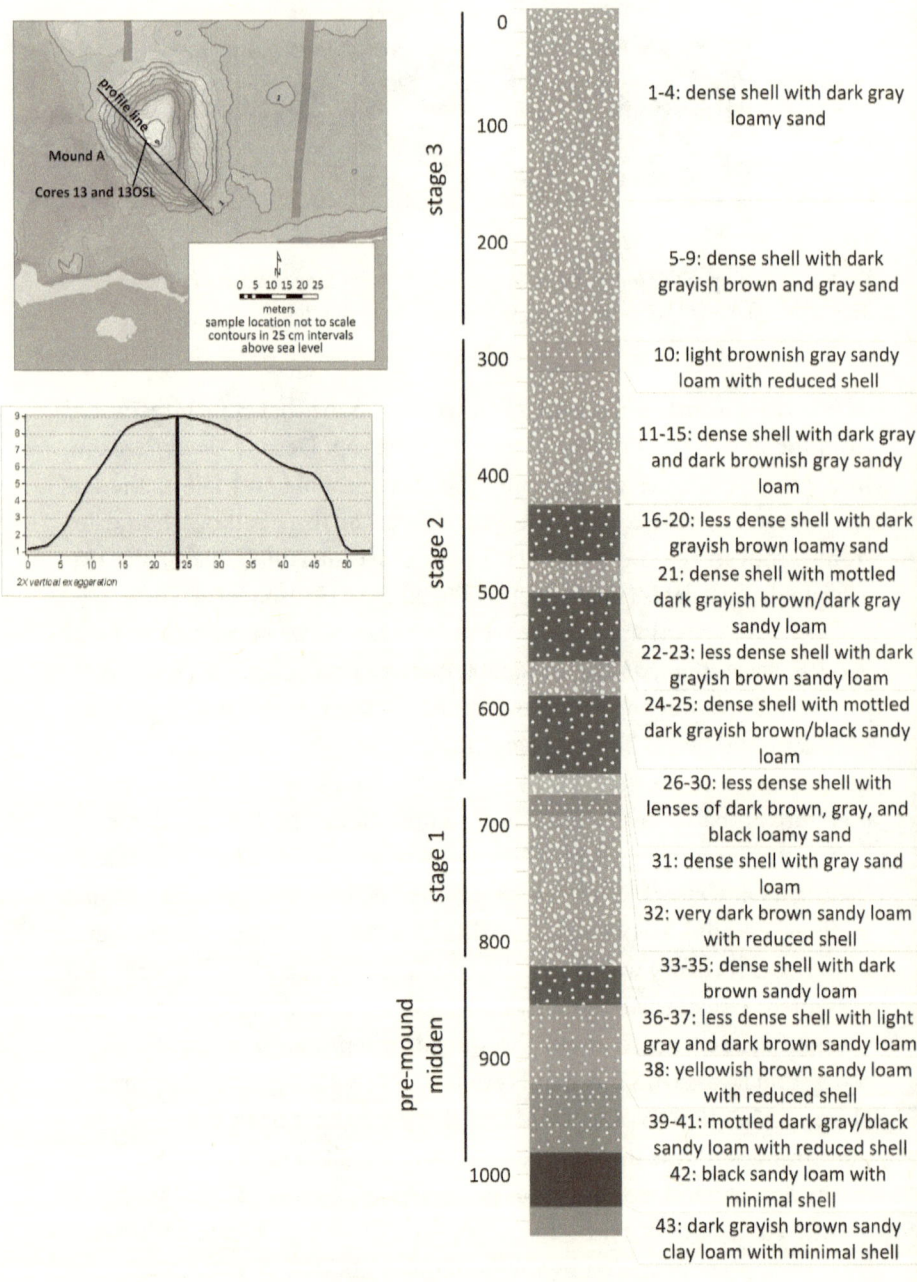

Figure 5.7. Generalized description of the soil core from Mound A at Crystal River.

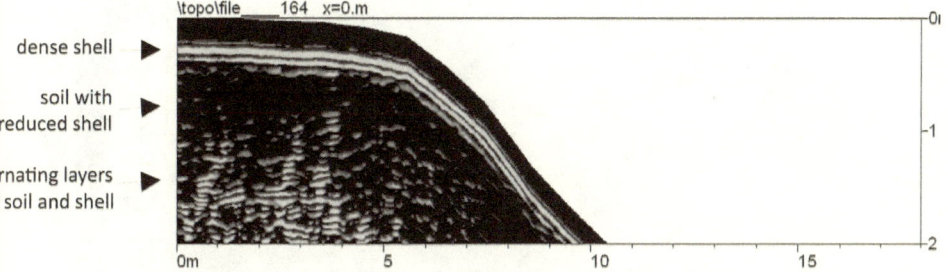

Figure 5.8. GPR profile from Mound A at Crystal River. This runs roughly south (*left*) to north (*right*), parallel with the stairs on the north slope of the mound.

dense shell and dark loamy sands with less shell in Layers 10–30. Finally, there is a late stage, represented by the dense shell in Layers 1–9.

This simplified model of the construction of Mound A is relatively consistent with the GPR profile (Figure 5.8), which shows a highly reflective core (our early stage of dense shell), superimposed by a less reflective layer (our middle stage of alternating shell and loamy sand), and finally a more reflective capping layer (our late-stage layer of dense shell). A photograph of Bullen's excavation cut in the ramp to Mound A (Figure 5.9) is also mostly consistent with this reconstruction, showing a dense shell layer (possibly associated with the earliest mound stage) superimposed by one with greater soil content (possibly representing our middle stage). The absence of an apparent third shell-dense layer in the ramp (corresponding with our upper stage) might be explained if this construction episode raised the height of the mound without also expanding it horizontally, thus requiring an expansion only of the top of the ramp (not represented in Bullen's cut).

The premound midden below Mound A is represented by one OSL date and one radiocarbon date with ranges coeval with Phases 1 and 2 of the midden chronology, respectively; a third OSL date produced a much older age estimate, perhaps as a result of disturbance (Pluckhahn, Hodson, et al. 2015; Pluckhahn and Thompson 2017). Unfortunately, we have no dates for the first mound stage above this pre-mound midden. However, our Bayesian model uses constraints provided by stratigraphically superior dates to estimate that its construction began between *cal A.D. 357 and 532 (95 percent probability)*, probably between *cal A.D. 398 and 480 (68 percent)* (Pluckhahn and Thompson 2017).

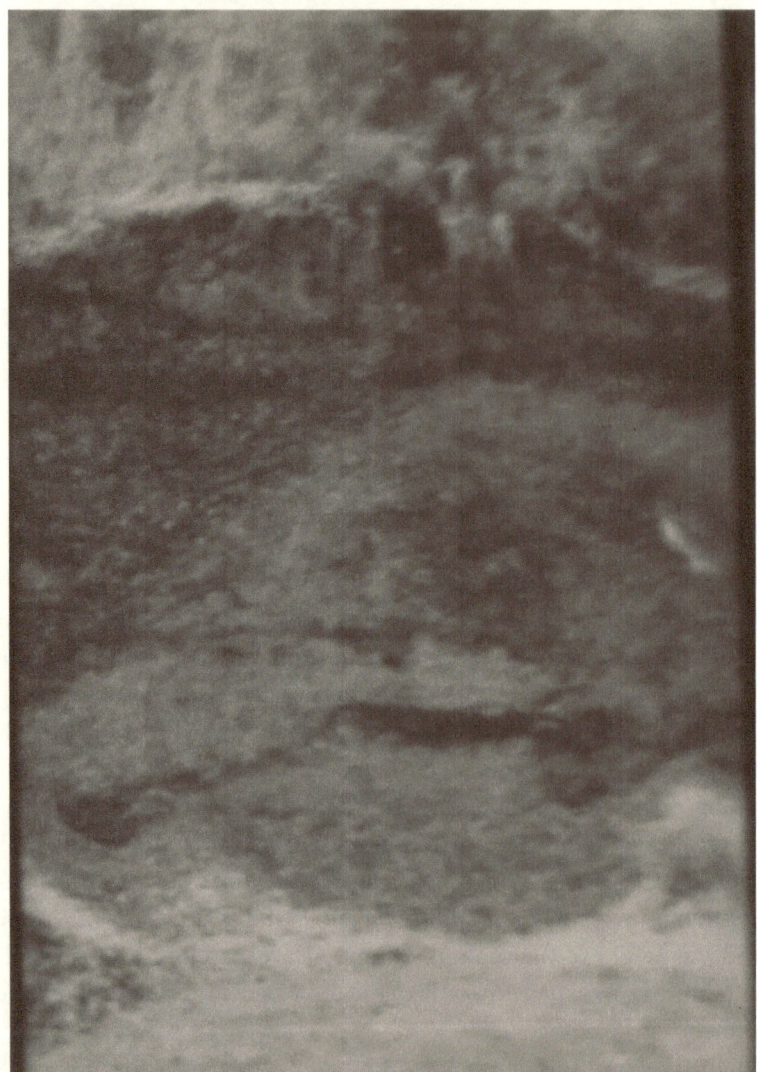

Figure 5.9. Photograph of Bullen's cut into the ramp on Mound A at Crystal River. Reproduced courtesy of the FLMNH (Negative PN94-228.878).

This second stage of mound construction is represented by alternating layers of dense shell and dark loamy sands with less shell in Layers 10–30. This construction episode is represented by two radiocarbon dates on soil-charcoal with ranges coeval with Phases 2 and 3 of the midden chronology (Pluckhahn and Thompson 2017). We also include one date retrieved by Bullen (1966b:865) on charcoal found 5.8 m (19 ft) below the top of the mound, with a calibrated range that spans Phases 3 and 4. The chronology of these three dates does not correspond with their stratigraphic position. This coupled with the incomplete zeroing of an OSL sample from Stratum 16, with an obviously overestimated age of almost 3,000 years before present, suggests that this construction episode included basket-loaded fill or redeposited midden (Pluckhahn, Hodson, et al. 2015; Pluckhahn and Thompson 2017) (other sites farther to the south along the Gulf exhibit a similar pattern of radiocarbon date reversals, with the implication that basket-loaded midden was used to construct these mounds [Thompson et al. 2016]). Regardless, our model suggests that the second mound stage was initiated between *cal A.D. 434 and 579 (95 percent)*, probably between *cal A.D. 481 and 548 (68 percent)* (Pluckhahn and Thompson 2017) (see Table 2.2). Thus, the first stage of Mound A was probably initiated during Phase 2 of the midden chronology, and the second stage in either Phase 2 or 3. As discussed in more detail in the next chapter, the dense shell layer that we take as the third and final mound construction episode dates to Phase 3.

The pottery assemblages from Mounds H and K, although limited in size, are remarkably similar to those from the Phase 2 midden and thus present an additional level of support for our dating. The FLMNH has collections from two units Bullen excavated on or near the summit of Mound H. Only 37 sherds are present, but the proportions are remarkably similar to the midden in regard to temper; 81 percent is limestone-tempered, 14 percent is sand, and 5 percent is spiculate. Also as with the Phase 2 midden, 97 percent of the Mound H assemblage is plain. Bullen excavated one unit in Mound K, and this assemblage is also small (n = 34) but again shows great consistency with the Phase 2 midden in the dominance of limestone (at 65 percent) over other tempers, and plain (at 97 percent) over other surface treatments.

The small assemblage from Mound A is less consistent with the pottery from the midden. Kemp (2015:56–57) documented 41 sherds surface-collected by Bullen (1951) and Smith (1951). In contrast with the midden, most are limestone-tempered. The discrepancies here again suggest the possibility that Mound A may have been constructed at least partially of redeposited midden. We find further support for this hypothesis in the isotopic studies of oysters (Thompson et al. 2015); in contrast with the other mounds we have sampled (which show harvesting only in cooler months), oyster samples from Mound A were determined to have been gathered across seasons—the pattern that might be expected if the people were gathering older midden to construct the mound.

Crystal River is, to our knowledge, the only Middle Woodland site in North America for which there is radiocarbon evidence for the construction of at least three platform mounds during the Middle Woodland period. It is all the more striking that these mounds seem to have been constructed in relatively short order. Why this seemingly new form of architecture, and at this historical juncture?

In the heyday of cultural historical archaeology in the middle twentieth century, the platform mounds at Crystal River presented a conundrum; Hopewellian artifacts clearly suggested a Middle Woodland date for Crystal River, but flat-topped mounds (as well as negative-painted pottery) suggested an association with the chiefdom-level societies of the Temple Mound, or Mississippian, period (Bullen 1951, 1953, 1966b; Smith 1951; Willey 1948a).

Bullen (1951) clung doggedly to the possibility that the platform mounds at Crystal River could be Mississippian, even while his own work clearly demonstrated that any such later occupation was too ephemeral to account for the mounds. Consistent with traditional understanding of the flat-topped monuments of the Mississippian period as "temple mounds" or chiefly residences, he proposed that Mound K may have served "as a foundation for a chief's or high priest's home" (Bullen 1965). This notion has been repeated in the interpretation of Mounds A, H, and K in signage and displays at the state park. Indeed, one former sign at Mound H presented information of rather dubious specificity regarding structures on the summit:

> The wide ramp gives access to the top of the mound where three houses stood. They contained sacred objects and the priest's paraphernalia. (McClendon 1972)

In fact, however, we see no clear evidence in either the GPR or coring data for the presence of structures on top of Mounds H and K. This appears to be typical of the platform mounds of the Woodland period (Knight 1990, 2001).

Others, such as McMichael (1960, 1964) and Ford (1966, 1969), suggested that the platform mounds were evidence of outside influence on the local, Woodland period community. Specifically, McMichael argued that flat-topped mounds and other unusual features were introduced to Crystal River by immigrants from Mesoamerica (probably the Maya lowlands), then spread north to the Midwest to stimulate the "Hopewell climax."

We now know that platform mounds are not exclusive to the Mississippian period; the existence of Woodland-period platform mounds has been demonstrated for dozens of sites in Southeast (Jefferies 1994; Knight 1990, 2001; Lindauer and Blitz 1997; Milanich et al. 1997; Pluckhahn 1996, 2003; Smith 1975:104–108; Wright 2014a, 2014b, 2016). Mounds A, H, and K were probably not the earliest such features in the region; at a minimum, the platform mounds at Mandeville (in southwestern Georgia), Pinson (in Tennessee), and Garden Creek (in North Carolina) would seem to date slightly earlier (Mainfort 2013; Smith 1975; Wright 2014a, 2014b). There is relatively good evidence of contact between Crystal River and Mandeville in the form of the sharing of rare negative-painted and incised ceramics (Smith 1975), and possible evidence for the same sort of contact with Garden Creek (Wright 2014a:287), so we don't dismiss the possibility that the idea of building platform mounds was borrowed from elsewhere. But it is probably safe to rule out McMichael's idea that Crystal River was a waypoint for Mesoamerican travelers; even Bullen (1960b) characterized this hypothesis as "a little enthusiastic."

More fundamentally, we might ask whether it is necessary to invoke any outside influences for platform mounds at Crystal River. Recall that the Main Burial Complex includes a small flat-topped mound of sorts; it just also happens to have been used for burials. Mounded platforms of earth are present in the construction sequences of several early burial mounds that took more conical forms when completed (Kellar et al. 1962a, 1962b; Sears 1956, 1982; Toth 1979). From this perspective, the development of free-standing platform mounds was also the reinterpretation of a long-standing tradition (Pluckhahn and Thompson 2017).

Another facet of this reinterpretation of tradition appears to have been the imposition of a more formal conception of space at Crystal River. While the plaza was likely already present in Phase 1, as indicated by the two burial mound complexes on either side, with the construction of Mounds H and K to the north and south (respectively), it was now much more clearly defined. Mound H and the plaza appear to have been functionally linked, as evidenced by the ramp that leads from the summit of the mound. This might be the earliest definitive evidence for a platform mound-plaza arrangement north of Mexico (Pluckhahn and Thompson

2017). The plaza was further defined by a causeway that linked Mounds G and H (Bullen 1965).

In that plazas are defined mainly by empty space, they are difficult to interpret archaeologically. The "square grounds" and "stomp grounds" of historic and contemporary Southeastern Indian societies may provide a fitting analogy in both form and function. Like the plazas of the Middle Woodland period, these were fastidiously maintained (Hudson 1976:367–68). Before important ceremonies the square grounds were swept clean, and a fresh layer of white sand was sometimes deposited (Witthoft 1949:57–59). Among the contemporary Yuchi in Oklahoma, continuous cleaning of the ceremonial grounds results in a circular ridge around the perimeter that helps to define the sacred precinct (Jackson 2003:56). For most of the historically documented native societies of the Southeast, the preeminent event associated with the square ground was the Green Corn Ceremony, which reinforced the corporate group identity and recreated the social order through rituals of purification (Hudson 1976:370–371; Jackson 1996, 2003:167–170, 203–205, 275–277; Witthoft 1949:69). A critical aspect of the Green Corn Ceremony was the making of a new fire (Hudson 1976:371–374). As a rite of purification and renewal, all of the fires in the village were extinguished. A priest started a new fire and carried it to the plaza in a ceramic vessel. The women of the village took some of the fire home with them to light new fires in their houses.

The inhabitants of Crystal River lacked maize agriculture, so the Green Corn Ceremony of the historic era obviously has no exact analogue in the Woodland period occupation at the site. But it seems reasonable to assume that the plaza at Crystal River was used for similar gatherings and ceremonies, perhaps triggered by some key event other than the first corn harvest. Given that the shell isotope data from the mounds indicate cool-weather collections, it may be that such events occurred during the late fall and winter harvests from the estuaries. We know from coring and resistivity survey that the plaza at Crystal River was kept free of debris such as shell or other artifacts, with a few small and localized exceptions (Blankenship 2013:74–81; Pluckhahn et al. 2009). For his master's thesis at USF, Alexander Delgado (2017) studied several of the anomalies in the plaza through geochemistry, microartifact analysis, and geophysics. Interestingly, one area in the southern portion of the plaza is notable for higher concentrations of artifacts, as well as for soil chemistry signatures suggestive of burning. Perhaps the new fire ceremony was in place for some time in the Southeast, although it would take much more work to say so conclusively.

Platform mounds seem to have been integrally related to the rituals and ceremonies associated with plazas. As we noted above, Knight's (1990, 2001) review suggests that structures were rarely constructed on the summits of Woodland period platform mounds. Instead, excavations on the summits of most of these mounds from this interval have revealed only evidence for scattered pits and large posts, many of which appear to have been periodically removed and replaced in a manner suggestive of rituals of renewal.

Another aspect of the marking of space during Phase 2 may have been the placement of stone markers, or "stelae." Stela 1 bears a carving of a human head (with eyes, mouth, ear spool, and flowing hair) and torso (Bullen 1966b) (Figure 5.10). Bullen (1966b) reported two radiocarbon assays on the same sample of charcoal using different counters and methods. Consistent with many radiocarbon dates from this era, the probability ranges are quite large, and we thus focus on the 68 percent ranges of cal A.D. 223 to 652 (for a subsample run in a less precise counter but with pretreatment to remove humic acids that might introduce more recent carbon) and cal A.D. 432 to 765 (for the other subsample, run in a more precise counter but without pretreatment) (Bullen 1966b:864).

There has been considerable debate regarding the authenticity of Stela 1 and its inscription (Milanich 1999:23; Weisman 1995a:62–65). Based partly on the stratigraphy he observed in his excavation at the base of the stela, as well as the presence of animal bones and flaked stone (perhaps suggestive of a small ritual cache) on a cobblestone pavement on its east side, Bullen (1965, 1966b) presents a case that the stone was not placed in its location in modern times. He also cited the recollections of the owner of the adjoining parcel, Mr. Cole, that the stone had been present when he purchased the property 11 years prior. As Bullen recorded on a notecard (Figure 5.11), Cole suggested that the carving of the face was also not recent, while the torso may have been added; this recollection matched Bullen's observation of differences in the carvings. We see no reason to question these observations. Unlike Milanich (1999:23), we are not troubled by the fact that Stela 1 was buried to a depth of only 48 cm (19 in); the elevation here is low, and our nearby core suggests no midden accumulation (Norman 2014:58–60). We also think it unlikely that the stone came to this location and position through natural processes. Further,

Figure 5.10. Ripley Bullen with Stela 1 at Crystal River in 1964, with inset of Stela 1 close-up. *Main photo*: Reproduced courtesy of the FLMNH (Negative PN94.228.1242). *Inset*: Limestone stela (Stela #1) at Crystal River State Park—Crystal River, Florida. 196-. Black & white photoprint, State Archives of Florida, Florida Memory.

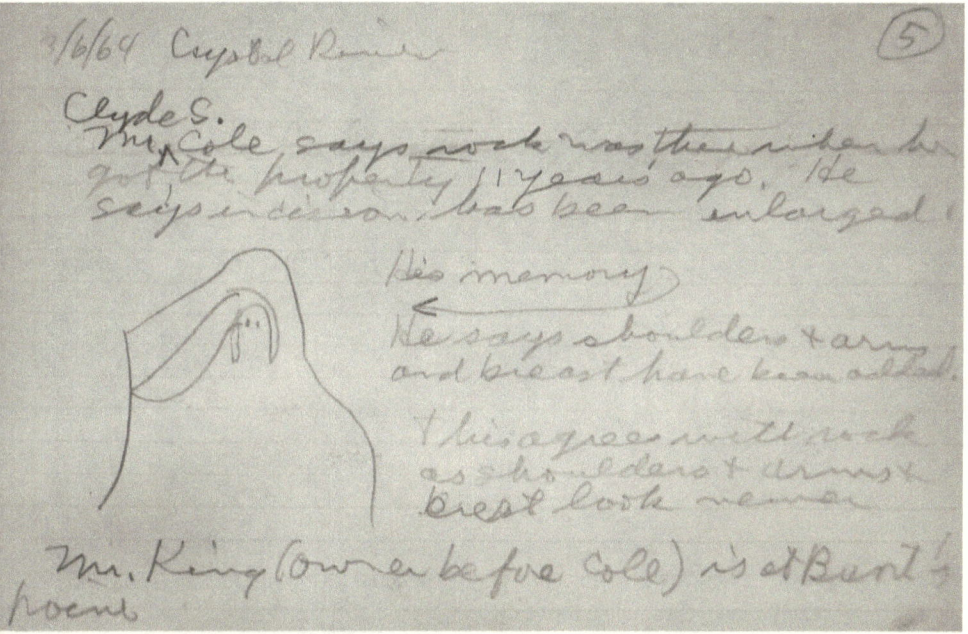

Figure 5.11. Bullen's notes on Stela 1, recorded in 1964 at the time of its discovery. Reproduced courtesy of the FLMNH.

given contemporary understanding of indigenous cave art in the Southeast (Simek et al. 2013; Simek et al. 2015), this inscribed stone appears less anomalous than it was once considered (although the face-forward perspective of the figure remains somewhat unusual for native art in this region).

Bullen (1966b:864) pointed out the spatial complementarity between mounds and stelae. The former ramp on Mound A appears to have pointed more or less to Stela 1; Hardman (1971) further suggested that the stone faces the rising sun on the summer solstice, and that this might have been observed from Mound A. As with Mound A and Stela 1, the ramp from Mound H leads directly to the plaza and also points more or less straight to Stela 2 (about midway through the plaza) and Mound K (at the southwestern end) (Bullen 1966b) (Figure 5.12). This stela is not carved, and limited excavations by Bullen produced only a small amount of material from its south side (Weisman 1995a:62). Other "stelae" have been reported from Crystal River, including one now buried near the museum that also bears an inscription, reportedly in the shape of a human hand (Weisman 1995a:64). However, this stone has been moved from its original location.

Figure 5.12. View to the southwest of Stela 2 at Crystal River, with Mounds J and K in background to right and left, respectively.

Given the appearance of this new architectural and spatial order at Crystal River, and presumably along with these an increase in the frequency and scale of public ceremony, it is somewhat surprising that the burials we can clearly associate with this interval lack the sort of accoutrements that we can reasonably associate with positions of status or leadership. As Weisman (1995a:7) observed for the Weeden Island period at Crystal River:

> The few recovered burials for which grave goods are known do not suggest that these individuals were possessed of inordinate wealth or occupied special positions of office or rank in society. In fact, these individuals seem less possessed of sacred or ritual connotations than do the Deptford burials in the deepest portion of the central sand mound, who had with them items of "superior quality" (Moore 1907) not found elsewhere on the site.

Although we must bear in mind the difficulties in clearly partitioning Moore's burials given the coarseness of his excavation and reporting, the difference is striking. But the change is not without precedent. Throughout the Weeden Island area, the items associated with individual graves tend to be both relatively few and comparatively modest; more impressive are the seemingly non-specific caches of pottery, aptly described by Moore (1902:161) as placed "for the dead in common" (see also Willey 1949a:405).

Still, as already noted, the Phase 2 burials are not entirely lacking in grave goods: shell is ubiquitous in later burials at Crystal River. Of the 30–40 individually described graves that Moore (1903, 1907) did not specify as coming from the central mound in the Main Burial Complex, and thus presumably falling later in the mound construction sequence, we would estimate that three-quarters were interred with shell ornaments or, less frequently, shell tools. Shell was virtually the only type of exotic found in the other burial mound (Mound G), although it was less prevalent here than in the Main Burial Complex (Weisman 1995a:58–59). These data suggest that marine shell became a more important commodity during Phase 2.

Sharon Goad (1978, 1979) made a case that the people of Crystal River traded cups and ornaments manufactured from large marine gastropods—especially lightning whelk—with Hopewellian communities in the Hopewell heartland. By controlling the movement of these unique coastal materials into the interior, Goad surmised, Crystal River was able to outcompete its Gulf Coast neighbors for valued nonlocal products such as copper. The monopoly that Crystal River enjoyed on the import of nonlocal goods was further supported by the community's more complex political organization relative to that of surrounding centers, which permitted greater elite control of trade (Goad 1978:178).

Goad's model has intuitive appeal. Moore's excavations in the Main Burial Complex produced shell cups, dippers, plummets, and gorgets of very fine craftsmanship (Figures 5.13 and 5.14). Marine shells and shell artifacts from the Gulf Coast are occasionally found at Hopewell sites many hundreds of miles into the interior, in Ohio and Illinois. Carr and Case (2006:229) suggest that in these contexts ceremonial leaders may have used conch shell dippers and spoons for serving important drinks. More generally, shell is common to burials across much of native North America (Trubitt 2003:261). In many areas, it seems to have been associated with water, creation, fertility, and rebirth, as well as with death and the underworld (Claassen 1998:203–209, 2015:167; Pietak 1998; Trubitt 2003:262).

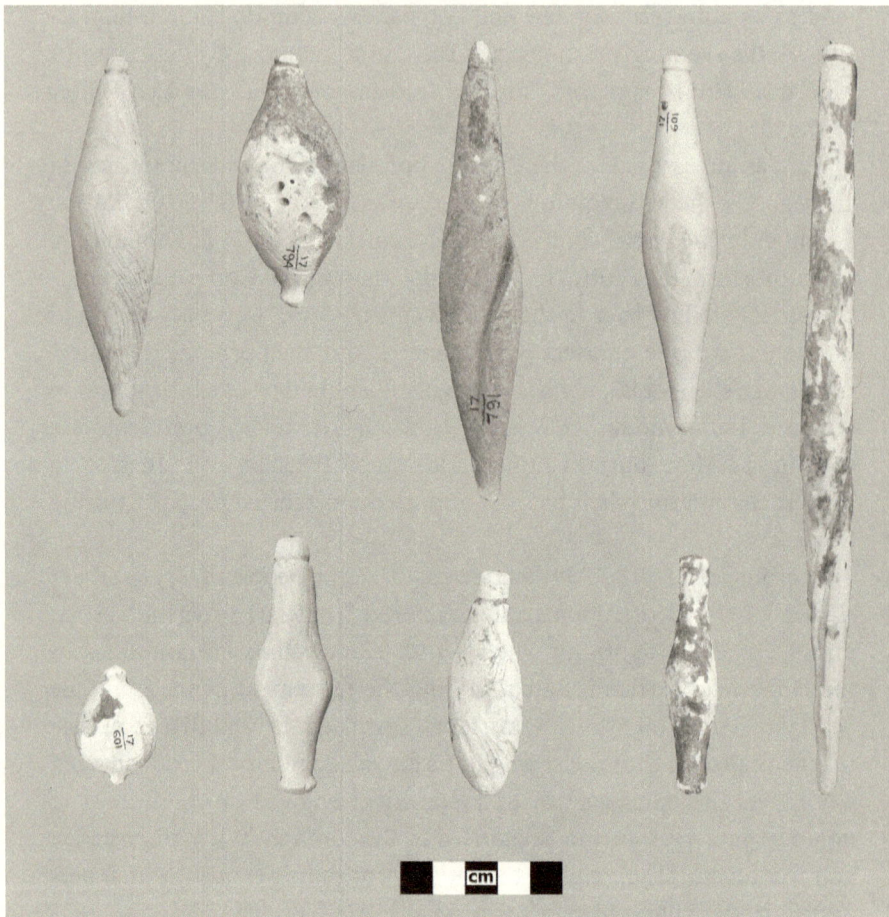

Figure 5.13. Selected shell plummets from Moore's work in the Main Burial Complex. National Museum of the American Indian, Smithsonian Institution (Catalog Numbers 170601.000, 170791.000, 170794.000, 170872.000, and 182256.000). Photographs by the authors.

But relatively little was known of Crystal River when Goad formulated her model, and we can now point to several fundamental problems. First, lightning whelks and comparably sized gastropods are rare to the central Gulf Coast, as documented by recent biological surveys (Stephenson et al. 2013). They are far more common to southwestern Florida and to the Apalachicola area of the Panhandle. Our testing suggests that this pattern is long-standing; we find very few lightning whelk in the middens at Crystal River (Blankenship 2013:80–81; Duke 2015:98–114). Thus, large

Figure 5.14. Selected shell gorgets from Moore's work in the Main Burial Complex. National Museum of the American Indian, Smithsonian Institution (Catalog Numbers 170368.000, 170374.000, 170375.000, 170604.000, 170606.000, 170608.000). Photographs by the authors.

marine gastropods were not a locally abundant resource that could be monopolized by elites.

Second, recent test excavations reveal only very limited evidence for the working of large marine gastropods into ornaments at Crystal River, in the form of a few ornament blanks and preforms fashioned from the outer whorls and somewhat more common whorl and columella fragments in middens (Blankenship 2013:64–68; O'Neal 2016:115–119; Pluckhahn, Menz, and O'Neal 2018). It is always possible that our sampling missed a small and concentrated workshop where lightning whelks were reduced to make cups and ornaments, but given that these gastropods appear always to have been rare in the area, we find this highly unlikely. Instead, we suspect that most of the marine shell cups and ornaments were imported from other areas as finished goods.

In addition to acquiring finished products from afar, a few local artisans may have finished imported shells on site, as indicated by the light quantity of blanks and manufacturing debris. This pattern of low-level spatially dispersed production holds true over other raw materials possibly used to make craft goods. Fragments of mica and quartz, both presumably obtained from sources to the north, are found in smaller quantities but occur with similar regularity in our test units in the midden. Limestone, which is naturally abundant in the area, is commonly found in larger quantities.

In their synthesis of archaeological approaches to trade, Oka and Kusimba (2008:361) (see also Costin 2001) note an abundance of recent work suggesting that craft specialists working at the household level frequently produce commodities for local, regional, and macroregional consumption. Such craft specialists may be only loosely organized by lineage or lateral relationships with other producers and distributors, under the sponsorship or encouragement—rather than outright control—of elites. The widespread distribution, limited quantity, and domestic context of large gastropod shell fragments and other crafting debris suggest small-scale, household-based production at Crystal River, rather than the type of elite-controlled manufacture envisioned by Goad (1978, 1979).

But this household craft production appears to have been too small in scale and intensity to account for the quantity of shell ornaments in burials at Crystal River, let alone the production for exchange to other communities in the region or beyond. Moreover, given the paucity of naturally occurring large gastropods in the immediate area, it seems unlikely that artisans from Crystal River could develop the knowledge or skills required to work such shells into finished ornaments. We thus suspect that households at Crystal River relied on the sort of lineage and lateral connections described by Oka and Kusimba (2008:361) to supply shell as raw material, finished shell ornaments and tools, and perhaps even shell-crafting specialists themselves.

Connections with communities to the south where large marine gastropods are more plentiful would seem to have been essential, and recent work provides intriguing evidence for linkages between Crystal River and specific sites in southern Florida. Kles (2013) has analyzed biological distance among skeletal populations from sites across Florida as revealed through craniometric data. Her analysis, while suggesting that the skeletal population from Crystal River exhibits a great deal of internal homogeneity, also reveals relatively close biological connections between Crystal River and the Yellow Bluffs mound site several hundred kilometers to the south. These data are consistent with the movement or intermarriage of people between Crystal River and an area where lightning whelk shells and shell-crafting traditions are more prevalent (Dietler 2008:163; Luer 2011).

George Luer (2013; Luer et al. 2015) has recently examined the distribution of a distinctive type of circular shell gorget he refers to as Tabbed Circular Artifacts (TCAs) found on sites in southern peninsular Florida. According to Luer, variation in the form and execution of these gorgets suggests local production at a number of different communities. However, Crystal River has produced more TCAs than any other single site, accounting for more than half of the 20 known examples (Figure 5.15). Moreover, Luer notes that the examples from Crystal River show consistency in form and fineness of execution that suggest they may have been made by the same artisan. It would thus appear that Crystal River had unparalleled access to either an artist or his or her wares. Intriguingly, one of the Crystal River specimens most closely resemble a TCA from the Miami Circle site (Luer 2013), suggesting a connection to the southeastern Florida coast where queen conch (*Lobatus gigas*) shells are common, and a tradition of shell tool manufacture using these large gastropods was well established (Dietler 2008:147).

Blankenship's (2013) recent reanalysis of the shell artifacts recovered by Bullen provides another glimpse of possible lateral connections with areas to the south. One of the shell artifacts recovered by Bullen from Moore's

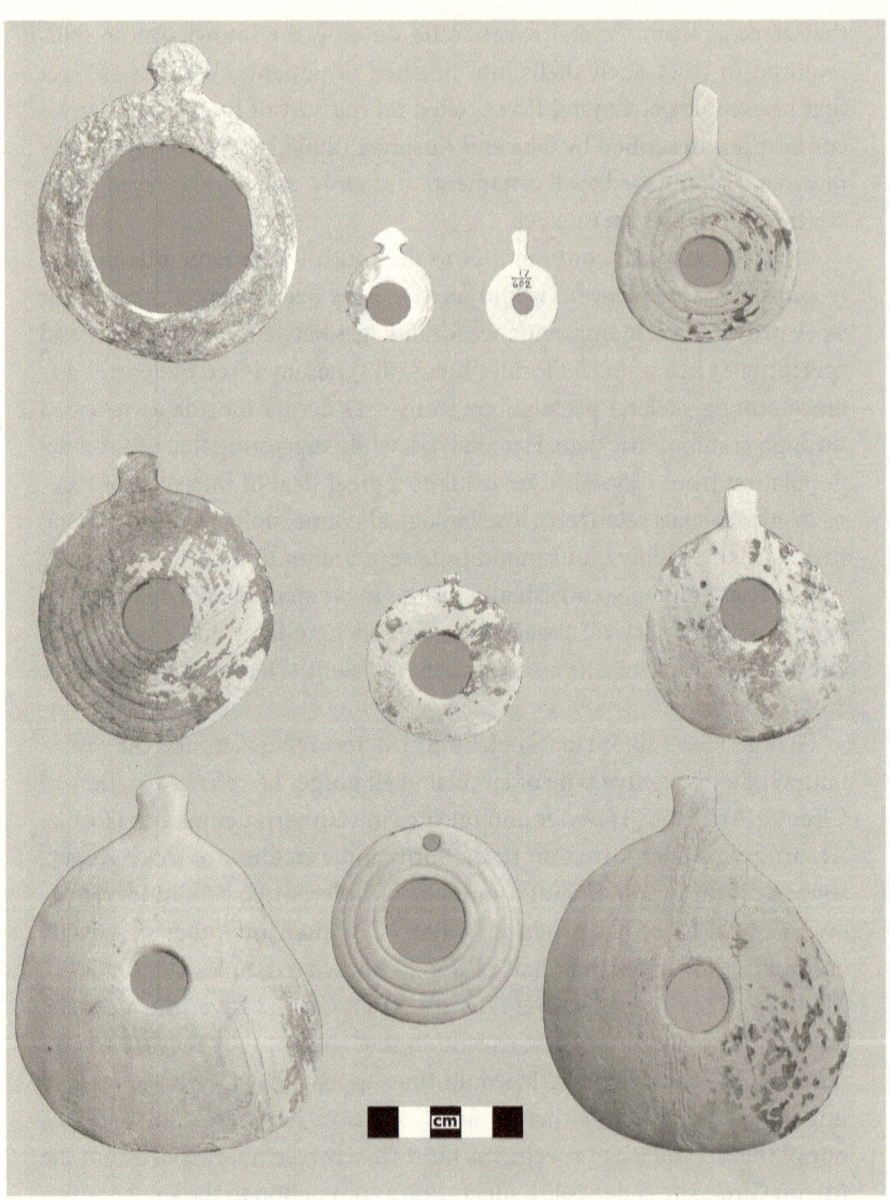

Figure 5.15. Tabbed Circular Artifacts (TCAs) from Moore's work in the Main Burial Complex. National Museum of the American Indian, Smithsonian Institution (Catalog Numbers 170366.000, 170371.000, 170372.000, 170373.000, 170602.000, and 170602.001). Photographs by the authors.

spoil has a shape suggestive of a large scallop but is more likely an outer body whorl of a large gastropod, possibly a queen conch, carved in imitation of a scallop (Blankenship 2013:63–64). The curving shape of the artifacts suggests the artisan may have been replicating the modern *Euvola* sp., although the thickness is more consistent with replication of the fossil scallop species (*Chesapecten* sp.). A complete scallop effigy was recovered from the Key Marco site in southwestern Florida (Gilliland 1975:Pl. 112c). This is the only other example of such an ornament that we have been able to identify, suggesting the possibility of a connection between these two sites or between these two sites and another source area in southern Florida.

Lithics provided another possible connection with sites to the south. Austin (2013) has documented chert from the Crystal River quarry cluster at the Pineland site. Perhaps people at Crystal River traded local cherts to residents of lithic-poor southwestern Florida in exchange for whelks.

The term "gateway interaction center" or "gateway community" is sometimes employed in archaeological discussions of Hopewell exchange (Anderson 1998; Emerson et al. 2013; Keith 2013; see Kohler [1991] and Wallis [2013] for applications to contemporaneous sites in Florida). As defined for archaeology by Hirth (1978:37), drawing mainly from the work of the geographer Burghardt (1971), gateway communities are presumed to develop "either as a response to increased trade or to the settling of sparsely populated frontier areas." Specifically, these communities develop at critical passages between areas of high craft productivity, or dense population, or high demand or supply for scarce resources. In addition, they are assumed to develop "at the interface of different technologies or levels of sociopolitical complexity." Gateway communities are assumed to be located to one side of a fan-shaped hinterland of other communities to which they are directly linked economically. Although lacking the term "gateway center," Ripley Bullen approached this concept in his discussion of the relationship between Crystal River and smaller sites such as Burtine Island:

> The Crystal River site was a ceremonial center that undoubtedly served a large area. The center had trade connections, either ceremonial or commercial, with Indians living at substantial distances from Florida. People from the hinterland, such as Burtine Island,

when they went to Crystal River were exposed to influences that originated at greater distances. It is also possible that Crystal River and other similar sites served not only as ceremonial centers but also as market places where people from the surrounding land exchanged their products on stated "market days." In either case, visits of Indians to Crystal River could easily explain the presence of trade sherds found at Burtine Island.

Several of the features of the gateway model make its extension to Crystal River (and potentially other Hopewellian centers as well) problematic. Nevertheless, from a less strict sense, it seems entirely plausible to us that Crystal River developed as a gateway or entrepôt between two areas with high craft productivity but relatively distinct resources and technologies: Weeden Island to the north in the Panhandle, and Glades to the south on the southwestern Florida coast. Wheeler (1996:32) suggests that this division developed during the Middle Woodland period, as Weeden Island communities to the north departed from long-standing artistic traditions:

> a major distinction between the two traditions lies in the parochial character of the Glades artists, who clung to the earlier media of wood and bone, with Weeden Island artists largely abandoning the earlier substrate to develop techniques of ceramic modeling and incising.

Wheeler notes that despite these differences in media, the two traditions were united by shared art and symbolic systems with deep roots.

The evidence suggests that Crystal River was drawing ideas, materials, and people from both of these traditions. Individuals and households at Crystal River likely established exchange relationships with others in southern Florida to acquire shells and shell ornaments and tools. Linkages with communities to the north are indicated by Weeden Island pottery and by small amounts of quartz and mica debris in the middens. This sort of exchange was likely tied to ceremonies that established and maintained alliances between villages (Knight 2001:327).

The development of a distinctive tradition of art by the villagers at Crystal River likely provided benefits beyond relationships with other communities. As we note in Chapter 8, distinctive artistic styles seem to be a common feature of early village societies. Belfer-Cohen and Bar-Yosef

(2000:25) suggest that this sort of artistic activity helps foster a sense of group identity and loyalty.

In sum, in Phase 2 people came together from formerly isolated settlements in the surrounding area to settle permanently in the village at Crystal River. This movement may have been, in part, a response to rising sea levels that threatened the security of living on islands, while simultaneously leading to more favorable conditions at Crystal River. But the growth of the community was almost certainly also because Crystal River had by this point emerged as an important place on the landscape, a nexus of ceremony and exchange that many people would have increasingly found a desirable place to live, in the same way today that people are attracted to vibrant, cosmopolitan cities. As Creese (2013) has described for Iroquoian societies of southern Ontario, early villages may be understood as "new kinds of creative entanglements with built space" and a sort of "place making practice" (see also Pluckhahn and Thompson 2013).

The increase in population undoubtedly meant that the early villagers were interacting more and more with people to whom they were not related by ties of blood or marriage. This must have presented challenges to cooperation, as Eerkens (2013:166) nicely summarizes:

> In societies where individuals have little or no authority to punish non-kin and widespread sharing and cooperation is the norm, an increase in the absolute number of non-kin in a community . . . will make free-riding an attractive option.

As Eerkens goes on, one potential solution to the free-rider dilemma is the establishment of formalized offices of leadership to enforce rules. In the previous chapter, we suggested that this might have been the case in Phase 1, based on changes in burial goods from religious to more secular. But these leadership positions were probably relatively poorly developed, as indicated by the lack of differentiation in village middens. Moreover, as we stated previously, there are few indications of such status in the burials that we are able to clearly associate with Phase 2, suggesting leadership roles may have assumed even less prominence during this interval.

Eerkens (2013), along with Stanish (2013) and many others, notes that a second solution to the free-rider dilemma is the adoption of a worldview or religion that incorporates a threat of punishment or taboo for those who do not follow the rules. This strategy might be manifest in the increase in public ritual in Phase 2. As Stanish (2013:88) observes, public ritual may provide an effective way to keep groups cooperating, by "establishing norms of work embedded in a ritual schedule and enforced through taboo."

We are accustomed to thinking of agriculture in terms of ritual cycles, but the same pattern holds for fishing in many maritime societies (Stanish 2013:89). Malinowski, in his ethnographic work on the Trobriand Islands (1918:22), noted that "*kalala* [mullet] fishing in Labai is surrounded with more numerous and stringent taboos and is more bound up with tradition and ceremonial than any other social activity in the Trobriands." As the full moon approached during mullet fishing season, the village magician performed a number of esoteric rites, and strangers were excluded from the beach, while men of the village were required to be present (Malinowski 1918:91). Firth (1929) noted similar rituals associated with fishing among the Maori in New Zealand. Persons who violated these rules and protocols, for example fishing out of turn, met with sanctions like having their canoes split to pieces (Stanish 2013:90).

Fishing and shellfishing may have been tied directly to public ritual; as we noted above, there is evidence from oyster isotope data that mound building was completed in cooler months of the year. Many of the fish that are prevalent in the middens at Crystal River, such as mullet and sheepshead, reach maximum availability about this same time as they spawn in estuaries (Widmer 1988:135–136). But we need not establish a direct correlation; a ritual cycle of mound building and ceremony might have given structure to the extended routines of fishing and shellfishing. In doing so it likely reinforced the necessity of cooperation.

While we have stressed the integrative nature of the ceremonies conducted on plazas and platform mounds, we recognize that these ceremonies equally provided arenas for displays of status, authority, and esoteric knowledge (Clark and Blake 1994). The labor necessary to construct and maintain mounds and plazas—no matter how communal in principle—certainly required some sort of authority to coordinate. And at a broader scale, we can imagine that the residents of the village at Crystal River and other sites with large-scale public works enjoyed a measure of prestige not associated with the inhabitants of smaller communities that lacked such facilities.

6

From Regional Center to Mound-Residential Compound (Phase 3)

One question we are often asked when we talk to the general public about archaeological sites like Crystal River goes something like this: why did people abandon this place? Or, restated slightly, why did people move away from here? It is a natural question to pose, but in our experience also one that, for several fundamental reasons, defies easy answer.

First, the unstated premise is usually that people moved away quickly, perhaps in reaction to some catastrophe. However, our temporal resolution in archaeology is frequently limited to changes on the order of a half century at best; thus, what appears sudden may have been more like a gradual attrition.

Next, the term "abandonment" implies that people never intended to return, or perhaps even relinquished any claim to the area. The former premise is unknowable, and the latter presumption is anathema to descendant communities who may still feel ties to places and landscapes (Colwell-Chanthaphonh and Ferguson 2006).

Finally and more fundamentally, the question assumes that settlements are somehow typically permanent—a view at odds with both the archaeological and historical records. Virtually every archaeological site was "abandoned" at some point, and the same is true of many of the towns and cities that we know from historical records. The assumption that our own modern communities are exempt from this same sort of abandonment reflects a hubris induced by historical amnesia.

Recent archaeological work suggests that people began moving away from Crystal River in Phase 3, which, according to our Bayesian modeling, began between *cal A.D. 478 and 634 (95 percent probability)*, probably between *cal A.D. 521 and 605 (68 percent)*, and ended between *cal A.D. 663 and 810 (95 percent)*, probably between *cal A.D. 671 and 747 (68 percent)* (Pluckhahn, Thompson, and Cherkinsky 2015) (see Table 2.1). Phase 3 lasted between *50 and 289 years (95 percent),* probably between *93 and 218 years (68 percent).* At Crystal River the village contracted to the area north of Mound A, and there was less midden deposition, suggesting a decline in population (Figure 6.1). Some of the former residents may have moved the short distance downstream to what we now know as the Roberts Island Shell Mound Complex, but which at the time was probably an inauspicious marsh island similar to many others in the area. Other former residents of Crystal River probably settled—or resettled—other small islands in the area.

Pottery again appears to track these changes in settlement. In Phase 3 midden assemblages, sand tempering of ceramics (at 83 percent) comes to dominate over limestone (16 percent), and there is a reduction in the proportion of mixed-temper sherds (Pluckhahn, Thompson, and Kemp 2017; Thompson 2016:89). The increase in sand at the expense of limestone is reminiscent of Phase 1; the trend suggests that this choice of temper was more common in periods when the population was dispersed on marsh islands closer to the Gulf, rather than concentrated on the mainland at areas like Crystal River (where limestone was probably easier to procure). The lesser proportion of mixed tempers could be consistent with potters in greater isolation from one another.

New research suggests that the shift in settlement at Crystal River in Phase 3 may have been coincident with similar changes at sites across the Weeden Island area of the northern peninsula and panhandle. Just to the north of Crystal River, at the Garden Patch site, Wallis and colleagues (2015) note a disruption in the village configuration at around cal A.D. 615. Russo and colleagues (2014) have suggested shifts in the village plans at sites in the Panhandle that are roughly concurrent with this trend. And recent research suggests that a reorganization of the village at Kolomoki, which Pluckhahn (2003:207–208) originally dated around A.D. 550, actually probably occurred a century or so later (Menz 2015; Pluckhahn, Menz, West, and Wallis 2018; West 2016). The causes of this apparent region-wide reorganization of settlement are unclear.

As with the growth of the village at Crystal River in the preceding phase, the decline in Phase 3 may be roughly coincident with climatic changes. Phase 3 overlaps a period of generally lower sea level and cooler temperatures referred to as the Vandal Minimum (Bryson 1994; Walker 2013). This interval—which is also generally associated with the decline

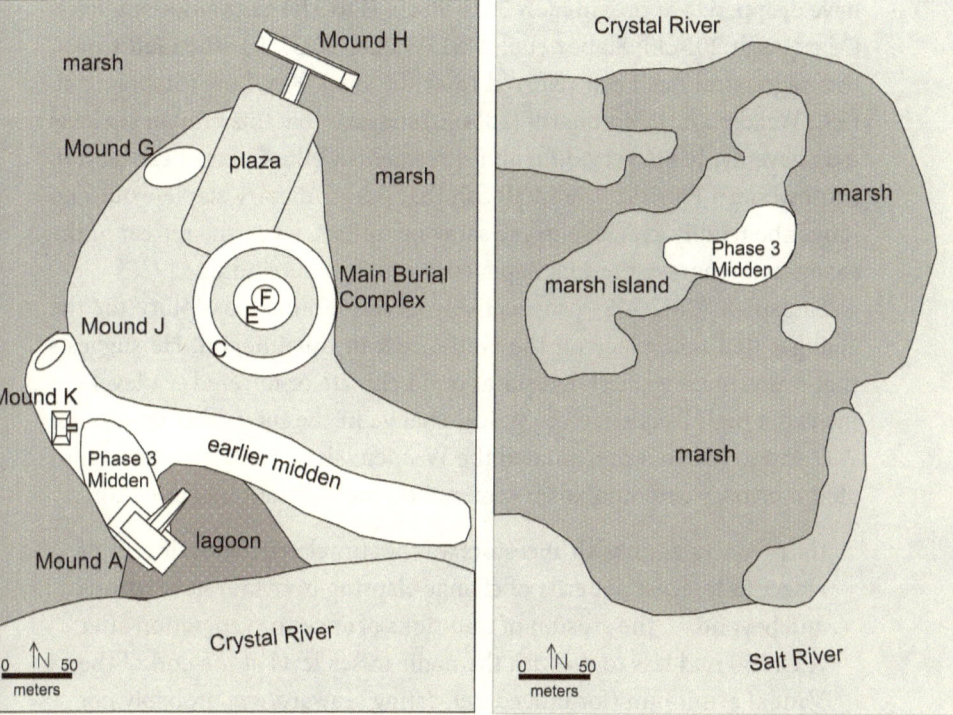

Figure 6.1. The settlement plans at Crystal River (*left*) and Roberts Island (*right*) during Phase 3.

of the Roman Empire, the beginning of the Dark Ages in Europe, and the end of the Classic period Maya florescence (among other cultural-historical milestones)—may have begun with a historically documented period of darkness and cold in the AD 530s (Baillie 1994; Rampino et al. 1988; Strothers 1984; Weisburd 1985). This prolonged period of reduced sunlight may have been caused by dust from a volcanic eruption, although this remains unproven (Baillie 1994).

The effects of the AD 530s event on the Gulf Coast have not been documented, but there is evidence in the region for a decline in sea level in the period between AD 550 and 850. Walker, Marquardt, and colleagues (Marquardt 2010:558–559; Walker 1992b; Walker et al. 1994) note a dramatic increase in the ratio of crown conchs (*Melongena corona*) to oysters on sites in Pine Island Sound in southwestern Florida; as these larger gastropods generally prefer higher salinity, they are possibly indicative of ecological destabilization resultant from a drop in sea level. Sea level may have dropped to approximately 30 to 90 cm (1 to 3 ft) below modern levels (Marquardt 2014:10; Stapor et al. 1991; Walker 2013). For the Gulf Coast, this regression has been referred to as the Buck Key Low (Stapor et al. 1991; Walker 2013). Marquardt (2014:10) suggests that this drop in sea level may have made life very difficult for residents of the Calusa heartland in southwestern Florida. The small fish that were a dietary staple would no longer be readily available in the same quantities, given the retreat of the mangrove-seagrass-mudflat habitats vital to fish nutrition.

Sassaman (2012:262) provocatively raises another possibility for the changes that take place on the Gulf Coast in this interval. He suggests that it was not a general deterioration in climate or lowered sea level but instead a high frequency of cyclical change in the interval from around A.D 450 to 750 that precipitated the Weeden Island tradition of accentuated mortuary ceremonialism centered on the veneration of ancestors:

> the preoccupation with ancestors was not unrelated to the efficacy of elders to forecast patterns of change elapsing over four generations and beyond... the erosion of traditions of ancestor veneration after A.D. 750 had less to do with the nadir in sea level at the end of the Vandal Minimum (for indeed, relocating seaward was probably not out of the question), but rather a loss of salience in elders to relate their memories of past experience to futures on the horizon.

Whatever the merits of Sassaman's hypothesis, the local manifestations of global changes in climate are not well understood. To the north of Crystal River at the mouth of the Suwanee, McFadden's (2015) soil studies document a transition from freshwater to brackish marsh conditions ca. A.D. 660–770, potentially contrary to both the general model of sea level decline and the specific evidence for this from southwestern Florida cited above. Jackson (2016:78–85) observed evidence for similarly anomalous wet conditions at Crystal River around this same time. Specifically, Stratum 2 in Core 48 in the marsh to the northeast of the site, with a radiocarbon age of cal A.D. 625 to 671 (95 percent probability), produced evidence for the growth of both freshwater wetland and salt-tolerant tree species. It is possible that factors other than changes in sea level, such as decreased rainfall or reduced spring flow, could account for the increase in salinity.

Assuming that seventh-century changes in climate or sea level, or both, made estuarine resources in proximity to Crystal River less productive, it would not be surprising if people began moving seaward to be in closer proximity to marine resources. Consistent with this, it is in Phase 3 that we see the earliest evidence for occupation at Roberts Island. In several of our shovel tests, we noted darker soil horizons with comparatively little shell but abundant artifacts buried 70–100 cmbs (2.3–3.3 ft). Soil-charcoal from deep in a shovel test on the eastern end of the island produced a calibrated date that overlaps with some of the latest retrieved from the middens at Crystal River (Pluckhahn, Thompson, and Cherkinsky 2015). Dates on soil-charcoal from the buried midden layer to the west, like those from the mounds themselves, are slightly later and suggest that most of the midden and monumental construction date to Phase 4, as discussed in the chapter to follow. We presume that people leaving Crystal River initiated the small Phase 3 settlement at Roberts Island, although this level of specificity is virtually impossible to prove archaeologically.

Other environmental changes may have contributed to the shift in settlement, including possible human-induced degradation of the mollusk resource base. Delgado (2013) measured samples of oysters from each of the four phases of occupation at Crystal River and Roberts Island. He found a decline in oyster length from earlier to later phases (mainly from Phase 3 to 4). This could be a sign that oysters were being harvested sooner in their life cycle, which in turn could be a sign of overpredation by people. There are some serious complications to this sort of analysis; among other factors that we must consider, oyster size is not a straightforward measurement, and oysters may have been harvested from different beds (Claassen 1998). But there are other, subtle indications that the higher and more nucleated population levels may have been placing greater stress on resources. Hardshell clam (*Mercenaria*), although never particularly common at Crystal River, are absent entirely from Phase 3 and later contexts (Duke 2015:Table 5.5; O'Neal 2016:114). It seems possible that these may have been subject to overharvesting by people living at Crystal River and related settlements in the area.

Of course, other social and environmental factors, some not readily observable in the archaeological record, undoubtedly also contributed to the decline in settlement at Crystal River during Phase 3. For example, Williams and Shapiro (1990) suggest that Mississippian villages cycled with the succession of leaders, and with the availability of game and firewood. Early villages of the Woodland period must have been prone to many of these same constraints. For Kolomoki, Pluckhahn (2003:217–218) has suggested that the scale of Middle Woodland ceremony and its likely appropriation by individuals or factions may have outstripped its erstwhile egalitarian ethos.

While all of these explanations are plausible, none clearly explains the changes that appear to have taken place at Crystal River and sites across the Gulf Coast and adjacent interior in the seventh century. A decline in sea level would certainly have affected much of the Gulf Coast, but would not seem to have directly affected communities in the interior, such as Kolomoki. The availability of game and firewood and the cycling of leaders are too localized to explain the concurrent changes in settlement. Nevertheless, it seems likely that some environmental or social change, even if only affecting a portion of this region, would have stimulated a wider social upheaval among communities that were closely linked by ties of kinship, ceremony, and exchange.

Whatever the cause, however, the decline in settlement at Crystal River does not conform to popular conceptions of collapse (see Tainter 2016). For one thing, by this point, the village had been permanently settled for five or six centuries—two or three times the number of years that the United States has been an independent nation. The longevity of Crystal River and other early villages is a point we return to in the final chapter.

Another reason we should not think of Phase 3 at Crystal River as a collapse is that while there may have been a decline in settlement, there is ample evidence that it continued as a place for ritual events. We suggest in the previous chapter that Mound E was likely added in Phase 2, but Moore's recovery of a number of Weeden Island vessels suggests that the use of this burial mound probably continued into Phase 3. The Mound E platform contained many secondary burials, as Moore (1903:382) noted:

> In the artificial elevation [Mound E], burials were very numerous, and to so great an extent had the ground been used that many graves, passing through the earlier ones, had caused great disturbance. In addition, numbers of disconnected bones lay, here and there, in the sand as though they had been gathered from the dead-house and scattered while the making of the elevation was in progress.

The apparent prevalence of secondary burials could be consistent with periodic burial rituals by people who had stored the remains of the dead for some time, perhaps at dispersed settlements.

There are also good indications that the use of the circular embankment as a burial facility continued into Phase 3. The pottery assemblage includes a number of Weeden Island types, including several that are generally regarded as becoming more frequent in the later Woodland (Kemp 2015:53–56). For example, Weeden Island Red and Wakulla Check Stamped are both relatively common at 15 and 6 percent, respectively.

In addition to these burial mounds, it appears, the residents of Crystal River also made additions to Mound J. As we noted in Chapters 2 and 4, the stratigraphy of this mound is difficult to interpret, and one of the three radiocarbon dates from the mound is problematic, but construction appears to have begun in Phase 2. However, the shell-dense layers at the top of the mound were added between *cal A.D. 426 and 653 (95 percent probability)*, probably between *cal A.D. 561 and 640 (68 percent)* (Pluckhahn and Thompson 2017) (see Table 2.2). We assume that the Phase 3 mound may have taken the form of a truncated pyramid, although it is now irregular in shape.

Perhaps the most dramatic statement to the continued relevance of Crystal River to the social landscape during Phase 3 was the completion of Mound A. We noted in the previous chapter the radiocarbon and OSL dates from this mound, and the results of our modeling suggest inhabitants initiated an early mound stage in Phase 2. We also noted that the modeling suggests that construction of the middle stage corresponds with either Phase 1 or 2 of the midden chronology. The upper stage is represented by the dense shell in Layers 1–9 (see Figure 5.6). Recovery in the core sections from this stage was poor, owing to the density of shell; as a result we have no dates from this stage (Pluckhahn and Thompson 2017). Owing to the lack of constraints, our model produces only a general estimate for the start of this stage between *cal A.D. 575 and 1758 (95 percent probability)*; it probably began between *cal A.D. 618 and 946 (68 percent)*. We think it likely that the upper stage was added in Phase 3.

Mound A is still imposing, perhaps especially when it is approached from the water, but it must have been particularly so before it was partially destroyed in the 1960s. The first written account of the mound comes from D. G. Brinton (1859:178–179), based on a visit in 1856–1857. In a slightly later publication, Brinton (1867:356–357) rather colorfully contrasted the appearance of Mound A (as well as the Turtle Mound near New Smyrna) with the more mundane and common "refuse heaps":

> By far the majority of these monuments of a past race are mere refuse heaps, the debris of villages of an icthyophagous [fish-eating]

population, showing no indications of having been designedly collected in heaps, true analogies of the kjoekken-moeddings [kitchen middens] of the age of stone; but in other instances it would appear that the Indians collected them into artificial mounds, forming a class of antiquities heretofore unnoticed by archaeologists. . . . The two most remarkable in the state are near New Smyrna, on the mosquito Lagoon, and near the mouth of the Crystal river, on the Gulf Coast. . . . Of the remarkable mound on Crystal River, four miles from its mouth, Mr. Dancy [former state geologist for Florida] writes: "The marsh of the river at that point is twenty yards wide to firm land, at which point this mound commences to rise. It is on all sides nearly perpendicular, the faces covered with brush and trees, to which the visitors have to cling to effect an ascent. It is about forty feet in height, the top surface nearly level, about thirty feet in diameter, and covered with magnolia, live oak, and other forest trees, some of them four feet in diameter. Its form is that of a truncated cone, and, as far as can be judged from external appearance, it is composed exclusively of oyster shells and vegetable mould. These shells are all separated. The mound was evidently thrown up by the Indians for a lookout, as the gulf can be seen from its summit. There are no oysters growing at this time within four or five miles of it." This is altogether different from the mere refuse heaps referred to elsewhere.

Randall (2015:21–28) offers a cogent critique of the use of terms like "refuse heap" and "kitchen midden" to characterize the numerous shell mounds of Florida, demonstrating how the use of such terms was bound to nineteenth-century notions of human progress that we now recognize as ethnocentric (or even racist). Still, it is hard to argue with Brinton that Mound A stands apart from most of the shell mounds of the coastal Southeast for its size, angularity, and setting (see Pluckhahn and Thompson 2014). We estimate that the mound has a volume of 9,002 m^3 (317,902 ft^3), the equivalent of 255,504 bushels of oysters.

Brinton's notion that mounds such as this served as lookouts was popular in the nineteenth century and remains so to an extent even today among the general public. The summit does provide a sweeping view of the adjacent marshes (Figure 6.2)—but not today as far as the Gulf. We

Figure 6.2. View from the summit of Mound A.

noted in the previous chapter the speculation by Hardman (1971) that the summit of Mound A may have been used to make observations in the opposite direction, to the rising sun on the summer solstice as marked by Stela 1. These speculations regarding the use of the summit of Mound A are intriguing, albeit difficult to substantiate.

We suspect the mound was intended primarily for other purposes. Specifically, the placement of the mound on a low spot near the river suggests to us that it was built to be seen, rather than to see from its summit. As described by Bullen (1953), Moore (1903), and Willey (1949b), a well-defined ramp extended down the east side of Mound A to the lagoon area. Willey (1949b) noted that at the time of his visit, the ramp approach was still "perfectly preserved" and that the only comparably well-preserved ramp was at the largest mound at the Mississippian period Moundville site in Alabama. The ramp appears to have been captured in a photo of the "Old Spanish Mound," as Mound A was formerly known (Figure 6.3). The unusual arrangement of the ramp relative to the lagoon suggests it

Figure 6.3. View of the ramp on Mound A. Note figure standing to right of ramp. Old Spanish mound near Crystal River, Florida. 19—?. Black-and-white postcard, State Archives of Florida, Florida Memory.

was meant to be seen and approached from the water, perhaps especially by visitors in canoes.

This strikes us as quite a different visitor experience than would have been associated with the smaller, earlier mounds. In a comparison of Woodland and Mississippian platform mounds, Lindauer and Blitz (1997) suggested that the former typically have summits that are small and open, thus providing unrestricted visual access from the plazas they frequently adjoin. In contrast, the summits of Mississippian platform mounds are generally larger and sometimes have evidence for fences or screens, suggesting the ceremonies conducted therein may have been less communal in nature.

This characterization seems valid for two of the three platform mounds at Crystal River; Mounds H and K both adjoin the plaza (the former more obviously than the latter), and both have summits that are quite narrow and low, so the ceremonies on their summits would be easily observable. However, none of these observations hold true for Mound A. Even today it is difficult to observe the summit from the ground or water immediately below, and this would most certainly have been the case before almost one-third of the mound was removed for fill.

Nevertheless, the mound would have certainly been an easily recognized landmark, and it remains so today. Cooney (2004) observes that visually distinctive elements of coastal topography such as points or promontories often serve to mark fishing grounds. People at Crystal River may have created a promontory of their own to stake such a claim. Visual anchors such as this may also mark territories or define "sight communities" (Bernardini and Peeples 2015).

We can't say much regarding features that might have been present on any of the mounds at Crystal River, but the location and size of Mound A in comparison with the two earlier platform mounds may mark a shift in the nature of ceremony, perhaps with greater control by a subset of the larger community. It is tempting to suggest that those select members of the community may have been those few who continued to live at Crystal River during Phase 3, in the area just north of Mound A. The small size of the Phase 3 settlement here suggests it was home to no more than a few households. The pattern is reminiscent of the "chiefly compounds" that have been observed in some parts of the American Southeast during the later Mississippian period—that is, mound centers with small occupations that are presumed to be those of a resident chief and his or her family (Williams 1995).

Save for the proximity to Mound A, however, there is nothing about the Phase 3 occupation area at Crystal River to suggest that the people who lived here held special status. The Phase 3 pottery assemblage from Crystal River is almost entirely plain and thus shows continuity with Phase 2 (interestingly, the Phase 3 assemblage from Roberts Island has higher proportions of complicated and check stamped and trace amounts of other decorative types). There are no other artifacts from our units here that suggest higher status.

Of course, it is still possible that the people who lived near Mound A at Crystal River during Phase 3 enjoyed greater prestige than those who resided elsewhere. If their prestige was tied to the leadership of ceremonies, and those ceremonies were restricted to certain times of the year, it may be that leadership was similarly contextual and situational. This would be consistent with lack of clear distinctions in burials, apart from the general division between those buried in mounds and those disposed of elsewhere.

Periods of transition are often difficult to characterize archaeologically, and this is certainly the case with Phase 3. On the one hand, people began moving away from Crystal River, to Roberts Island and other areas along the coast. On the other, they continued to congregate at Crystal River for ceremonies that included feasting and the construction of monuments.

The shift in settlement may have been related to broad-scale changes in sea level and climate, specifically the lower sea levels and generally cooler and drier—but also more variable—conditions associated with the Vandal Minimum, or with overuse of resources. But as we intimated above, there are problems with the extension of these environmentally based lines of reasoning to changes that appear to be typical of the broader region. A combination of ecological and social factors seems likely.

As Belfer-Cohen and Bar-Yosef (2000:24) observe, competition may favor the formation of villages, but these are also difficult to maintain, in part because they involve more decision-making institutions, and thus more potential for these to be in conflict (see also Fletcher 1995; Kowalewski 2013; Johnson 1982). As Belfer-Cohen and Bar-Yosef (2000:24) further argue, larger groups may become an economic disadvantage as marginal returns diminish, as might have been the case at Crystal River with even a relatively modest deterioration of the resource base.

A decline in or increasing unpredictability of resources returns may have also imperiled the social relations of production. Bettinger (2015:60) has recently noted that the packing together of previously isolated groups required a restructuring of social relations, most notably "the institution that individuals who camped in the same place were, merely by virtue of that, members of a sociopolitical unit whose reason for being was cooperation and obligate food sharing for the common good." Strong social ties that reinforced generalized reciprocity appear to have prevailed in Phases 1 and 2, but in Phase 3 people may have turned increasingly to the alternative strategy of looser social ties, less sharing of production and consumption, and greater isolation among kin groups.

Seemingly contradictory to this interpretation, Phase 3 witnessed the completion of one of the largest platform mounds ever completed in the coastal Southeast. However, we have speculated that Mound A, with its high and expansive summit, could have been used for rituals that were obscure to the people who stood or canoed below; thus, it could mark a shift to a less communal expression of ceremony. We are also struck by the reduction of settlement to the area immediately north of the mound, perhaps indicating that Crystal River was now home to a small group of people who directed these ceremonies.

Unfortunately, we currently lack the evidence to clearly interpret these patterns. What is clear, however, is that new ceremonial centers were beginning to compete with Crystal River, a trend that would accelerate in the centuries to follow.

7

New Centers Emerge (Phase 4)

In the introduction to their 1961 article summarizing archaeological investigations at the Wash Island site, Adelaide and Ripley Bullen (1961:69) paused to describe a new find in the same general vicinity:

> A short distance inland from the water at a location called "Shell Mounds," between the Salt and Crystal Rivers, is an excellent temple mound previously, we believe, unrecorded. Its flat top covers an area about 40 by 60 feet [12 to 18 m], with the long axis extending in a north-south direction, and reaches an elevation of 12 to 15 feet [3.7 to 4.6 m] above the surrounding terrain. There is a suggestion of a ramp on the east side while the other sides are all rather steep and straight.

The Bullens' excitement at this discovery, although understated, is obvious; finding a well-preserved but previously unrecorded platform mound was even at the time—and especially today—a rare find on the Gulf Coast. Roberts Island, as the Shell Mounds came to be known, evaded archaeological attention for another 35 years, when it was revisited by Brent Weisman (1995b). Recognizing that "the mound and midden . . . areas are culturally and temporally associated and reflect an organized site plan," Weisman (1995b:2) grouped a series of separately recorded sites into a singular complex. Like the Bullens, Weisman (1995b:3) was impressed by the state of preservation:

> To the best of my knowledge, the Roberts Island Shell Mound Complex is the best preserved example of an aboriginal ceremonial and village mound complex on the entire Florida Gulf Coast. Unlike comparable major site complexes . . . at Roberts Island pothunting has been negligible or nonexistent, and impacts from construction

or other activities have been very limited. The preservation quality is of the highest order.

Also like the Bullens, Weisman (1995b:3) was unable to date the mounds, noting only that resolving the relationship between the seemingly contemporaneous Roberts Island and Crystal River sites should be a research question of major importance.

As we noted in Chapter 6 (see also Pluckhahn, Thompson, and Cherkinsky 2015), radiocarbon dates suggest that people began living at Roberts Island during our Phase 3. However, additional evidence suggests that it was during the subsequent phase that native peoples constructed the mounds and midden (Pluckhahn, Hodson, et al. 2015; Pluckhahn et al. 2016. This final phase of occupation at Crystal River and Roberts Island started between *cal A.D. 723 and 881 (95 percent probability)*, probably between *cal A.D. 779 and 867 (68 percent)*. It ended between *cal A.D. 891 and 1060 (95 percent)*, probably between *cal A.D. 902 and 982 (68 percent)*. Phase 4 lasted between *23 and 305 years (95 percent)*, probably between *62 and 207 years (68 percent)*.

This range firmly dates the major occupation of Roberts Island to the Late Woodland period, one of the great disjunctures in the archaeology of the American Eastern Woodlands. While the periods before and after this experienced florescences of mound building and long-distance exchange, the Late Woodland appears archaeologically as a sort of "dark ages," owing to the cessation of these activities and the seeming blandness of material culture. James Griffin (1952:361–362), in his landmark synthesis of the prehistory of the Southeast, made only passing reference to this as "a period of rest and quiescence." Stephen Williams (1963) famously referred to the societies of the Late Woodland as "the good grey cultures," presumably for the seeming redundancy and plainness.

More recent authors suggest that earlier perceptions of sameness stemmed largely from a lack of data and preoccupation with the periods bracketing the Late Woodland; as McElrath et al. (2000:10) observe, "the good gray cultures should more appropriately be viewed as a multicolored, patchwork quilt." Moreover, archaeologists now recognize that the Late Woodland witnessed, rather than a period of quiescence, three major transformations: a major demographic shift, recognized by changes in settlement following the decline of Middle Woodland lifeways; the widespread adoption of the bow and arrow; and, finally, the adoption of maize-based economies (McElrath et al. 2000). However, the timing and extent of these transformations varied widely across eastern North America.

The Late Woodland transformations are arguably best documented for the American Bottom region at the confluence of the Missouri and Mississippi rivers in southern Illinois. The Late Woodland settlement shift here began in the fourth century (McElrath et al. 2000:13–14) but accelerated with the widespread adoption of the bow and arrow around A.D. 600 (McElrath et al. 2000:17–18). After A.D. 850 there were dense, nucleated populations and an increasing reliance on maize (Kelly et al. 1987; Kelly et al. 1990). From these antecedents, a new Mississippian identity and lifestyle would emerge in a "big bang" at the Cahokia site near modern St. Louis, around AD 1050 (Pauketat 1994, 2004).

Interestingly, there appears to have been no strong tradition of mound building in the American Bottom in the century or so leading up to the big bang. In contrast, in the related Coles Creek and Plumb Bayou areas of the lower Mississippi and Arkansas River valleys (respectively), mound construction appears to have continued virtually unabated through the last centuries of the first millennium at sites like Toltec near modern Little Rock (Nassaney 1992, 2000; Rolingson 2012), and Feltus near modern Natchez (Kassabaum 2014), among many others that remain less well known archaeologically. Otherwise, however, the Late Woodland transformations largely paralleled those in the American Bottom.

The Weeden Island complex of the northern Gulf Coast has often been viewed as a bridge spanning the "climaxes" of the Middle Woodland and Mississippian periods (e.g., Muller 1997:123; Nassaney and Cobb 1991:314; Willey 1966:289). However, as we have noted elsewhere (Pluckhahn et al. 2016), this Weeden Island "exceptionalism" represents something of a half-truth, in that while it seems certain that mound construction and exchange continued later in this region than in much of the region, these appear to have waned here too by around A.D. 800 (see also Milanich et al. 1997; Pluckhahn 2003:215–216; Pluckhahn, Menz, West, and Wallis 2018). This change has been attributed to the adoption of maize (Kohler 1991; Percy and Brose 1974), but the evidence suggests that corn was uncommon in the region until Middle Mississippian times, and even then probably only on the northern Gulf Coast (Ashley and Rolland 2009; Mickwee 2009; Milanich 1974).

This makes the timing of Roberts Island all the more peculiar. Why did mound construction continue here even as it declined elsewhere in the Weeden Island area, and across much of eastern North America? One possible explanation is its connections to the south. The southern peninsular Gulf Coast was no exception to the generalized Late Woodland "decline." Summarizing radiocarbon evidence from archaeological sites from the Tampa Bay area, Austin and colleagues (2014:97–103) note relatively few dated components in the interval from around A.D. 600 to 800. They relate this pattern to the abandonment of many settlements in the face of the deterioration of climate and lowered sea levels of the Buck Key Low, which they suggest may have altered the marine ecology and negatively impacted the subsistence base of fish and shellfish. Farther south in the Calusa heartland, environmental conditions in Pine Island Sound became so dire in the ninth century (Caloosatachee IIB-a,b) that people probably abandoned the Pineland complex altogether, moving west to Useppa Island (Marquardt and Walker 2013:836–837)—a migration not unlike what we have proposed for the initial settlement of Roberts Island in Phase 3.

Yet these societies to the south appear to have rebounded relatively quickly with the onset of more favorable conditions associated with the Medieval Warm period. The Bayshore Homes mound and village complex in Tampa Bay, abandoned during the Buck Key Low, was reoccupied at around A.D. 950, and a similar pattern played out at the village represented by the Yat Kitischee site (Austin et al. 2014:102–103). New settlements, such as the Anderson site, were founded in the area by around A.D. 1000. In the Calusa heartland, the pattern was slower to develop. But the Pineland site appears to have been resettled in the tenth century (Caloosahatchee IIB-c,d) (Marquardt and Walker 2013:837).

Crystal River and Roberts Island were peripheral to the Caloosahatchee and related traditions to the south, just as they were to the Weeden Island complex centered to their north. However, the people who resided here may have leveraged this position to their advantage. While the network of Weeden Island interaction was strong, they appear to have looked north. But as Weeden Island mound ceremonialism faded in the eighth and ninth centuries, they may have increased their connections to the south.

As epitomized by sites in Charlotte Harbor and the Ten Thousand Islands, native peoples of the Caloosahatchee tradition of southwestern Florida constructed massive complexes of shell, in forms unique in North America, if not in the world (Cushing 1897; Marquardt 2010, 2014;

Schober 2014; Schwadron 2010; Thompson 2017; Thompson et al. 2016; Widmer 1988). The core areas of these complexes are typically composed of vast shell fields and shell midden-mounds. Narrow, linear shell ridges often radiate out from these shell fields like tentacles on an octopus; these might have served as tidal fish weirs or the foundations of houses (Schwadron 2010:294). Perhaps one of the more interesting features is the "water courts," circular depressions enclosed by shell walls. Some of these are multichambered. These features may have functioned as fish ponds, water retention areas, or canoe basins (Cushing 1897; Marquardt 2010:561; Schwadron 2010:292; Thompson 2017).

It is likely that some of the mounds and ridges on these Caloosahatchee complexes served as the bases for large long houses. Such houses may have been home to large extended families or perhaps corporate groups. Ethnohistorical descriptions of the population and number of houses at Mound Key, the capital of the Calusa polity at the time of European contact in the sixteenth century, suggest there were as many as 63 individuals to a structure (Thompson et al. 2014:63). While few structures have been excavated in the Calusa region, limited excavations and GPR at the Pineland site revealed a large domestic structure dating to Caloosahatchee IIA-Early (A.D. 500 to 650) (Thompson et al. 2014:71). It may be that the shift from early, smaller, single-family dwellings to extended-family long houses accompanied shifts in the environment (i.e., cooler and a lowering of sea level); once climatic conditions and sea levels returned to more favorable conditions around A.D. 850, surplus labor could be devoted to other large-scale communal undertakings, such as canal construction and water courts (Thompson et al. 2014:71).

By Phase 4, Crystal River appears to have been abandoned except for a small area of occupation immediately north of Mound A (Figure 7.1). This area of occupation is even smaller than that we discussed for Phase 3 and may represent a continuing "caretaker" population or family group, such as has been suggested for the ceremonial core of Chaco Canyon in the American Southwest (Saitta 1997:13). If so, we may never know who exactly these remnant inhabitants were or what role they played in the continued occupation of Crystal River. What is certain, however, is that we see no evidence for the initiation of new mound construction at Crystal River, although the modeled end dates for the upper stages of Mound A extend into this interval (Pluckhahn and Thompson 2017).

Conversely, this was the period when native people constructed

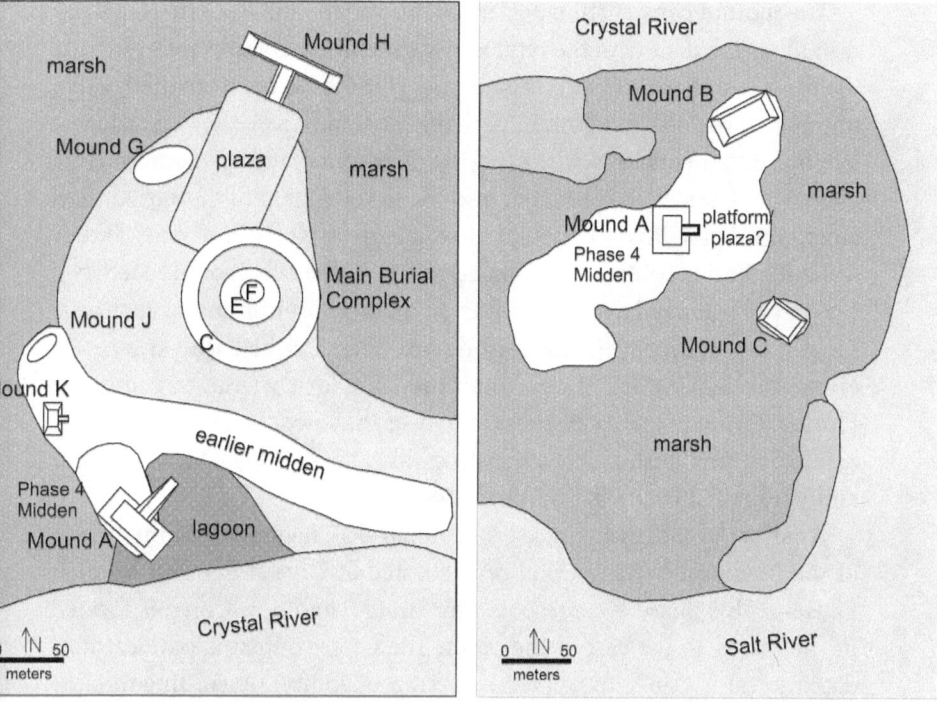

Figure 7.1. The settlement plans at Crystal River (*left*) and Roberts Island (*right*) during Phase 4.

mounds and deposited most of the midden at Roberts Island (Pluckhahn, Hodson, et al. 2015; Pluckhahn, Thompson, and Cherkinsky 2015). Indeed, the "island" at Roberts Island would not exist today were it not for the construction that took place during Phase 4. As we noted in the previous chapter, in the basal layers of our shovel tests at Roberts Island we commonly encountered a layer of dark, largely shell-free soil layer that we have radiocarbon-dated to Phase 3. This is generally covered by a minimum of 1 m (3.1 ft) of shell midden. This ridge of shell midden extends northeast to southwest, measuring approximately 200 m (656 ft) long, 20–50 m (65–164 ft) wide, and around 1.7 ha (4 ac) in total area. The highest point of the ridge, apart from the mounds we describe below, is a dome-shaped prominence measuring about 20 m east–west and 25 m north–south, with an elevation of about 2.9 m (10 ft) amsl. Shovel test excavations suggest this is a midden pile rather than a burial mound—as might be assumed from its appearance.

The mound construction and midden formation at Roberts Island are roughly coincident with the return of warmer temperatures referred to as the Medieval Warm period. The warmer climate has been credited with a number of societal milestones, perhaps most famously the expansion of Viking settlements to North America (Newfoundland) (Dugmore et al. 2012; Mikkelsen et al. 2008), but also the development of the agricultural chiefdoms of the Mississippian period in eastern North America (Anderson 2012; Foster 2012). As we alluded to above, the effects of the Medieval Warm period may have been felt even among tropical hunter-gatherer-fishers; this warmer climate episode has been credited with the development of larger populations and more complex societies in southwest Florida, owing to increased productivity of shallow seagrass meadows inhabited by small fish and large gastropods (Dietler 2008:444; Marquardt and Walker 2013:880–883; Widmer 1988).

Analysis of pollen by Jackson (2016:86–95) suggests that the effects of the Medieval Warm period reverberated at Crystal River in Midden Phase 4. This phase is represented by Strata 5 and 6 in Core 55, located in the marsh to the east of the plaza. The latter context is radiocarbon-dated to cal A.D. 878 to 982 (95 percent probability). According to Jackson, sparse arboreal representation and the dominance of the moderately salt-tolerant sedges suggest that wetlands adjacent to the site experienced substantial tidal influence, while the abundance of freshwater-dependent marsh plants suggests that brackish water rarely penetrated the wetlands landward of the midden.

A wetter and warmer climate likely accelerated a shift in subsistence toward marine resources. This is most readily apparent in the vast quantities of oyster shells (and to a far lesser extent those of other mollusks) that make up the midden and mounds. Comparing the quantities of invertebrates and vertebrate fishes across time, Duke (2015) noted a trend toward an increase in the abundance of invertebrates—particularly bivalves, and especially oyster. The contribution of bivalves to biomass is 74 percent for the Phase 1 sample, increases slightly to 76 percent for Phase 2 and again to 82 percent for Phase 3, then rises more steeply to 95 percent in Phase 4. An increase in oyster collection was clearly the main constituent of this trend, with the biomass trend for this species paralleling that for bivalves generally.

Shell hammers may provide an indirect measure of the increasing importance of shellfish in Phase 4. These tools, consisting of conch shells that were hafted to a wooden handle, are far more prevalent in this phase than in any previous (O'Neal 2016:112–113); indeed, they litter the surface of Roberts Island. Menz (2013, 2016) studied the use-wear on a large sample from the surface of the site and compared it to the wear patterns observed on replica tools that he had used for a variety of tasks (e.g., working wood, breaking shell). His analysis suggested that these ubiquitous tools might have been used for processing oysters—probably breaking up larger clusters.

Not surprisingly, perhaps, people who resided at Roberts Island during Phase 4 seem to have been procuring oysters from areas closer to the Gulf than was the case in earlier phases. Recent analysis of oyster isotopes indicate that the samples from Roberts Island are disproportionately from higher-saline environments relative to those from earlier time periods (Lulewicz et al. 2017). Duke's (2015:121–124) analysis of temporal trends in the size of crown conch at Crystal River and Roberts Island lends some additional support to this observation. The mean size of crown conch increased over time; larger crown conch are typically found on the more substantial oyster reefs typical of the river mouths, due to the higher availability of prey.

The increase in the importance of shellfish was accompanied by a decrease in the contribution of vertebrate taxa (Compton 2014; Duke 2015:Tables 5.8, 5.9). Still, vertebrate fauna remains are plentiful in the midden, as stated. Compton's (2014) analysis of a sample of the vertebrate fauna from Roberts Island identified 41 taxa representing at least 124 individuals. But aquatic taxa make up 85 percent of the vertebrate species identified, 99 percent of specimens, 95 percent of individuals, and 89 percent of estimated biomass. This overwhelming dominance of aquatic resources among vertebrate fauna is due primarily to the abundance of fishes and turtles. Fishes are by far the most abundant group in terms of numbers of individuals (88 percent) and identified specimens (88 percent). Twenty-seven fish taxa representing 18 fish families are present. Most abundant are the sea catfishes and mullets, representing nearly 70 percent of the fish specimens identified by count and weight. Compton notes a second tier of fish abundance that includes the drums and croakers (Sciaenidae) and porgies (Sparidae), and a third tier grouping that includes the gars (Lepisosteidae), tenpounders (Elopidae), needlefishes (Belonidae), and sunfishes (Centrarchidae).

Turtles represent 17 percent of the species identified, 11 percent of specimens, 6 percent of individuals, and 58 percent of estimated biomass. Sea turtles are represented by two species, the loggerhead sea turtle (*Caretta caretta*) and the green sea turtle (*Chelonia mydas*). Freshwater turtles present in the assemblage include snapping turtles (*Chelydra serpentina*), American mud turtles (*Kinosternon* spp.), and cooters (*Pseudemys* sp.).

Reptiles other than turtles include only the American alligator, which is represented by just two specimens. Birds are also uncommon; they are represented by only two taxa: true ducks and plumed egrets. Finally, mammals are the least-represented vertebrate group in the assemblage, with only 15 total specimens. The four mammalian species represented include eastern gray squirrel (*Sciurus carolinensis*), Hispid cotton rat (*Sigmodon hispidus*), raccoon, and white-tailed deer. Of these, only the white-tailed deer is represented by more than one specimen (NISP = 7).

Together, these faunal data suggest that the inhabitants of Roberts Island and the people who came together there for ceremonies primarily focused their resource procurement activities in the estuarine and marine habitats of Crystal Bay and its associated marshes. Assuming that people "shopped locally," this subsistence strategy is consistent with a settlement pattern composed of households dotting the marsh islands along the coast and estuaries. As has also been assumed for southwestern Florida (Widmer 1988), people in this area during Phase 4 were likely catching most of the fish in nets. Consistent with this, the faunal assemblage from Roberts Island is lacking in the bones of rays and skates that were present in earlier assemblages from Crystal River (Duke 2015:Tables 5.8, 5.9), and which were probably not captured in nets (Widmer 1988:251–252). Their paucity in later phases corresponds with the disappearance of bipointed bone points (O'Neal 2016:Table 4.3), suggesting these tools were probably used to spear these animals and fell out of favor as nets became more commonly employed.

We have thus far treated Roberts Island as a "shell midden," and this is an accurate label in that the sediments are composed principally of oyster shells and small fragments of bone—the obvious remains of meals. But it is clear to us that much of this sediment is not the result of the gradual accretion of ordinary household refuse, as the term "shell midden" implies (Randall 2015:29–33). In contrast with the buried Phase 3 midden layer, as well as most of the midden at Crystal River, portions of the shell midden here contain little soil and few artifacts other than shell and bone (Gilleland 2013). The absence of ceramics, in particular, would suggest that this deposition was not associated with in situ habitation. This is especially true of the middle levels in our shovel tests, suggesting that at some point the island was deliberately built up, probably through the deposition of feasting remains. And the observation holds particularly true for the middle levels in our shovel tests on the eastern edge of the midden. At some point during Phase 4, this portion of the site appears to have been deliberately formed into an elevated plaza.

We don't think that Roberts Island was occupied only for feasting and ceremony during Phase 4, however. A high density of ceramics in the upper levels of Shovel Test 11 point to the possibility of a residence in this area west of the mound. We also encountered a relatively high density of ceramics and shell tools in our trench in the depression at the southwestern end of the ridge of shell midden. This depression resembles the "water courts" observed more frequently on sites in southwest Florida, and the timing of Phase 4 is consistent with features there; Schwadron (2010:289) suggests that water courts date from about A.D. 600 to A.D. 1400 (late Glades I to Glades IIIa).

The central depression in the "water court" at Roberts Island runs northeast–southwest and measures about 20 × 6 m (65 × 20 ft); the elevation inside the depression is about 1 m (3.3 ft) amsl, compared with about 2.3 m (7.5 ft) amsl on the roughly circular midden defining the feature (Figure 7.2). Although the formation and function of this depression are unclear, the concentration of pottery and shell tools suggests the possibility of a structure in this location, perhaps similar to the large multifamily houses noted earlier for this time period on the southwestern Gulf Coast. Specifically, it seems possible that shell accumulated around the edges of a large circular to oval structure on stilts; the area directly beneath may have been used as an activity area or for storage, as evidenced by the higher densities of pottery and shell tools. If we are correct, the water court could represent the presence of at least one resident household at Roberts Island. However, the size and shape of the presumed structure here could be seen as indicative of some type of special-purpose structure, such as a council house. Similar structures have been identified elsewhere in the coastal Southeast (see Thompson 2009).

With regard to possible habitation at Roberts Island, we also note that beyond the "water court" at the southwestern end of the shell midden are one or two narrow ridges of shell extending southeast (see Figure 2.5).

Figure 7.2. View of Trench 2 and the "water court" area on Roberts Island.

These bear a resemblance to the linear shell middens more commonly found in southwest Florida, although at only 2–3 m (6–10 ft) wide (at least above the current water table), they are far narrower than the those reported by Schwadron (2010). However, the timing is again consistent; Schwadron (2010:389) places the finger ridges in southwest Florida in the interval from around A.D. 900 to A.D. 1290 (Glades IIb to Glades IIIa), consistent with Phase 4. Following the interpretation of similar features, the ridges of shell at Roberts Island may have accumulated below linear houses built on pilings. If true, these linear ridges might account for a few households. However, we can't rule out other possibilities, such as their use as fish weirs or even as a formal entranceway.

So it seems probable that at least a small number of people were living at Roberts Island during Phase 4, even if we can't presently point to clear structural remains. Still, it also seems clear that Roberts Island may have functioned primarily as a ceremonial center, as evidenced by the apparent rapid deposition of shell midden and the arrangement of mounds at the northern end of the site.

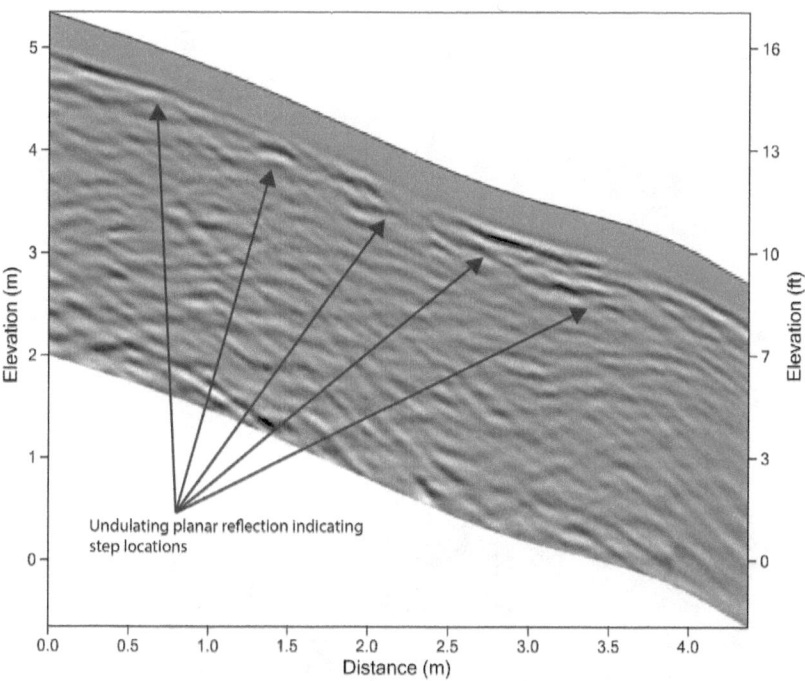

Figure 7.3. Reflection (corrected for topography) of a GPR transect on the western side of Mound A at Roberts Island, drawing attention to a series of relatively shallow anomalies.

Mound A, the largest and best-preserved of these mounds, measures about 29 × 32 m (95 × 105 ft) at its base and 14 × 21 m (39 × 69 ft) at its summit, which is about 4 m (13 ft) higher than the surrounding ground surface. Unlike any of the mounds at Crystal River, its axes are oriented precisely with the cardinal directions, with the long axis running north–south. True to previous descriptions (Bullen and Bullen 1961:69), midway along the eastern slope of Mound A is a discontinuity in elevation, suggestive of a ramp (as with several of the mounds at Crystal River). The presumed ramp connects the mound to the previously described flat, plaza-like midden deposit that extends about 40 m (131 ft) east before trailing off into marsh.

To better understand the timing and methods of mound construction, Mound A was investigated with a combination of GPR survey and small-scale excavation (Pluckhahn et al. 2016). Figure 7.3 documents the reflection (corrected for topography) of a GPR transect on the western side of

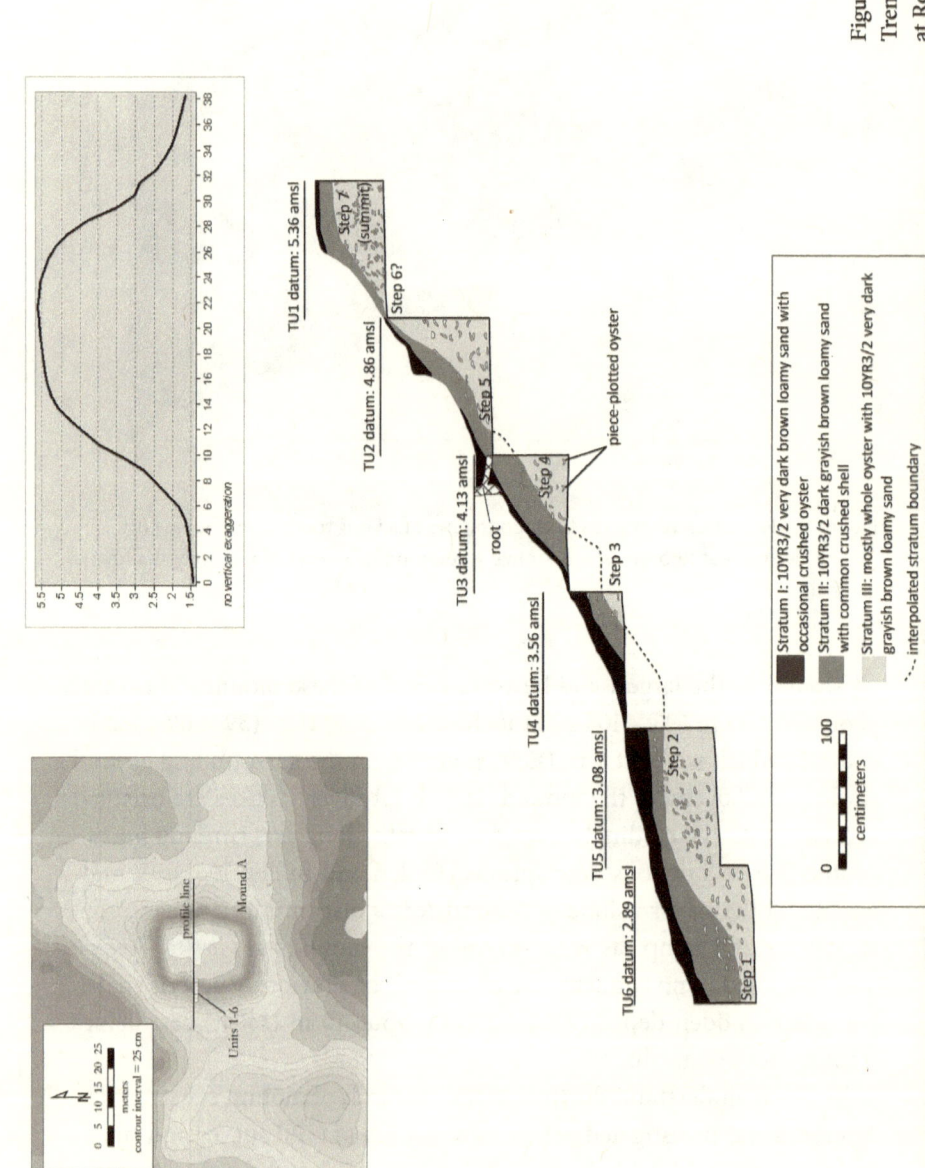

Figure 7.4. Profile of Trench 1 in Mound A at Roberts Island.

Mound A, drawing attention to a series of relatively shallow anomalies. The only other significant anomalies lie near the lower limit of our radar profiles and are thus difficult to interpret but which could possibly indicate the existence of a low "primary" mound stage. In general, however, the radar profile suggested that the mound fill is composed of homogeneous fill.

We excavated a 1-×-6-m (3-×-20-ft) trench directly adjacent to the previously described GPR transect on the western slope of Mound A (Figure 7.4). The trench profile suggested that the mound was built almost entirely of oyster shell, with very little soil save for the topsoil above. Oyster shell was a common building material for the prehistoric societies of the Atlantic and Gulf coasts; in this regard, the construction of the mound fit the expected pattern. However, closer examination of the stratigraphy of the trench revealed that rather than paralleling the modern ground surface, the contact between the overlying topsoil and the mound core consisted of a series of alternating horizontal and vertical surfaces consistent with the GPR profile and possibly representing a stepped form of construction (Pluckhahn et al. 2016). Beginning from the bottom of the mound at left (west) in Unit 6, the stratigraphic boundary marked by the dense oyster shell of Stratum III exhibits a roughly horizontal surface, followed by a point of inflection to a slope of approximately 45 degrees, followed by another point of inflection to another nearly horizontal surface, and continuing in this pattern to the top of the mound to the right (east) in Unit 1. Considering the trench profile as a whole, we think there were between two and six steps on the slope of the mound between the base and summit (Figure 7.5). Although possible stepped construction has been observed at a few later (Mississippian) mounds in the region (Williams 1999:17), this is the first example identified for the Woodland period, and the first of any time period made from shell.

The fact that the fill of Mound A was composed almost exclusively of oyster shells presented a challenge for dating of the mound. However, with the assistance of Jack Rink, we were able to collect samples of oyster shells with adherent sand grains for OSL dating. The samples had to be taken at night, so that the electron trap of the sand grains would not be reset by light—an adventure we like to refer to as our foray into "vampire archaeology." OSL dating of these sand grains adhering to shells in Stratum III produced age estimates falling in the last two centuries of the first millennium A.D. and the first two centuries of the second (Hodson

Figure 7.5. Trench 1, partially backfilled with oyster shell to show apparent stepped construction.

2012:22; Pluckhahn, Hodson, et al. 2015; Pluckhahn et al. 2016). A radiocarbon date on a deer bone found amongst the oyster shells at the base of our trench has a roughly equivalent calibrated range. Bayesian modeling of these three dates as *terminus post quem* suggests construction began between *cal A.D. 791 and 1115 (95 percent probability)*, probably between *cal A.D. 865 and 1045 (95 percent)* (see Table 2.2).

Several lines of evidence support the inference drawn from the lack of stratigraphic breaks that Mound A was completed quickly (Pluckhahn et al. 2016). First, the fill of the mound consisted mainly of "clean" oyster shell with very little sediment and relatively few artifacts (but see Marquardt [2010:554] for a discussion of the problems with this term and the inference of rapid accumulation). Christina Perry Sampson (2015) compared the size of oyster shells from mound and midden contexts at Roberts Island site 8CI41. Her analysis revealed significantly greater variation in the shells from midden layers; such a pattern might be expected if the mound construction corresponded to a relatively short interval in the seasonal growth cycles of oysters. As a corollary to this, Thompson et al.

(2015)'s isotope studies to determine season of capture for oyster found significant discrepancies between mound and midden samples from Roberts Island. In contrast with the samples from the midden, which appear to have been procured year-round, the samples from the mound were harvested exclusively in the fall/winter and winter. This does not prove they were collected in a single season, but it does raise this possibility.

From the adjoining plaza near Mound A there is another projection of the shell ridge northeast to Mound B. As we noted in Chapter 2, this mound was greatly disturbed by the construction of a house on its summit in the 1950s. In their initial description of this mound, Bullen and Bullen (1961:69) seemed divided regarding the amount of disturbance the construction of this house had inflicted:

> Nearby is another large shell mound with a flat top about 125 to 150 feet [38 to 46 m] across. However, it seems doubtful that this second mound represents a ceremonial structure. More likely its top was leveled for the construction of the large frame house it still supports.

Unfortunately, we know of no maps or photographs documenting the appearance of Mound B before this disturbance, at least definitively. But there is a 1922 photograph in the J. K. Small collection of the Florida Memory archives that we think might be an image of Mound B before it was significantly damaged (Figure 7.6). Unfortunately, the photo bears only the same identifiers used for several others in this collection:

> Shell mounds and kitchen-middens . . . Photographed in Salt River coastwise lagoons, south of Crystal River, Florida . . . August 1922 . . . The only high land in the region.

The topography of the mound that is depicted in this photo is reminiscent of Roberts Island, with a small inlet beyond the mound to the left. However, there are also some discrepancies, such as what appear to be shell deposits depicted to the right of the mound where there is mainly only marsh today (although there are several smaller rises, and Weisman [1995b] was told by local informants that these included human burials). The shell mound in the photo appears to have been flat-topped, but with a dome-shaped pile of shell on top of the platform. This could be an architectural feature, or a pile of feasting remains, or a remnant of mining or other disturbances to the summit even before the photo was taken in 1922. Unfortunately, we will likely never know for certain if this is Mound B at

Figure 7.6. Photograph of a shell mound in the Crystal River area, possibly Mound B at Roberts Island. Photograph by John Kunkel Small, 1869–1938, Shell mounds and kitchen-middens, 1922, Black & white nitrate photonegative, State Archives of Florida, Florida Memory.

Roberts Island or some other mound in the area that met a similar—or worse—fate.

Despite the disturbances to the summit of Mound B, it is otherwise relatively well preserved. The mound appears rectangular and oriented northeast–southwest at an angle of around 60 degrees. As we noted in Chapter 2, it measures 40 m x 18 m (131 × 59 ft) at the summit, 56 × 30 m (183 × 98 ft) at the base, and stands about 2 m (6.6 ft) above the surrounding marsh. Its western edge displays a sharp corner reminiscent of Mound A and several of the mounds at Crystal River. The shape and orthogonality suggest to us that it was indeed a flat-topped mound.

We placed a 1-×-4-m (3-×-13-ft) trench on the southern slope near the southwest corner of the mound, from the summit to near the base (Figure 7.7) (see also Pluckhahn et al. 2016). As with Mound A, our trench here indicated that the mound was constructed almost entirely of oyster shells. Also like Mound A, this mound appears to have been stepped. Although the evidence here was more equivocal, owing to the lesser slope and the fact that our trench was slightly oblique to the main axis of the mound,

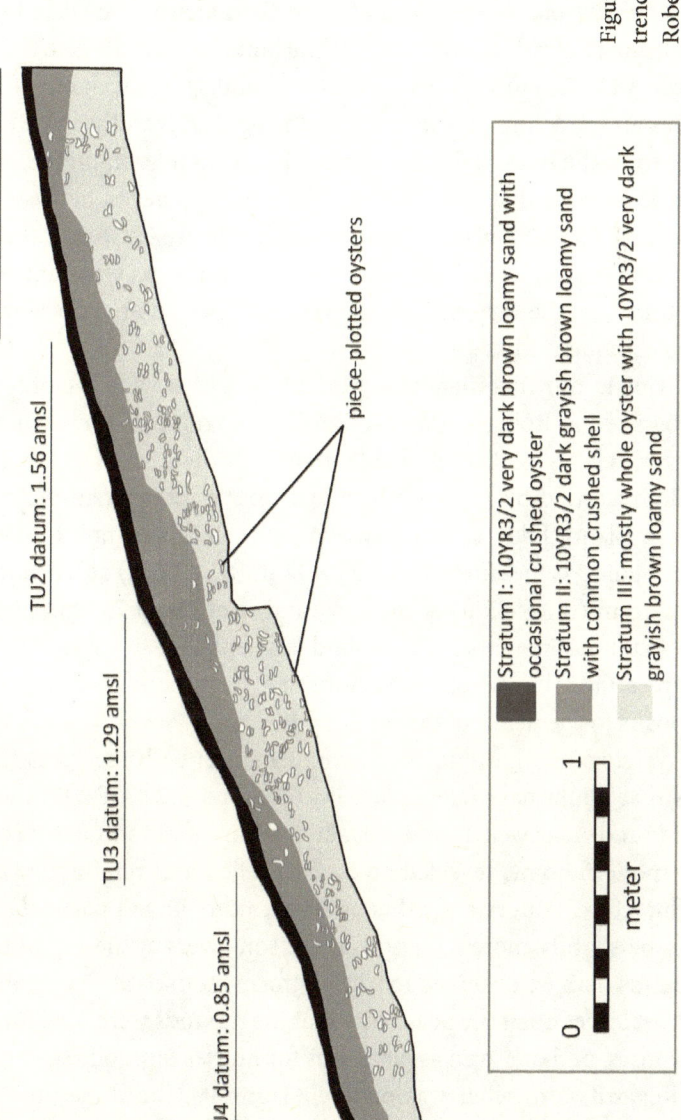

Figure 7.7. Profile of the trench on Mound B at Roberts Island.

the profile revealed five possible steps. We hypothesize that there might have been one or two more, given that our trench did not reach the base of the mound and the possibility that the summit was truncated by modern disturbances.

Similar to Mound A, the fill of Mound B consisted almost exclusively of oyster shells; but we were again fortunate to identify one deer bone from our trench for radiocarbon dating. The bone produced a date with a range of cal A.D. 1025 to 1155 (95 percent probability) (Pluckhahn et al. 2016). Bayesian modeling produces limited insights, given that this is a single date from the mound fill, but using this date as a *terminus post quem* our model suggests that construction of the mound began between *cal A.D. 1034 and 1200 (95 percent probability)*, probably between *cal A.D. 1055 and 1165 (68 percent)*. This suggests that the mound was built soon after Mound A, at the very end of the Woodland period or at the beginning of the subsequent Mississippian period.

Prior to our investigations, Mounds A and B were the only mounds recognized at Roberts Island. LiDAR data, confirmed by archaeological survey, reveals another probable mound to the east on site 8CI39, originally recorded by Ripley Bullen and now a rather inauspicious, small marsh island. Like the other two mounds in this complex, Mound C is rectangular. It measures about 25 × 17 m (82 × 56 ft) at the summit and 33 × 26 m (108 × 85 ft) at the base, and rises about 75 cm (2.5 ft) above the surrounding marsh. The mound is oriented at an angle of around 120 degrees. One shovel test on the summit of the mound revealed dense shell deposits to the depth of the water table.

We currently have no specific information with regard to the activities that might have taken place on these mounds. GPR on the summit of Mound A, as well as on the small portion of Mound B not covered by the modern home, revealed no distinct reflections reminiscent of formal architecture. Pottery and other artifacts, although not particularly dense, may be slightly more common in the soil layers at the top of these two mounds than we observed for the platform mounds at Crystal River. This at least leaves open the possibility that the mounds were used for different purposes, perhaps even as platforms for houses or public structures.

Regardless of what was on their summits, the three mounds were clearly built for ceremonial purposes and with deliberate forethought. In addition to the stepped construction of Mound A and its alignment with the cardinal directions, there is greater patterning that suggests the

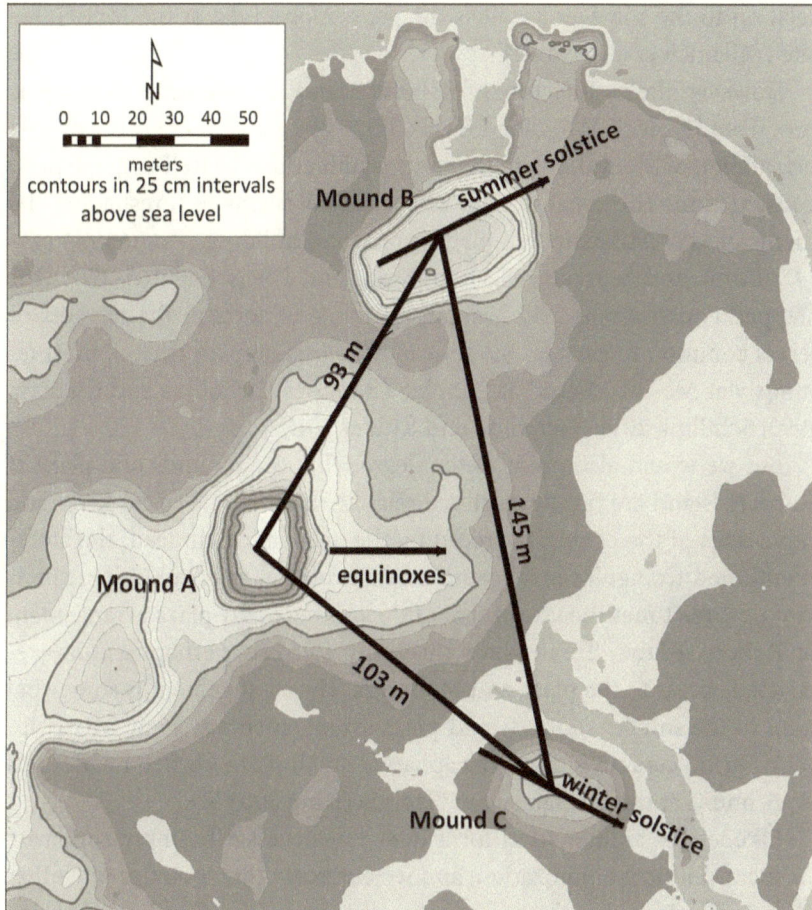

Figure 7.8. Spatial relationships among the mounds at Roberts Island and possible relations to astronomical events.

mounds formed an integrated ceremonial complex. Mounds B and C are in roughly complementary positions with respect to Mound A at distances of 93 and 103 m (305 and 338 ft), respectively (Figure 7.8). They are also at roughly complementary angles to each other and Mound A. There is also evidence that the mounds were arranged with respect to astronomical concerns. The possible stairs, or ramp, on Mound A, as well as the adjoining plaza, are oriented due east with the rising sun on the equinox. Mounds B and C appear to be oriented roughly to the rising and setting sun at the solstices. The triangular arrangement of mounds here and their relation to the solstices parallels the pattern observed at the McKeithen site (Milanich et al. 1994:92).

However, the architecture of Roberts Island also seems to us a departure from "typical" Woodland forms. First, of course, there is the precise orientation of Mound A with the cardinal directions, as well as the stepped construction. The concern with directionality seems to foreshadow elements of later Mississippian platform mound building (Payne 1994:143–147; Payne and Scarry 1998:39–41; Stout and Lewis 1998:165–170). The stepped construction may have an analogue of sorts in the terraces or levels common to earthen mounds of the Mississippian period, most famously at Monks Mound at Cahokia (Bareis 1975; Collins and Chalfant 1993; Schilling 2013; Sherwood and Kidder 2011).

But we would also point to the degree that the mounds and plaza at Roberts Island are tightly clustered relative to those at Crystal River and other sites of the centuries preceding the occupation. Indeed, the aforementioned triangular arrangement of mounds at the McKeithen site is two or three times the size of that of the mounds-and-plaza arrangement at Roberts Island. This tighter clustering suggests perhaps a more restricted access to the plaza and Mound A. The arrangement is somewhat akin to the smaller mounds-and-plaza arrangements at some Mississippian period centers, such as the apparent small plaza formed by Mounds A, B, and C at the Etowah site in Georgia (King 2003:51).

Likeness of architectural form does not necessarily imply similarity in socio-political organization, and we currently can't point to any other clear indications that the community at Roberts Island and neighboring islands was organized hierarchically, with something akin to the "chiefs" of the Mississippian period. However, it is commonly agreed that it was about this time that chiefdoms developed in southwest Florida (Marquardt 2014; Patton 2001; Widmer 1988). Widmer (1988) credits the development of these chiefdoms to steady population growth over the course of the Woodland period, leading to a filling in of the landscape, or a "population circumscription" as it commonly referred to by archaeologists. With the landscape full and population levels approaching carrying capacity, villages could no longer easily "fission" (bud off) to form new villages when conflicts developed. This encouraged the development of centralized political authority to manage the harvesting of critical resources, implement group labor activities, and coordinate defense (Widmer 1988:222–223).

Marquardt (2014:10) has recently appraised Widmer's model based on more recent work in the area. While agreeing that chiefdoms developed around A.D. 800 in the Caloosahatchee area, he takes issue with crediting this development to circumscription and conflict; although plausible, it "has yet to be demonstrated that key resources were limited enough to necessitate the imposition of this level of coercive power." As Marquardt notes, there is no evidence for palisaded villages or skeletal trauma.

Many of these same objections predicate application of Widmer's model to Roberts Island and associated settlements. While settlement data for the region is lacking in many respects, we see no evidence that the population of this area had reached carrying capacity or that the landscape was necessarily filled. The plaza at Roberts Island may have had restricted access, as we noted above, but the settlement was almost certainly not palisaded. True arrowheads, in the form of triangular Pinellas points, appeared for the first time during this period in southwest Florida (Dietler 2008:445), and there is an example from one of our shovel tests at Roberts Island (O'Neal 2016), but this hardly constitutes evidence for intensive conflict. Still, as we noted above with regard to the faunal and isotope data, there appears to have been a shift to the reliance on oysters, especially those from beds farther offshore. These oyster beds represent an example of a "zero sum resource," meaning one that is relatively fixed and overexploitable to the point of low or no regeneration (Carballo 2013:10). Resources of this type may be subject to corporate ownership and exclusion, although they may also be managed as a common property resource through collective social institutions or leaders with threat of sanction (Ostrom 1990).

As an alternative to Widmer's model, Marquardt (2014:12–13) suggests that deteriorating natural resources ca. A.D. 500–850 fostered a higher level of coordination and technological innovation, as evidenced by canal building, trade, and water storage facilities (water courts). As conditions improved with the onset of the Medieval Warm period, interregional connectivity intensified and contributed to the development of hierarchical social organization through both greater cooperation and competition. As we noted earlier, this might have also been linked to shifts in household organization, specifically a transition from single-family residence to larger co-resident corporate groups (Thompson et al. 2014).

We have noted above several lines of possible connection between Roberts Island and the Caloosahatchee area that seem consistent with the heightened connectivity that Marquardt hypothesizes. We would also note the recovery from Roberts Island of a cube of galena, an item of trade that has also been found on Caloosahatchee IIB and III sites (Marquardt 2014:14). However, we currently don't see evidence from either faunal (Compton 2014; Duke 2015) or pollen (Jackson 2016) data that environmental conditions in the Crystal River area deteriorated quite as badly in the interval from A.D. 500 to 850 as seems to have been the case in southwest Florida. We also can't speak of any major technological changes; there are no canals at Roberts Island or elsewhere on the central Gulf Coast, and the single "water court" was probably not a water storage facility.

Nevertheless, portions of the models proposed by both Widmer and Marquardt seem consistent with developments during Phase 4 at Roberts Island. We noted above the increased reliance on oysters, particularly those from higher-saline habitats closer to the Gulf (Thompson et al. 2015). But it is also worth noting that recent isotope study suggests that oyster shells from Roberts Island display less variability in terms of habitat relative to those from earlier contexts at Crystal River (Lulewicz et al. 2017). This could be consistent with the sort of fixed-resource ownership central to Widmer's model of the development of political hierarchy, as well as Marquardt's hypothesis of more-coordinated labor. Specifically, we suggest the possibility that in earlier phases small subsistence production groups (individual households or a few related households) worked mainly independently to target dispersed resources that were collectively owned and managed by the community, with considerable sharing of the returns reinforced by social and religious institutions. Conversely, in Phase 4 larger corporate kin groups (such as matrilineages) may have worked more independently, targeting specific resource locales that they owned and managed for themselves, and to the exclusion of other such groups. These kin groups may have merged together to retain exclusive access to resource areas they could not defend on their own, perhaps initially into something akin to the loosely confederated "tribelets" of aboriginal California (Bettinger 2015:145) (and possibly represented by Roberts Island and related settlements) but later into the more hierarchical and territorial chiefdoms of the Mississippian period.

Dietler (2008) has proposed another model for the development of chiefdoms in the Caloosahatchee area around A.D. 800. Noting an increase in the quantities of shell cutting-edge tools at certain sites in the area—especially mound centers—he suggests that elites monopolized the production of these woodworking tools. Dietler believes that elites furnished these tools to woodworkers, who in turn provided them with canoes, religious items, and labor to construct monuments. As we have already mentioned, shell tools litter the surface of Roberts Island. However, these are not the *Busycon* cutting-edge tools that are most useful for woodworking (Dietler 2008). They might have been used mainly for breaking up large clusters of oysters (Menz 2013, 2016), although we can't rule out the possibility that they were employed in some sort of craft production, as we mention again below.

Patton (2001) provides yet another take on the development of chiefdoms in the Caloosahatchee area in the interval coeval with Phase 4 at Roberts Island. While not discounting the influences of environment and resource productivity, he stresses the religious-based foundations of leadership that had developed earlier in the Woodland period. Specifically, he suggests that Caloosahatchee elites transitioned from mortuary specialists to the controllers of critical productive goods and services. Particularly important was the control of lightning whelk shells, in demand both in local exchange (primarily for their use as tools) and in interregional exchange (mainly as symbolic artifacts, and as evidenced by their recovery in burials at sites in the interior).

Patton's model is attractive for explaining possible changes in the nature of leadership at Roberts Island, in that there was clearly a precedent here for leadership positions based in mortuary rituals. Lightning whelk was not available locally, but communities at Roberts Island would have been well positioned to serve as mediators between the source areas in southwest Florida and areas of the interior where shells were in demand. People living here may have used this location to fill other trade niches as well. For example, shell beads are at least slightly more common in the midden at Roberts Island than at Crystal River. We also recovered a chert microdrill of a form similar to that which has been identified as a specialized tool for working shell in several areas of North America (Trubitt 2003:253).

However, we probably don't need to invoke ecological, economic, or religious reasons for the changes that take place at Roberts Island in Phase 4. As more complex societies formed to the south, and perhaps elsewhere in the region, the community here may have emulated them, lest they gradually lose population to the attraction of emerging centers elsewhere. We recall that the late Charles Hudson sometimes likened the advent of

Mississippian societies to the development of the I-formation in high school football in the 1950s: once one team adopted this offense, others had to follow suit to remain competitive.

As we have lamented elsewhere (Pluckhahn et al. 2016), central and southwestern Florida are rarely included in discussions of the Late Woodland period or Mississippian origins, probably because of their geographic isolation from the Mississippian heartland in the American Bottom and the seeming dissimilarities in subsistence and material culture. But we suspect that there must have been exchanges of materials and information—whether direct or indirect—between these regions. Marine shell beads (probably from Gulf Coast sources) and ceramic effigies of whelk shell cups appear in terminal Late Woodland Lindeman phase contexts at Range and other sites in the American Bottom (Marquardt and Kozuch 2016; Kozuch 2013). We have not yet sourced the cube of galena found at Roberts Island, but Austin and colleagues' (2000) analysis (see also Donop et al. 2016) suggests that much of the galena from Florida sites can be traced to southeastern Missouri—probably the same source as for the galena found in the nearby American Bottom (Austin et al. 2000; Pauketat et al. 1998:39; Walthall 1981). In the context of these connections, we should perhaps not be surprised that Mississippian peoples may have drawn on a tradition of platform mound construction that was maintained, and perhaps elaborated on, by the people at sites like Roberts Island. At the least, central and southwestern Florida should not be so easily excluded from discussions of the geopolitics of the terminal Late Woodland and Mississippian emergence. As Patton (2001:357–8) has suggested, "Perhaps . . . the process of political development in the lower Mississippian Southeast was stimulated by precocious Gulf-coastal political complexity."

Somewhat ironically, then, the same forces that precipitated the development of more complex societies in southwestern Florida and in portions of the interior Southeast may have ultimately led to the decline of Roberts Island. The Mississippian population centers that developed after the big bang at Cahokia around A.D. 1050 were probably powerful attractors. One such population center appears to be represented by the Safety Harbor culture in the Tampa Bay area to the south (Austin and Mitchem 2014; Austin et al. 2014; Mitchem 1989). Another was the Fort Walton area of the Panhandle to the north (Marrinan and White 2007; White 2014). Mississippian (Safety Harbor) components have been recorded for the

Crystal River area, including a cemetery excavated by Rainey (1935) at the Buzzard's Island site just upstream. For the most part, however, the available settlement data suggest this area was gradually depopulated over the course of the Mississippian period. Where during the Woodland period it seems that villages were more or less spread across the length of the Gulf Coast, with the Mississippian period these settlements were more concentrated in certain locations, with vast expanses of unoccupied terrain between these clusters. The novel institutions and communities that people at Crystal River and Roberts Island constructed over the course of the Woodland period were instrumental to the Mississippian way of life, even as they were fundamentally altered.

8

The Early Village at Crystal River in Broader Perspective

Approaching Crystal River as a case study in the historical process of becoming villagers, rather than from the rubric of "complex hunter-gatherers," as might be conventionally expected, allows us to avoid problems with the latter term and its conceptualization, as we discussed in Chapter 1. However complex we characterize societies of this sort, the term "hunter-gather" arguably retains a diminutive connotation, owing to the legacy of evolutionary thinking. More to the point, we think it more illuminating to position Crystal River with respect to early villages of similar scale and complexity, even if it does not necessarily share the same subsistence base.

The early-village approach also places Crystal River in a context that encourages consideration of the full suite of novel social and ecological challenges that sedentary villagers must have confronted (Bandy and Fox 2010:2). We have tried to give equal consideration to both sorts of challenges. The people of Crystal River adapted to changing environmental conditions, some—such as storm surges—that were perhaps very rapid and others longer term, some the result of planetary processes, and other perhaps the result of their own or their ancestors' agency. But the people of Crystal River and Roberts Island also adapted to living together in social groups that were larger, more permanent, and more varied.

Framing Crystal River as a case study in the formation of early village societies also has the advantage of allowing us to engage with current debates regarding the role of competition and cooperation in the development of human societies. We give weight to both competition and cooperation, drawing insights from both evolutionary and more historical perspectives on this matter. The village at Crystal River appears to have formed in the absence of any severe conflict in the region, although we don't rule out competition for either subsistence resources or prestige goods in a landscape that was becoming increasingly filled. Ritual seems to have been key to both the foundation and maintenance of cooperation at the village and regional levels, although it is clear that some individuals, as well as some larger social groups and perhaps even whole communities, may have been in competition for prestige. With the eventual dissolution of the village, such tensions may have been exacerbated.

The final advantage of our framing of this study around the process of becoming villagers is that it provides a means for placing the history of Crystal River in a larger framework. Our understanding of this history of Crystal River is based on nearly a decade of archaeological field and laboratory work, as described in Chapter 2. Recognizing that Crystal River is a protected site with a troubled history of poorly controlled and inadequately reported excavations, we have emphasized minimally invasive fieldwork and the analysis of previous collections. Still, our work provides a relatively fine level of spatial and temporal control. Indeed, with regard to the latter, the more than 60 radiocarbon dates from Crystal River alone represent a tenfold increase over the dates that have been previously obtained, making Crystal River among the most thoroughly dated archaeological sites in eastern North America.

Chapters 3–7 traced the history of the early village at Crystal River. Although we have at times engaged with the broader literature on early village societies, our emphasis thus far has been on *how* rather than *why* the people of Crystal River became villagers. This approach is typical of the paradigmatic turn that Pauketat (2001a, 2001b) has termed "historical processualism." We are not new to this perspective. Pluckhahn (2002, 2003)—perhaps one of the earliest adopters of historical processualism—used this perspective to demonstrate how the interpretation of one of Crystal River's contemporaries, the Kolomoki site in Georgia, was misled by typological thinking. Thompson (2007; Thompson and Andrus 2011), in his work at the Late Archaic shell rings on Sapelo Island on the coast of Georgia, employed a similar approach to describe variability in the formation histories of such structures.

Yet we also acknowledge that emphasis on local histories alone runs the risk of parochialism. As Kowalewski (2006:94–95) notes:

> Anthropology is more than the sum of all local histories; it is something more like the multiplication of histories, in which there are

regularities in pattern and process and experiences shared by virtue of similar cause and effect as well as common tradition.

Robb and Pauketat (2013:5), while perhaps not sharing Kowalewski's vision for the foundations or aims of anthropology, have similarly bemoaned the recent tendency in archaeology to redefine "all the big questions of the past to be little questions."

This call for greater attention to "pattern and process and experiences" does not mean unbridled theorizing or generalization, but instead the identification of regularities in well-documented case studies. We think Kowalewski's recent work on "coalescent societies" exemplifies this approach. Drawing from Ethridge and Hudson's (2002) use of this term to describe the social formations of the early historic American Southeast, Kowalewski showed how the concept could be applied more broadly to describe a historical pattern of indigenous response to upheaval, especially demographic collapse in the colonial milieu but also social collapse in the era before contact. Since its initial fleshing out by Kowalewski, the concept of coalescent societies has been applied widely (and perhaps at times a bit uncritically) to societies of the late precontact and early historic eras in the Southeast (e.g., Lawres 2014; Regnier 2014) and across much of North America (Birch 2012; Hill et al. 2004).

In the remainder of this concluding chapter, we take a similar approach to the identification of pattern and process in the development of early village societies. Building from our work at Crystal River, we look for regularities that might be typical of this transition on the Gulf Coast, consistent with the notion that population aggregations such as this one are often not isolated but instead part of a regional process (Kowalewski 2013:203). We focus particularly on an unfortunately limited number of sites where archaeological investigations provide sufficient spatial and temporal control to reconstruct the lived experience of the process of early village formation: the Garden Patch site to the north of Crystal River on the Gulf Coast, as recently described by Wallis and colleagues (Wallis and McFadden 2013, 2014, 2016; Wallis et al. 2015); the McKeithen site in the interior of the Florida peninsula, as documented by Milanich and colleagues (1997); and the Kolomoki site in southwestern Georgia, as revealed by work by Pluckhahn (2003, 2010a, 2010b, 2013) and Sears (1956), and more recently by Menz (2015) and West (2016), both singly and in combination with Pluckhahn and Wallis (Pluckhahn et al. 2018). Drawing primarily from these case studies, we present eight postulates about early village societies on the Gulf Coast.

Although we limit our search for process mainly to our region of study, we also look to the literature from other areas of the world to judge which of these postulates might be more broadly generalizable and, on the other hand, which may be unique to the particular historical development of Crystal River and neighboring early villages. Here, we are reliant on those areas of the world where archaeologists have approached the topic of early villages in greatest detail: the Basketmaker and Pithouse periods in the American Southwest (Kohler et al. 2004; Kohler and Varien 2012; Mabry et al. 1997; Rautman 2014, 2016; Wilshusen 1991; Wilshusen and Potter 2010); the Formative era in highland Mesoamerica (Flannery 1976; Lesure et al. 2013; Marcus 2008; Marcus and Flannery 1996; Whalen 1983) and highland South America (Bandy 2004, 2006); and the Neolithic Near East (Byrd 1994, 2005; Hole et al. 1969; Kuijt 2000; Nelson 2004).

Our format draws from Kowalewski's approach to coalescent societies, as do some of our postulates. This is not surprising, given that early village formation was also a kind of coalescence, but we think a process sufficiently different from those described under the label of coalescent societies to merit unique description. Unlike coalescent societies, the aggregation into early villages was presumably not—at least in most cases—a response to demographic decline or socio-political collapse.

As we point out below, there are a number of convergences in terms of the processes that led to the emergence of early villages in various regions throughout the world. However, there also appear to be some components of the history of Crystal River that have no analogue, or at the very least are not well represented in other areas of study. At the conclusion of the chapter, we consider what these similarities and differences mean for the study of early village societies and exactly what we have learned about this process from our work at Crystal River.

1. Early Villages on the Gulf Coast Developed from Vacant Ceremonial Centers

As described in Chapter 3, current radiocarbon evidence suggests that at least two burial mound features (Mounds C and F) were initiated at Crystal River several centuries before the village was first occupied even seasonally. Although some of these dates from these mounds are potentially problematic, recent analysis of ceramic vessels recovered from one of the burial mounds provides support for the early construction of the burial mounds, in that the assemblages lean disproportionately to early, podal-supported vessel forms that are rare in the village.

Similarly, at Kolomoki radiocarbon dates from the burial mounds (Mounds D and E) or specialized deposits below them are among the earliest from the site (Pluckhahn 2003:Table 2.3; Pluckhahn, Menz, West, and Wallis 2018). The pattern is less clear for Garden Patch and McKeithen, although there are anomalously early dates from mounds at these sites (Milanich et al. 1997:104; Wallis et al. 2015); at the least it appears that mound construction was coincident with village formation. Farther afield, but remaining for the moment in the American Southeast, Wright (2013:142–143) describes ritual feasting in the pre-mound layers at the Garden Creek site in North Carolina and laments the insufficient published details on similar patterns at other sites in the region.

The literature on early villages elsewhere in the world does not seem to support the broader applicability of this postulate; we see no evidence that early villages in the American Southwest, Mexico, South America, or the Near East routinely developed from vacant ceremonial centers (although in the latter area there are separate sites focused mainly on ritual, such as Göbekli Teppe [Goring-Morris and Belfer-Cohen 2010:60]). Perhaps the historical trajectory of village formation on the Gulf Coast differs on this point because of the reliance on fishing-hunting-gathering, with a resultant slower pace in their commitment to sedentism than is evident for Neolithic farmers (Bandy 2005, 2008). Unlike for emergent agricultural villages, growing populations along the Gulf Coast had vast areas of plentiful resources to take advantage of before population pressure exerted any noticeable effects. We touch on this point in Chapter 3 in our argument for the location of Crystal River as being just one of a host of locales suitable for the growth of such a center with respect to natural resources.

We suspect that ceremonial centers in our region might have provided something like a neutral ground for the foundation of inclusive communities from more diverse and dispersed origins. One might also imagine that an origin rooted in ritual provided the nascent leadership with something akin to a divine or ancestral charter in the absence of clear hereditary claims to such privilege. The eventual transition to early villages may have been more than simply fortuitous. As we noted in Chapter 3, Clay (2013:70) has suggested that some Hopewell burial mounds were planned for extended ritual. Similarly, Creese (2013) describes the buildings on some early village sites as "anticipatory" in the sense that these were "planned and constructed to accommodate anticipated long-term reoccupation and maintenance" by an enduring social group.

2. Once Settled, Early Villages on the Gulf Coast Developed Quickly and in Parallel with Neighboring Peers

Radiocarbon evidence suggests that the midden at Crystal River grew quickly in thickness and areal extent in the two earliest phases of occupation, as we described in Chapters 4 and 5. Carbon dates from the lower levels of widely spaced test units are roughly contemporaneous, indicating that the arcuate village plan developed early, rather than from gradual expansion.

Although Kolomoki is less intensively dated than Crystal River, Pluckhahn (2003:183–198) has suggested from ceramic evidence that the circular village there developed relatively rapidly in the interval from around A.D. 350 to 550. More recent work suggests that this period of rapid growth was later in time but probably more sudden (Menz 2015; Pluckhahn, Menz, West, and Wallis 2018; West 2016). Milanich and colleagues (1997:89) see a similarly speedy growth in the village at McKeithen. Wallis and colleagues (2015) have recently extended the same pattern to Garden Patch, describing rapid village formation beginning in the fourth century.

This pattern of brisk growth of early villages seems extendable to other areas of the world. Rautman (2014:189) notes that at least some of the villages in the American Southwest grew dramatically in a short amount of time. Goring-Morris and Bar-Cohen (2010:67) use the term "exponential" to describe the increase in the number, size, and scale of Neolithic villages in the Near East.

The rapidity of village development suggests that these communities were the product of coordinated strategies of aggregation, rather than a slow and steady process of population growth or settlement relocation. The seeming contemporaneity across widely spaced village centers indicates that this was a strategy that rippled across regions. The pattern seems consistent with the portrayal of early villages, at least at a regional level, as defensive groups (Roscoe 2013).

3. Early Villages on the Gulf Coast Exhibited Formal, Open Arrangements of Households

The pattern for the Woodland period on the northern Gulf Coast and adjacent interior regions is now well established, with an overwhelming predominance of circular or U-shaped villages (Bense 1998; Milanich et al. 1997; Pluckhahn 2003, 2010b; Russo et al. 2006; Stephenson et al. 2002; Willey 1949a:403). Kolomoki is exceptional for its size, with a village nearly a kilometer in diameter and a plaza minimally measuring 300 m long (Pluckhahn 2003, 2010b), but in form it is similar to McKeithen (Milanich et al. 1997), Garden Patch (Wallis et al. 2015), and dozens of sites in the region. Wallis and colleagues (2015) suggest that the circular village at Garden Patch "followed a pre-conceived site plan." At Crystal River (Pluckhahn, Thompson, and Cherkinsky 2015), and perhaps generally on sites of the southern peninsular Gulf Coast, the trend is to arcuate rather than circular shell middens, but the formality and openness of the arrangement is comparable.

The pattern of open arrangements of houses around common areas is characteristic of early villages in the American Southwest (Rautman 2014) and highland Mesoamerica (Flannery 1976). It is less clearly the case for highland South America, but this may be because domestic areas there are less frequently exposed in their entirety (Bandy 2006). It is clearly not the case for Neolithic sites in the Near East. For example, at Hallan Çemi in eastern Anatolia, one of the earliest villages in the region, houses faced away from each other and from open areas, a layout that would have promoted household privacy (Rosenberg and Redding 2000:57).

In his survey and exploration of settlement types, Ole Grøn (1991:107–108) notes that the pattern of houses arranged in a circular fashion (e.g., around a plaza) is typical of more or less egalitarian social relationships. Kowalewski (2006:117) describes open layouts as a distinguishing feature of coalescent societies and credits this design to the promotion of community integration. We, along with others, have argued the same for early villages in our region (Pluckhahn 2003, 2010b; Pluckhahn, Menz, West, and Wallis 2018; Sanger 2015; Thompson 2006, 2007).

However, we recognize that this integration was achieved not simply through fostering a common identity, and a review of similar patterns on early villages elsewhere serves as a reminder of this. Rautman (2016:125) suggests that while circular villages might appear to be an expression of integrated and communal society in which individual needs were subsumed to those of the larger social group, they were tied to demographic change, social uncertainty, and conflict; she calls circular villages "an uneasy but workable group identity." Graves and Van Keuren (2011:264) propose that the panoptic, plaza-oriented village layouts of Pueblo communities in the American Southwest reflect the perpetuation of a social order wherein "the practices of individuals and groups that constitute whole communities are constantly monitored." Such monitoring may have been an important means of maintaining order in communities that lacked clearly established leadership hierarchies.

We also recognize that at Crystal River and other mound-village locales there would seem to have been more tensions as the creation of public architecture both physically and symbolically altered the landscape. As Grøn (1991:108) notes, equality in status in a circular village is predicated on the assumption that dwellings face one another on visually and physically open isotropic surfaces. The arcuate layout of Crystal River, as well as the altered landscape with its large public architecture, would have promoted openness to the site while at the same moment elevating certain households, individuals, and groups in prestige.

4. Early Villages on the Gulf Coast Included Integrative Public Architecture

The circular villages of the northern Gulf Coast define empty spaces commonly interpreted as plazas (Bense 1998; Milanich et al. 1997; Pluckhahn 2003, 2010b; Russo et al. 2006). Excavations in several of the plazas on Middle Woodland sites in the region have typically revealed few, if any, features (Milanich et al. 1997; Pluckhahn 2003). One exception is the Bernath Place site, where Bense (1998) identified more than 100 burials within the central plaza. At Garden Patch and McKeithen and most other circular villages in the region, the plazas are proportional to the village and of sufficient size to have incorporated at least the local population, while the huge plaza at Kolomoki could have easily held many thousands of people more than the few hundred who are estimated to have resided there permanently (Pluckhahn 2003:190–191). The plaza at Crystal River is unusual in that is defined by mounds rather than midden. Still, like the plaza at Kolomoki and others in the region, it is relatively large and unrestricted.

As with the open village plan, we see the large and unrestricted plazas as evidence of deliberate strategy of community integration. Beyond the monitoring we describe above, the centralization of community ceremonial space may be evidence of symbolic "bonding" that strengthened ties between members of social groups (Kolb and Snead 1997:621), a bond further reinforced through community-wide performance and ceremony (Pluckhahn 2010a, 2010b).

Pluckhahn (2010b) has drawn analogy between plazas and the kivas found in early villages in the American Southwest, which are often assumed to have played an important role in integrating societies through their use in rituals by either the community as a whole or by representatives of the community (Adler and Wilshusen 1990; Bandy 2004:330; Stanish 2004:17–18; Wilshusen 1991). In the Neolithic Near East, public architecture most famously included silos, walls, and towers at sites like Jericho (Belfer-Cohen and Bar-Yosef 2000:30) (although the famous early village at Çatalhöyük apparently lacks communal structures [Hastorf 2010:147]). These are less clearly integrative in the sense of providing a forum for interaction for the community or constituent representatives. But Rosenberg and Redding (2000:48–49) note other public structures that may have been more amenable to this function. At early village sites in highland Mexico, public structures on raised platforms have been interpreted as men's houses (Marcus and Flannery 1996:87). In highland South America, plazas and sunken courtyards provided space for large-scale ceremony and feasting (Cohen 2010; Hastorf 2010).

5. Early Villages on the Gulf Coast Were Organized as Dualities

We have already mentioned the predominant pattern of circular or U-shaped villages; at Kolomoki the two halves of the village are opposed across a central axis composed of mounds and plaza, an arrangement that Pluckhahn and colleagues (Pluckhahn, Menz, West, and Wallis 2018) (see also Menz 2015:78–79; Pluckhahn 2003:189–190; West 2016:155–157) have interpreted as possible evidence of dual organization. Similar oppositions can be inferred from the placement of the two burial mounds and from the arrangement of crypts within the largest of these. Milanich and colleagues

(1997:189–190) describe a very similar bilateral symmetry to the layout of mounds and village at McKeithen. Crystal River lacks clear duality in the village layout, but as we discussed in Chapter 3, exhibits similar opposition in burial facilities, with mounds flanking opposite sides of the plaza; radiocarbon dates suggest the mounds are at least partially contemporaneous (Pluckhahn and Thompson 2017; Pluckhahn et al. 2010).

Evidence for dual organization is less clear for early village societies elsewhere. However, Rosenberg and Redding (2000:48–49) also note dual organization of public buildings at Hallan Çemi in the Near East. Kowalewski (2006), drawing from the ethnographies of Maybury-Lewis (1979a, 1979b) and others, describes similar evidence for dual organization in coalescent societies in Amazonia. As he suggests for that region, the dual organization of early villages in the Southeast and elsewhere may have been another tool for promoting the integration of formerly disparate groups into singular communities through complementary social and ceremonial obligations.

6. Early Villages on the Gulf Coast Included Collective Burial Facilities with Commingled Remains

Gordon Willey (1949a:404), based on his work at many burial mounds in the region, noted that in the Middle Woodland on the Gulf Coast "nearly all gifts to the dead were placed in a common mass deposit." The pattern is clearest at Kolomoki and sites of the northern Gulf Coast, where mass pottery deposits were commonly placed on the east side of mounds, separate from the burials. Interments most frequently took the form of secondary bundle burials, often placed in groups and occasionally clustered in pits or log-lined crypts. We suspect that the commingling of remains in a discrete cemetery was a strategy of incorporation, while also recognizing that many individuals were apparently excluded from this form of burial, as Clay (2014) has observed, and as we discussed in Chapter 3.

The closest analogue for this postulate may be with the Neolithic societies of the Near East, where Belfer-Cohen and Bar-Yosef (2000:26) note more mixed burials, especially secondary, in early village contexts. Kuijt (2000:143–144) suggests that secondary burial permits the scheduling of mortuary ceremonies at pre-arranged times that do not conflict with other tasks and also facilitates participation in community events that cross-cut kin and household (Kuijt 2000:144). Elsewhere, Whalen (1983:38) notes the appearance of formal, spatially discrete, specialized burial areas with both primary and secondary interments in discrete cemeteries in early villages in highland Mesoamerica. He suggests that these communal village cemeteries would have asserted the unity of the community.

7. Early Villagers on the Gulf Coast Crafted Distinctive Art That Was Widely Traded

The Middle Woodland penchant for the crafting and exchange of symbolically charged items is well established (Carr 2006; Seeman 1979). Crystal River is widely regarded as the southernmost major expression of Hopewellian trade, thanks to the large and diverse assemblage of copper and other exotic artifacts recovered by Moore (1901, 1907, 1918). Kolomoki, Garden Patch, and McKeithen have produced smaller but comparable assemblages of Hopewellian trade goods. Crystal River has produced, in addition to those from afar, copious quantities of shell cups, dippers, and gorgets. As we discuss in Chapter 5, recent work by Luer (2013) suggests the possibility that artisans at Crystal River crafted a distinctive type of circular shell gorget. However, exchange was not limited to exotics. The formation of early villages at Crystal River and other sites on the Gulf Coast was coincident with the appearance of the distinctive Swift Creek and Weeden Island pottery styles. Recent analyses by Wallis et al. (2016) indicate the regular movement of utilitarian Swift Creek pottery across hundreds of kilometers, with documented connections between Kolomoki, Garden Patch, and McKeithen.

This postulate appears generalizable to early village societies in other areas of the world. In highland South America, the development of the Yaya-Mama Religious Tradition, an artistic canon manifested in stone sculpture, ritual paraphernalia, public architecture, and iconography, is coincident with increases in village size (Cohen 2010:82–84). Ritual objects and pottery in the Olmec style are found at early villages in highland Mexico (Coe and Diehl 1980; Marcus and Flannery 1996). Rautman (2014:228) observes a standardized iconography found on pottery across a wide area of the American Southwest during the period of early village formation.

Kowalewski (2006:117) describes intensification of trade as a distinguishing feature of coalescent societies. We suspect that more formalized exchange relationships became of increasing importance as settlement contracted into fewer and more widely spaced villages. Belfer-Cohen and Bar-Yosef (2000:25) suggest that artistic activity creates a sense of group identity and loyalty.

8. Early Villages on the Gulf Coast Persist for Relatively Long Periods of Time

Crystal River epitomizes this trend, with extensive radiocarbon dating suggesting an occupational history of at least 600 years; settlement was more intensive in some phases than in others, but there were apparently no major periods of abandonment across this interval (Pluckhahn, Thompson, and Cherkinsky 2015). McKeithen may have had a similar longevity, although the radiocarbon evidence here is less conclusive. Kolomoki was occupied for at least 500 years, albeit with pronounced settlement shifts and perhaps at least one interval of abandonment (Pluckhahn, Menz, West, and Wallis 2018). Garden Patch was occupied for 300 years, abandoned for an interval of one or two centuries, and then reoccupied (Wallis et al. 2015). Longevity is relative, but it seems clear that the early villages of the Middle Woodland period persisted longer than their later Mississippian counterparts, which were notoriously prone to cycling on the order of a century or less (Anderson 1994).

It is unclear if the resilience of early villages in our region is typical of those elsewhere. Bandy and Fox (2010:15) suggest that in general early village societies were prone to fissioning. Yet many of the early villages in highland Mexico (Marcus and Flannery 1996) and the Near East seem to have had similarly long trajectories. We suspect that in our study area, this longevity may owe in part to leadership by collective, rather than individuals (Carr and Case 2006). This emphasis on horizontal over vertical connectivity, coupled with a diversified hunting-gathering-fishing subsistence base, may have also lent a greater degree of resilience to perturbations in climate (see Turck and Thompson 2016; Thompson and Turck 2009 regarding hunter-gatherer resilience).

Comparison of Crystal River and contemporaneous sites of the Gulf Coast with early village societies elsewhere thus reveals both similarities and differences. While we eschew viewing Crystal River as simply another example of so-called complex hunter-gatherers, we recognize that the marine and estuarine resources that formed the basis of the Crystal

River economy represent a resource base fundamentally different from that of domestic plant and animals, and this undoubtedly accounts for some of the differences observed between Crystal River and early village societies elsewhere in the world. However, for us the key difference is not that one resource base was "wild" and the other "domesticated." We suspect instead that the crucial differences may arise from variation in the temporality, technology, and sociality of production activities.

With regard to the former, the focus on marine and estuarine resources by the residents of Crystal River may have elicited different temporal rhythms than those that characterized early villages that relied on domesticated plants. While some of the fishes they depended on have annual cycles of availability not unlike those of domesticated plants, these are generally less predictable in time and space, and may conflict with one another in terms of scheduling (Widmer 1988:267). Sudden cold spells and influxes of freshwater introduced additional variability. Fishers had to pay attention to tidal regimes, including not only daily tidal variation but also lunar and seasonal patterns.

In terms of technology, many of the shellfish and some fishes that early villagers at Crystal River targeted could have been procured by individuals or small groups with simple technologies such as spears or lines. This is perhaps analogous to the relatively simple technologies associated with most horticulture. However, with the exception of shellfish like oysters, the locations of these resources are more variable. Moreover, some of the targeted species may have required both more labor and more labor-intensive technologies (e.g., boats, nets, and weirs) to produce and deploy.

Finally, some of the smaller fish that were favored by the early villagers at Crystal River could be smoked and stored for later consumption, perhaps in a manner not too dissimilar to crops. We wonder too if some animals such as turtles could have even been kept in pens like domesticated animals, as they were by historic-era settlers in the area. The people of Crystal River might also have been able to store wild plant foods like tubers. Nevertheless, it seems clear that most of the marine and estuarine resources that were the staples of people at Crystal River would have had to have been consumed immediately, unlike the domesticated plants and animals available to many early villagers elsewhere.

In light of these differences, village life here may have necessitated somewhat unique social institutions. Still we are struck more by the similarities than the differences between Crystal River and other early village societies, and these reinforce for us the understanding that the commitment to sedentary living in larger social groups was a more salient characteristic than subsistence. It is these convergences and departures that make Crystal River an important example of how the process of early villages played out differentially in the human past.

Afterword

Why Early Villages Still Matter

As one of the pivotal processes in the development of human societies, early villages are a worthy topic of study in their own right. However, we suggest that the lessons we learn from the archaeological study of early villages are not strictly academic but also reverberate in modern political discourse. While we would not characterize this study as a work of activist archaeology, we are convinced that archaeology can and should contribute to contemporary issues (Dawdy 2009; Pyburn 2007; Sabloff 2008). To be clear, we are not suggesting that the lessons we can learn from the archaeology of early villages are necessarily prescriptive; indeed, we are skeptical that small-scale social formations can provide much in the way of specific remedies to the problems faced by an ever more urbanized population of more than seven billion people. But we agree with Saitta (2013:144) that "we should not minimize the potential of public scholarship for producing critical thought about how the contemporary world came to be and how alternative arrangements for organizing human social life have different consequences and effects in the world." We find particular resonance for our study in two separate yet related issues of modern concern.

First, the previously discussed debate over the roles of competition and cooperation in the development of human societies has been implicated in contemporary political discourse regarding individual versus collective responsibility for social welfare. Proponents of the former position, some working from assumptions about innate competitiveness that mirror those of evolutionary scientists, believe that societies flourish when they are rooted in personal rights and responsibilities. These critics of social welfare programs sometimes look for evidence for their position in the historical record. Perhaps the most famous example is Marvin Olasky, whose book *The Tragedy of American Compassion* (Olasky 1992) has been praised by conservative politicians and formed the intellectual basis of President George W. Bush's "compassionate conservatism" (Grann 1999; Konczal 2014; Schwartz 1998). Olafsky argues that the system of private charitable organizations in place in America in the nineteenth century did a better job providing for the poor than the twentieth-century "welfare state," largely because the former placed greater moral demands on recipients of aid. Similarly, but emphasizing the personal responsibilities assumed to come with private property, David Schmidtz (1998) describes the initial failure of the Jamestown and Plymouth colonies as an indictment of communal social experiments, and the eventual success of these settlements as a triumph of private ownership. As with Olafsky's treatise, this argument has found currency with conservative commentators (Keating 2014).

Rooting suggestions for contemporary public policy in history or prehistory should be done with caution; historians and archaeologists know that reading the past is rarely straightforward. Konczal (2014) argues that Olafsky's premise is incorrect as a matter of history, in that "it ignores the complex interaction between public and private social insurance that has always existed in the United States." Schwartz (1990) presents an alternative reading of nineteenth-century reformers to illustrate that the attempt to "make the poor less poor by making them virtuous" was an outcome "devoutly to be wished, but seldom achieved." Similarly, the interpretation of Plymouth and Jamestown as exemplars of the failures of collective social welfare ignores key pieces of historical context. First, these settlements were actually common stock corporations with clear aspirations of profit, rather than communes (Bunker 2010; Kelso 2006). Next, Bunker (2010) suggests that while it may be true that the communal system of land tenure at Plymouth discouraged land improvement, this was mainly because parcels were rotated among families (who thus saw little justification for making improvements). Finally, William Kelso's (2006) archaeological excavations at Jamestown indicate that the early settlers did not lack in industriousness, and that the "failure" of the settlement owed more to factors of climate, geology, and geography. Perhaps the lesson here is that historians and archaeologists who work on small-scale social formations would do well to consider the implications of their work for contemporary debates regarding social welfare and collective government, lest others do it for them.

It is difficult to reconstruct systems of tenure of land, estuarine, and marine resources from the archaeological record for Crystal River and Roberts Island. The same is true for the organization of labor to harvest these resources. We suggested in Chapter 3 that people began cooperating in mortuary ceremonies and mound construction projects before they began working collectively toward subsistence-related ends, as indicated by the fact that the population was initially dispersed around a vacant ceremonial center. We assume that as people began to settle at the site more permanently in Phases 1 and 2 they probably began fishing collectively more frequently, and there is some evidence for this in the faunal data showing an increase in fish that would have likely been trapped in nets, the production and employment of which may have required more coordinated labor by larger groups. At the same time, isotopic studies of oysters from these phases at Crystal River indicate collection from varying habitats, suggesting productive groups likely shared access to particular resource locations. However, the oyster isotope data for Phases 3 and 4 suggest less variation in habitat, raising the possibility that as the population dispersed again and the new center emerged at Roberts Island, particular groups might have taken ownership of fixed shellfishing locations. Thus, in earlier phases smaller small groups (individual households or a few related households) appear to have worked mainly independently to satisfy their subsistence needs, targeting resources that were loosely owned and managed by the community as a whole. By our latest phase, however, larger corporate groups may have worked cooperatively on resources that they owned and managed for themselves, to the exclusion of other such groups. We take two lessons from this case study with regard to collective welfare.

First, collective ownership in this case was apparently effective, in that it persisted in one form or another for at least several centuries. There is some evidence of overharvesting, in the form of a decline in the average size of oysters and the disappearance of hardshell clams, but we don't see evidence for severe degradation of the resource base—there was no apparent "tragedy of the commons" (Hardin 1968) here. Likewise, there are indications from burials of variation in status and perhaps wealth, but differences among households appear to have been relatively minimal.

However, our second lesson is that the development and maintenance of systems of collective ownership and production were not easy. Assuming that at some level evolutionary theorists are correct in that ritual and mound construction are a form of costly signaling to discourage free-riders, or at least a means to establish a common worldview and moral order to facilitate group labor as suggested by some collective action theorists, the scale of these activities at Crystal River would seem to suggest that the system required considerable and sustained effort. And while this strategy apparently worked for several centuries, it may have been fragile enough to fall apart in Phases 3 and 4, perhaps in response to the environmental perturbations that we see evidence for in these intervals. We are reminded here of Blanton and Fargher's caution (2013:115) that cooperation at societal scales comes about "only with difficulty and against great odds ... often requiring cultural and social restructuring of society from top to bottom." Put another way, as Kowalewski (2013:215) has recently stated, "the process required extraordinary physical and social work."

We think our research also has implications for another strand of contemporary political discourse, specifically the human role in, and response to, environmental change. In his 1929 book *From Eden to Sahara, Florida's Tragedy*, botanist John Small (1929:36) lamented the accelerating human toll on the landscape of Crystal River:

> The preceding pages refer much to Florida's yesterday through the kitchen-middens. Approaching the head of the river the view of the large pencil factory at Crystal River brought to mind the evolution of Florida's today and reminded us of the fast approaching extermination of native floral life in Florida. The red-cedar is being used up for lead-pencils—or should we say has been; the pine for fruit-crates, the hickory for wheel-spokes and tool-handles. The animals, even in the deepest hammocks, are likewise being exterminated—for "sport"; and the ground itself is being drained and burned until it is unproductive. What is to be Florida's tomorrow?

Small's question rings even more urgently today than it did 90 years ago. As we write this book, scientists have only relatively recently proposed the concept of the Anthropocene, the modern geologic epoch for which there is abundant evidence that humanity has come to play a pivotal role in all of the Earth's systems, although its start date is hotly debated (Certini and Scalenghe 2011; Crutzen and Steffen 2003; Ruddiman et al.

2011; Ruddiman et al. 2015). With the steady accumulation of supporting evidence, the concept is finding widespread acceptance among scientists; however, the vast majority of the work has privileged an emphasis on atmospheric alterations by humans as the primary marker of the Anthropocene. As more archaeologists have begun to engage with this discussion, new lines of evidence are now beginning to be considered that illustrate the complex ways humans altered their environments in the past. These new markers of the Anthropocene include animal and plant domestication, extinctions, transportation of species, and, most important for our purposes, the deposition of anthropogenic sediments (e.g., shell) (Braje and Erlandson 2013; Edgeworth 2014; Erlandson 2013; Erlandson and Braje 2013; Smith and Zeder 2013). The looming question is what—if anything—might be done to reverse or mitigate its manifestation in warming temperatures and rising sea levels. Meanwhile, political debate—at least in the United States—continues to revolve around whether these effects are even real, let alone human-induced. The disconnect between science and public discourse stems at least partially from our lack of appreciation of the degree to which people of the past have played a role in, and adapted to, environmental change—a problem that Swanson (2017) has recently described as the "banality of the anthropocene."

Early villages were arguably a key development in the changes that characterize the Anthropocene. Crystal River and Roberts Island preserve a record of human response to environmental change across the first millennium A.D. Climate change and sea level undoubtedly played key roles in many of the historical developments we have described in this book, although we must bear in mind that the relationship between climate and historical events and trends is not straightforward, as we have tried to emphasize through the use of conditional language. For one thing, the resolution of both archaeological phases and climatic periods is frequently so coarse that correlating the two is often rather like hitting the proverbial broad side of a barn. For another, intervals like the Roman Warm period are generalizations that sometimes include significant variation; as Sassaman and colleagues (2011:260) have suggested, we might do better to focus on the degree of variability within these intervals than on the overall trend.

Bearing in mind these caveats, the initial settling of the Crystal River site, and particularly the influx of people in Phase 2, may be related to a pulse in sea level that made life more difficult on islands especially prone to tidal flooding. The building up of the shell midden in Phase 2 may have been a strategy for dealing with increased sea levels. More generally, the period of major settlement and mound building at Crystal River corresponds roughly with the generally favorable conditions of the Roman Warm period, and the period of decline in Phase 3 with the drier conditions of the Vandal Minimum.

Van de Noort (2011:1045) has noted that "living by the coast is in itself a matter of exercising agency: coastal communities could have decided to move inland rather than adapt to new conditions created by the impact of climate change." Generations of people who lived at Crystal River chose to remain despite the disruptions caused by climate change, including fluctuations in sea level that were probably equivalent to the conservative projection of a 1-m (3-ft) rise in our current century. However, they significantly adjusted their lives and livelihoods in response to these changes, apparently aggregating into villages when sea level rose and often dispersing into smaller settlements when it fell. These adjustments were no doubt difficult; the residents of these communities were heavily invested in both the natural and the human-made infrastructure—from oyster beds to spawning grounds, and from fish weirs to houses and mounds. But, at least in terms of economics, their investment was incommensurate with those who reside along this coast today. The question that now demands attention is, How will we adjust to the changes that could come on the next high tide?

References Cited

Archival and Artifact Collections Consulted

Citrus County Historical Society, Inc., Old Courthouse Heritage Museum, Inverness, Florida, archival records

Crystal River Archaeological State Park, Crystal River, Florida, archival records and object collections

Crystal River Preserve State Park, Crystal River, Florida, archival records and object collections

Florida Department of State, Division of Historical Resources, Tallahassee, Florida: Florida Master Site File and State of Florida Archaeological Collections

Florida Museum of Natural History, University of Florida, Gainesville, Florida Archaeology Collections and archival records of the Anthropology Division

National Museum of the American Indian, Cultural Resources Center, Suitland, Maryland, object collections and photo archives

Published Sources

Abrams, Elliot M.
2009   Hopewell Archaeology: A View from the Northern Woodlands. *Journal of Archaeological Research* 17:169–204.

Adler, Michael A., and Richard H. Wilshusen
1990   Large-Scale Integrative Facilities in Tribal Societies: Cross-Cultural and Southwestern US Examples. *World Archaeology* 22:133–146.

Andersen, Hans-Erik, Robert J. McGaughey, Stephen E. Reutebuch, Gerard Schreuder, and James Agee
2006   The Use of High-Resolution Remotely Sensed Data in Estimating Crown Fire Behavior Variables: Final Report to the Joint Fire Science Program. JFSP Project 01-1-4-07. Electronic document, http://forsys.cfr.washington.edu/JFSP06/index.htm.

Anderson, David G.
1994   *The Savannah River Chiefdoms: Political Change in the Late Prehistoric Southeast*. University of Alabama Press, Tuscaloosa.

1998 Swift Creek in a Regional Perspective. In *A World Engraved: Archaeology of the Swift Creek Culture*, edited by Mark Williams and David T. Elliott, pp. 274–300. University of Alabama Press, Tuscaloosa.

2012 Monumentality in Eastern North America during the Mississippian Period. In *Early New World Monumentality*, edited by Richard L. Burger and Robert M. Rosenswig, pp. 78–110. University Press of Florida, Gainesville.

Anderson, David G., and Kenneth E. Sassaman

2012 *Recent Developments in Southeastern Archaeology: From Colonization to Complexity*. Society for American Archaeology Press, Washington, D.C.

Anonymous

1995 Crystal River Auger Samples. Manuscript on file at the Florida Bureau of Archaeological Research, Tallahassee.

Arnold, Jeanne E.

1993 Labor and the Rise of Complex Hunter-Gatherers. *Journal of Anthropological Archaeology* 12:75–119.

1996a The Archaeology of Complex Hunter-Gatherers. *Journal of Archaeological Method and Theory* 3:77–126.

1996b Organizational Transformations: Power and Labor among Complex Hunter-Gatherers and Other Intermediate Societies. In *Emergent Complexity: The Evolution of Intermediate Societies*, edited Jeanne E. Arnold, pp. 59–73. International Monographs in Prehistory, Ann Arbor.

Asch, David L., and Nancy B. Asch

1985 Prehistoric Plant Cultivation in West-Central Illinois. In *Prehistoric Food Production in North America*, edited by Richard I. Ford, pp. 149–203. Anthropological Paper 75. Museum of Anthropology, University of Michigan, Ann Arbor.

Ashley, Keith, and Vicki Rolland

2009 Where Is the Corn in Precolumbian Peninsular Florida? Paper presented at the 74th Annual Meeting of the Society for American Archaeology, Atlanta.

Austin, Robert J.

2013 Lithic Acquisition and Use at Pineland. In *The Archaeology of Pineland: A Coastal Southwest Florida Site Complex, A.D. 50–1710*, edited by William H. Marquardt and Karen J. Walker, pp. 657–718. Institute of Archaeology andPaleoenvironmental Studies Monograph 4. University of Florida, Gainesville.

Austin, Robert J., Ronald M. Farquhar, and Karen J. Walker

2000 Isotope Analysis of Galena from Prehistoric Archaeological Sites in South Florida. *Florida Scientist* 63:123–131.

Austin, Robert J., and Jeffrey M. Mitchem

2014 Chronology, Site Formation, and the Woodland–Mississippian Transition at Bayshore Homes, Florida. *Southeastern Archaeology* 33:68–86.

Austin, Robert J., Jeffrey M. Mitchem, and Brent R. Weisman

2014 Radiocarbon Dates and the Late Prehistory of Tampa Bay. In *New Histories of Pre-Columbian Florida*, edited by Neill J. Wallis and Asa R. Randall, pp. 38–61. University Press of Florida, Gainesville.

Axelrod, Robert
1984   *The Evolution of Cooperation.* Basic Books, New York.
1997   *The Complexity of Cooperation: Agent-Based Models of Competition and Collaboration.* Princeton University Press, Princeton.
Bahn, Paul
1989   *Bluff Your Way in Archaeology.* Ravette Books, London.
Baillie, M.G.L.
1994   Dendrochronology Raises Questions about the Nature of the AD 536 Dust-Veil Event. *Holocene* 4:212–217.
Balsillie, James H., and Joseph F. Donoghue
2004   *High Resolution Sea-Level History for the Gulf of Mexico since the Last Glacial Maximum.* Report of Investigations No. 103. Florida Geological Survey, Tallahassee.
Bandy, Matthew S.
2004   Fissioning, Scalar Stress, and Social Evolution in Early Village Societies. *American Anthropologist* 106:322–333.
2005   New World Settlement Evidence for a Two-Stage Neolithic Demographic Transition. *Current Anthropology* 46:109–115.
2006   Early Village Society in the Formative Period. In *Andean Archaeology III: North and South*, edited by William H. Isbell and Helaine Silverman, pp. 210–236. Springer, New York.
2008   Global Patterns of Early Village Development. In *The Neolithic Demographic Transition and Its Consequences*, edited by Jean-Pierre Bocquet-Appel and Ofer Bar-Yosef, pp. 333–358. Springer, New York.
2010   Population Growth, Village Fissioning, and Alternative Early Village Trajectories. In *Becoming Villagers: Comparing Early Village Societies*, edited by Matthew S. Bandy and Jake R. Fox, pp. 19–36. University of Arizona Press, Tucson.
Bandy, Matthew S., and Jake R. Fox
2010   Becoming Villagers: The Evolution of Early Village Societies. In *Becoming Villagers: Comparing Early Village Societies*, edited by Matthew S. Bandy and Jake R. Fox, pp. 1–18. University of Arizona Press, Tucson.
Bandy, Matthew S., and Jake R. Fox (editors)
2010   *Becoming Villagers: Comparing Early Village Societies.* University of Arizona Press, Tucson.
Barbour, George M.
1964   *Florida for Tourists, Invalids, and Settlers.* Originally published 1882. Facsimile edition, University of Florida Press, Gainesville.
Bareis, Charles J.
1975   Report of 1972 University of Illinois–Urbana Excavations at the Cahokia Site. In *Cahokia Archaeology*, edited by Melvin L. Fowler, pp. 11–15. Papers in Anthropology Vol. 3. Illinois State Museum, Springfield.
Bayliss, Alex, Johannes van der Plicht, Christopher Bronk Ramsey, Gerry McCormack, Frances Healy, and Alasdair Whittle
2011   Towards Generational Time-Scales: The Quantitative Interpretation of Archae-

ological Chronologies. In *Gathering Time: Dating the Early Neolithic Enclosures of Southern Britain and Ireland*, edited by Alasdair Whittle, Frances Healy, and Alex Bayliss, pp. 17–59. Oxbow Books, Oxford.

Beck, Robin A., Jr., and James A. Brown
2011   Political Economy and the Routinization of Religious Movements: A View from the Eastern Woodlands. *Archeological Papers of the American Anthropological Association* 21:72–88.

Behrendt, Barbara
2000   Land Set to Whisper of Its Past. *St. Petersburg Times* April 4, 2000.

Belfer-Cohen, Anna, and Ofer Bar-Yosef
2000   Early Sedentism in the Near East: A Bumpy Ride to Village Life. In *Life in Neolithic Farming Communities: Social Organization, Identity, and Differentiation*, edited by Ian Kuijt, pp. 19–38. Kluwer Academic/Plenum, New York.

Bender, Barbara
1990   The Dynamics of Nonhierarchical Societies. In *The Evolution of Political Systems: Sociopolitics in Small-Scale Sedentary Societies*, edited by Steadman Upham, pp. 247–263. Cambridge University, Cambridge.

Bense, Judith A.
1985   *Hawkshaw: Prehistory and History in an Urban Neighborhood in Pensacola, Florida*. Report of Investigations 1. Office of Cultural and Archaeological Research, University of West Florida, Pensacola.
1998   Santa Rosa–Swift Creek in Northwestern Florida. In *A World Engraved: Archaeology of the Swift Creek Culture*, edited by Mark Williams and David T. Elliott, pp. 247–273. University of Alabama Press, Tuscaloosa.

Bernardini, Wesley, and Matthew A. Peeples
2015   Sight Communities: The Social Significance of Shared Visual Landmarks. *American Antiquity* 80:215–235.

Bettencourt, Luís M. A.
2013   The Origins of Scaling in Cities. *Science* 340:1438–1441.

Bettinger, Robert L.
2015   *Orderly Anarchy: Sociopolitical Evolution in Aboriginal California*. University of California Press, Berkeley.

Binford, Lewis R.
2001   *Constructing Frames of Reference: An Analytical Method for Archaeological Theory Building Using Ethnographic and Environmental Data Sets*. University of California Press, Berkeley.

Birch, Jennifer
2012   Coalescent Communities: Settlement Aggregation and Social Integration in Iroquoian Ontario. *American Antiquity* 77:646–670.

Birch, Jennifer, and Ronald F. Williamson
2015   Navigating Ancestral Landscapes in the Northern Iroquoian World. *Journal of Anthropological Archaeology* 39:139–150.

Blankenship, Beth
2013   The Hopewellian Influence at Crystal River, Florida: Testing the Marine Shell

Artifact Production Hypothesis. Unpublished master's thesis, Department of Anthropology, University of South Florida, Tampa.

Blanton, Richard E., and Lane F. Fargher
2008 *Collective Action in the Formation of Pre-modern States*. Springer, New York.
2016 *How Humans Cooperate: Confronting the Challenges of Collective Action*. University Press of Colorado, Boulder.

Bonhage-Freund, Mary Theresa, and Jeffrey A. Kurland
1994 Tit-for-Tat among the Iroquois: A Game Theoretic Perspective on Inter-Tribal Political Organization. *Journal of Anthropological Archaeology* 13:278–305.

Bourdieu, Pierre
1977 *Outline of a Theory of Practice*. Cambridge University Press, Cambridge.
1980 *The Logic of Practice*. Sanford University Press, Stanford.

Braje, Todd J., and Jon M. Erlandson
2013 Looking Forward, Looking Back: Humans, Anthropogenic Change, and the Anthropocene. *Anthropocene* 4:116–121.

Braun, David P.
1986 Midwestern Hopewellian Exchange and Supralocal Interaction. In *Peer Polity Interaction and Socio-political Change*, edited by Colin Renfrew and John .F. Cherry, pp. 117–126. Cambridge University Press, Cambridge.

Brinton, Daniel G.
1859 *Notes on the Floridian Peninsula, Its Literary History, Indian Tribes and Antiquities*. Joseph Sabin, Philadelphia.
1867 Artificial Shell Deposits of the United States. In *Annual Report of the Board of Regents of the Smithsonian Institution Showing the Operations, Expenditures, and Condition of the Institution for the Year 1866*, pp. 356–358. Government Printing Office, Washington, D.C.

Bronk Ramsey, C.
2009 Bayesian Analysis of Radiocarbon Dates. *Radiocarbon* 51:337–360.
2014 OxCal 4.2 Manual. Electronic document, https://c14.arch.ox.ac.uk/oxcalhelp/hlp_contents.html.

Brose, David S.
1979 An Interpretation of the Hopewellian Traits in Florida. In *Hopewell Archaeology: The Chillicothe Conference*, edited by David S. Brose and N'omi Greber, pp. 141–49. Kent State University Press, Kent, Ohio.

Brose, David S., and George Percy
1974 Weeden Island Ceremonialism: A Reappraisal. Paper presented at the 39th Annual Meeting of the Society for American Archaeology, Washington, D.C.

Brown, Antony, Phillip Toms, Chris Carey, and Eddie Rhodes
2013 Geomorphology of the Anthropocene: Time-Transgressive Discontinuities of Human-induced Alluviation. *Anthropocene* 1:3–13.

Brown, James A.
1985 Long-Term Trends to Sedentism and the Emergence of Complexity in the American Midwest. In *Prehistoric Hunter-Gatherers: The Emergence of Cultural*

Complexity, edited by T. Douglas Price and James A. Brown, pp. 435–442. Academic Press, San Diego.

1997 The Archaeology of Ancient Religion in the Eastern Woodlands. *Annual Review of Anthropology* 26:465–485.

2006 The Shamanic Element in Hopewellian Period Ritual. In *Recreating Hopewell: New Perspectives on Middle Woodland in Eastern North America*, edited by Douglas K. Charles and Jane E. Buikstra, pp. 475–488. University Press of Florida, Gainesville.

Bryson, Reid A.

1994 On Integrating Climatic Change and Culture Change Studies. *Human Ecology* 22:115–128.

Buikstra, Jane E., and Douglas K. Charles

1999 Centering the Ancestors: Cemeteries, Mounds and Sacred Landscapes of the Ancient North American Midcontinent. In *Archaeologies of Landscape: Contemporary Perspectives*, edited by Wendy Ashmore and A. Bernard Knapp, pp. 201–228. Blackwell Oxford.

Bullen, Adelaide K., and Ripley P. Bullen

1961 Wash Island in Crystal River. *Florida Anthropologist* 14:69–73.

Bullen, Ripley P.

1951 The Enigmatic Crystal River Site. *American Antiquity* 17:142–143.

1953 The Famous Crystal River Site. *Florida Anthropologist* 6:9–37.

1960a The Famous Crystal River Site: Its Potentialities as a Florida State Park. Manuscript on file at the Florida Museum of Natural History, Gainesville.

1960b Suggestions for the Development of the Crystal River Site as an On-Location Exhibit Area. Manuscript on file at the Florida Museum of Natural History, Gainesville.

1965 Recent Additional Information. An addendum to a brochure from the Crystal River Indian Mound Museum. Reproduced in *Famous Florida Sites: Crystal River and Mount Royal*, edited by Jerald T. Milanich, pp. 225–226. University Press of Florida, Gainesville.

1966a Burtine Island, Citrus County, Florida. Contributions of the Florida State Museum, Social Sciences, No. 14. University of Florida, Gainesville.

1966b Stelae at the Crystal River Site, Florida. *American Antiquity* 31:861–865.

1967 A Florida Folsom(?) Point from the Crystal River Mounds Museum. *Florida Anthropologist* 20 (Brief Notes):2–89.

Bunker, Nick

2010 *Making Haste from Babylon: The Mayflower Pilgrims and Their World: A New History*. Alfred A. Knopf, New York.

Burghardt, Andrew F.

1971 A Hypothesis about Gateway Cities. *Annals of the Association of American Geographers* 61:269–285.

Burks, Jarrod

2014 Geophysical Survey at Ohio Earthworks: Updating Nineteenth Century Maps and Filling the "Empty" Spaces. *Archaeological Prospection* 21:5–13.

Byrd, Brian F.
1994 Public and Private, Domestic and Corporate: The Emergence of the Southwest Asian Village. *American Antiquity* 59:639–666.
2005 *Early Village Life at Beidha, Jordan: Neolithic Spatial Organization and Vernacular Architecture: The Excavations of Mrs. Diana Kirkbride-Helbæk*. British Academy Monographs in Archaeology Book 14. Oxford University Press, New York.

Caldwell, Joseph
1964 Interaction Spheres in Prehistory. In *Hopewellian Studies*, edited by Joseph R. Caldwell and Robert L. Hall, pp.133–143. Scientific Papers 12. Illinois State Museum, Springfield.

Carballo, David M.
2013 Cultural and Evolutionary Dynamics of Cooperation in Archaeological Perspective. In *Cooperation and Collective Action: Archaeological Perspectives*, edited by David M. Carballo, pp. 3–33. University Press of Colorado, Boulder.

Carballo, David M., Paul Roscoe, and Gary M. Feinman
2014 Cooperation and Collective Action in the Cultural Evolution of Complex Societies. *Journal of Archaeological Method and Theory* 21:98–133.

Carr, Christopher
2006a Rethinking Interregional Hopewellian "Interaction." In *Gathering Hopewell: Society, Ritual, and Ritual Interaction*, edited by Christopher Carr and D. Troy Case, pp. 575–623. Springer, New York.
2006b Salient Issues in the Social and Political Organizations of Northern Hopewellian Peoples. In *Gathering Hopewell: Society, Ritual, and Ritual Interaction*, edited by Christopher Carr and D. Troy Case, pp. 73–118. Springer, New York.
2008a Coming to Know Ohio Hopewell Peoples Better: Topics for Future Research, Masters' Theses, and Doctoral Dissertations. In *The Scioto Hopewell and Their Neighbors: Bioarchaeological Documentation and Cultural Understanding*, edited by Christopher Carr, pp. 603–690. Springer, New York.
2008b Social and Ritual Organization. In *The Scioto Hopewell and Their Neighbors: Bioarchaeological Documentation and Cultural Understanding*, edited by Christopher Carr, pp 151–288. Springer, New York.

Carr, Christopher, and D. Troy Case
2006 The Nature of Leadership in Ohio Hopewell Societies. In *Gathering Hopewell: Society, Ritual, and Ritual Interaction*, edited by Christopher Carr and D. Troy Case, pp. 177–237. Springer, New York.
2008 Documenting the Lives of Ohio Hopewell People: Philosophical and Empirical Foundations. In *The Scioto Hopewell and Their Neighbors: Bioarchaeological Documentation and Cultural Understanding*, edited by D. Troy Case and Christopher Carr, pp. 3–34. Springer, New York.

Carr, Christopher, Beau J. Goldstein, and Jaimin D. Weets
2006 Estimating the Sizes and Social Compositions of Mortuary-Related Gatherings at Scioto Hopewell Earthwork-Mound Sites. In *Gathering Hopewell: Society,*

Ritual, and Ritual Interaction, edited by Christopher Carr and D. Troy Case, pp. 480–532. Springer, New York.

Certini, Giacomo, and Riccardo Scalenghe
2011 Anthropogenic Soils Are the Golden Spikes for the Anthropocene. *Holocene* 21:1269–1274.

Cherkinsky, Alexander, Thomas J. Pluckhahn, and Victor D. Thompson
2014 Variation in Radiocarbon Age Determinations from the Crystal River Archaeological Site, Florida. *Radiocarbon* 56:1–10.

Claassen, Cheryl
1998 *Shells*. Cambridge University Press, Cambridge.
2015 *Beliefs and Rituals in Archaic Eastern North America: An Interpretive Guide*. University of Alabama Press, Tuscaloosa.

Clark, Anthony
1990 *Seeing beneath the Soil: Prospecting Methods in Archaeology*. 2nd ed. B. T. Batsford, London.

Clark, John E., and Michael Blake
1994 The Power of Prestige: Competitive Generosity and the Emergence of Ranked Societies in Lowland Mesoamerica. In *Factional Competition and Political Development in the New World*, edited by Elizabeth M. Brumfiel and John W. Fox, pp. 17–30. Cambridge University Press, Cambridge.

Clausen, C. J., A. D. Cohen, Cesare Emiliani, J. A. Holmanand, J. J. Stipp
1979 Little Salt Spring, Florida: A Unique Underwater Site. *Science* 203:609–614.

Clay, Brenda J.
1992 Other Times, Other Places: Agency and the Big Man in Central New Ireland. *Man* 27:719–733.

Clay, R. Berle
1987 Circles and Ovals: Two Types of Adena Space. *Southeastern Archaeology* 6:46–56.
2013 Like a Dead Dog: Strategic Ritual Choice in the Mortuary Enterprise. In *Early and Middle Woodland Landscapes of the Southeast*, edited by Alice P. Wright and Edward R. Henry, pp. 56–70. University Press of Florida, Gainesville.
2014 What Does Mortuary Variability in the Ohio Valley Middle Woodland Mean? Agency, Its Projects, and Interpretive Ambiguity. *Southeastern Archaeology* 33:143–152.

Cobb, Charles R.
2003 Mississippian Chiefdoms: How Complex? *Annual Review of Anthropology* 32:63–84.

Coe, Michael D., and Richard A. Diehl
1980 *In the Land of the Olmec: The Archaeology of San Lorenzo Tenochtitlán*, Vol. 1. University of Texas, Austin.

Cohen, Amanda B.
2010 "Ritualization" in Early Village Society: The Case of the Lake Titicaca Basin Formative. In *Becoming Villagers: Comparing Early Village Societies*, edited by

Matthew S. Bandy and Jake R. Fox, pp. 81–99. University of Arizona Press, Tucson.

Collins, James M., and Michael L. Chalfant
1993   A Second-Terrace Perspective on Monks Mound. *American Antiquity* 58:319–332.

Collins, Lori D., and Travis F. Doering
2009   High Definition Digital Documentation at the Crystal River Archaeological Site (8CI1). *Florida Anthropologist* 62:47–68.

Collins, Lori D., Jeffrey P. DuVernay, Steven Fernandez, and Kelly A. Driscoll
2012   *Archaeological Resource Sensitivity Modeling in Florida State Parks District 2: The Northeast Florida Region.* Alliance for Integrated Spatial Technologies, University of South Florida, Tampa. Submitted to the Florida Bureau of Archaeological Research, Tallahassee.

Colwell-Chanthaphonh, Chip, and T. J. Ferguson
2006   Rethinking Abandonment in Archaeological Contexts. *SAA Archaeological Record* 6:37–41.

Compton, J. Matthew
2014   *Animal Remains from 2011 Excavations at the Roberts Island Shell Mound Complex (8CI41), Citrus County, Florida.* Southeastern Zooarchaeological Research, LLC, Raleigh. Report submitted to the Department of Anthropology, University of South Florida, Tampa.

Conyers, Lawrence B.
2013   *Ground-Penetrating Radar for Archaeology.* AltaMira Press, Lanham.

Cook, Robert A., Aaron R. Comstock, Kristie R. Martin, Jarrod Burks, Wendy Church, and Melissa French
2015   Early Village Life in Southeastern Indiana: Recent Field Investigations at the Guard Site (12D29). *Southeastern Archaeology* 34:95–115.

Cooke, Charles Wythe
1945   *Geology of Florida.* Geological Bulletin No. 29. Florida Geological Survey, Tallahassee.

Coon, Matthew S.
2009   Variation in Ohio Hopewell Political Economies. *American Antiquity* 74:49–76.

Cooney, Gabriel
2004   Introduction: Seeing Land from the Sea. *World Archaeology* 35:323–328.

Cordell, Ann
2016   *Variability in Clay Resources from the Vicinity of Crystal River, Citrus County, Florida.* Report on file, Florida Museum of Natural History-Ceramic Technology Laboratory, Gainesville.

Costin, Cathy
2001   Craft Production Systems. In *Archaeology at the Millennium: A Sourcebook,* edited by Gary Feinman and T. Douglas Price, pp. 273–327. Kluwer Academic/Plenum Press, New York.

Cowardin, Lewis M., Virginia Carter, Francis C. Golet
1979   *Classification of Wetlands and Deepwater Habitats of the United States.* US Department of the Interior, Fish and Wildlife Service, Washington, D.C.

Creese, John L.
2013   Rethinking Early Village Development in Southern Ontario: Toward a History of Place-Making. *Canadian Journal of Archaeology* 37:185–218.

Crutzen, Paul J.
2006   The "Anthropocene." In *Earth System Science in the Anthropocene*, edited by Eckart Ehlers and Thomas Krafft, pp. 13–18. Springer, Berlin.

Crutzen, Paul J., and Will Steffen
2003   How Long Have We Been in the Anthropocene Era? *Climatic Change* 61:251–257.

Cumbaa, Stephen L.
1980   Aboriginal Use of Marine Mammals in the Southeastern United States. *Southeastern Archaeological Conference Bulletin* 17:6–10.

Cushing, Frank Hamilton
1897   *Exploration of Ancient Key-Dwellers' Remains on the Gulf Coast of Florida.* MacCalla, Philadelphia.

Dawdy, Shannon Lee
2009   Millennial Archaeology: Locating the Discipline in the Age of Insecurity. *Archaeological Dialogues* 16:131–142.

Dean, Jonathan, and Gary D. Ellis
2004   *Archaeological Reconnaissance of the South Buffer Preserve, Crystal Riverbank Tract, St. Martins Marsh Aquatic Preserve/Crystal River State Buffer Preserve, Citrus County, Florida.* Gulf Archaeology Research Institute, Crystal River, Florida. Submitted to St. Martins Marsh Aquatic Preserve/Crystal River State Buffer Preserve, Citrus County, Florida.

Dean, Jonathan, Gary D. Ellis, Randy Martin, and Ken Nash
2004   *Archaeological Reconnaissance of the South Withlacoochee Tract, St. Martins Marsh Aquatic Preserve/Crystal River State Buffer Preserve, Citrus County, Florida.* Gulf Archaeology Research Institute, Crystal River, Florida. Submitted to St. Martins Marsh Aquatic Preserve/Crystal River State Buffer Preserve, Citrus County, Florida.

Dekle, Victoria G.
2013   Ritual Life and Landscape at Tunacunnhee. In *Early and Middle Woodland Landscapes of the Southeast*, edited by Alice P. Wright and Edward R. Henry, pp. 196–203. University Press of Florida, Gainesville.

Delgado, Alexander
2013   Oyster Exploitation in the Woodland Period at Crystal River (8CI1): An Investigation into the Image of the Ecological Indian. Unpublished honor's thesis, Department of Anthropology, University of South Florida, Tampa.
2017   More than Just Empty Space? Integrated Geoarchaeological Investigations of a Woodland-Period Plaza at Crystal River (8CI1). Unpublished master's thesis, Department of Anthropology, University of South Florida, Tampa.

DeMarrais, Elizabeth
2016   Making Pacts and Cooperative Acts: The Archaeology of Coalition and Consensus. *World Archaeology* 48:1–13.

Devlet, Ekaterina
2001   Rock Art and the Material Culture of Siberian and Central Asian Shamanism. In *The Archaeology of Shamanism*, edited by Neil S. Price, pp. 43–55. Routledge, London.

Diamond, Jared
2005   *Collapse: How Societies Choose to Fail or Succeed*. Penguin, New York.

Dietler, John Eric
2008   Craft Specialization and the Emergence of Political Complexity in Southwest Florida. Ph.D. dissertation, Department of Anthropology, University of California, Los Angeles.

Donop, Mark C., George D. Kamenov, Tiffany E. Birakis, and Matthew D. Woodside
2016   A Rare Galena Artifact from Palmetto Mound (8LV2), Levy County, Florida. *Florida Anthropologist* 69:164–173.

Doran, Glen
2002   Introduction to Wet Sites and Windover (8BR246) Investigations. In *Windover: Multidisciplinary Investigations of an Early Archaic Florida Cemetery*, edited by Glen Doran, pp. 1–38. University Press of Florida, Gainesville.

Dugmore, Andrew J., Thomas H. McGovern, Orri Vésteinsson, Jette Arneborg, Richard Streeter, and Christian Keller
2012   Cultural Adaptation, Compounding Vulnerabilities and Conjunctures in Norse Greenland. *Proceedings of the National Academy of Sciences* 109:3658–3663.

Duke, C. Trevor
2015   Identifying Humanized Ecosystems: Anthropogenic Impacts, Intentionality, and Resource Acquisition at Crystal River (8CI1) and Roberts Island (8CI41). Unpublished master's thesis, Department of Anthropology, University of South Florida, Tampa.

Dunn, Hampton
1977   *Back Home: A History of Citrus County, Florida*. Citrus County Bicentennial Steering Committee. Inverness, Florida.

Dye, David H.
2009   *War Paths, Peace Paths: An Archaeology of Cooperation and Conflict in Native Eastern North America*. AltaMira Press, Lanham.

Eckert, Suzanne L.
2012   Choosing Clays and Painting Pots in the Fourteenth-Century Zuni Region. In *Potters and Communities of Practice: Glaze Paint and Polychrome Pottery in the American Southwest, A.D. 1250 to 1700*, edited by Linda S. Cordell and Judith A. Habcht-Mauche, pp. 55–64. Anthropological Papers of the University of Arizona No. 75. University of Arizona Press, Tucson.

Edgeworth, Matt
2014   The Relationship between Archaeological Stratigraphy and Artificial Ground and

Its Significance in the Anthropocene. Special Publications Vol. 395, No. 1, 91–108. Geological Society, London.

Eerkens, Jelmer W.
2013   Free-Riding, Cooperation, and Population Growth: The Evolution of Privatization and Leaders in Owens Valley, California. In *Cooperation and Collective Action: Archaeological Perspectives*, edited by David M. Carballo, pp. 151–174. University Press of Colorado, Boulder.

Eliade, Mircea
1964   *Shamanism: Archaic Techniques of Ecstasy.* Routledge & Kegan Paul, London.

Ellis, Gary D.
1999   *Crystal River State Archaeological Site, Seawall Restoration Project, Summary Report.* Gulf Archaeology Research Institute, Crystal River, Florida. Submitted to Crystal River Preserve State Park, Crystal River, Florida.
2004   *Storm Damage Assessment on Mound G, Crystal River State Archaeological Park, Crystal River, Florida.* Gulf Archaeology Research Institute, Crystal River, Florida. Submitted to Crystal River Preserve State Park, Crystal River, Florida.
2008a *Action Report and Storm Damage Assessment, Wash Island, Crystal River Preserve State Park, Crystal River, Florida.* Gulf Archaeology Research Institute, Crystal River, Florida. Submitted to Crystal River Preserve State Park, Crystal River, Florida.
2008b *Storm Damage Assessment-Tree Fall, Crystal River State Archaeological Park, Crystal River, Florida.* Gulf Archaeology Research Institute, Crystal River, Florida. Submitted to Crystal River Preserve State Park, Crystal River, Florida.

Ellis, Gary D., and Jonathan Dean
2004   *Archaeological Reconnaissance of the Inter-Island Group, St. Martins Marsh Aquatic Preserve/Crystal River State Buffer Preserve, Citrus County, Florida.* Gulf Archaeology Research Institute, Crystal River, Florida. Submitted to St. Martins Marsh Aquatic Preserve/Crystal River State Buffer Preserve, Citrus County, FL.

Ellis, Gary D., Jonathan Dean, and Randy Martin
2003   *Displaced Midden Recovery Project, Crystal River Mounds State Archaeological Site.* Gulf Archaeology Research Institute, Crystal River, Florida. Submitted to Crystal River Preserve State Park, Crystal River, Florida.

Ellis, Gary D., Robin L. Denson, and Russell A. Dorsey
1995   *Phase II Archaeological Study, Citrus County, Florida.* Ellis Archaeology, Lecanto, FL. Submitted to Citrus County Board of Commissioners, Inverness, Florida.

Ellis, Gary D., Russell A. Dorsey, and Robin L. Denson
1993   *Archaeological Study of Citrus County, Phase I.* Ellis Archaeology, Lecanto, FL. Submitted to Citrus County Board of Commissioners, Inverness, Florida.

Emerson, Thomas E., Kenneth B. Farnsworth, Sarah U. Wisseman, and Randall E. Hughes
2013   The Allure of the Exotic: Reexamining the Use of Local and Distant Pipestone Quarries in Ohio Hopewell Pipe Caches. *American Antiquity* 78:48–67.

Erlandson, Jon M.
2001 The Archaeology of Aquatic Adaptations: Paradigms for a New Millennium. *Journal of Archaeological Research* 9:287–350.
2013 Shell Middens and Other Anthropogenic Soils as Global Stratigraphic Signatures of the Anthropocene. *Anthropocene* 4:24–32.
Erlandson, Jon M., and Todd J. Braje
2013 Archeology and the Anthropocene. *Anthropocene* 4:1–7.
Estabrook, Richard W.
2011 Social Landscapes of Transegalitarian Societies: An Analysis of the Chipped Stone Artifact Assemblage from the Crystal River Site (8CI1), Citrus County, Florida. Ph.D. dissertation, Department of Anthropology, University of South Florida, Tampa.
Ethridge, Robbie, and Charles Hudson (editors)
2002 *The Transformation of the Southeastern Indians, 1540–1760.* University Press of Mississippi, Jackson.
Fewkes, J. Walter
1924 Preliminary Archeological Explorations at Weeden Island, Florida. *Smithsonian Miscellaneous Collections* 76(13):1–26.
Firth, Raymond
1929 *Primitive Economics of the New Zealand Maori.* Dutton, New York.
Flannery, Kent V.
1976 *The Early Mesoamerican Village.* Academic Press, New York.
Fletcher, Roland
1995 *The Limits of Settlement Growth: A Theoretical Outline.* Cambridge University Press, New York.
Florida Department of Environmental Protection
2000 *Crystal River State Archaeological Site: Unit Management Plan.* Florida Department of Environmental Protection, Division of Recreation and Parks, Tallahassee, Florida.
Ford, James A.
1966 Early Formative Cultures in Georgia and Florida. *American Antiquity* 31:781–799.
1969 *A Comparison of Formative Cultures in the Americas.* Smithsonian Contributions to Anthropology Vol. 11. Smithsonian Institution Press, Washington, D.C.
Ford, James A., and Gordon R. Willey
1941 An Interpretation of the Prehistory of the Eastern United States. *American Anthropologist* 43:325–363.
Foster, William C.
2012 *Climate and Culture Change in North America AD 900–1600.* University of Texas Press, Austin.
Fradkin, Arlene
1976 The Wightman Site: A Study of Prehistoric Culture and Environment on Sanibel Island, Lee County, Florida. Unpublished master's thesis, Department of Anthropology, University of Florida, Gainesville.

Garraty, Christopher
2013	Social Identity and Political Competition in a Culturally Diverse Landscape: Decorated Pottery from the Mescal War Site, Southeastern Arizona. *Journal of Arizona Archaeology* 2:163–177.

Gater, John, and Chris Gaffney
2003	*Revealing the Buried Past: Geophysics for Archaeologists*. Tempus, Wiltshire.

Gibson, Jon L.
2001	*The Ancient Mounds of Poverty Point: Place of Rings*. University Press of Florida, Gainesville.

Giddens, Anthony
1979	*Central Problems in Social Theory: Action, Structure, and Contradiction in Social Analysis*. University of California Press, Berkeley.
1984	*The Constitution of Society: Outline of a Theory of Structuration*. University of California Press, Berkeley.

Gilleland, Sarah
2013	Finding the Floor: Construction History at Roberts Island. Unpublished honor's thesis, Department of Anthropology, University of South Florida, Tampa.

Gilliland, Marion Spjut
1975	*The Material Culture of Key Marco, Florida*. University Presses of Florida, Gainesville.

Gilman, Antonio
1981	The Development of Social Stratification in Bronze Age Europe. *Current Anthropology* 22:1–24.

Glowacki, Mary
2002	Field Report for Crystal River State Archaeological Site (8CI1): Monitoring of Units Dug for Seawall Anchors. Report on file at the Florida Bureau of Archaeological Research, Tallahassee.

Goad, Sharon
1978	Exchange Networks in the Prehistoric Southeastern United States. Ph.D. dissertation, University of Georgia, Athens. University Microfilms, Ann Arbor.
1979	Middle Woodland Exchange in the Prehistoric Southeastern United States. In *Hopewell Archaeology: The Chillicothe Conference*, edited by David S. Brose and N'omi B. Greber, pp. pp. 239–246. Kent State University Press, Kent, Ohio.

Goldstein, Lynne
1976	Spatial Structure and Social Organization. Ph.D. dissertation, Department of Anthropology, Northwestern University, Evanston.
1980	*Mississippian Mortuary Practices: A Case Study of Two Cemeteries in the Lower Illinois Valley*. Scientific Papers No. 4. Northwestern University Archeological Program, Evanston.
1981	One-Dimensional Archaeology and Multi-Dimensional People: Spatial Organization and Mortuary Analysis. In *The Archaeology of Death*, edited by Robert Chapman, Ian Kinnes, and Klavs Randsborg, pp. 53–69. Cambridge University Press, Cambridge.

Goodbred, Steven Lee, Jr.
1995   Geologic Controls on the Holocene Evolution of an Open-Marine Marsh System Fronting a Shallow—Water Embayment: Waccasassa Bay, West-Central Florida. Unpublished master's thesis, Department of Marine Science, University of South Florida, Tampa.

Goodbred, Steven, Eric Wright, and Albert Hine
1998   Sea-Level Change and Storm-Surge Deposition in a Late Holocene Florida Salt Marsh. *Journal of Sedimentary Research* 68:240–252.

Goring-Morris, Nigel, and Anna Belfer-Cohen
2010   "Great Expectations," or the Inevitable Collapse of the Early Neolithic in the Near East. In *Becoming Villagers: Comparing Early Village Societies*, edited by Matthew S. Bandy and Jake R. Fox, pp. 62–80. University of Arizona Press, Tucson.

Grann, David
1999   "Where We Got Compassion." *New York Times Magazine* 12 September. New York.

Graves, William M., and Scott Van Keuren
2011   Ancestral Pueblo Villages and the Panoptic Gaze of the Commune. *Cambridge Archaeological Journal* 21:263–282.

Green, Victoria D.
1993   Endemic Syphilis: A Prehistoric Controversy at Crystal River, Florida. Unpublished senior thesis, Hampshire College, Amherst, Massachusetts.

Greenman, Emerson F.
1938   Hopewellian Traits in Florida. *American Antiquity* 3:327–332.

Griffin, James B.
1946   Cultural Change and Continuity in Eastern United States Archaeology. In *Man in Northeastern North America*, edited by Frederick Johnson, pp. 37–95. Vol. 35, Papers of the Robert S. Peabody Foundation for Archaeology, Phillips Academy, Andover.
1952   Culture Periods in Eastern United States Archaeology. In *Archaeology of Eastern United States*, edited by James B. Griffin, pp. 352–364. University of Chicago Press, Chicago.

Griffin, James B., and Ripley P. Bullen
1950   *The Safety Harbor Site, Pinellas County, Florida*. Publication No. 2. Florida Anthropological Society, Gainesville.

Grøn, Ole
1991   A Method for Reconstruction of Social Structure in Prehistoric Societies and Examples of Practical Application. In *Social Space: Human Spatial Behaviour in Dwellings and Settlements; Proceedings of an Interdisciplinary Conference*, edited by Ole Grøn, Ericka Engelstad and Inge Lindblom, pp. 100–117. Odense University Press, Odense.

Gunn, Joel D. (editor)
2000   *The Years without Summer: Tracing AD 536 and Its Aftermath*. BAR International Series 872. Archaeopress, Oxford.

Hadden, Carla S.
2015   Coastal Subsistence and Settlement Systems on the Northern Gulf of Mexico, USA. Unpublished Ph.D. dissertation, Department of Anthropology, University of Georgia, Athens.

Hall, Robert
1979   In Search of the Ideology of Adena-Hopewell Climax. In *Hopewell Archaeology: The Chillicothe Conference*, edited by David S. Brose and N'omi Greber, pp. 258–265. Kent State University Press, Kent, Ohio.
1997   *Archaeology of the Soul: North American Indian Belief and Ritual*. University of Illinois Press, Urbana.

Hamilton, Fran
1999   Southeastern Archaic Mounds: Example of Elaboration in a Temporally Fluctuating Environment. *Journal of Anthropological Archaeology* 18:344–355.

Hardin, Garrett
1968   The Tragedy of the Commons. *Science* 162:1243–1248.

Hardman, Clark, Jr.
1971   The Primitive Solar Observatory at Crystal River and Its Implications. *Florida Anthropologist* 24:135–168.

Harner, Michael
1980   *The Way of the Shaman: A Guide to Power and Healing*. Harper and Row, San Francisco.

Hastorf, Christine A.
2010   Sea Changes in Stable Communities: What Do Small Changes in Practices at Catalhoyuk and Chiripa Imply about Community Making? In *Becoming Villagers: Comparing Early Village Societies*, edited by Matthew S. Bandy and Jake R. Fox, pp. 140–164. University of Arizona Press, Tucson.

Hayden, Brian
1995   Pathways to Power: Principles for Creating Socioeconomic Inequalities. In *Foundations of Social Inequality*, edited by T. Douglas Price and Gary M. Feinman, pp. 15–86. Plenum Press, New York.

Hegmon, Michelle
2003   Setting Theoretical Egos Aside: Issues and Theory in North American Archaeology. *American Antiquity* 68:213–244.

Helms, Mary W.
2014   *Ulysses' Sail: An Ethnographic Odyssey of Power, Knowledge, and Geographical Distance*. Princeton University Press, Princeton.

Henry, Edward R., Nicolas R. Laracuente, Jared S. Case, and Jay K. Johnson
2014   Incorporating Multistaged Geophysical Data into Regional-Scale Models: A Case Study from an Adena Burial Mound in Central Kentucky. *Archaeological Prospection* 21:15–26.

Hill, J. Brett, Jeffery J. Clark, William H. Doelle, and Patrick D. Lyons
2004   Prehistoric Demography in the Southwest: Migration, Coalescence, and Hohokam Population Decline. *American Antiquity* 69:689–716.

Hillyard, M. B.
1887   *The New South: A Description of the Southern States, Noting Each State Separately, and Giving Their Most Distinctive Features and Most Salient Characteristics.* Manfacturers' Record, Baltimore.

Hine, Albert C., and Daniel F. Belknap
1986   Recent Geologic History and Modern Sedimentary Processes of the Pasco, Hernando, and Citrus County Coastline: West Central Florida. Report 79. Florida Sea Grant Collge, Gainesville.

Hirth, Kenneth G.
1978   Interregional Trade and the Formation of Prehistoric Gateway Communities. *American Antiquity* 43:35–45.

Hodson, Alex
2012   The Crystal River Project: Determining the Ages of Two Ceremonial Mounds in Florida Using Optically Stimulated Luminescence Dating. Unpublished honor's thesis, School of Geography and Earth Sciences, McMaster University, Hamilton.

Hoese, H. Dickson, and Richard H. Moore
1998   *Fishes of the Gulf of Mexico: Texas, Louisiana, and Adjacent Waters.* 2nd ed. Texas A&M University Press, College Station.

Hole, Frank, Kent V. Flannery, and James A. Neely
1969   *Prehistory and Human Ecology of the Deh Luran Plain: An Early Village Sequence from Khuzistan, Iran.* Memoirs of the Museum of Anthropology No. 1. University of Michigan, Ann Arbor.

Hudson, Charles
1976   *The Southeastern Indians.* University of Tennessee Press, Knoxville.
1998   *Knights of Spain, Warriors of the Sun: Hernando de Soto and the South's Ancient Chiefdoms.* University of Georgia Press, Athens.

Hutchinson, Dale L.
2004   *Bioarchaeology of the Florida Gulf Coast: Adaptation, Conflict and Change.* University Press of Florida, Gainesville.

Hutton, Joan
1986   Bedrock Control, Sedimentation and Holocene Evolution of the Marsh Archipelago Coast, West-Central Florida. Unpublished master's thesis, School of Marine Science, University of South Florida, Tampa.

Ingold, Tim
1999   On the Social Relations of the Hunter-Gatherer Band. In *The Cambridge Encyclopedia of Hunters and Gatherers*, edited by Richard B. Lee and Richard Daly, pp. 399–410. Cambridge University Press, Cambridge.
2000   *The Perception of the Environment: Essays in Livelihood, Dwelling, and Skill.* Routledge, New York.

Intergovernmental Panel on Climate Change (IPCC)
2014   *Climate Change 2014: IPCC Fifth Assessment Synthesis Report.* United Nations Intergovernmental Panel on Climate Change, New York. Electronic document, http://www.ipcc.ch/ report/ar5/syr/.

Jackson, Jason Baird
1996   "Everybody Has a Part to Play, Even the Little Bitty Ones": Notes on the Social Organization of Yuchi Ceremonialism. *Florida Anthropologist* 49:121–130.
2003   *Yuchi Ceremonial Life: Performance, Meaning, and Tradition in a Contemporary American Indian Community*. University of Nebraska Press, Lincoln.

Jackson, Kendal R.
2016   The Archaeo-Palynology of Crystal River Site (8Ci1), Citrus County, Florida. Unpublished master's thesis, Department of Anthropology, University of South Florida, Tampa.

Jefferies, Richard W.
1976   *The Tunacunnhee Site: Evidence of Hopewell Interaction in Northwest Georgia*. Anthropological Papers No. 1. Department of Anthropology, University of Georgia, Athens.
1994   The Swift Creek Site and Woodland Platform Mounds in the Southeastern United States. In *Ocmulgee Archaeology 1936–1986*, edited by David J. Hally, pp. 71–83. University of Georgia Press, Athens.

Johnson, Gregory A.
1982   Organizational Structure and Scalar Stress. In *Theory and Explanation in Archaeology*, edited by Colin Renfrew, Michael Rowlands, and Barbara A. Segraves-Whallon, pp. 389–421. Academic Press, New York.

Judd, Lilith
1997   The Fracture Rate of Two Pre-Contact Florida Populations: The Crystal River Burial Mound G and Palmer Site Burial Mound. Unpublished senior thesis, Department of Anthropology, University of Florida, Gainesville.

Kantner, John
1996   Political Competition among the Chaco Anasazi of the American Southwest. *Journal of Anthropological Archaeology* 15:41–105.

Karnoutsos, Carmela
2007   Dixon Crucible Company/Dixon Mills. Electronic document, http://www.njcu.edu/programs/jchistory/pages/d_pages/dixon_crucible_company.htm, accessed 3/13/2013.

Kassabaum, Megan Crandal
2014   Feasting and Communal Ritual in the Lower Mississippi Valley, AD 700–1000. Ph.D. dissertation, Department of Anthropology, University of North Carolina, Chapel Hill.

Katzmarzyk, Cheryl
1998   Evidence of Stress in a Precolumbian Population from Mound G at the Crystal River Site, Florida. Unpublished master's thesis, Department of Anthropology, University of Florida, Gainesville.

Keating, Joshua
2014   The People's Republic of Plymouth. *Slate*, November 25. Electronic document, http://www.slate.com/articles/life/holidays/2014/11/thanksgiving_socialism_the_strange_and_persistent_right_wing_myth_that_thanksgiving.html.

Keith, Scot
2013   The Woodland Period Cultural Landscape of the Leake Site Complex. In *Early and Middle Woodland Landscapes of the Southeast*, edited by Alice P. Wright and Edward R. Henry, pp. 138–152. University Press of Florida, Gainesville.
Kellar, James H., A. R. Kelly, and Edward V. McMichael
1962a   *Final Report on Archaeological Explorations at the Mandeville Site, 9 Cla 1.* Laboratory of Archaeology Report No. 8. University of Georgia, Athens.
1962b   The Mandeville Site in Southwest Georgia. *American Antiquity* 27:336–355.
Kelly, John E., Andrew C. Fortier, Stephen J. Ozuk, and Joyce A. Williams
1987   *The Range Site: Archaic through Late Woodland Occupations.* American Bottom Archaeology FAI-270 Site Reports Vol. 16. University of Illinois Press, Urbana.
Kelly, John E., Stephen J. Ozuk, and Joyce Williams
1990   *The Range Site 2: The Emergent Mississippian Dohack and Range Phase Occupations.* American Bottom Archaeology FAI-270 Site Reports Vol. 20. University of Illinois Press, Urbana.
Kelso, William M.
2006   *Jamestown: The Buried Truth.* University of Virginia Press, Charlottesville.
Kemp, Kassie C.
2015   Pottery Exchange and Interaction at the Crystal River Site (8CI1), Florida. Unpublished master's thesis, Department of Anthropology, University of South Florida, Tampa.
Kennett, Douglas J.
2005   *The Island Chumash: Behavioral Ecology of a Maritime Society.* University of California Press, Berkeley.
Kidder, Tristram R.
2004   Plazas as Architecture: An Example from the Raffman Site in Northeast Louisiana. *American Antiquity* 69:513–532.
2010   Hunter-Gatherer Ritual and Complexity: New Evidence from Poverty Point, Louisiana. In *Ancient Complexities: New Perspectives in Precolumbian North America*, edited by Susan M. Alt, pp. 32–51. University of Utah Press, Salt Lake City.
2011   Transforming Hunter-Gatherer History at Poverty Point. In *Hunter-Gatherer Archaeology as Historical Process*, edited by Kenneth E. Sassaman and Donald H. Holly Jr., pp. 95–119. University of Arizona Press, Tucson.
Kidder, Tristram R., Katherine A. Adelsberger, Lee J. Arco, and Timothy M. Schilling
2008   Basin-Scale Reconstruction of the Geological Context of Human Settlement: An Example from the Lower Mississippi Valley, USA. *Quaternary Science Reviews* 27:1255–1270.
King, Adam
2003   *Etowah: The Political History of a Chiefdom Capital.* University of Alabama Press, Tuscaloosa.
Kles, Maranda Almy
2013   Human Biological Variation and Biological Distance in Pre-contact Florida: A Morphometric Examination of Biological and Cultural Continuity and

Change. Unpublished Ph.D. dissertation, Department of Anthropology, University of Florida, Gainesville.

Knight, Vernon J., Jr.
1989   Some Speculations on Mississippian Monsters. In *The Southeastern Ceremonial Complex: Artifacts and Analysis*, edited by Patricia Galloway, pp. 205–210. University of Nebraska Press, Lincoln.
1990   *Excavation of the Truncated Mound at the Walling Site: Middle Woodland Culture and Copena in the Tennessee Valley.* Report of Investigations 56. Division of Archaeology, Alabama State Museum of Natural History, University of Alabama, Tuscaloosa.
2001   Feasting and the Emergence of Platform Mound Ceremonialism in Eastern North America. In *Feasts: Archaeological and Ethnographic Perspectives on Food, Politics, and Power*, edited by Michael Dietler and Brian Hayden, pp. 311–333. Smithsonian Institution Press, Washington, D.C.

Knight, Vernon J., Jr., and Tim S. Mistovich
1984   *Walter F. George Lake: Archaeological Survey of Fee Owned Lands, Alabama and Georgia.* Report of Investigations 42. Office of Archaeological Research, University of Alabama, Tuscaloosa.

Kohler, Timothy A.
1991   The Demise of Weeden Island, and Post–Weeden Island Cultural Stability, in Non-Mississippianized Northern Florida. In *Stability, Transformation, and Variation: The Late Woodland Southeast*, edited by Michael S. Nassaney and Charles R. Cobb, pp. 91–110. Plenum Press, New York.
2004   Introduction. In *Archaeology of Bandelier National Monument: Village Formation on the Pajarito Plateau, New Mexico*, edited by Timothy A. Kohler, pp. 1–17. University of New Mexico Press, Albuquerque.

Kohler, Timothy A., Stephanie VanBuskirk, and Samantha Ruscavage-Barz
2004   Vessels and Villages: Evidence for Conformist Transmission in Early Village Aggregations on the Pajarito Plateau, New Mexico. *Journal of Anthropological Archaeology* 23:100–118.

Kohler, Timothy A., Matthew W. Van Pelt, and Lorene Y. L. Yap
2000   Reciprocity and Its Limits: Considerations for a Study of the Prehispanic Pueblo World. In *Alternative Leadership Strategies in the Prehispanic Southwest*, edited by Barbara J. Mills, pp. 180–206. University of Arizona Press, Tucson.

Kohler, Timothy A., and Carla Van West
1996   The Calculus of Self-Interest in the Development of Cooperation: Sociopolitical Development and Risk among the Northern Anasazi. In *Evolving Complexity and Environmental Risk in the Prehistoric Southwest*, edited by Joseph A. Tainter and Bonnie Bagley Tainter, pp. 169–196. Studies in the Sciences of Complexity Proceedings 24. Addison-Wesley, Reading, Massachusetts.

Kohler, Timothy A., and Mark D. Varien (editors)
2012   *Emergence and Collapse of Early Villages: Models of Central Mesa Verde Archaeology.* University of California Press, Berkeley.

Kolb, Michael J., and James E. Snead
1997 It's a Small World after All: Comparative Analyses of Community Organization in Archaeology. *American Antiquity* 62:609–628.

Konczal, Mike
2014 The Conservative Myth of a Social Safety Net Built on Charity. *Atlantic*, March 24. Electronic document, http://www.theatlantic.com/politics/archive/2014/03/the-conservative-myth-of-a-social-safety-net-built-on-charity/284552/.

Kowalewski, Stephen A.
2006 Coalescent Societies. In *Light on the Path: The Anthropology and History of the Southeastern Indians*, edited by Thomas J. Pluckhahn and Robbie Ethridge, pp. 94–122. University of Alabama Press, Tuscaloosa.
2012 Two Metaphors and a Myth. *Social Evolution and History* 11(2):63–66.
2013 The Work of Making Community. In *From Prehistoric Villages to Cities: Settlement Aggregation and Community Transformation*, edited by Jennifer Birch, pp. 201–218. Routledge, New York.

Kozuch, Laura
2013 Ceramic Shell Cup Effigies from Illinois and Their Implications. *Southeastern Archaeology* 32:29–45.

Kuijt, Ian
1996 Negotiating Equality through Ritual: A Consideration of Late Natufian and Prepottery Neolithic A Period Mortuary Practices. *Journal of Anthropological Archaeology* 15:313–336.
2000 Keeping the Peace: Ritual, Skull Caching, and Community Organization in the Levantine Neolithic. In *Life in Neolithic Farming Communities: Social Organization, Identity, and Differentiation*, edited by Ian Kuijt, pp. 137–162. Kluwer Academic/Plenum, New York.

Kuijt, Ian (editor)
1996 *Life in Neolithic Farming Communities: Social Organization, Identity, and Differentiation*. Kluwer Academic/Plenum, New York.

Laist, David W., and John E. Reynolds III
2005 Influence of Power Plants and Other Warm-Water Refuges on Florida Manatees. *Marine Mammal Science* 21:739–764.

Lane, Paul J.
2015 Archaeology in the Age of the Anthropocene: A Critical Assessment of Its Scope and Societal Contributions. *Journal of Field Archaeology* 40:485–498.

Lave, Jean, and Etienne Wenger
1991 *Situated Learning: Legitimate Peripheral Participation*. Cambridge University Press, Cambridge.

Lawres, Nathan R.
2014 Reconceptualizing the Landscape: Changing Patterns of Land Use in a Coalescent Culture. *Journal of Anthropological Research* 70:543–572.

Leacock, Eleanor, and Richard Lee (editors)
1982 *Politics and History in Band Societies*. Cambridge University Press, Cambridge.

Lee, Richard B.
1990   Primitive Communism and the Origins of Social Inequality. In *The Evolution of Political Systems: Sociopolitics in Small-Scale Sedentary Societies*, edited by Steadman Upham, pp. 225–246. Cambridge University Press, Cambridge.
1988   Reflections on Primitive Communism. *Hunters and Gatherers* 1:252–268.
1992   Art, Science, or Politics? The Crisis in Hunter-Gatherer Studies. *American Anthropologist* 94:31–54.

Leone, Mark P., and Parker B. Potter Jr. (editors)
1999   *Historical Archaeologies of Capitalism*. Kluwer Academic/Plenum, New York.

Lesure, Richard G., Thomas A. Wake, Aleksander Borejsza, Jennifer Carballo, David M. Carballo, Isabel Rodríguez López, and Mauro de Ángeles Guzmán
2013   Swidden Agriculture, Village Longevity, and Social Relations in Formative Central Tlaxcala: Towards an Understanding of Macroregional Structure. *Journal of Anthropological Archaeology* 32:224–241.

Levi, Margaret
1988   *Of Rule and Revenue*. University of California Press, Berkeley.

Lindauer, Owen, and John H. Blitz
1997   Higher Ground: The Archaeology of North American Platform Mounds. *Journal of Archaeological Research* 5:169–207.

Little, Maran Elaine
2015   Coastal Weeden Island Subsistence Economy and Occupation: A Zooarchaeological Analysis of Strange's Ring Midden (8By1355), Bay County, Florida. Unpublished master's thesis, Department of Anthropology, University of Georgia, Athens.

Little, Maran E., and Elizabeth J. Reitz
2015   *Vertebrate Remains from the Crystal River Site (8Cl1), Unit 1, Phase 1*. Georgia Museum of Natural History, University of Georgia, Athens. Report submitted to the Department of Anthropology, University of South Florida, Tampa.

Luer, George M.
2011   The Yellow Bluffs Mound Revisited: A Manasota Period Burial Mound in Sarasota. *Florida Anthropologist* 64:5–32.
2013   Tabbed Circular Artifacts in Florida: An Intriguing Type of Gorget and Pendant. *Florida Anthropologist* 66:103–128.

Luer, George M., and Marion M. Almy
1982   A Definition of the Manasota Culture. *Florida Anthropologist* 35:34–58.

Luer, George M., Todd Lumley, and April Lumley
2015   A Tabbed Circular Artifact from the Florida Panhandle. *Florida Anthropologist* 68:65–74.

Lulewicz, Isabelle, Victor D. Thompson, Thomas J. Pluckhahn, Oindrila Das, and Fred T. Andrus
2017   Exploring Oyster (*Crassostrea virginica*) Habitat Collection via Oxygen Isotope Geochemistry and Its Implications for Ritual and Mound Construction at Crystal River and Roberts Island, Florida. *Journal of Island and Coastal Archaeology*, https://doi.org/10.1080/15564894.2017.1363096.

Lyons, Patrick D., and Jeffery J. Clark
2012   A Community of Practice in Diaspora: The Rise and Demise of Roosevelt Red Ware. In *Potters and Communities of Practice: Glaze Paint and Polychrome Pottery in the American Southwest, A.D. 1250 to 1700*, edited by Linda S. Cordell and Judith A. Habcht-Mauche, pp. 19–33. Anthropological Papers of the University of Arizona No. 75. University of Arizona Press, Tucson.

Mabry, Jonathan, Deborah Swartz, Jeffery Clark, Helga Wocherl, and Michael Lindeman
1997   *Archaeological Investigations of Early Village Sites in the Middle Santa Cruz Valley: Descriptions of the Santa Cruz Bend, Square Hearth, Stone Pipe, and Canal Sites*. Anthropological Papers No. 18. Center for Desert Archaeology, Tucson.

Mabulla, Audax Z.
ca. 1990 Skeletal Markers of Occupational Stress in Prehistoric Crystal River Population. Manuscript on file at the Florida Museum of Natural History, Gainesville.

Mainfort, Robert C., Jr. (editor)
2013   *Pinson Mounds: Middle Woodland Ceremonialism in the Midsouth*. University of Arkansas Press, Fayetteville.

Mainfort, Robert C., Jr., and Charles H. McNutt
2013   Calibrated Radiocarbon Chronology for Pinson Mounds and Related Sites. In *Pinson Mounds: Middle Woodland Ceremonialism in the Midsouth*, edited by Robert C. Mainfort Jr., pp. 191–201. University of Arkansas Press, Fayetteville.

Malinowski, Bronislaw
1918   Fishing in the Trobriand Islands. *Man* 18:87–92.

Marcus, Joyce
2008   The Archaeological Evidence for Social Evolution. *Annual Review of Anthropology* 37:251–266.

Marcus, Joyce, and Kent V. Flannery
1996   *Zapotec Civilization: How Urban Society Evolved in Mexico's Oaxaca Valley*. Thames and Hudson, London.

Marean, Curtis W.
2014   The Origins and Significance of Coastal Resource Use in Africa and Western Eurasia. *Journal of Human Evolution* 77:17–40.
2015   The Most Invasive Species of All. *Scientific American* 313(2):32–39.

Marquardt, William H.
2010   Shell Mounds in the Southeast: Middens, Monuments, Temple Mounds, Rings, or Works? *American Antiquity* 75:551–570.
2013   The Pineland Site Complex: Theoretical and Cultural Contexts. In *The Archaeology of Pineland: A Coastal Southwest Florida Site Complex, A.D. 50–1710*, edited by William H. Marquardt and Karen J. Walker, pp. 1–22. Institute of Archaeology and Paleoenvironmental Studies Monograph 4. University of Florida, Gainesville.
2014   Tracking the Calusa: A Retrospective. *Southeastern Archaeology* 33:1–24.

Marquardt, William H., and Laura Kozuch
2016   The Lightning Whelk: An Enduring Icon of Southeastern North American Spirituality. *Journal of Anthropological Archaeology* 42:1–26.

Marquardt, William H., and Karen J. Walker
2012   Southwest Florida during the Mississippian Period. In *Late Prehistoric Florida: Archaeology at the Edge of the Mississippian World*, edited by Keith H. Ashley and Nancy Marie White, pp. 29–61. University Press of Florida, Gainesville.
2013   The Pineland Site Complex: An Environmental and Cultural History. In *The Archaeology of Pineland: A Coastal Southwest Florida Site Complex, A.D. 50–1710*, edited by William H. Marquardt and Karen J. Walker, pp. 793–920. Institute of Archaeology and Paleoenvironmental Studies Monograph 4. University of Florida, Gainesville.

Marrinan, Rochelle A., and Nancy Marie White
2007   Modeling Fort Walton Culture in Northwest Florida. *Southeastern Archaeology* 26:292–318.

Mattson, Robert A., Thomas K. Frazer, Jason Hale, Seth Blitch, and Lisa Ahijevych
2006   Florida Big Bend. In *Seagrass Status and Trends in the Northern Gulf of Mexico: 1940–2002*, edited by Larry Handley, D. Altsman, and R. DeMay, pp. 171–188. U.S. Geological Survey Scientific Investigations Report 2006–5287 5287 and U.S. Environmental Protection Agency 855-R-04-003.

Maybury-Lewis, David
1979a   Conclusion. In *Dialectical Societies: The Gê and Bororo of Central Brazil*, edited by David Maybury-Lewis, pp. 301–312. Harvard University Press, Cambridge.
1979b   Introduction. In *Dialectical Societies: The Gê and Bororo of Central Brazil*, edited by D. Maybury-Lewis, pp. 1–13. Harvard University Press, Cambridge.

Mayewski, Paul A., Eelco E. Rohling, J. Curt Stager, Wibjörn Karlén, Kirk A. Maasch, L. David Meeker, Eric A. Meyerson, Francoise Gasse, Shirley van Kreveld, Karin Holmgren, Julia Lee-Thorp, Gunhild Rosqvist, Frank Rack, Michael Staubwasser, Ralph R. Schneider, and Eric J. Steig
2004   Holocene Climate Variability. *Quaternary Research* 62:243–255.

McClendon, Tom
1972   *Trail and Sign at Crystal River State Park—Crystal River, Florida*. Black & white photoprint, 5 x 4 in. State Archives of Florida, Florida Memory. https://www.floridamemory.com/items/show/86877, accessed October 10, 2017.

McElrath, Dale L., Thomas E. Emerson, and Andrew C. Fortier
2000   Social Evolution or Social Response? A Fresh Look at the "Good Gray Cultures" after Four Decades of Midwest Research. In *Late Woodland Societies: Tradition and Transformation across the Midcontinent*, edited by Thomas E. Emerson, Dale L. McElrath, and Andrew C. Fortier, pp. 3–36. University of Nebraska Press, Lincoln.

McFadden, Paulette S.
2015   Late Holocene Coastal Evolution and Human Occupation on the Northern Gulf Coast of Florida. Ph.D. dissertation, Department of Anthropology, University of Florida, Gainesville.
2016   Coastal Dynamics and Pre-Columbian Human Occupation in Horseshoe Cove on the Northern Gulf Coast of Florida, USA. *Geoarchaeology: An International Journal* 31:355–375.

McGuire, Randall H.
1992 *A Marxist Archaeology*. Academic Press, San Diego.
McGuire, Randall H., and Robert Paynter (editors)
1991 *The Archaeology of Inequality*. Basil Blackwell, Inc. Cambridge, Massachusetts.
McMichael, Edward V.
1960 The Anatomy of a Tradition: A Study of Southeastern Stamped Pottery. Ph.D. dissertation, Department of Anthropology, Indiana University, Bloomington. University Microfilms, Ann Arbor.
1964 Veracruz, the Crystal River Complex, and the Hopewellian Climax. In *Hopewellian Studies*, edited by Joseph R. Caldwell and Robert L. Hall, pp. 123–132. Scientific Papers Vol. 12. Illinois State Museum, Springfield.
McNiven, Ian
2004 Saltwater People: Spiritscapes, Maritime Rituals and the Archaeology of Australian Indigenous Seascapes. *World Archaeology* 35:329–349.
Meier, Fred
1972 Ending the Vietnam War Is Easier. *Ocala Star-Banner*, Friday, October 20, 1972:2A, vol. 29. Ocala, Florida.
Menz, Martin W.
2013 The Use-Life and Times of the Type-G Shell Hammer: A Descriptive and Experimental Analysis of Shell Hammers from Roberts Island (8CI41). Unpublished honor's thesis, Department of Anthropology, University of South Florida, Tampa.
2015 Like Blood from a Stone: Teasing Out Social Difference from Lithic Production Debris at Kolomoki (9ER1). Unpublished master's thesis, Department of Anthropology, University of South Florida, Tampa.
2016 The Use-Life and Times of the Type-G Shell Hammer: A Replicative Experiment and Use-Wear Analysis of Shell Tools from Crystal River (8CI1) and Roberts Island (8CI41). *Florida Anthropologist* 69:129–144.
Mickwee, Christopher L.
2009 Wakulla in the Sandhills: Analysis of a Late Weeden Island Occupation in the Northwest Florida Interior Uplands. Paper presented at the Annual Meeting of the Florida Anthropological Society, Pensacola.
Mikkelsen, Naja, Antoon Kuijpers, and Jette Arneborg
2008 The Norse in Greenland and Late Holocene Sea-Level Change. *Polar Record* 44:45–50.
Milanich, Jerald T.
1974 Life in a 9th Century Indian Household, a Weeden Island Fall–Winter Site on the Upper Apalachicola River, Florida. *Florida Bureau of Historic Sites and Properties Bulletin* 4:1–44.
1977 Ripley Pierce Bullen, 1902–1976. *Florida Anthropologist* 30:34–35.
1979 Origins and Prehistoric Distributions of Black Drink and the Ceremonial Drinking Cup. In *Black Drink: A Native American Tea*, edited by Charles M. Hudson, pp. 83–119. University of Georgia Press, Athens.
1994 *Archaeology of Precolumbian Florida*. University Press of Florida, Gainesville.

1999   Introduction. In *Famous Florida Sites: Crystal River and Mount Royal*, edited by Jerald T. Milanich, pp. 1–28. University Press of Florida, Gainesville.
2007   Gordon R. Willey and the Archaeology of the Florida Gulf Coast. In *Gordon R. Willey and American Archaeology: Contemporary Perspectives*, edited by Jeremy A. Sabloff and William L. Fash, pp. 15–25. University of Oklahoma Press, Norman.

Milanich, Jerald T., Jefferson Chapman, Ann S. Cordell, H. Stephen Hale, and Rochelle A. Marrinan
1984   Prehistoric Development of Calusa Society in Southwest Florida: Excavations on Useppa Island. In *Perspectives on Gulf Coast Prehistory*, edited by Dave D. Davis, pp. 258–314. University Presses of Florida, Gainesville.

Milanich, Jerald T., Ann S. Cordell, Vernon J. Knight Jr., Timothy A. Kohler, and Brenda J. Sigler-Lavelle
1997   *Archaeology of Northern Florida, A.D. 200–900: The McKeithen Weeden Island Culture*. Academic Press, New York. Originally published 1984.

Mitchem, Jeffrey McClain
1988   Some Alternative Interpretations of Safety Harbor Burial Mounds. *Florida Scientist* 51:100–107.
1989   Redefining Safety Harbor: Late Prehistoric/Protohistoric Archaeology in West Peninsular Florida. Unpublished Ph.D. dissertation, Department of Anthropology, University of Florida, Gainesville.

Mitchem, Jeffrey M., and Brent R. Weisman
1987   Changing Settlement Patterns and Pottery Types in the Withlacoochee Cove. *Florida Anthropologist* 40:154–166.

Monés, Micah P., Neill J. Wallis, and Kenneth E. Sassaman
2012   *Archaeological Investigations at Deer Island, Levy County, Florida*. Technical Report 15. Laboratory of Southeastern Archaeology, Department of Anthropology, University of Florida.

Moore, Clarence Bloomfield
1901   Certain Aboriginal Remains of the Northwest Florida Coast. Part I. *Journal of the Academy of Natural Sciences of Philadelphia*, second series 11:421–497.
1902   Certain Aboriginal Remains of the Northwest Florida Coast. Part II. *Journal of the Academy of Natural Sciences of Philadelphia*, second series 12:127–358.
1903   Certain Aboriginal Mounds of the Central Florida West-Coast. *Journal of the Academy of Natural Sciences of Philadelphia* 12:361–438.
1907   Crystal River Revisited. *Journal of the Academy of Natural Sciences of Philadelphia*, second series 13:406–25.
1918   The Northwestern Florida Coast Revisited. *Journal of the Academy of Natural Sciences of Philadelphia*, second series 16:514–81.

Moore, J. C.
1951a   The Range of the Florida Manatee. *Quarterly Journal of the Florida Academy of Science* 14:1–19.
1951b   The Status of Manatees in the Everglades National Park, with Notes on Its Natural History. *Journal of Mammalogy* 32:22–36.

Moss, Madonna L.
2011   *Northwest Coast: Archaeology as Deep History*. SAA Press, Washington, D.C.

Muller, Jon
1997   *Mississippian Political Economy*. Plenum Press, New York.

Murphy, J. M.
1987 [1890]   Turtling in Florida. Reproduced in *Tales of Old Florida*, edited by Frank Oppel and Tony Meisel, pp. 75–84. Castle Books, Edison, New Jersey.

Myers, Fred R.
1988   Critical Trends in the Study of Hunter-Gatherers. *Annual Review of Anthropology* 17:261–282.

Nassaney, Michael S.
1992   Communal Societies and the Emergence of Elites in the Prehistoric American Southeast. In *Lords of the Southeast: Social Inequality and the Native Elites of Southeastern North America*, edited by Alex Barker and Timothy Pauketat, pp. 111–143. Archaeological Papers No. 3. American Anthropological Association, Washington, D.C.
2000   The Late Woodland Southeast. In *Late Woodland Societies: Tradition and Transformation across the Midcontinent*, edited by Thomas E. Emerson, Dale L. McElrath, and Andrew C. Fortier, pp. 713–30. University of Nebraska Press, Lincoln.
2001   A Historical-Processual Development of Late Woodland Societies. In *The Archaeology of Traditions: Agency and History Before and After Columbus*, edited by T.R. Pauketat, pp. 157–173. University Press of Florida, Gainesville.

Nassaney, Michael S., and Charles R. Cobb
1991   Patterns and Processes of Late Woodland Development in the Greater Southeastern United States. In *Stability, Transformation, and Variation: The Late Woodland Southeast*, edited by Michael S. Nassaney and Charles R. Cobb, pp. 285–322. Plenum Press, New York.

Neill, Wilfred T., and J. C. McKay
1968   A Supposed "Florida Folsom" Point: A Refutation. *Florida Anthropologist* 21:122–123.

Nelson, Sarah M.
2004   *Korean Social Archaeology: Early Villages*. Jimoondang, Seoul.

Neusius, Sarah W., and G. Timothy Gross
2007   *Seeking Our Past: An Introduction to North American Archaeology*. Oxford University Press, New York.

Norman, Sean
2014   Modeling the Relationship between Climate Change and Landscape Modification at the Crystal River Site (8CI1), Florida. Unpublished master's thesis, Department of Anthropology, University of South Florida, Tampa.

Ocala Star-Banner [Ocala, Florida]
1965   Former Californian Plans Two Trailer Parks. Thursday, November 25:1A. Ocala, Florida.

Oka, Rahul, and Chapurukha M. Kusimba
2008   The Archaeology of Trading Systems, Part 1: Towards a New Trade Synthesis. *Journal of Archaeological Research* 16:339–395.

Olasky, Marvin
1992   *The Tragedy of American Compassion*. Regnery, Washington, D.C.

O'Neal, Lori
2016   What's in Your Toolbox? Examining Tool Choices at Two Middle and Late Woodland–Period Sites on Florida's Central Gulf Coast. Unpublished master's thesis, Department of Anthropology, University of South Florida, Tampa.

Ortman, Scott G., and Grant D. Coffey
2017   Settlement Scaling in Middle-Range Societies. *American Antiquity* 82:662–682.

Ortman, Scott G., Kaitlyn E. Davis, José Lobo, Michael E. Smith, Luís M. A. Bettencourt, and Aaron Trumbo
2016   Settlement Scaling and Economic Change in the Central Andes. *Journal of Archaeological Science* 73:94–106.

Ostrom, Elinor
1990   *Governing the Commons: The Evolution of Institutions for Collective Action*. Cambridge University Press, Cambridge.
2000   Collective Action and the Evolution of Social Norms. *Journal of Economic Perspectives* 14(3):137–158.

Otto, Martha Potter
1975   A New Engraved Adena Tablet. *Ohio Archaeologist* 25:31–36.

Parker Pearson, Mike
2008   *The Archaeology of Death and Burial*. Texas A&M University Press, College Station.

Pattillo, Mark E., Thomas E. Czapla, David M. Nelson, and Mark E. Monaco
1997   *Distribution and Abundance of Fishes and Invertebrates in Gulf of Mexico Estuaries: II: Species Life History Summaries*. ELMR Report No. 11. National Oceanic and Atmospheric Administration (NOAA), National Ocean Service (NOS), Strategic Environmental Assessments Division, Silver Spring, Maryland.

Patton, R. B.
2001   The Spatial Structure and Process of Nonagricultural Production: Settlement Patterns and Political Development in Precolumbian Southwest Florida. Ph.D. dissertation, Department of Anthropology, University of Florida, Gainesville.

Pauketat, Timothy R.
1994   *The Ascent of Chiefs: Cahokia and Mississippian Politics in Native North America*. University of Alabama Press, Tuscaloosa.
2000   Tragedy of the Commoners. In *Agency in Archaeology*, edited by Marcia-Anne Dobres and John Robb, pp. 113–129. Routledge, New York.
2001a   A New Tradition in Archaeology. In *The Archaeology of Traditions: Agency and History before and after Columbus*, edited by Timothy R. Pauketat, pp. 1–16. University Press of Florida, Gainesville.

2001b   Practice and History in Archaeology: An Emerging Paradigm. *Anthropological Theory* 1:73–98.
2003   Resettled Farmers and the Making of a Mississippian Polity. *American Antiquity* 68:39–66.
2004   *Ancient Cahokia and the Mississippians*. Cambridge University Press, Cambridge.
2007   *Chiefdoms and Other Archaeological Delusions*. AltaMira Press, Lanham.
2009   Foreword. In *War Paths, Peace Paths: An Archaeology of Cooperation and Conflict in Native Eastern North America*, by David H. Dye, pp. xi–xiii. AltaMira Press, Lanham.
2012   *An Archaeology of the Cosmos: Rethinking Agency and Religion in Ancient America*. Routledge, New York.

Pauketat, Timothy R., and Susan M. Alt
2005   Agency in a Postmold? Physicality and the Archaeology of Culture-making. *Journal of Archaeological Method and Theory* 12:213–237.

Pauketat, Timothy R., Preston T. Miracle, and Sandra L. Dunavan
1998   *The Archaeology of Downtown Cahokia: The Tract 15A and Dunham Tract Excavations*. University of Illinois Press, Urbana.

Payne, Claudine
1994   Mississippian Capitals: An Archaeological Investigation of PreColumbian Political Structure. Ph.D. dissertation, Department of Anthropology, University of Florida, Gainesville.

Payne, Claudine, and John F. Scarry
1998   Town Structure at the Edge of the Mississippian World. In *Mississippian Towns and Sacred Spaces: Searching for an Architectural Grammar*, edited by R. Barry Lewis and Charles Stout, pp. 22–48. University of Alabama Press, Tuscaloosa.

Peacock, Evan, and Janet Rafferty
2013   The Bet Hedging Model as an Explanatory Framework for the Evolution of Mound Building in the Southeastern United States. In *Beyond Barrows: Current Research on the Structuration and Perception of the Prehistoric Landscape through Monuments*, edited by David Fontijn, Arjan J. Louwen, Sasja Van Der Vaart, and Karstan Wentink, pp. 251–279. Sidestone Press, Leiden.

Pearson, James L.
2002   *Shamanism and the Ancient Mind: A Cognitive Approach to Archaeology*. Rowman Altamira, Walnut Creek, California.

Peebles, Christopher S., and Susan M. Kus
1977   Some Archaeological Correlates of Ranked Societies. *American Antiquity* 42:421–448.

Pennisi, Elizabeth
2005   How Did Cooperative Behaviors Evolve? *Science* 309(5731):93.

Percy, George W., and David S. Brose
1974   Weeden Island Ecology, Subsistence and Village Life: A Comparison of Coastal and Inland Manifestations in Northwestern and Central Gulf Coast Florida

and Adjacent Sections of Alabama and Georgia. Paper presented at the 39th Annual Meeting of the Society for American Archaeology, Washington, D.C.

Perillo, Gerardo M. E.
1995 Definitions and Geomorphologic Classifications of Estuaries. *Developments in Sedimentology* 53:17–47.

Phillips, Philip, and James A. Brown
1978 *Pre-Columbian Shell Engravings from the Craig Mound at Spiro, Oklahoma*, Part 1. Peabody Museum Press, Cambridge.

Phillips, Philip, James A. Ford, and James B. Griffin
1951 *Archaeological Survey in the Lower Mississippi Alluvial Valley, 1940–1947*. Papers of the Peabody Museum of American Archaeology and Ethnology Vol. 25. Harvard University, Cambridge.

Pietak, Lynn M.
1998 Body Symbolism and Cultural Aesthetics: The Use of Shell Beads and Ornaments by Delaware and Munsee Groups. *North American Archaeologist* 19:135–161.

Pluckhahn, Thomas J.
1996 Joseph Caldwell's Summerour Mound and Late Woodland Platform Mounds in the Southeastern United States. *Southeastern Archaeology* 15:191–210.
2002 Kolomoki: Settlement, Ceremony, and Status in the Deep South, ca. 350 to 750 A.D. Ph.D. dissertation, Department of Anthropology, University of Georgia, Athens.
2003 *Kolomoki: Settlement, Ceremony, and Status in the Deep South, ca. 350 to 750 A.D.* University of Alabama Press, Tuscaloosa.
2007 "The Mounds Themselves Might Be Perfectly Happy in Their Surroundings": The "Kolomoki Problem" in Notes and Letters. *Florida Anthropologist* 60:63–76.
2010a Practicing Complexity (Past and Present) at Kolomoki. In *Ancient Complexities: New Perspectives in Precolumbian North America*, edited by Susan M. Alt, pp. 52–72. University of Utah Press, Salt Lake City.
2010b The Sacred and the Secular Revisited: The Essential Tensions of Early Village Societies in the Southeastern U.S. In *Becoming Villagers: Comparing Early Village Societies*, edited by Matthew S. Bandy and Jake R. Fox, pp. 100–118. University of Arizona Press, Tucson.
2013 Cooperation and Competition among Late Woodland Households at Kolomoki, Georgia. In *Cooperation and Collective Action: Archaeological Perspectives*, edited by David M. Carballo, pp. 175–196. University Press of Colorado, Boulder.

Pluckhahn, Thomas J., Alex D. Hodson, W. Jack Rink, Victor D. Thompson, Robert R. Hendricks, Glen Doran, Grayal Farr, Alexander Cherkinsky, and Sean P. Norman
2015 Radiocarbon and Luminescence Age Determinations on Mounds at Crystal River and Roberts Island, Florida, USA. *Geoarchaeology: An International Journal* 30:238–260.

Pluckhahn, Thomas J., Martin Menz, and Lori O'Neal
2018 Crafting Everyday Matters in the Middle and Late Woodland Periods. In *Investigating the Ordinary: Everyday Matters in Southeast Archaeology*, edited by Sarah E. Price and Philip J. Carr, pp. 112–123. University Press of Florida, Gainesville.

Pluckhahn, Thomas J., Martin Menz, Shaun E. West, and Neill J. Wallis
2018 A New History of Community Formation and Change at Kolomoki (9ER1). *American Antiquity*, in press.

Pluckhahn, Thomas J., Rachel Thompson, and Kassie Kemp
2017 Constructing Community at Civic-Ceremonial Centers: Pottery-Making Practices at Crystal River and Roberts Island. *Southeastern Archaeology* 36:110–121.

Pluckhahn, Thomas J., and Victor D. Thompson
2009 Mapping Crystal River: Past, Present, and Future. *Florida Anthropologist* 62:3–22.
2013 Constituting Similarity and Difference in the Deep South: The Ritual and Domestic Landscapes of Kolomoki, Crystal River, and Fort Center. In *Landscapes and People of the Early and Middle Woodland Southeast*, edited by Alice P. Wright and Edward R. Henry, pp. 181–195. University Press of Florida, Gainesville.
2017 Woodland-Period Mound Building as Historical Tradition: Dating the Mounds and Monuments at Crystal River (8CI1). *Journal of Archaeological Science: Reports* 15:73–94.

Pluckhahn, Thomas J., Victor D. Thompson, and Alexander Cherkinsky
2015 The Temporality of Shell-Bearing Landscapes at Crystal River, Florida. *Journal of Anthropological Archaeology* 37:19–36.

Pluckhahn, Thomas J., Victor D. Thompson, Nicolas Laracuente, Sarah Mitchell, Amanda Roberts, and Adrianne Sams
2009 *Archaeological Investigations at the Famous Crystal River Site (8CI1) (2008 Field Season), Citrus County, Florida*. Department of Anthropology, University of South Florida, Tampa. Submitted to Bureau of Natural & Cultural Resources, Division of Recreation and Parks, Florida Department of Environmental Protection, Tallahassee.

Pluckhahn, Thomas J., Victor D. Thompson, and W. Jack Rink
2016 Evidence for Stepped Pyramids of Shell in the Woodland Period of Eastern North America. *American Antiquity* 81:345–363.

Pluckhahn, Thomas J., Victor D. Thompson, and Brent R. Weisman
2010 A New View of History and Process at Crystal River. *Southeastern Archaeology* 29:164–181.

Potter, James M., and Elizabeth M. Perry
2011 Mortuary Features and Identity Construction in an Early Village Community in the American Southwest. *American Antiquity* 76:529–546.

Prentiss, William C., and Ian Kuijt
2004 Introduction: The Archaeology of the Plateau Region of Northwestern North America—Approaches to the Evolution of Complex Hunter-Gatherers. In

Complex Hunter-Gatherers: Evolution and Organization of Prehistoric Communities on the Plateau of Northwestern North America, edited by William C. Prentiss and Ian Kuijt, pp. vii–xviii. University of Utah Press, Salt Lake City.

Price, T. Douglas
1985   Affluent Foragers of Mesolithic Southern Scandinavia. In *Prehistoric Hunter-Gatherers: The Emergence of Cultural Complexity*, edited by T. Douglas Price and James A. Brown, pp. 341–363. Academic Press, San Diego.
2006   *Principles of Archaeology*. McGraw Hill, Boston.

Pritchard, Donald W.
1967   What Is an Estuary: Physical Viewpoint. In *Estuaries*, edited by George H. Lauff, pp. 3–5. American Association for the Advancement of Science, Washington, D.C.

Purdy, Barbara A.
2008   *Florida's People during the Last Ice Age*. University Press of Florida, Gainesville.

Pyburn, K. Anne
2007   Archeology as Activism. In *Cultural Heritage and Human Rights*, edited by Helaine Silverman and D. Fairchild Ruggles, pp. 172–183. Springer, New York.

Raab, L. Mark
1992   An Optimal Foraging Analysis of Prehistoric Shellfish Collecting on San Clemente Island, California. *Journal of Ethnobiology* 12:63–80.

Rainey, Froelich G.
1935   An Indian Burial Site at Crystal River, Florida. *Florida Historical Quarterly* 13:185–192.

Rampino, Michael R., Stephen Self, and Richard B. Stothers
1988   Volcanic Winters. *Annual Review of Earth and Planetary Sciences* 16:73–99.

Randall, Asa R.
2015   *Constructing Histories: Archaic Freshwater Shell Mounds and Social Landscapes of the St. Johns River, Florida*. University Press of Florida, Gainesville.

Randall, Asa R., and Kenneth E. Sassaman
2010   (E)mergent Complexities during the Archaic Period in Northeast Florida. In *Ancient Complexities: New Perspectives in Precolumbian North America*, edited by Susan M. Alt, pp. 8–31. University of Utah Press, Salt Lake City.

Rautman, Alison E.
2014   *Constructing Community: The Archaeology of Early Villages in Central New Mexico*. University of Arizona Press, Tucson.
2016   "Circling the Wagons" and Community Formation: Interpreting Circular Villages in the Archaeological Record. *World Archaeology* 48:125–143.

Regnier, Amanda L.
2014   *Reconstructing Tascalusa's Chiefdom: Pottery Styles and the Social Composition of Late Mississippian Communities along the Alabama River*. University of Alabama Press, Tuscaloosa.

Reimer, P. J., M.G.L. Baillie, E. Bard, A. Bayliss, J. W. Beck, C. J. H. Bertrand, P. G. Blackwell, C. E. Buck, G. S. Burr, K. B. Cutler, P. E. Damon, R. L. Edwards, R. G. Fairbanks, M. Friedrich, T. P. Guilderson, A. G. Hogg, K. A. Hughen, B. Kromer,

F. G. McCormac, S. W. Manning, C. B. Ramsey, R. W. Reimer, S. Remmele, J. R. Southon, M. Stuiver, S. Talamo, F. W. Taylor, J. van der Plicht, C. E. and Weyhenmeyer

2004   IntCal04 Terrestrial Radiocarbon Age Calibration, 26–0 ka BP. *Radiocarbon* 46:1029–1058.

Reis, Robert Lawrence

2013   Hopewell Panpipe, Music, Art, and Expression: An Exploration of Music In Hopewell Culture. Unpublished master's thesis, Department of Sociology and Archaeology, University of Wisconsin–La Crosse.

Reitz, Elizabeth J., and Kelly B. Brown

2015   *Vertebrate Remains from the Crystal River Site (8Cl1), Unit 5, Phases 1 and 2. Georgia Museum of Natural History, University of Georgia, Athens.* Report submitted to the Department of Anthropology, University of South Florida, Tampa.

Reitz, Elizabeth J., Carla S. Hadden, Maran E. Little, Gregory A. Waselkov, C. Frederick T. Andrus, and Evan Peacock

2013   *Final Project Report: Woodland Seasonality on the Northern Coast of the Gulf of Mexico.* Final technical report submitted to the National Science Foundation for project title "Collaborative Research Project: Woodland Subsistence Seasonality on the Northern Gulf Coast" (Award #BCS 1026167). Manuscript on file, Zooarchaeology Laboratory, Georgia Museum of Natural History, University of Georgia, Athens.

Richerson, Peter J., Robert T. Boyd, and Joseph Henrich

2003   Cultural Evolution of Human Cooperation. In *Genetic and Cultural Evolution of Cooperation*, edited by Peter Hammerstein, pp. 357–388. MIT Press and Preie Universität, Cambridge and Berlin.

Robb, John, and Timothy R. Pauketat

2013   From Moments to Millennia: Theorizing Scale and Change in Human History. In *Big Histories, Human Lives: Tackling Problems of Scale in Archaeology*, edited by John Robb and Timothy R. Pauketat, pp. 3–33. SAR Press, Santa Fe.

Robbin, Daniel M.

1984   A New Holocene Sea Level Curve for the Upper Florida Keys and Florida Reef Tract. In *Environments of South Florida, Present and Past II*, edited by Patrick Gleason, pp. 437–457. Miami Geological Society, Miami.

Roddick, Andrew Paul

2009   Communities of Pottery Production and Consumption on the Taraco Peninsula, Bolivia 200 BC–300 AD. Unpublished Ph.D. dissertation, Department of Anthropology, University of California.

Rolingson, Martha Ann

2012   *Toltec Mounds: Archeology of the Mound-and-Plaza Complex.* Arkansas Archeological Survey, Fayetteville.

Romain, William F.

2009   *Shamans of the Lost World: A Cognitive Approach to the Prehistoric Religion of the Ohio Hopewell.* Altamira Press, Lanham.

Roscoe, Paul
2009 Social Signaling and the Organization of Small-Scale Society. *Journal of Archaeological Method and Theory* 16:69–116.
2013 War, Collective Action, and the "Evolution" of Human Polities. In *Cooperation and Collective Action: Archaeological Perspectives*, edited by David M. Carballo, pp. 57–82. University Press of Colorado, Boulder.

Rosenberg, Michael, and Richard W. Redding
2000 Hallan Çemi and Early Village Organization in Eastern Anatolia. In *Life in Neolithic Farming Communities: Social Organization, Identity, and Differentiation*, edited by Ian Kuijt, pp. 39–62. Kluwer Academic/Plenum, New York.

Ruby, Bret J., Christopher Carr, and Douglas K. Charles
2005 Community Organizations in the Scioto, Mann and Havana Hopewellian Regions: A Comparative Perspective. In *Gathering Hopewell: Society, Ritual, and Ritual Interaction*, edited by Christopher Carr and D. Troy Case, pp. 119–176. New York: Kluwer Academic/Plenum.

Ruddiman, William F., Michel C. Crucifix, and F. A. Oldfield
2011 Introduction to the Early-Anthropocene. Special issue. *Holocene* 21:713.

Ruddiman, William F., Erie C. Ellis, Jed O. Kaplan, and Dorian Q. Fuller
2015 Defining the Epoch We Live In. *Science* 348(6230):38–39.

Ruhl, Donna
1981 An Investigation into the Relationships between Midwestern Hopewell and Southeastern Prehistory. Unpublished master's thesis, Department of Anthropology, Florida Atlantic University, Boca Raton.

Russo, Michael
1991 Archaic Sedentism on the Florida Coast: A Case Study from Horr's Island. Ph.D. dissertation, Department of Anthropology, University of Florida, Gainesville.
1994 Why We Don't Believe in Archaic Ceremonial Mounds and Why We Should: The Case from Florida. *Southeastern Archaeology* 13:93–108.

Russo, Michael, Craig Dengel, and Jeffrey Shanks
2014 Northwest Florida Woodland Mounds and Middens: The Sacred and Not So Secular. In *New Histories of Pre-Columbian Florida*, edited by Neill J. Wallis and Asa R. Randall, pp. 121–142. University Press of Florida, Gainesville.

Russo, Michael, and Gregory Heide
2001 Shell Rings of the Southeast US. *Antiquity* 75:491–492.

Russo, Michael, Margo Schwadron, and Emily M. Yates
2006 *Archeological Investigation of the Bayview Site (8BY137), a Weeden Island Ring Midden, Tyndall Air Force Base, Panama City, Florida*. National Park Service, Southeast Archeological Center, Tallahassee. Submitted to Tyndall Air Force Base, Panama City, Florida.

Sabloff, Jeremy A.
2008 *Archaeology Matters: Action Archaeology in the Modern World*. Left Coast Press, Walnut Creek, California.

Saitta, Dean J.
1997   Power, Labor, and the Dynamics of Change in Chacoan Political Economy. *American Antiquity* 62:7–26.
2007   *The Archaeology of Collective Action*. University Press of Florida, Gainesville.
2013   Agency and Collective Action: Insights from North American Historical Archaeology. In *Cooperation and Collective Action: Archaeological Perspectives*, edited by David M. Carballo, pp. 129–150. University Press of Colorado, Boulder.

Sampson, Christina Perry
2015   Oyster Demographics and the Creation of Coastal Monuments at Roberts Island Mound Complex, Florida. *Southeastern Archaeology* 34:84–94.

Sanger, Matthew Clair
2015   Life in the Round: Shell Rings of the Georgia Bight. Ph.D. dissertation, Department of Anthropology, Columbia University, New York.

Sassaman, Kenneth E.
1993   *Early Pottery in the Southeast: Tradition and Innovation in Cooking Technology*. University of Alabama Press, Tuscaloosa.
2004   Complex Hunter-Gatherers in Evolution and History: A North American Perspective. *Journal of Archaeological Research* 12:227–280.
2005   Poverty Point as Structure, Event, Process. *Journal of Archaeological Method and Theory* 12:335–364.
2006   *People of the Shoals: Stallings Culture of the Savannah River Valley*. University Press of Florida, Gainesville.
2010   *The Eastern Archaic, Historicized*. Altamira Press, Lanham.
2012   Futurologists Look Back. *Archaeologies* 8:250–268.

Sassaman, Kenneth E., and Donald H. Holly Jr.
2011   Transformative Hunter-Gatherer Archaeology in North America. In *Hunter-Gatherer Archaeology as Historical Process*, edited by Kenneth E. Sassaman and Donald H. Holly Jr., pp. 1–16. University of Arizona Press, Tucson.

Sassaman, Kenneth E., Paulette S. McFadden, and Micah P. Monés
2011   Lower Suwannee Archaeological Survey 2009–2010: Investigations at Cat Island (8DI29), Little Bradford Island (8DI32), and Richards Island (8LV137). Technical Report 10, Laboratory of Southeastern Archaeology, Department of Anthropology, University of Florida, Gainesville.

Sassaman, Kenneth E., Paulette S. McFadden, Micah P. Monés, Andrea Palmiotto, and Asa R. Randall
2014   Northern Gulf Coastal Archaeology of the Here and Now. In *New Histories of Precolumbian Florida*, edited by Neill J. Wallis and Asa R. Randall, pp. 143–162. University Press of Florida, Gainesville.

Sassaman, Kenneth E., Andrea Palmiotto, Ginessa J. Mahar, Micah P. Monés, and Paulette S. McFadden
2013   Archaeological Investigations at Shell Mound (8LV42), Levy County, Florida: 2012 Testing. Technical Report 16, Laboratory of Southeastern Archaeology, Department of Anthropology, University of Florida, Gainesville.

Sassaman, Kenneth E., and Asa R. Randall
2012   Shell Mounds of the Middle St. Johns Basin, Northeast Florida. In *Early New World Monumentality*, edited by Richard L. Burger and Robert M. Rosenwig, pp. 53–72. University Press of Florida, Gainesville.

Sassaman, Kenneth E., and Wictoria Rudolphi
2001   Communities of Practice in the Early Pottery Traditions of the American Southeast. *Journal of Anthropological Research* 57:407–425.

Saxe, Arthur A.
1970   Social Dimensions of Mortuary Practices. Ph.D. disssertation, Department of Anthropology, University of Michigan, Ann Arbor.

Schilling, Timothy
2013   The Chronology of Monks Mound. *Southeastern Archaeology* 32:14–28.

Schmidtz, David
1998   Taking Responsibility. In *Social Welfare and Individual Responsibility*, by David Schmidtz and Robert E. Goodin, pp. 1–94. Cambridge University Press, New York.

Schober, Theresa
2014   Deconstructing and Reconstructing Caloosahatchee Shell Mound Building. In *New Histories of Pre-Columbian Florida*. In *New Histories of Precolumbian Florida*, edited by Neill J. Wallis and Asa R. Randall, pp. 38–61. University Press of Florida, Gainesville.

Scholl, David W., Frank C. Craighead, and Minze Stuiver
1969   Florida Submergence Curve Revisited: Its Relation to Sedimentation Rates. *Science* 163:562–564.

Schroeder, William W., and William J. Wiseman Jr.
1999   Geology and Hydrodynamics of Gulf of Mexico Estuaries. In *Biogeochemistry of Gulf of Mexico Estuaries*, edited by Thomas S. Bianchi, Jonathan R. Pennock, and Robert R. Twilley, pp. 3–30. John Wiley and Sons, New York.

Schwadron, Margo
2010   Landscapes of Maritime Complexity: Prehistoric Shell Work Sites of the Ten Thousand Islands, Florida. Ph.D. dissertation, University of Leicester, Leicester.

Schwartz, Joel
1998   Moral Reform—Learning from the Past. *Public Interest* 131:71–91.

Sears, William H.
1956   *Excavations at Kolomoki: Final Report*. University of Georgia Press, Athens.
1962   Hopewellian Affiliations of Certain Sites on the Gulf Coast of Florida. *American Antiquity* 28:5–18.

Sears, William H. (editor)
1982   *Fort Center: An Archaeological Site in the Lake Okeechobee Basin*. University Presses of Florida, Gainesville.

Seeman, Mark F.
1979   *The Hopewell Interaction Sphere: The Evidence for Inter-Regional Trade and Structural Complexity*. Ph.D. dissertation, Department of Anthropology, Indiana University, Bloomington. University Microfilms, Ann Arbor.

1988 Ohio Hopewell Trophy-Skull Artifacts as Evidence for Competition in Middle Woodland Societies circa 50 BC–AD 350. *American Antiquity* 53:565–577.

1995 When Words Are Not Enough: Hopewell Interregionalism and the Use of Material Symbols at the GE Mound. In *Native American Interactions: Multiscalar Analyses and Interpretations in the Eastern Woodlands*, edited by Michael S. Nassaney and Kenneth E. Sassaman, pp. 122–143. University of Tennessee Press, Knoxville.

Seeman, Mark F., and James Branch

2006 The Mounded Landscapes of Ohio: Hopewell Patterns and Placements. In *Recreating Hopewell: New Perspectives on Middle Woodland in Eastern North America*, edited by Douglas K. Charles and Jane E. Buikstra, pp. 106–121. University Press of Florida, Gainesville.

Sewell, William H., Jr.

2005 *The Logics of History: Social Theory and Social Transformation*. University of Chicago Press, Chicago.

Sherwood, Sarah C., and Tristram R. Kidder

2011 The DaVincis of Dirt: Geoarchaeological Perspectives on Native American Mound Building in the Mississippi River Basin. *Journal of Anthropological Archaeology* 30:69–87.

Silverberg, Robert

1986 *The Mound Builders*. Ohio University Press, Athens.

Simek, Jan F., Alan Cressler, and Nicholas P. Herrmann

2015 Prehistoric Rock Art from Painted Bluff and the Landscape of North Alabama Rock Art. *Southeastern Archaeology* 32:218–234.

Simek, Jan F., Alan Cressler, Nicholas P. Herrmann, and Sarah C. Sherwood

2013 Sacred Landscapes of the Southeastern USA: Prehistoric Rock and Cave Art in Tennessee. *Antiquity* 87:430–446.

Simons, Robert W.

1990 Terrestrial and Freshwater Habitats. In *An Ecological Characterization of the Florida Springs Coast: Pithlachascotee to Waccasassa Rivers*, edited by Steven H. Wolfe, pp. 99–157. USFWS Biological Report 90 (21). U.S. Fish and Wildlife Service, National Wetlands Research Center, Slidell, Louisiana.

Small, John K.

1924 The Land Where Spring Meets Autumn. *Journal of the New York Botanical Garden* 25:53–94.

1929 *From Eden to Sahara, Florida's Tragedy*. Science Press, Lancaster, Pennsylvania.

Smith, Betty A.

1975 A Re-analysis of the Mandeville Site, 9Cy1, Focusing on Its Internal History and External Relations. Unpublished Ph.D. dissertation, Department of Anthropology, University of Georgia, Athens.

1979 The Hopewell Connection in Southwest Georgia. In *Hopewell Archaeology: The Chillicothe Conference*, edited by David S. Brose and N'omi Greber, pp. 181–87. Kent State University Press, Kent, Ohio.

Smith, Bruce D.
1986   The Archaeology of the Southeastern United States: From Dalton to DeSoto, 10,500 to 500 B.P. *Advances in World Archaeology* 5:1–91.

Smith, Bruce D., and Martha A. Zeder
2013   The Onset of the Anthropocene. *Anthropocene* 4:8–13.

Smith, Eric A.
2003   Human Cooperation: Perspectives from Behavioral Ecology. In *Genetic and Cultural Evolution of Cooperation*, edited by Peter Hammerstein, pp. 401–427. MIT Press and Preie Universität, Cambridge and Berlin.

Smith, Eric A., and Rebecca Bliege Bird
2000   Turtle Hunting and Tombstone Opening: Public Generosity as Costly Signaling. *Evolution and Human Behavior* 21:245–261.
2005   Costly Signaling and Cooperative Behavior. In *Moral Sentiments and Material Interests: The Foundations of Cooperation in Economic Life*, edited by Herbert Gintis, Samuel Bowles, Robert Boyd, and Ernst Fehr, pp. 115–148. MIT Press, Cambridge.

Smith, Hale G.
1951   Crystal River, Revisited, Revisited, Revisited. *American Antiquity* 17:143–144.

Somers, Lewis
2006   Resistivity Survey. In *Remote Sensing in Archaeology: An Explicitly North American Perspective*, edited by Jay K. Johnson, pp. 109–130. University of Alabama Press, Tuscaloosa.

Spencer, Charles S.
2013   The Competitive Context of Cooperation in Pre-Hispanic Barinas, Venezuela: A Multi-Level Selection Approach. In *Cooperation and Collective Action: Archaeological Perspectives*, edited by David M. Carballo, pp. 197–222. University Press of Colorado, Boulder.

Stanish, Charles
2004   The Evolution of Chiefdoms: An Economic Anthropological Model. In *Archaeological Perspectives on Political Economies*, edited by Gary M. Feinman and Linda M. Nicholas, pp. 7–24. University of Utah Press, Salt Lake City.
2013   The Ritualized Economy and Cooperative Labor in Intermediate Societies. In *Cooperation and Collective Action: Archaeological Perspectives*, edited by David M. Carballo, pp. 83–92. University Press of Colorado, Boulder.

Stanish, Charles, and Kevin J. Haley
2005   Power, Fairness, and Architecture: Modeling Early Chiefdom Development in the Central Andes. *Archeological Papers of the American Anthropological Association* 14:53–70.

Stapor, Frank W., Thomas D. Matthews, and Fonta E. Lindfors-Kearns
1991   Barrier-Island Progradation and Holocene Sea-Level History in Southwest Florida. *Journal of Coastal Research* 7:815–838.

Steckel, Richard H.
2007   Big Social Science History. *Social Science History* 31:1–34.

Stephenson, Keith, Judith A. Bense, and Frankie Snow
2002   Aspects of Deptford and Swift Creek of the South Atlantic and Gulf Coastal Plains. In *The Woodland Southeast*, edited by David G. Anderson and Robert C. Mainfort Jr., pp. 318–351. University of Alabama Press, Tuscaloosa.

Stephenson, Sarah P., Nancy E. Sheridan, Stephen P. Geiger, and William S. Arnold.
2013   Abundance and Distribution of Large Marine Gastropods in Nearshore Seagrass Beds along the Gulf Coast of Florida. *Journal of Shellfish Research* 32:305–313.

Steponaitis, Vincas P.
1986   Prehistoric Archaeology in the Southeastern United States, 1970–1985. *Annual Review of Anthropology* 15:363–404.

Steward, Julian
1955   *Theory of Culture Change*. University of Illinois Press, Urbana.

Stothers, Richard B.
1984   Mystery Cloud of AD 536. *Nature* 307(5949):344–345.

Stout, Charles, and R. Barry Lewis
1998   Mississippian Towns in Kentucky. In *Mississippian Towns and Sacred Spaces: Searching for an Architectural Grammar*, edited by R. Barry Lewis and Charles Stout, pp. 151–178. University of Alabama Press, Tuscaloosa.

St. Petersburg Times
1998   A Storm with No Name. http://www.sptimes.com/StormWatch/SW.3.html.

Stuiver, Minze, and Paula J. Reimer
1993   Extended 14C Database and Revised CALIB Radiocarbon Calibration Program. *Radiocarbon* 35:215–230.

Swanson, Heather Anne
2017   The Banality of the Anthropocene. Dispatches, *Cultural Anthropology*, February 22, 2017. https://culanth.org/fieldsights/1074-the-banality-of-the-anthropocene.

Tainter, Joseph A.
2016   Why Collapse Is So Difficult to Understand. In *Beyond Collapse: Archaeological Perspectives on Resilience, Revitalization, and Reorganization in Complex Societies*, edited by Ronald Sonny Faulseit, pp. 27–42. University of Southern Illinois Press, Carbondale.

Tanner, William F.
1960   Florida Coastal Classification. *Gulf Coast Association of Geological Societies Transactions* 10:259–266.
1991   The "Gulf of Mexico" Late Holocene Sea Level Curve and River Delta History. *Transactions of the Gulf Coast Association of Geological Societies* 41:583–589.
1992   Late Holocene Sea-Level Changes from Grain-Size Data: Evidence from the Gulf of Mexico. *Holocene* 2:249–254.
1993   An 8000-Year Record of Sea Level Change from Grain Size Parameters: Data from Beach Ridges in Denmark. *Holocene* 3:220–231.

Thomas, Chad R., Christopher Carr, and Cynthia Keller
2006 Animal-Totemic Clans of Ohio Hopewell Peoples. In *Gathering Hopewell: Society, Ritual, and Ritual Interaction*, edited by Christopher Carr and D. Troy Case, pp. 339–385. Springer, New York.

Thomas, David Hurst
2008 Aboriginal Foraging Strategies on St. Catherines Island. In *Native American Landscapes of St. Catherines Island, Georgia: I: The Theoretical Framework*, edited by David Hurst Thomas, pp. 62–73. Anthropological Paper No. 88. American Museum of Natural History, New York.

Thompson, Rachel E.
2016 Understanding Identity through Ceramic Analysis at the Crystal River and Roberts Island Sites. Unpublished master's thesis, Department of Anthropology, University of South Florida, Tampa.

Thompson, Victor D.
2007 Articulating Activity Areas and Formation Processes at the Sapelo Island Shell Ring Complex. *Southeastern Archaeology* 26:91–107.
2010 The Rhythms of Space-Time and the Making of Monuments and Places during the Archaic. In *Trend, Tradition, and Turmoil: What Happened to the Southeastern Archaic?* edited by David Hurst Thomas and Matthew Sanger, pp. 217–227. Anthropological Papers No. 93. American Museum of Natural History, New York.
2017 Conceptualizing Anthropogenic Islands through LiDAR in Southern Florida. In *New Approaches to Anthropological Remote Sensing*, edited by Duncan McKinnon and Bryan Haley, pp. 127–140. University of Alabama Press, Tuscaloosa.

Thompson, Victor D., and C. Fred T. Andrus
2011 Evaluating Mobility, Monumentality, and Feasting at the Sapelo Shell Ring Complex. *American Antiquity* 76:315–344.

Thompson, Victor D., William H. Marquardt, Alexander Cherkinsky, Amanda D. Roberts Thompson, Karen J. Walker, Lee A. Newsom
2016 From Shell Midden to Shell Mound: The Geoarchaeology of Mound Key, an Anthropogenic Island in Southwest Florida, USA. *PLOS One* 11: e0154611. doi:10.1371/journal. pone.0154611

Thompson, Victor D., William H. Marquardt, and Karen J. Walker
2014 A Remote Sensing Perspective on Shoreline Modification, Canal Construction and Household Trajectories at Pineland along Florida's Southwestern Gulf Coast. *Archaeological Prospection* 21:59–73.

Thompson, Victor D., and Thomas J. Pluckhahn
2010 History, Complex Hunter-Gatherers, and the Mounds and Monuments of Crystal River, Florida: A Geophysical Perspective. *Journal of Island and Coastal Archaeology* 5:33–51.
2012 Monumentalization and Ritual Landscapes at Fort Center in the Lake Okeechobee Basin of South Florida. *Journal of Anthropological Archaeology* 31:49–65.

Thompson, Victor D., Thomas J. Pluckhahn, Oindrila Das, and C. Fred T. Andrus
2015   Assessing Village Life and Monument Construction (cal. AD 65–1070) along the Central Gulf Coast of Florida through Stable Isotope Geochemistry. *Journal of Archaeological Science: Reports* 4:111–123.
Thompson, Victor D., Matthew D. Reynolds, Bryan Haley, Richard Jefferies, Jay K. Johnson, and Laura Humphries
2004   The Sapelo Shell Rings: Shallow Geophysics on a Georgia Sea Island. *Southeastern Archaeology* 23:192–201.
Thompson, Victor D., and John A. Turck
2009   Adaptive Cycles of Coastal Hunter-gatherers. *American Antiquity* 74:255–278.
Thulman, David K.
2004   A Reconstruction of the Natural History of the West Indian Manatee in Florida in the Past 12,000 Years from Archaeological, Ethnographic, and Other Data. Unpublished manuscript in possession of the author.
Tolius, Alfred F.
1973   Appraisal of Theron A. White Property, Crystal River State Archaeological Site, Crystal River, Citrus County, Florida. Manuscript on file, Crystal River Archaeological State Park, Crystal River.
Toth, Alan
1979   The Marksville Connection. In *Hopewell Archaeology: The Chillicothe Conference*, edited by David S. Brose and N'omi Greber, pp. 188–199. Kent State University Press, Kent, Ohio.
Trinkley, Michael B.
1980   Investigation of the Woodland Period along the South Carolina Coast. Unpublished Ph.D. dissertation, Department of Anthropology, University of North Carolina, Chapel Hill.
1985   The Form and Function of South Carolina's Early Woodland Shell Rings. In *Structure and Process in Southeastern Archaeology*, edited by Roy S. Dickens Jr., and H. Trawick Ward, pp. 102–118. University of Alabama Press, Tuscaloosa.
Trubitt, Mary Beth D.
2003   The Production and Exchange of Marine Shell Prestige Goods. *Journal of Archaeological Research* 11:243–277.
Tschinkel, Walter R., Tyler Murdock, Joshua R. King, and Christina Kwapich
2012   Ant Distribution in Relation to Ground Water in North Florida Pine Flatwoods. *Journal of Insect Science* 12:1–20.
Turck, John A., and Victor D. Thompson
2016   Revisiting the Resilience of Late Archaic Hunter-Gatherers along the Georgia Coast. *Journal of Anthropological Archaeology* 43:39–55.
United States Geological Survey (USGS)
2005   *Preliminary Integrated Geologic Map Databases for the United States: Alabama, Florida, Georgia, Mississippi, North Carolina, and South Carolina*. USGS Open-File Report 2005–1323. Electronic document, https://pubs.usgs.gov/of/2005/1323/.

Van de Noort, Robert
2011   Conceptualising Climate Change Archaeology. *Antiquity* 85:1039–1048.
VanPool, Christine S.
2003   The Shaman-Priests of Casas Grandes. *American Antiquity* 68:696–717.
2009   The Signs of the Sacred: Identifying Shamans Using Archaeological Evidence. *Journal of Anthropological Archaeology* 28:177–190.
VanPool, Christine S., and Todd L. VanPool
2007   *Signs of the Casas Grandes Shamans*. University of Utah Press, Salt Lake City.
Varien, Mark D., and James M. Potter (editors)
2008   The Social Construction of Communities: Agency, Structure, and Identity in the Prehispanic Southwest. Rowman Altamira Press, Lanham.
Vince, Susan W., Stephen R. Humphrey, and Robert W. Simons
1989   *The Ecology of Hydric Hammocks: A Community Profile*. Report No. BR-85(7.26). Fish and Wildlife Service, Washington, D.C., and Florida Museum of Natural History, Gainesville.
Walker, Karen J.
1992a   The Zooarchaeology of Charlotte Harbor's Prehistoric Maritime Adaptation: Spatial and Temporal Perspectives. Ph.D. dissertation, Department of Anthropology, University of Florida, Gainesville.
1992b   The Zooarchaeology of Charlotte Harbor's Prehistoric Maritime Adaptation: Spatial and Temporal Perspectives. In *Culture and Environment in the Domain of the Calusa*, edited by William H. Marquardt, pp. 265–366. Institute of Archaeology and Paleoenvironmental Studies Monograph 1. Florida Museum of Natural History, University of Florida, Gainesville.
2000   A Cooling Episode in Southwest Florida during the Sixth and Seventh Centuries A.D. In *The Years without Summer: Tracing A.D. 536 and Its Aftermath*, edited by Joel D. Gunn, pp. 119–127. International Series 872. British Archaeological Reports. David Brown Book Company, Oakville, Connecticut.
2013   The Pineland Site Complex: Environmental Contexts. In *The Archaeology of Pineland: A Coastal Southwest Florida Site Complex, AD 50–1710*, edited by William H. Marquardt and Karen J. Walker, pp. 23–52. Institute of Archaeology and Paleoenvironmental Studies Monograph 4. University of Florida, Gainesville.
Walker, Karen J., Frank W. Stapor Jr., and William H. Marquardt
1994   Episodic Sea Levels and Human Occupation at Southwest Florida's Wightman Site. *Florida Anthropologist* 47:161–179.
1995   Archaeological Evidence for a 1750–1450 BP Higher-than-Present Sea Level along Florida's Gulf Coast. In *Holocene Cycles: Climate, Sea Levels, and Sedimentation*, edited by C. W. Finkl Jr., pp. 205–218. *Journal of Coastal Research*, special issue no. 17. Coastal Education and Reserch Foundation, n.p.
Wallis, Neill J.
2013   Swift Creek and Weeden Island Mortuary Landscapes of Interaction. In *Early and Middle Woodland Landscapes of the Southeast*, edited by Alice P. Wright and Edward R. Henry, pp. 204–218. University Press of Florida, Gainesville.

Wallis, Neill J., Ann S. Cordell, and James B. Stoltman
2014 Foundations of the Cades Pond Culture in North-Central Florida: The River Styx Site (8Al458). *Southeastern Archaeology* 33:168–188.

Wallis, Neill J., and Paulette S. McFadden
2013 Archaeological Investigations at the Garden Patch Site (8DI4), Dixie County, Florida. Division of Anthropology Miscellaneous Report No. 63. Florida Museum of Natural History, University of Florida, Gainesville.
2014 Suwannee Valley Archaeological Field School 2013: The Garden Patch Site (8DI4). Division of Anthropology Miscellaneous Report No. 64. Florida Museum of Natural History, University of Florida, Gainesville.
2016 Recovering the Forgotten Woodland Mound Excavations at Garden Patch (8DI4). *Southeastern Archaeology* 35:194–212.

Wallis, Neill J., Paulette S. McFadden, and Hayley M. Singleton
2015 Radiocarbon Dating the Pace of Monument Construction and Village Aggregation at Garden Patch: A Ceremonial Center on the Florida Gulf Coast. *Journal of Archaeological Science: Reports* 2:507–516.

Wallis, Neill, Thomas Pluckhahn, and Michael D. Glascock
2016 Interaction Networks of the Woodland Period American Southeast: Neutron Activation Analysis of Swift Creek Complicated Stamped Pottery. *American Antiquity* 81:717–736.

Walthall, John A.
1981 *Galena and Aboriginal Trade in Eastern North America*. Scientific Papers Vol. XVII. Illinois State Museum, Springfield.

Wang, Ting, Donna Surge, and Karen Jo Walker
2011 Isotopic Evidence for Climate Change during the Vandal Minimum from *Ariopsis felis* Otoliths and *Mercenaria campechiensis* Shells, Southwest Florida, USA. *Holocene* 21:1081–1091.
2013 Seasonal Climate Change across the Roman Warm Period/Vandal Minimum Transition Using Isotope Sclerochronology in Archaeological Shells and Otoliths, Southwest Florida, USA. *Quaternary International* 308:230–241.

Waselkov, Gregory A.
1987 Shellfish Gathering and Shell Midden Archaeology. *Advances in Archaeological Method and Theory* 10:93–210.

Waselkov, Gregory A., and Kathryn E. Holland Braund (editors)
1995 *William Bartram on the Southeastern Indians*. University of Nebraska Press, Lincoln.

Waters, C. N., J. A. Zalasiewicz, M. Williams, M. A. Ellis, and A. M. Snelling
2014 A Stratigraphical Basis for the Anthropocene? *Geological Society, London, Special Publications* 395:1–21.

Wax, Amy L.
2000 Rethinking Welfare Rights: Reciprocity Norms, Reactive Attitudes, and the Political Economy of Welfare Reform. *Law and Contemporary Problems* 63:257–297.

Webb, William S., and Charles E. Snow
1945   *The Adena People*. Reports in Anthropology No. 6. University of Kentucky, Lexington.

Weber, Max
1947   *The Theory of Social and Economic Organization*. Free Press, New York.

Weisburd, S.
1985   Excavating Words: A Geological Tool. *Science News* 127:91–96.

Weisman, Brent R.
1985   WRAC at Crystal River Archaeological Site. *Withlacoochee River Archaeology Council News* 2(3):9–10.
1986   The Cove of the Withlacoochee: A First look at the Archaeology of an Interior Florida Wetland. *Florida Anthropologist* 39:4–23.
1987   *A Cultural Resource Inventory of the Crystal River Archaeological Site (8Ci-1), Citrus County, Florida*. Report submitted to the Florida Division of Natural Resources, Bureau of Land and Aquatic Resources Management, Tallahassee, Florida.
1990   CARL Inventory Project, Report of Activities, Crystal River State Preserve. Manuscript No. 2293, Florida Master Site File, Tallahassee.
1992   Impacts to Archaeological Remains of Proposed Planting Activities, Crystal River Site. Manuscript No. 3111, Florida Master Site File, Tallahassee.
1993   Report of Disturbance to the Crystal River Mounds, Crystal River State Archaeological Site, Caused by the Storm of March 12–13, 1993. Manuscript No. 5398, Florida Master Site File, Tallahassee.
1995a   *Crystal River: A Ceremonial Mound Center on the Florida Gulf Coast*. Florida Archaeology Series No. 8, Division of Historical Resources, Florida Department of State, Tallahassee.
1995b   The Roberts Island Shell Mound Complex and Its Archaeological Significance. Manuscript No. 4365, Florida Master Site File, Tallahassee.

Weisman, Brent R., Lori Collins, and Travis Doering
2007   *Mapping the Moundbuilders: Revisiting the National Landmark Site of Crystal River (8CI1), Florida, Using Integrated Spatial Technologies*. University of South Florida, Tampa. Submitted to Division of Historic Resources Grants in Aid, Survey and Planning Program, Tallahassee.

Weisman, Brent R., and Christine L. Newman
1991   An Inventory and Evaluation of Archaeological and Historical Resources on Crystal River State Reserve. Manuscript No. 3181, Florida Master Site File, Tallahassee.

Wendrich, Willeke
2012a   Archaeology and Apprenticeship: Body Knowledge, Identity, and Communities of Practice. In *Archaeology and Apprenticeship: Body Knowledge, Identity, and Communities of Practice*, edited by Willeke Wendrich, pp. 1–19. University of Arizona Press, Tucson.

2012b   Recognizing Knowledge Transfer in the Archaeological Record. In *Archaeology and Apprenticeship: Body Knowledge, Identity, and Communities of Practice*, edited by Willeke Wendrich, pp. 255–262. University of Arizona Press, Tucson.

Wenger, Etienne
1998   *Communities of Practice: Learning, Meaning, and Identity*. Cambridge University Press, New York.

West, Shaun E.
2016   Investigating Early Village Community Formation and Development at Kolomoki (9ER1). Master's thesis, Department of Anthropology, University of South Florida, Tampa.

Whalen, Michael E.
1983   Reconstructing Early Formative Village Organization in Oaxaca, Mexico. *American Antiquity* 48:17–43.

Wheeler, Ryan
1996   Ancient Art of the Florida Peninsula: 500 BC to AD 1763. Unpublished Ph.D. dissertation, Department of Anthropology, University of Florida, Gainesville.
2001   Shovel Testing for Fence Relocation Project, Crystal River State Archaeological Site (8CI1). Manuscript No. 6618, Florida Master Site File, Tallahassee.

White, Mel
2013   When Push Comes to Shove. *National Geographic* 223:82–97.

White, Nancy Marie
2014   Woodland and Mississippian in Northwest Florida: Part of the South but Different. In *New Histories of Pre-Columbian Florida*, edited by Neill J. Wallis and Asa R. Randall, pp. 223–242. University Press of Florida, Gainesville.

White, William A.
1970   *The Geomorphology of the Florida Peninsula*. Geological Bulletin No. 51. Bureau of Geology, Division of Interior Resources, Florida Department of Natural Resources, Tallahassee.

Widmer, Randolph J.
1988   *The Evolution of Calusa: A Nonagricultural Chiefdom of the Southwest Florida Coast*. University of Alabama Press, Tuscaloosa.

Wilkerson, S. Jeffrey K.
1978   Obituary: Ripley Pierce Bullen, 1902–1976. *American Antiquity* 43:622–631.

Willey, Gordon R.
1948a   The Cultural Context of the Crystal River Negative-Painted Style. *American Antiquity* 13:325–328.
1948b   Cultural Sequence in the Manatee Region of West Florida. *American Antiquity* 13:209–218.
1948c   A Prototype for the Southern Cult. *American Antiquity* 13:328–330.
1949a   *Archeology of the Florida Gulf Coast*. Smithsonian Miscellaneous Collections 113. Washington, D.C.
1949b   Crystal River, Florida: A 1949 Visit. *Florida Anthropologist* 2:41–46.
1966   *An Introduction to American Archaeology: 1: North and Middle America*. Prentice-Hall, Englewood Cliffs.

Willey, Gordon R., and Philip Phillips
1944   Negative-Painted Pottery from Crystal River, Florida. *American Antiquity* 10:173–185.
1958   *Method and Theory in American Archaeology*. University of Chicago Press, Chicago.
Williams, Kimberlyn, Katherine C. Ewel, Richard P. Stumpf, Francis E. Putz, and Thomas W. Workman
1999   Sea-Level Rise and Coastal Forest Retreat on the West Coast of Florida, USA. *Ecology* 80:2045–2063.
Williams, Mark
1995   Chiefly Compounds. In *Mississippian Communities and Households*, edited by J. Daniel Rogers and Bruce D. Smith, pp. 124–134. University of Alabama Press, Tuscaloosa.
1999   *Lamar Revisited: 1996 Test Excavations at the Lamar Site*. LAMAR Institute Publication 43. Electronic document, http://shapiro.anthro.uga.edu/Lamar/images/PDFs/publication_43.pdf.
Williams, Mark, and Gary Shapiro
1990   Paired Towns. In *Lamar Archaeology, Mississippian Chiefdoms in the Deep South*, edited by Mark Williams and Gary Shapiro, pp. 163–174. University of Alabama Press, Tuscaloosa.
Williams, Stephen
1963   The Eastern United States. In *Early Indian Farmers and Villages and Communities*, edited by William Haag, pp. 267–325. National Park Service, Washington, D.C.
Williamson, Ray A.
1984   *Living the Sky*. Houghton Mifflin, Boston.
Wilshusen, Richard H.
1991   Early Villages in the American Southwest: Cross-Cultural and Archaeological Perspectives. Ph.D. dissertation, Department of Anthropology, University of Colorado, Boulder.
Wilshusen, Richard H., and James M. Potter
2010   The Emergence of Early Villages in the American Southwest: Cultural Issues and Historical Perspectives. In *Becoming Villagers: Comparing Early Village Societies*, edited by Matthew S. Bandy and Jake R. Fox, pp. 1–18. University of Arizona Press, Tucson.
Wilson, Peter J.
1988   *The Domestication of the Human Species*. Yale University Press, New Haven.
Witthoft, John
1949   *Green Corn Ceremonialism in the Eastern Woodlands*. Occasional Contributions from the Museum of Anthropology of the University of Michigan No. 13, University of Michigan Press, Ann Arbor.

Wolfe, Steven H. (editor)
1990   *An Ecological Characterization of the Florida Springs Coast: Pithlachascotee to Waccasassa Rivers*. USFWS Biological Report 90 (21). U.S. Fish and Wildlife Service, National Wetlands Research Center, Slidell, Louisiana.

Wolfe, Steven H., Jeffrey A. Reidenauer, and Michael S. Flannery
1990   Saltwater Wetland, Estuarine, and Marine Habitats. In *An Ecological Characterization of the Florida Springs Coast: Pithlachascotee to Waccasassa Rivers*, edited by Steven H. Wolfe, pp. 158–210. USFWS Biological Report 90 (21). U.S. Fish and Wildlife Service, National Wetlands Research Center, Slidell, Louisiana.

Wright, Alice P.
2013   Persistent Place, Shifting Practice: The Premound Landscape at the Garden Creek Site, North Carolina. In *Early and Middle Woodland Landscapes of the Southeast*, edited by Alice P. Wright and Edward R. Henry, pp. 56–70. University Press of Florida, Gainesville.
2014a History, Monumentality, and Interaction in the Appalachian Summit Middle Woodland. *American Antiquity* 79:277–294.
2014b Inscribing Interaction: Middle Woodland Monumentality in the Appalachian Summit, 100 BC–AD 400. Ph.D. dissertation, Department of Anthropology, University of Michigan, Ann Arbor.
2016   Local and "Global" Perspectives on the Middle Woodland Southeast. *Journal of Archaeological Research* 25:37–83.

Wright, Eric E., Albert C. Hine, Stephen L. Goodbred Jr., Stanley D. Locker
2005   The Effect of Sea-Level and Climate Change on the Development of a Mixed Siliciclastic-Carbonate, Deltaic Coastline: Suwannee River, Florida, U.S.A. *Journal of Sedimentary Research* 75:621–635.

Yerkes, Richard W.
1988   Introduction. In *Interpretations of Culture Change in the Eastern Woodlands during the Late Woodland Period*, edited by Richard W. Yerkes, pp. 1–6. Ohio State University, Columbus.

Index

Page numbers marked with *i* refer to illustrations and those marked with *t* refer to tables.

Actor-based approaches. *See* Agency
Adaptation, 96, 194, 213–14
Adena tradition, 78, 92, 99
Adornment (personal), 87, 89, 92–93
Agency, 21–22, 76, 194, 214
Agriculture, 1, 8, 13, 17–18, 34, 140, 154, 174, 198
Alabama, 84, 163
Alabama, University of, 104
Alligators, 30, 123, 176
Amazonia, 203
American mud turtles, 176
Anatolia, 200
Ancestors, 42, 82, 158, 194, 198
Andrus, Fred, 104
Anthropocene, 212–13
Anthropogenic sediments and landscapes, 61, 213
Apalachicola area, 146
Appalachian Mountains, 84, 96
Archaic period, 1–4, 74, 78, 82, 103, 195
Architecture, 138, 144, 183, 186, 188; monumental, 15, 138; public, 1, 22, 47, 98, 201–2, 204. *See also* Burial mounds; Platform mounds; Shell mounds
Arkansas River Valley, 170
Armadillos, 57
Artists and artisans. *See* Craft production and specialization
Atlantic coast, 117, 181

Austin, Robert, 151, 171, 192
Australia, 115–16, 121
Autonomous villages. *See* Early villages

Bahn, Paul, 92
Bartram, William, 94
Basketmaker period, 8, 197
Bayesian analysis, 66–67, 70, 128, 133, 135, 155, 186. *See also* Crystal River (site); Optically Stimulated Luminescence dates; Phases; Roberts Island (site and Shell Mound Complex)
Bayport Mound site, 7*i*, 82
Bayshore Homes site, 171
Beads, 89, 93, 95, 112–13, 191–92
Bernath Place site, 201
Bettinger, Robert, 166, 190
Bilobed arrow motif (on pottery), 94
Biomass, 105, 114, 122, 174–76
Bitumen, 89
Bivalves, 28, 174. *See also* Hardshell clam; Marsh clams; Oyster; Shell
Blankenship, Beth, 54, 149
Block-Sterns site, 7*i*
Blue crabs, 28
Boulders. *See* Stelae
Bow and arrow, 170, 189
Box turtles, 123
Breastplate (copper), 12*i*, 96
Brinton, D. G., 25, 161–62
Brooksville Ridge section, 26, 27*i*, 98
Brose, David S., 96
Buck Key Low. *See* Vandal Minimum
Bullen, Adelaide, 4, 30, 80, 168–69, 183

Bullen, Ripley: description of Crystal River as a center for trade and ceremony, 151–52; discovery of Roberts Island, 4, 30, 39, 168–69, 183, 186; investigations at the Burtine and Wash Island sites, 80; investigations at Crystal River, 13–15, 25, 35, 43–48, 55, 68, 74, 77–80, 108–9, 111, 114, 119, 123–26, 133, 135–43, 149, 163; investigations at other sites in the vicinity of Crystal River, 82–83. *See also* Crystal River (site); Roberts Island (site and Shell Mound Complex)
Bulrushes, 28
Burghardt, Andrew F., 151
Burial goods, 79, 83, 91, 112, 125, 127, 153, 191. *See also* Burial mounds; Burials; Main Burial Complex; Mounds C–G (Crystal River site)
Burial mounds, 52, 82–83, 96, 124–25, 127, 165, 198, 203–4. *See also* Burial goods; Burials; Main Burial Complex; Mounds C–G (Crystal River site)
Burials, 74, 105, 201, 204, 211; excavated by Bullen, 45, 77–79; excavated by Moore, 10–13, 30, 40, 84–93; in situ display at Crystal River, 35; at Roberts Island, 183. *See also* Burial goods; Burial mounds; Main Burial Complex; Mounds C–G (Crystal River site)
Burtine Island site, 80, 151–52
Buzzard's Island site, 193

Caches: in association with stelae, 141; of ceramics, 125–26, 145; of dolphin teeth, 114
Cahokia Site, 7*i*, 170, 188, 192
California, 15, 190
Caloosahatchee phases and ceramics, 5–6*t*, 171–72, 189–91. *See also* Ceramics
Calusa, 74, 123, 158, 171–72
Cannel coal, 96
Canoes, 120, 154, 164, 166, 172, 191
Cape Canaveral, 78
Carballo, David M., 8–9, 20–22, 115, 189
Carnivore teeth, 91–93, 114
Carr, Christopher, 97, 100, 109, 113, 145
Cassina (black drink), 93
Çatalhöyük site, 202
Catfish, hardhead, 123, 175

Catlinite, 84, 89*i*
Cattail, 28
Cedar, 28, 34, 75, 212
Cedar Key, 9, 98
Celts, 127
Central Highlands (geomorphic division), 26
Central-Peninsular Gulf Coast, 5–6*t*. *See also* Peninsular Florida
Ceramics, 13, 90*i*, 91, 95*i*, 112, 125, 127, 140, 192, 199; analysis of collections by CREVAP, 47–48, 54, 64, 5–6*t*; as a chronological marker for mound construction, 77–79, 198; chronology of diagnostic ceramic types, 2–3*t*; confusion regarding pottery types at Crystal River, 42–43; invention of in the American Southeast, 1; as a marker of more permanent settlement, 121–22, 177; as a marker of trade or interaction, 84, 87, 108–9, 111–13, 139, 152, 156; as markers of identity or social difference, 81, 111; petrography, 109; potters and potting traditions, 108–9, 111, 156; tempering agents, 5–6*t*, 108–11, 122, 137, 156. *See also* Caches; Crystal River (site); Effigy vessels; Pipes; Roberts Island (site and Shell Mound Complex)
Ceremonial exchange, 96–98. *See also* Ceremonies; Exchange
Ceremonial leaders, 145, 165. *See also* Ceremonies; Leader(ship); Rituals
Ceremonies, 23, 125, 127–28, 144, 154, 160, 171; in association with ancestor worship, 158; in association with early villages, 197–99; in association with plazas, 139–41; among contemporary Native Americans, 140; exclusivity of, 164–66; as a tool for solidarity building, 83, 116, 152, 154, 202–3; scalar issues, 159–60. *See also* Crystal River (site); Green Corn Ceremony; Hopewell(ian) culture or tradition; Rituals; Roberts Island (site and Shell Mound Complex)
Chaco Canyon, 172
Charlotte Harbor, 75, 171
Chattahoochee River Valley, 100
Cherts, 151, 191

Chiefdoms, 1, 17, 138, 174, 188–91. *See also* Chiefly compounds; Leader(ship); Mississippian period; Status
Chiefly compounds, 165
Chronology: major periods in prehistory and history, 2–3*t*; temporal divisions of the Woodland and Mississippian periods, 5–6*t*. *See also* Bayesian analysis; Ceramics; Crystal River (site); Optically Stimulated Luminescence dates; Phases; Roberts Island (site and Shell Mound Complex)
Circular embankments, 78. *See also* Main Burial Complex; Mound C (Crystal River site)
Citronelle gravels, 84, 89*i*
Citrus County, 25, 34, 39
Citrus County Historical Society, 34–35, 39
Clans, 81–82, 92, 116. *See also* Kinship; Lineages; Segmentary structure
Clay, R. Berle, 99, 198, 203
Climate change, 40, 73, 117–18, 156, 158, 166, 171–72, 174, 205, 210, 213–14. *See also* Medieval Warm period; Roman Warm period; Sea levels; Vandal Minimum
Coalescent societies, 196–97, 200, 203–4. *See also* Collective social groups; Cooperation
Coles Creek, 170
Collective action theory, 9, 20
Collective social groups, 8–9, 19–21, 24, 83, 99, 189, 203, 205, 209–12. *See also* Coalescent societies; Cooperation
Colubridae, 123
Columellae, 127, 148. *See also* Gastropods; Shell; Whelk
Communal labor, 99, 154, 172
Communal societies. *See* Collective social groups
Communal structures, 202. *See also* Mounds; Plazas; Public architecture
Competition: as a factor in the location of Crystal River, 76; as a focus of study by CREVAP, 47; debate regarding importance to human societies, 8–9, 19–20, 22, 166, 194–95, 209; in the Late Woodland period, 189; between Middle Woodland centers, 100. *See also* Cooperation

Complex hunter-gatherers, 4, 8, 15–17, 194, 205
Complex societies, 21–22, 188–92. *See also* Chiefdoms; Complex hunter-gatherers
Compton, Matthew, 66, 175
Conchs, 113, 145, 149, 151, 157, 174–75. *See also* Gastropods; Shell
Cooperation: challenges to, 153, 212; debate regarding importance to human societies, 8–9, 19–20, 22, 194–95, 209; as a focus of study by CREVAP, 47; in labor projects, 99; in relation to social hierarchy, 189; in ritual and mortuary ceremonies, 115, 154; in subsistence, 115, 166; scalar increases in, 115. *See also* Coalescent societies; Collective social groups
Cooters, 176
Copena area, 96
Copper, 11, 12*i*, 79, 84, 87*i*, 89*i*, 91*i*, 92, 94, 96–98, 100, 112–13, 145, 204
Cordage, 89, 91
Cordell, Ann, 109
Cordgrass, 28
Cores and coring. *See* Crystal River (site); Crystal River Early Village Archaeological Project; Roberts Island (site and Shell Mound Complex)
Corn. *See* Green Corn Ceremony; Maize
Cosmology, 21
Cove of the Withlacoochee, 80
Craft production and specialization, 148–49, 151–53, 191, 204
Crawfish, 121
Creation myth. *See* Earth Diver myth
Creese, John, 153, 199
Croakers, 175
Crown conch. *See* Conchs
Crypts, 202–3
Crystal River (city), 34, 71
Crystal River (site): "abandonment" of, 32, 34, 155–56, 159–61, 172; as a ceremonial center, 76–77, 80–81, 98–100, 103, 105, 108–9, 115, 119, 124, 140, 151–53, 166–67; as an enigma, 9, 14–15, 25; as a National Historic Landmark, 38; descriptions of CREVAP excavations and analysis, 46–61, 64–70; environmental setting, 25–30, 71–76, 98, 118–19, 156–59; evidence for

Crystal River (site)—*continued*
houses, 106–8; fame of, 4; history of excavations, 4, 9, 40–46, 84–94, 126–27; history of ownership, 34–35, 37–38; presumed connections to Mesoamerica, 14, 45, 139; revised chronology for, 66–70, 77–80, 102–3, 119, 126, 128, 131, 135–37, 155–56, 161; seasonality of occupation, 103–6, 108, 115, 119, 121–23, 197; subsistence remains, 105, 113–15, 116, 122–23; village form, 103, 119–21. *See also* Lagoon area (at Crystal River site); Main Burial Complex; Mounds A–K (Crystal River site); Plazas; Shell middens

Crystal River Early Village Archaeological Project (CREVAP), 23, 46–47, 75, 101, 108

Crystal River Mobile Home Park, 37–39, 48, 54, 56–57, 117. *See also* Lagoon area (at Crystal River site)

Crystal River quarry cluster, 151

Cultural historical archaeology, 13–14, 138

Deer, 30, 92, 105, 114, 116, 122–23, 133, 176, 182, 186

Deer Island site, 7*i*, 78

Defleshing, 94, 11

Delgado, Alexander, 140, 159

DeMarrais, Elizabeth, 20–21

Deptford period and ceramics, 6*t*, 42, 78, 80–81, 106, 108–11, 144. *See also* Ceramics

Diamond, Jared, 124

Diamondback terrapins, 123

Dietler, John, 189–91

Diffusion, 13

Dixon Crucible Co., 39

Dolomite, 28

Dolphin, 92, 114, 116, 123

Dual organization, 127, 202–3

Duke, Trevor, 66, 174–75

Dunellon Gap, 27*i*

Dyer, George, 35, 44–45, 79

Early Archaic period, 3*t*

Early villages, 1; aggregation or nucleation into, 1, 17–18, 108, 116, 122, 196–97, 199; autonomy of, 18; defined, 17–18; development from vacant ceremonial centers, 197–99; as exemplified at Crystal River and Roberts Island, 22–23; factors possibly effecting longevity, 159, 205; form and arrangements of households, 200–201; in global perspective, 8, 194–207; as a regional process, 1–2, 199; tendency to have collective burial facilities, 203–4; tendency to have distinctive artistic traditions, 204–5; tendency to have integrative public architecture, 201–2; tendency toward dual organization and bilateral symmetry in village plans, 202–3. *See also* Crystal River (site); Roberts Island (site and Shell Mound Complex)

Ear spool: copper, 96; representation on stelae, 141

Earth Diver myth, 121

Eastern gray squirrel, 176

Eastern North America, 66, 89, 170–71, 174, 195. *See also* Eastern Woodlands

Eastern oysters. *See* Oyster

Eastern Woodlands, 92, 169. *See also* Eastern North America

Eerkens, Jelmer, 153

Effigy vessels, 91, 126, 151, 192. *See also* Ceramics; Weeden Island period and ceramics

Egalitarian, 23, 160, 200

Egrets (plumed), 176

Ellis, Gary, 46, 54, 80, 114

Enclosures, 1, 78

Englewood period and ceramics, 5*t*. *See also* Ceramics

Environment. *See* Climate change; Crystal River (site); Estuaries; Forests; Marsh; Roberts Island (site and Shell Mound Complex); Sea levels; Wetlands

Eocene age, 28

Equinox, 187

Esoteric knowledge, 92, 154. *See also* Ceremonies; Leader(ship); Rituals

Estuaries, 16, 18, 28, 29*i*, 30, 66, 73–74, 98–99, 105, 123, 140, 154, 158, 176, 205–6, 211. *See also* Marsh; Wetlands

Etowah site, 188

Evolutionary approaches, 8–9, 18–20, 115, 194, 209, 212. *See also* Competition; Cooperation; Free-rider dilemma

Exchange, 160; between Crystal River and

southwestern Florida, 151–52; decline in Late Woodland period, 169–70; extralocal and long-distance, 1, 4, 12, 15, 16, 22, 40, 79, 84–85, 92–93, 96–98, 100, 112, 124, 127, 145, 151, 191–92, 204; as a feature common to early village societies, 204–5; production for, 148
Exclusionary political strategies, 17, 22, 189–90, 211. *See also* Competition; Leader(ship)

Factions, 20, 98, 160. *See also* Competition; Exclusionary political strategies
Fargher, Lane, 9, 20–21, 212
Farmers (Neolithic), 198
Farming. *See* Agriculture
Feasts and feasting, 47, 83, 99, 103, 116, 166, 177, 183, 198, 202. *See also* Ceremonies; Rituals
Feltus site, 7*i*, 170
Fertility, 22, 145
Fewkes, J. W., 124
Fiddler crab, 28
Fissioning, 188, 205
Flaked stone. *See* Lithics
Florida Master Site File, 30
Florida Memory archives, 183
Florida Museum of Natural History, 15, 137
Florida Panhandle, 100, 125–26, 146, 152, 156, 192
Forests, 28, 76, 93, 98–99, 122–23, 162
Formative period (Mesoamerica), 8, 197
Fort Center site, 7*i*, 78
Fort Walton period and ceramics, 5*t*, 192
Free-rider dilemma, 19–20, 153, 212. *See also* Competition; Cooperation; Evolutionary approaches; Game Theory

Galena, 190, 192
Game theory, 19–20. *See also* Competition; Cooperation; Evolutionary approaches; Free-rider dilemma
Garden Creek site, 7*i*, 139, 198
Gars, 175
Gastropods, 145–49, 151, 157, 174. *See also* Conchs; Shell; Whelk
Gateway interaction center, 151–52. *See also* Exchange

Geophysical survey, 46, 51; methods, 48–49; results, 50i, 106, 107*i*, 128, 131, 133, 135, 138, 140, 172, 179, 181, 186. *See also* Crystal River (site); Mounds A–C (Roberts Island site); Mounds A–K (Crystal River site); Plazas; Roberts Island (site and Shell Mound Complex)
Georgia, 78, 100, 106, 113, 139, 188, 195–96
Glades period or ceramics, 5*t*, 152, 177–78
Göbekli Teppe, 198
Golden shiners, 123
"Gopher" (steamship), 9
Gopher tortoise, 123
Granites, 84
Grasses, 28, 117
Great Lakes, 84
Green Corn Ceremony, 140
Greenman, Emerson, 13, 42
Green sea turtle, 176
Griffin, James, 169
Ground-penetrating radar. *See* Geophysical survey
Gulf Coast, 34, 73–75, 80, 100; archaeological sites, 82, 96–97, 112–13, 118, 123–25, 127, 145–46, 158, 160, 162, 168, 170–71, 177, 181, 190, 193, 196; as an area of study, 4, 22–23, 42, 124; characteristics of early villages on, 196–206; chronology for, 5–6*t*; contributions to Mississippian political development, 192; environmental characteristics, 25–26, 28, 71–72, 76, 109, 115, 157–58; as a source for marine shell in the American Bottom, 192. *See also* Gulf Coast Lowlands; Gulf of Mexico
Gulf Coastal Lowlands, 26, 27*i*
Gulf of Mexico, 9, 26, 76, 118

Habitus, 21
Hallan Çemi site, 200, 203
Hammocks, 28, 76, 80, 98, 119, 212
Hardshell clam, 159, 211. *See also* Bivalves; Shell
Hematite, 89
Hendricks, Robert, 54
Hickory, 212
Hierarchical social and political organization, 18, 201, 188, 190. *See also* Chiefdoms; Leader(ship); Status

Hispid cotton rat, 176
Historical process, 4, 17–18, 22–24, 194
Historical processualism, 195
Historic period, 2*t*, 21, 92–95, 121, 140, 172
Hodson, Alex, 54
Holocene, 73
Homo sapiens, 19
Homosassa River, 75
Hopewell(ian) culture or tradition, 15, 22, 46; as a sphere of interaction and exchange, 4, 96–97, 112–13, 124, 148, 151–52; "climax" of, 14, 139; decline of, 124; earthworks associated with, 76, 82, 99, 198; exchange, 96–97; nature of leadership, 92–96, 100; orientation toward, 113; natural features, 76; representation at Crystal River and in Florida, 4, 12–13, 42, 79, 85, 92–98, 100, 112, 138, 204. *See also* Hopewell period; Hopewell site; Middle Woodland period
Hopewell Interaction Sphere. *See* Hopewell(ian) culture or tradition
Hopewell period, 15, 46, 82, 100
Hopewell site, 12
Horticulture, 1, 15–16, 206. *See also* Agriculture
Households, 34, 165, 176–78; and craft specialization, 148–49; differentiation in wealth or status, 99, 113–14, 204, 211; social and economic ties among, 99, 109, 115–16, 149, 152, 189–90, 200–201, 204, 211
Hudson, Charles, 191, 196
Hunter-gatherers, 73, 115, 121, 174, 194, 205. *See also* Complex hunter-gatherers
Hypersociality, 19

Iconography, 91, 204
Identity, 81, 99, 140, 153, 170, 200–201, 205
Ideologies, 21, 23, 95–96
Igneous stone, 84
Illinois, 13, 145, 170
Incised pottery, 91, 94, 124–25, 139, 152. *See also* Ceramics; Weeden Island period and ceramics
Indians (contemporary), 97, 115, 140, 146–47
Ingold, Tim, 8, 16–17
Interpretive ambiguity, 99

Invertebrate(s), 64, 66, 174
Iroquoian societies, 153

Jackson, Kendal, 54, 71, 73–74, 174
Jamestown site, 210
Jericho site, 202

Katzmarzyk, Cheryl, 47, 68, 78–79
Kelso, William, 210
Kemp, Kassie, 47, 108–9, 126, 137
Key Marco site, 151
Kings Bay, 26
Kinship, 21, 81, 99, 160; fictive kin, 82
Kitchen middens, 162, 183–84, 212. *See also* Shell; Shell middens
Kivas, 202
Kolomoki site, 7*i*, 156, 159–60, 195–96, 198–205
Kowalewski, Stephen A., 122, 195–97, 200, 203–4, 212
Kuijt, Ian, 16, 203

Lagoon area (at Crystal River site), 31*i*, 37–38, 54, 55*i*, 103, 106, 108, 117, 120, 163
Largemouth bass, 123
Laser scanning. *See* LiDAR
Late Archaic period, 2*t*, 74, 78, 103, 195
Late Pacific period (Northwest Coast or Southern California), 15
Late Woodland period, 2*t*, 13, 124, 169–71, 192
Leader(ship): by shaman, priests, or religious specialists, 92–97, 100, 113, 138, 140, 165, 191, 198; by collective, 189–90, 205; in early village societies generally, 201; relationship to moundbuilding, 83; as exemplified by control over exotic goods or esoteric knowledge, 96–97, 145; institutionalization of authority, 100, 113, 116, 153; relationship to mortuary ceremony, 83–84, 144; succession and cycling, 83, 159, 160; threat of sanction, 189; as understood by collective action theorists, 20. *See also* Chiefdoms
Leake Site Complex, 7*i*, 113
LeMoyne, Jacques, 89
Letchworth site, 7*i*

Levant region, 15
LiDAR, 46, 48, 186
Lightning whelk. *See* Whelk
Limestone: artifacts made of, 12, 84, 85*i*, 93, 148; ceramic temper, 108–9, 111, 122, 137, 156; geologic substrate, 28, 45, 66, 71–73, 77, 109, 119, 131. *See also* Stelae
Lindeman phase, 192
Lineages, 81–82,f 148–49. *See also* Clans; Kinship; Marriage; Matrilineages; Segmentary structure
Lithics (flaked stone), 47, 85, 141, 151. *See also* Pinellas projectile points; Projectile points
Live oak, 28, 118–19, 162
Loggerhead sea turtle. *See* Sea turtle
Louisiana, 1, 84
Luer, George, 149, 204
Lulewicz, Isabelle Holland, 103–4

Magnolia, 28, 75, 162
Main Burial Complex, 11–13, 30, 31*i*, 35, 41*i*, 43, 55*i*, 56*i*, 79, 81*i*, 104*i*, 120*i*, 157*i*, 173*i*; Bullen's excavations in, 77–79; chronology of, 77–80, 108, 111–12, 126, 160–61, 197–98; differences in burial goods and treatments, 96, 98–99, 111–13, 125–27, 144–47, 150*i*; Moore's excavations in, 11–13, 40, 41*i*, 42, 46, 79–80, 84–93, 114, 125–27, 144, 150*i*, 160–61; orientation of village toward, 103; as a prototype for Platform mounds, 139; relationship to Mound G, 81, 111, 139, 202–3. *See also* Burial mounds; Burials; Mounds C, E, and F (Crystal River site)
Maize, 140, 170
Malinowski, Bronislaw, 154
Mammals, 30, 66, 99, 123, 176
Manasota periods and ceramics, 5–6*t*. *See also* Ceramics
Manatees, 71–72, 74–75, 92
Mandeville site, 7*i*, 100, 124, 139
Mangrove, 28, 158
Maori, 154
Marean, Curtis W., 19
Marquardt, William, 74, 123, 157–58, 188–90

Marriage, 149, 153. *See also* Clans; Kinship; Lineages; Matrilineages
Marsh, 28, 30, 74, 118, 156, 158, 162, 174, 176, 179, 183–84, 186. *See also* Estuaries; Wetlands
Marsh clams, 28
Marsh elder, 28
Marsh islands, 80, 111, 118, 123, 156, 176
Marsh wrens, 30
Marxism, 21
Maryland, 47, 84
Matrilineages, 190. *See also* Clans; Kinship; Lineages; Marriage; Segmentary structure
Maya, 157. *See also* Mesoamerica
McKeithen site, 7*i*, 125, 188, 196, 198–201, 203–5
McMaster University, 54
McMichael, Edward V., 14, 138–39
McNiven, Ian, 116, 120
Meat, 105, 114–15
Medieval Warm period, 171, 174, 189. *See also* Climate change; Sea levels
Mesoamerica: as an example of early villages, 8, 197–98, 200, 202, 204–5; presumed connections to Crystal River, 14, 45, 139. *See also* Maya
Mesolithic, 15
Meteoric iron, 92
Mexico. *See* Mesoamerica
Miami Circle site, 7*i*, 149
Mica, 87, 96, 148, 152
Microartifact analysis, 140
Microdrill, 191
Midcontinent. *See* Midwest
Midden. *See* Shell middens
Midden B. *See* Mound B (Crystal River site)
Middle Archaic period, 3*t*
Middle Woodland period, 2*t*, 4, 13, 15, 76, 82, 93, 96, 103, 124, 138, 140, 152, 159, 169–70, 201, 203–5
Midwest, 12, 14, 76, 78, 82, 92–93, 99, 113, 124, 139
Milanich, Jerald T., 12, 42, 76–77, 98, 100, 106, 108, 123, 125, 196, 199, 202
Minimum Number of Individuals (MNI), 105

Minnesota, 84
Mississippi, 84, 170
Mississippian period, 1–2, 5–6, 13, 42, 91, 93–94, 138–39, 159, 163–64, 170, 174, 181, 186, 188, 190, 192–93
Missouri, 170, 192
Mitchem, Jeffrey, 45, 80
Modular organization, 115
Mollusk(s), 159, 174
Monks Mound, 188
Monumental architecture, 1, 13, 15–16, 30, 73–74, 78, 82–83, 120–21, 138–39, 161–62, 166, 191. *See also* Burial mounds; Mounds; Mounds A–C (Roberts Island site); Mounds A–K (Crystal River site); Platform mounds; Shell mounds
Moore, Clarence B.: curation and analyses of artifacts from his excavation, 15, 46–47, 84–92, 149–50; investigations at Crystal River site, 4, 9–13, 25, 34, 40–43, 77, 79, 83–84, 93–95, 98, 112–14, 125–27, 145–47, 160, 163, 204; investigations of other sites in the region, 82, 96–97, 125. *See also* Crystal River (site)
Mortuary archaeology, 83. *See also* Burial mounds; Burials
Mortuary mounds, contexts, and ceremonies, 95, 98, 105, 115–16, 124, 127–28, 158, 191, 203, 211. *See also* Burial goods; Burial mounds; Burials; Ceremonies; Mortuary archaeology; Mortuary specialists; Rituals
Mortuary specialists, 191. *See also* Ceremonies; Leader(ship); Rituals
Moss, Madonna, 16
Mound A (Crystal River site), 9, 10*i*, 25, 31*i*, 35–38, 42–46, 48, 51, 54, 55*i*, 59, 69*t*, 103, 106, 107*i*, 117, 119, 120*i*, 133–36, 143, 156, 157*i*, 161–66, 172, 173*i*. *See also* Crystal River (site); Main Burial Complex; Platform mounds; Plazas
Mound A (Roberts Island site), 30, 32*i*, 33*i*, 64, 65*i*, 69*t*, 163*i*, 164*i*, 173*i*, 179–88. *See also* Platform mounds; Roberts Island (site and Shell Mound Complex)
Mound B (midden) (Crystal River site), 14*i*, 31*i*, 43, 44*i*, 51*i*, 103, 104*i*, 120*i*, 157*i*, 173*i*. *See also* Crystal River (site); Shell middens
Mound B (Roberts Island site), 30, 32*i*, 33*i*, 64, 65*i*, 69*t*, 183–84, 173*i*, 184*i*, 185*i*, 186, 187*i*. *See also* Platform mounds; Roberts Island (site and Shell Mound Complex)
Mound C (Crystal River site), 11, 31*i*, 35, 40, 41*i*, 43, 44*i*, 45, 69*t*, 77–80, 81*i*, 99, 100, 104*i*, 120*i*, 125–26, 157*i*, 160, 173*i*. *See also* Circular embankments; Main Burial Complex
Mound C (Roberts Island site), 30, 32, 34*i*, 173*i*, 186–87. *See also* Platform mounds; Roberts Island (site and Shell Mound Complex)
Mound E (Crystal River site), 11, 31*i*, 40, 41*i*, 43, 44*i*, 69*t*, 79, 120*i*, 126–27, 104*i*, 157*i*, 160, 173*i*. *See also* Burial mounds; Burials; Crystal River (site); Main Burial Complex; Platform mounds
Mound F (Crystal River site), 11, 12, 31*i*, 40, 41*i*, 44*i*, 43, 45, 69*t*, 79, 81*i*, 83–84, 92–94, 96, 98–99, 104*i*, 112–13, 120*i*, 127, 157*i*, 173*i*. *See also* Burial mounds; Burials; Crystal River (site); Main Burial Complex; Platform mounds
Mound G (Crystal River site), 30, 31*i*, 41*i*, 44*i*, 45, 50*i*, 69*t*, 78–79, 81, 104*i*, 108, 111–12, 117, 126, 140, 145, 157*i*, 173*i*. *See also* Burial mounds; Burials; Crystal River (site); Main Burial Complex
Mound H (Crystal River site), 10, 30, 31*i*, 41*i*, 43, 44*i*, 49, 68, 69*t*, 72, 55*i*, 129*i*, 131–33, 137–39, 140, 143, 157*i*, 173*i*. *See also* Crystal River (site); Main Burial Complex; Platform mounds; Plazas
Mound J (Crystal River site), 31*i*, 43, 44*i*, 48, 50*i*, 55*i*, 68, 69*t*, 103, 104*i*, 108, 120*i*, 128, 157*i*, 161, 173*i*. *See also* Crystal River (site); Main Burial Complex; Platform mounds
Mound K (Crystal River site), 13, 14*i*, 31*i*, 43, 44*i*, 50*i*, 51, 55, 56*i*, 69*t*, 107*i*, 120*i*, 128, 130*i*, 131, 133, 137–38, 143, 157*i*, 173*i*. *See also* Crystal River (site); Main Burial Complex; Platform mounds; Plazas
Mound Key site, 7*i*, 172
Mounds: association of mound building with favorable climatic intervals, 213–14;

association with plazas, 139, 202–3; coincidence of mound construction and early village formation, 197–99; decline in construction during the Late Woodland period, 170–71; elaboration of mounds at Crystal River site, 4; as lookouts, 162; mound building as evidence of cooperation, 211; mound building as evidence of costly signaling, 212; myths associated with, 25; necessity of authority to coordinate construction, 154; possible functions associated with mounds and mound building, 82–84; ritual cycles of mound building and feasting, 154. *See also* Burial mounds; Main Burial Complex; Mounds A–C (Roberts Island site); Mounds A–K (Crystal River site); Platform mounds; Shell mounds

Moundville site, 163

Mullet, 116, 123, 154, 175

Natchez, 170

National Museum of the American Indian (NMAI), 15, 47, 89, 114

National Science Foundation (NSF), 47

Natufian period, 15

Needlefishes, 175

Neolithic period, 8, 18, 197–200, 202–3

Newfoundland, 174

New Guinea, 115

Nonvenomous snakes, 123

Norman, Sean, 54, 71–72, 109, 133, 141

North Carolina, 139, 198

Number of Individual Specimens Present (NISP), 114, 176

Ocala Group, 28

Ohio, 12–13, 42, 94, 96, 145. *See also* Midwest

Oklahoma, 140

Olasky, Marvin, 210

Oligocene age, 28

Olmec, 204. *See also* Mesoamerica

Ontario, 153

Ontologies, 76

Optically Stimulated Luminescence (OSL) dates, 54. *See also* Bayesian analysis; Chronology; Crystal River (site); Phases;

Roberts Island (site and Shell Mound Complex)

Osprey, 30

Ostrom, Elinor, 20, 189

Otter, 123

Oxygen isotopes, 103–4, 108, 121, 137, 140, 154, 175, 183, 189–90, 211. *See also* Oyster

Oyster: association with feasting, 83, 116; bars, beds, bioherms and reefs, 28, 73–74, 83, 98, 175, 189, 214; growth patterns and utility for seasonality studies, 104, 121, 137–38, 154, 175, 183, 190, 211; intensified use of during Late Woodland period, 174, 189–90; possible evidence for overharvesting, 159, 211; procurement and processing of, 175, 191, 206. *See also* Resources; Shell middens; Shell mounds; Shell; Shellfish

Ozark Mountains, 84

Paleoindian period, 1, 3*t*, 72–74

Palisaded villages, 189

Palmetto Mound site, 7*i*, 82

Palms, 28, 75. *See also* Sabal palm

Pamlico terrace, 27

Panpipes, 94, 96

Pasco period and ceramics, 5–6*t*, 42, 110*i*. *See also* Ceramics

Patton, Robert B., 188, 191–92

Pauketat, Timothy, 9, 76, 195–96

Pendants: copper, 92; quartz crystal, 93; shell, 112, 127; stone, 84, 89, 91–92. *See also* Plummets; Shell gorgets; Tabbed Circular Artifacts

Peninsular Florida, 5–6*t*, 13, 25–26, 78, 84, 100, 125, 149, 156, 171, 196, 200

Phases: methods of defining, 66–70; of midden deposition, 66–68; of mound construction, 68–70, 79. *See also* Chronology; Crystal River (site); Roberts Island (site and Shell Mound Complex)

Piedmont region, 84

Pierce Mound site, 7*i*, 82, 100

Pilgrimages. *See* Rituals

Pine, 28

Pine Island Sound, 157, 171

Pineland site, 7*i*, 151, 171–72

Pinellas period and ceramics, 5–6*t*

Pinellas projectile points, 189
Pinson Mounds site, 7*i*, 66, 139
Pipes, 97; ceramic, 93; stone, 84, 93, 96
Pit features, 56–57, 101, 105, 141, 203
Pithouse period (American Southwest), 8, 197
Platform mounds: association with integrative ceremonies, 154; comparison of Woodland and Mississippian, 164, 188, 192; low platforms in early stages of, 128, 131; "new" form of architecture at the Crystal River site, 138–39; problems for interpretation, 13–14, 138–39; relationship to plazas, 141; as a Woodland period innovation, 1; as foundations for men's houses, 202. *See also* Mounds; Mounds A–C (Roberts Island site); Mounds A, E, H, J, and K (Crystal River site); Shell mounds
Plazas: association with platform mounds, 141, 143, 164, 179, 188; at the Crystal River site, 30, 31*i*, 49*i*, 50*i*, 79, 81, 98, 112, 139–41, 143, 157*i*, 173*i*; as features common to early villages, 200–203; interpretation of, 140–41, 154; at the Roberts Island site, 30, 32*i*, 164, 173*i*, 177, 179, 183, 187–89. *See also* Crystal River (site); Green Corn Ceremony; Rituals; Roberts Island (site and Shell Mound Complex)
Pleistocene Epoch, 27, 71, 131
Plumb Bayou culture, 170
Plumed egrets, 176
Plummets, 77, 84–87, 89, 91, 93, 96, 100, 145–46
Pollen analysis, 52, 54, 71, 73–74, 174, 190
Population: aggregation and nucleation, 122, 159, 170, 196; Circumscription, 55*i*, 99, 188; density, 18, 22, 82–83, 96, 98–99, 108, 198. *See also* Early villages
Porgies, 175
Portals to other worlds, 103
Pottery. *See* Ceramics
Poverty Point site, 1, 7*i*
Prentiss, William, 16
Prestige, 92, 115, 154, 165
Prestige goods, 22, 47, 99, 195. *See also* Leader(ship); Status

Priests. *See* Leader(ship)
Projectile points, 87. *See also* Pinellas projectile points
Public architecture, 1, 22, 47, 98, 201–2, 204. *See also* Kivas; Mounds; Platform mounds; Plazas
Pueblo communities (American Southwest), 201
Puma, 92
Punctate pottery, 5–6*t*, 124–25
Putnam, Frederick Ward, 12

Quartz crystals, 12, 84, 88*i*, 93, 112, 148, 152
Queen conch. *See* Conchs

Raccoon, 30, 176
Radiocarbon dates. *See* Chronology; Crystal River (site); Phases; Roberts Island (site and Shell Mound Complex)
Rainey, Froelich, 193
Randall, Asa R., 162, 176
Rautman, Alison, 23, 116, 199–200, 204
Rebirth, 145
Reciprocity, 47, 166
Red cedar, 28
Redding, Richard, 18, 202–3
Reis, Robert Lawrence, 94
Relational ontologies, 76
Religious specialists. *See* Leader(ship)
Reptiles, 30, 176
Resilience, 23, 205
Resistance survey. *See* Geophysical survey
Resources: overuse of, 159, 166, 189, 211; ownership of, 35, 82, 189, 210–11. *See also* Oyster
Rink, Jack, 54, 181
Rituals: as an all-purpose explanation in archaeology, 92; association with mounds and mortuary activities, 121, 127, 141, 144, 154, 160, 166, 198; association with stela, 141; as a characteristic of Hopewell and Middle Woodland societies, 76, 92; Crystal River as a ritual center, 77, 160; as a divine charter for the foundation of early villages, 198–99; as a form of costly signaling, 19, 212; as a means of building solidarity or fostering cooperation, 21–22, 195, 202; as a means

of managing seascapes and access to resources, 116, 154; as a means of shamanic transformation, 92; paraphernalia, 93–94, 97, 100, 138, 204; performances and public display, 93, 154; pilgrimages, 97; rites of purification and renewal, 140–41. *See also* Burial mounds; Ceremonies; Green Corn Ceremony; Leader(ship); Mounds; Platform mounds; Plazas
Ritual specialists. *See* Leader(ship)
River Styx site, 7*i*, 78
Robb, John, 196
Roberts Island (site and Shell Mound Complex): as a ceremonial center, 168, 176–78, 183, 186–87, 211; CREVAP excavations and analyses, 61–70; depopulation and abandonment, 32, 34, 192–93; eligibility for the National Register of Historic Places, 40; environmental setting, 25–30, 158–59, 174; history of ownership, 39; history of prior investigations, 4; mound alignments, 179, 186–88; revised chronology for, 66–70, 159, 169, 173, 182, 186; subsistence remains, 174–76; village form, prior, 176–78. *See also* Mounds A–C (Roberts Island site); Plazas; Shell middens
Roman Empire, 157
Roman Warm period, 74, 118, 213–14. *See also* Climate change; Sea levels
Rosenberg, Michael, 202–3
Routinization, 113
Rushes, 28
Russo, Michael, 156

Sabal palm, 28
Safety Harbor period or culture, 5–6*t*, 43, 45, 82, 192
Safford Mound site, 7*i*, 82
Saitta, Dean, 209
Saltgrass, 28
Santa Rosa ceramics, 42–43. *See also* Ceramics
Santa Rosa-Swift Creek ceramics, 42–43. *See also* Ceramics
Sapelo Island, 195
Sassaman, Kenneth, 4, 16–17, 78, 118, 121, 158, 213

Saw palmetto, 28
Scallop, 151
Schmidtz, David, 210
Schwadron, Margot, 177–78
Schwartz, Joel, 210
Scioto region. *See* Ohio
Seagrass, 158, 174
Sea levels: contemporary changes in, 118, 213–14; reconstruction of changes in the past, 71, 73–74, 82–83, 101, 118, 124, 156–58; response and adaption to changes in, 99, 120, 123, 153, 158, 160, 166, 171–72, 214. *See also* Climate change; Medieval Warm period; Roman Warm period; Tidal variation; Vandal Minimum
Sears, William, 196
Seascapes, 116
Sea turtle, 114, 123
Secondary burials, 112, 127, 160, 203–4
Sedentary village. *See* Early villages
Sedentism, 1, 17–18, 121–22, 194, 198, 207
Sedges, 28, 174
Seeman, Mark, 96–97
Segmentary structure, 115. *See also* Clans; Kinship
Seminole Indians, 93, 115
Settlers (historic), 32, 75, 206, 210
Shaman. *See* Ceremonies; Leader(ship); Rituals
Shamanic sacra, 95
Shapiro, Gary, 159
Sharks, 92
Sheepshead, 154
Shell: artifacts, 11–12, 30, 47, 64, 66, 87, 89, 91, 93–94, 96, 98, 112–13, 121, 127–28, 140, 145–48, 150*i*, 174–77, 190–92, 204; density in mounds and middens, 48, 51, 54, 56–57, 59, 61, 64, 66, 83, 101–3, 106, 107*i*, 119–20, 128, 152, 159, 161, 176; suitability for radiocarbon dating, 66–67, 77, 124; as a trade commodity, 96–98, 145, 152; utility for studies of seasonality, 104, 121, 140, 190. *See also* Oyster; Shell cups; Shellfish; Shell gorgets; Shell middens; Shell mounds; Shell rings; Tabbed Circular Artifacts
Shell cups, 93–94, 145, 148, 192, 204

Shellfish, 99, 101, 103, 116, 154, 171, 174–75, 206, 211. *See also* Gastropods; Mollusk(s); Oyster; Whelk

Shell gorgets, 91, 93, 96, 127, 145, 147*i*, 149, 204. *See also* Shell; Tabbed Circular Artifacts

Shell middens: description and chronology of the midden at Crystal River site, 13–14, 30, 43, 45–46, 52, 54–57, 61, 73–74, 77–78, 80, 102–3, 101–9, 111, 117, 119–22, 128, 131, 133, 135–38, 141, 146, 148, 152–54, 156, 159, 161–62, 199–201, 214; description and chronology of the midden at Roberts Island site, 4, 30, 168–69, 172–79, 182–83, 191; description of the middens at the Wash Island and Burtine Island sites, 80; difficulty in excavating and interpreting, 101; lack of "pure" Deptford, 149; methods for developing a chronology of midden deposition, 66–67, 68*t*, 70; middens, 80–81; use of geophysical survey to identify, 46, 48–49, 51*i*, 107*i*. *See also* Oyster; Shell; Shell mounds; Shell rings

Shell mounds, 1, 4, 9, 11, 37, 40, 43, 51, 99, 125, 131, 133–37, 162, 168, 171–74, 181–84, 186; mining for fill, 37–38, 54; relation to Earth Diver myth, 121. *See also* Oyster; Shell; Shell middens; Shell rings

Shell Mound site, 7*i*, 78

Shell rings, 74, 78, 195

Shovel tests. *See* Crystal River (site); Crystal River Early Village Archaeological Project; Roberts Island (site and Shell Mound Complex)

Sight communities, 165

Signage and displays, 138

Sinistral (left-handed) opening, 93

Skates, 176

Small, John, 42, 212

Smith, Hale, 13–14, 19, 25, 39, 43, 46, 74, 100, 115, 124, 137–39, 213

Smithsonian Institution, 85–91, 124, 146–47, 150

Snapping turtles, 176

Social cohesion approaches, 20. *See also* Collective action theory; Competition; Cooperation

Sociality, 16–17, 23, 206

Social rules and obligations, 16–17, 203. *See also* Competition; Cooperation

Sodalities, 92

Softshell turtles, 123

Soil chemistry, 48, 140

Solstices, 143, 163, 187–88

South America, 8, 197–98, 200, 202, 204

Southard, Elizabeth, 104

Southern magnolia, 28

Southwest (United States), 8, 172, 197–202, 204

Southwestern Florida, 5–6*t*, 74, 118, 123, 146, 151–52, 157–58, 171, 174, 176–78, 188–92. *See also* Caloosahatchee phases and ceramics

Southwestern Georgia, 100, 139, 196

Spears, 87, 176, 206

Spirit adoption, 97

Stanish, Charles, 154

State Archives of Florida, Florida Memory, 142, 164, 183–84

Status, 16, 39, 71, 83, 97, 100, 112–15, 144, 153–54, 165, 201, 211. *See also* Households; Leader(ship)

Stelae, 14, 30, 40, 45; Stela 1, 31*i*, 141–43, 163; Stela 2, 31*i*, 143–44; Stela 3, 31*i*

Steward, Julian, 18

St. Johns period and ceramics, 5*t*, 42, 110*i*

Storage, 177, 189–90

Storm of the Century, 46, 117

Storm surges, 117–19, 194. *See also* Climate change; Sea levels

St. Petersburg (city), 124

Subsistence, 16, 18, 48, 99, 104, 115, 171, 174, 176, 190, 192, 195, 205, 207, 211. *See also* Crystal River (site); Roberts Island (site and Shell Mound Complex)

Sunfishes, 123, 175

Supernatural beings, 91

Superstorm of March 1993, 46, 117

Suwannee River, 73, 118, 158

Swamp bay, 28, 30

Sweet bay, 28

Swift Creek ceramics, 5–6*t*, 42–43, 109–11, 204. *See also* Ceramics

Tabbed Circular Artifacts (TCAs), 149–50

Taboo, 153–54

Tampa Bay area, 9, 82, 171, 192
Tanner, William, 73
Technologies: associated with fishing and shellfishing, 206; differences between hunter-gatherers and farmers; differences between Weeden Island and Glades traditions, 151–52; innovations and social change, 189–90
Temple mound. *See* Platform mounds
Temple Mound period, 138. *See also* Mississippian period
Tennessee, 66, 96, 139
Tenpounders, 175
Ten Thousand Islands, 171
Terrapins, 123
Terrestrial animals, 28, 66, 105, 122
Territoriality, 82–83, 165, 190
Test units. *See* Crystal River (site); Crystal River Early Village Archaeological Project; Roberts Island (site and Shell Mound Complex)
Tetrapodal vessels, 77
Thompson, Rachel, 64
Three Sisters Spring, 72*i*
Thulman, David, 75
Tidal variation, 76, 206
Timber, 35
Tobacco, 93
Toltec site, 7*i*, 170
Topographic mapping, 43, 46
Topography, 165, 179, 183
Tornado, 45, 117
Torres Strait, 115
Tortoises, 123
Trade. *See* Exchange
Tragedy of the commons, 211
Trailer park. *See* Crystal River Mobile Home Park
Transportation, 76, 213
Trenches. *See* Crystal River (site); Roberts Island (site and Shell Mound Complex)
Tribelets, 190
Tribes, 17
Trobriand Islands, 154
Tubers, 206
Tunnacunnhee site, 7*i*, 113
Turkey, 123
Turner Mound site, 12

Turtle Mound site, 161
Turtles, 91, 114–16, 175–76, 206

Underworld, 145
University of Alabama, 104
University of Georgia (UGA), 104
University of South Florida, 104
Useppa Island, 171

Vandal Minimum, 156–58, 166, 171, 214. *See also* Climate change; Sea levels
VanPool, Christine, 94–95
Venomous (Viperidae) snakes, 123
Vertebrate fishes, 66, 174–76
Vibracore, 54

Waccasassa Bay, 118
Wakulla Check Stamped, 5–6, 161
Walker, Karen, 74, 157
Wallis, Neill, 156, 196, 199–200, 202, 204
Warfare, 22, 91
Waring, Antonio, Jr., 42
Wash Island site, 80, 168
Wealth, 100, 113, 144, 211
Weather events, 71, 75, 117–18, 140
Weber, Max, 113
Weeden Island period and ceramics, 5–6*t*, 42–43, 82, 111, 124–26, 144, 152, 156, 158, 160–61, 170–71, 204. *See also* Caches; Ceramics
Weirs, 115, 172, 178, 206, 214
Weisman, Brent, 4, 25, 45–46, 168
Wetlands, 28–29, 30, 35, 54, 78, 158, 174. *See also* Estuaries; Marsh
Whalen, Michael, 204
Wheeler, Ryan, 152
Whelk, 93, 127, 145–46, 148, 151, 148–49, 191–92
Widmer, Randolf, 188–90
Willey, Gordon, 12–13, 25, 42–43, 81, 125, 163, 203
Williams, Stephen, 159, 169
Williston member, 28
Willoughby, Charles, 12
Windover Pond site, 7*i*, 78
Woodland period, archaeology of, 46, 66, 79–80, 92, 105, 140–41, 193; mounds, 13, 128, 138–39, 181, 186, 188; as period when

early villages become established, 1–2, 18, 159; population growth during, 188; societies of, 4, 8, 17, 191, 200; temporal divisions, 2*t*, 5–6*t*. *See also* Late Woodland period; Middle Woodland period
Wrens, 30
Wright, Alice, 73, 198
Wulfert High. *See* Roman Warm period

Yat Kitischee site, 171
Yaupon holly, 93
Yaya-Mama Religious Tradition, 204. *See also* South America
Yellow Bluffs site, 7*i*, 149
Yent Mound site, 7*i*, 82, 100
Yuchi, 140

Thomas J. Pluckhahn is professor of anthropology at the University of South Florida. He specializes in the anthropological archaeology of the American Southeast, with particular focus on the ceramics, households, monuments, and landscapes of the Woodland and Mississippian periods.

Victor D. Thompson is professor of archaeology at the University of Georgia. He specializes in the political and historical ecology of native coastal populations of the American Southeast, incorporating geoarchaeology and archaeological science methods in this research.

RIPLEY P. BULLEN SERIES

Florida Museum of Natural History
Edited by Neill J. Wallis and Charles R. Cobb

Tacachale: Essays on the Indians of Florida and Southeastern Georgia during the Historic Period, edited by Jerald T. Milanich and Samuel Proctor (1978)

Aboriginal Subsistence Technology on the Southeastern Coastal Plain during the Late Prehistoric Period, by Lewis H. Larson (1980)

Cemochechobee: Archaeology of a Mississippian Ceremonial Center on the Chattahoochee River, by Frank T. Schnell, Vernon J. Knight Jr., and Gail S. Schnell (1981)

Fort Center: An Archaeological Site in the Lake Okeechobee Basin, by William H. Sears, with contributions by Elsie O'R. Sears and Karl T. Steinen (1982)

Perspectives on Gulf Coast Prehistory, edited by Dave D. Davis (1984)

Archaeology of Aboriginal Culture Change in the Interior Southeast: Depopulation during the Early Historic Period, by Marvin T. Smith (1987)

Apalachee: The Land between the Rivers, by John H. Hann (1988)

Key Marco's Buried Treasure: Archaeology and Adventure in the Nineteenth Century, by Marion Spjut Gilliland (1989)

First Encounters: Spanish Explorations in the Caribbean and the United States, 1492–1570, edited by Jerald T. Milanich and Susan Milbrath (1989)

Missions to the Calusa, edited and translated by John H. Hann, with an introduction by William H. Marquardt (1991; first paperback edition 2024)

Excavations on the Franciscan Frontier: Archaeology at the Fig Springs Mission, by Brent Richards Weisman (1992)

The People Who Discovered Columbus: The Prehistory of the Bahamas, by William F. Keegan (1992)

Hernando de Soto and the Indians of Florida, by Jerald T. Milanich and Charles Hudson (1992)

Foraging and Farming in the Eastern Woodlands, edited by C. Margaret Scarry (1993)

Puerto Real: The Archaeology of a Sixteenth-Century Spanish Town in Hispaniola, edited by Kathleen Deagan (1995)

Political Structure and Change in the Prehistoric Southeastern United States, edited by John F. Scarry (1996)

Bioarchaeology of Native American Adaptation in the Spanish Borderlands, edited by Brenda J. Baker and Lisa Kealhofer (1996)

A History of the Timucua Indians and Missions, by John H. Hann (1996)

Archaeology of the Mid-Holocene Southeast, edited by Kenneth E. Sassaman and David G. Anderson (1996)

The Indigenous People of the Caribbean, edited by Samuel M. Wilson (1997; first paperback edition, 1999)

Hernando de Soto among the Apalachee: The Archaeology of the First Winter Encampment, by Charles R. Ewen and John H. Hann (1998)

The Timucuan Chiefdoms of Spanish Florida, by John E. Worth: vol. 1, *Assimilation*; vol. 2, *Resistance and Destruction* (1998; first paperback edition, 2020)

Ancient Earthen Enclosures of the Eastern Woodlands, edited by Robert C. Mainfort Jr. and Lynne P. Sullivan (1998)

An Environmental History of Northeast Florida, by James J. Miller (1998)

Precolumbian Architecture in Eastern North America, by William N. Morgan (1999)
Archaeology of Colonial Pensacola, edited by Judith A. Bense (1999)
Grit-Tempered: Early Women Archaeologists in the Southeastern United States, edited by Nancy Marie White, Lynne P. Sullivan, and Rochelle A. Marrinan (1999; first paperback edition, 2001)
Coosa: The Rise and Fall of a Southeastern Mississippian Chiefdom, by Marvin T. Smith (2000)
Religion, Power, and Politics in Colonial St. Augustine, by Robert L. Kapitzke (2001)
Bioarchaeology of Spanish Florida: The Impact of Colonialism, edited by Clark Spencer Larsen (2001)
Archaeological Studies of Gender in the Southeastern United States, edited by Jane M. Eastman and Christopher B. Rodning (2001)
The Archaeology of Traditions: Agency and History Before and After Columbus, edited by Timothy R. Pauketat (2001)
Foraging, Farming, and Coastal Biocultural Adaptation in Late Prehistoric North Carolina, by Dale L. Hutchinson (2002)
Windover: Multidisciplinary Investigations of an Early Archaic Florida Cemetery, edited by Glen H. Doran (2002)
Archaeology of the Everglades, by John W. Griffin (2002; first paperback edition, 2017)
Pioneer in Space and Time: John Mann Goggin and the Development of Florida Archaeology, by Brent Richards Weisman (2002)
Indians of Central and South Florida, 1513–1763, by John H. Hann (2003)
Presidio Santa María de Galve: A Struggle for Survival in Colonial Spanish Pensacola, edited by Judith A. Bense (2003)
Bioarchaeology of the Florida Gulf Coast: Adaptation, Conflict, and Change, by Dale L. Hutchinson (2004; first paperback edition, 2020)
The Myth of Syphilis: The Natural History of Treponematosis in North America, edited by Mary Lucas Powell and Della Collins Cook (2005)
The Florida Journals of Frank Hamilton Cushing, edited by Phyllis E. Kolianos and Brent R. Weisman (2005)
The Lost Florida Manuscript of Frank Hamilton Cushing, edited by Phyllis E. Kolianos and Brent R. Weisman (2005)
The Native American World Beyond Apalachee: West Florida and the Chattahoochee Valley, by John H. Hann (2006)
Tatham Mound and the Bioarchaeology of European Contact: Disease and Depopulation in Central Gulf Coast Florida, by Dale L. Hutchinson (2007)
Taíno Indian Myth and Practice: The Arrival of the Stranger King, by William F. Keegan (2007; first paperback edition, 2022)
An Archaeology of Black Markets: Local Ceramics and Economies in Eighteenth-Century Jamaica, by Mark W. Hauser (2008; first paperback edition, 2013)
Mississippian Mortuary Practices: Beyond Hierarchy and the Representationist Perspective, edited by Lynne P. Sullivan and Robert C. Mainfort Jr. (2010; first paperback edition, 2012)
Bioarchaeology of Ethnogenesis in the Colonial Southeast, by Christopher M. Stojanowski (2010; first paperback edition, 2013)
French Colonial Archaeology in the Southeast and Caribbean, edited by Kenneth G. Kelly and Meredith D. Hardy (2011; first paperback edition, 2015)
Late Prehistoric Florida: Archaeology at the Edge of the Mississippian World, edited by Keith Ashley and Nancy Marie White (2012; first paperback edition, 2015)

Early and Middle Woodland Landscapes of the Southeast, edited by Alice P. Wright and Edward R. Henry (2013; first paperback edition, 2019)

Trends and Traditions in Southeastern Zooarchaeology, edited by Tanya M. Peres (2014)

New Histories of Pre-Columbian Florida, edited by Neill J. Wallis and Asa R. Randall (2014; first paperback edition, 2016)

Discovering Florida: First-Contact Narratives from Spanish Expeditions along the Lower Gulf Coast, edited and translated by John E. Worth (2014; first paperback edition, 2016)

Constructing Histories: Archaic Freshwater Shell Mounds and Social Landscapes of the St. Johns River, Florida, by Asa R. Randall (2015)

Archaeology of Early Colonial Interaction at El Chorro de Maíta, Cuba, by Roberto Valcárcel Rojas (2016)

Fort San Juan and the Limits of Empire: Colonialism and Household Practice at the Berry Site, edited by Robin A. Beck, Christopher B. Rodning, and David G. Moore (2016)

Rethinking Moundville and Its Hinterland, edited by Vincas P. Steponaitis and C. Margaret Scarry (2016; first paperback edition, 2019)

Gathering at Silver Glen: Community and History in Late Archaic Florida, by Zackary I. Gilmore (2016)

Paleoindian Societies of the Coastal Southeast, by James S. Dunbar (2016; first paperback edition, 2019)

Cuban Archaeology in the Caribbean, edited by Ivan Roksandic (2016)

Handbook of Ceramic Animal Symbols in the Ancient Lesser Antilles, by Lawrence Waldron (2016)

Archaeologies of Slavery and Freedom in the Caribbean: Exploring the Spaces in Between, edited by Lynsey A. Bates, John M. Chenoweth, and James A. Delle (2016; first paperback edition, 2018)

Setting the Table: Ceramics, Dining, and Cultural Exchange in Andalucía and La Florida, by Kathryn L. Ness (2017)

Simplicity, Equality, and Slavery: An Archaeology of Quakerism in the British Virgin Islands, 1740–1780, by John M. Chenoweth (2017)

Fit for War: Sustenance and Order in the Mid-Eighteenth-Century Catawba Nation, by Mary Elizabeth Fitts (2017)

Water from Stone: Archaeology and Conservation at Florida's Springs, by Jason O'Donoughue (2017)

Mississippian Beginnings, edited by Gregory D. Wilson (2017; first paperback edition, 2019)

Harney Flats: A Florida Paleoindian Site, by I. Randolph Daniel Jr. and Michael Wisenbaker (2017)

Honoring Ancestors in Sacred Space: The Archaeology of an Eighteenth-Century African-Bahamian Cemetery, by Grace Turner (2017; first paperback edition, 2023)

Investigating the Ordinary: Everyday Matters in Southeast Archaeology, edited by Sarah E. Price and Philip J. Carr (2018; first paperback edition, 2024)

New Histories of Village Life at Crystal River, by Thomas J. Pluckhahn and Victor D. Thompson (2018; first paperback edition 2025)

Early Human Life on the Southeastern Coastal Plain, edited by Albert C. Goodyear and Christopher R. Moore (2018; first paperback edition, 2021)

The Archaeology of Villages in Eastern North America, edited by Jennifer Birch and Victor D. Thompson (2018)

The Cumberland River Archaic of Middle Tennessee, edited by Tanya M. Peres and Aaron Deter-Wolf (2019)

Pre-Columbian Art of the Caribbean, by Lawrence Waldron (2019)

Iconography and Wetsite Archaeology of Florida's Watery Realms, edited by Ryan Wheeler and Joanna Ostapkowicz (2019)

New Directions in the Search for the First Floridians, edited by David K. Thulman and Ervan G. Garrison (2019)

Archaeology of Domestic Landscapes of the Enslaved in the Caribbean, edited by James A. Delle and Elizabeth C. Clay (2019; first paperback edition, 2022)

Authority, Autonomy, and the Archaeology of a Mississippian Community, by Erin S. Nelson (2019; first paperback edition, 2024)

Cahokia in Context: Hegemony and Diaspora, edited by Charles H. McNutt and Ryan M. Parish (2020)

Bears: Archaeological and Ethnohistorical Perspectives in Native Eastern North America, edited by Heather A. Lapham and Gregory A. Waselkov (2020; first paperback edition, 2024)

Contact, Colonialism, and Native Communities in the Southeastern United States, edited by Edmond A. Boudreaux III, Maureen Meyers, and Jay K. Johnson (2020)

An Archaeology and History of a Caribbean Sugar Plantation on Antigua, edited by Georgia L. Fox (2020)

Modeling Entradas: Sixteenth-Century Assemblages in North America, edited by Clay Mathers (2020)

Archaeology in Dominica: Everyday Ecologies and Economies at Morne Patate, edited by Mark W. Hauser and Diane Wallman (2020)

The Making of Mississippian Tradition, by Christina M. Friberg (2020)

The Historical Turn in Southeastern Archaeology, edited by Robbie Ethridge and Eric E. Bowne (2020)

Falls of the Ohio Archaeology: Archaeology of Native American Settlement, edited by David Pollack, Anne Tobbe Bader, and Justin N. Carlson (2021)

A History of Platform Mound Ceremonialism: Finding Meaning in Elevated Ground, by Megan C. Kassabaum (2021)

New Methods and Theories for Analyzing Mississippian Imagery, edited by Bretton T. Giles and Shawn P. Lambert (2021)

Methods, Mounds, and Missions: New Contributions to Florida Archaeology, edited by Ann S. Cordell and Jeffrey M. Mitchem (2021)

Unearthing the Missions of Spanish Florida, edited by Tanya M. Peres and Rochelle A. Marrinan (2021)

Presidios of Spanish West Florida, by Judith A. Bense (2022)

En Bas Saline: A Taíno Town before and after Columbus, by Kathleen Deagan (2023)

Mississippian Women, edited by Rachel V. Briggs, Michaelyn Harle, and Lynne P. Sullivan (2024)

An Archaeology of Woodland Transformation: Social Movements, Identities, and Pottery Production on the Gulf Coast, by Jessica A. Jenkins (2025)

The Mann Phase: Hopewell Culture in Southwestern Indiana, by Michael Strezewski (2025)

www.ingramcontent.com/pod-product-compliance
Lightning Source LLC
Chambersburg PA
CBHW021851230426
43671CB00006B/341